Scotch Rite

Masonry Illustrated.

THE COMPLETE RITUAL

OF THE

Ancient and Accepted Scottish Rite,

PROFUSELY ILLUSTRATED.

By A SOVEREIGN GRAND COMMANDER, 33°

WITH AN HISTORICAL SKETCH OF THE ORDER, INTRODUCTION
AND CRITICAL ANALYSIS OF EACH DEGREE

—BY—

President J. Blanchard of Wheaton College.

OVER FOUR HUNDRED QUOTATIONS FROM STANDARD
MASONIC AUTHORITIES CONFIRM THE ACCURACY
OF THE RITUAL AND SHOW THE CHARACTER
OF MASONIC TEACHING AND DOCTRINE

VOLUME 2

NINETEENTH TO THIRTY-THIRD DEGREE INCLUSIVE.

NOMENCLATURE AND CLASSIFICATION OF THE GRADES IN FREEMASONRY

SYMBOLIC GRADES

Conferred only in regular Lodges of Master Masons, duly constituted by Grand Lodges

1° Entered Apprentice   2° Fellowcraft
3° Master Mason

INEFFABLE GRADES

4° Secret Master
5° Perfect Master
6° Intimate Secretary
7° Provost and Judge
8° Intendant of the building

9° Master Elect of Nine
10° Master Elect of Fifteen
11° Sublime Master Elected
12° Grand Master Architect
13° Master of the Ninth Arch

14° Grand Elect Mason

Conferred in a Lodge of Perfection, 14°, duly constituted under authority of the Supreme Council of the 33°.

ANCIENT HISTORICAL AND TRADITIONAL GRADES

15° Knight of the East or Sword   16° Prince of Jerusalem

Conferred in a Council, Princes of Jerusalem, 16°.

APOCALYPTIC AND CHRISTIAN GRADES

17° Knight of the East and West
18° Knight of Rose Croix de H-R-D-M

Conferred in a Chapter of Rose Croix de H-R-D-M, 18°

MODERN HISTORICAL, CHIVALRIC, AND PHILOSOPHICAL GRADES

19° Grand Pontiff
20° Master ad Vitam
21° Patriarch Noachite
22° Prince of Libanus
23° Chief of the Tabernacle
24° Prince of the Tabernacle
25° Knight of the Brazen Serpent
26° Prince of Mercy

27° Commander of the Temple
28° Knight of the Sun
29° Knight of St. Andrew
30° Grand Elect Kadosh or Knight of the White and Black Eagle
31° Grand Inspector Inquisitor Commander
32° Sublime Prince of the Royal Secret

Conferred in a Consistory, Sublime Princes of the Royal Secret, 32°

OFFICIAL GRADES

33° Sovereign Grand Inspector General

Conferred only by the SUPREME COUNCIL, 33° and upon those who may be elected to receive it by that high body which assembles yearly.

PUBLISHER'S PREFACE

SECOND VOLUME.

This Second Volume is simply a continuation of the First one. The magnitude of the work, (aggregating over One Thousand Pages,) rendered a division into two Volumes desirable. The Introduction, Historical Sketch and Preface found in the First Volume are for the entire Work.

Attention is again called to the fact that the *First Three Masonic Degrees,* termed the "Blue Lodge Degrees," are not given in this work, because those degrees are common to all the different Masonic Rites, and are very fully and accurately given in *Freemasonry Illustrated,* as advertised in the back part of this Volume. The reader will however find the *"Secret Work"* of those degrees given in the last Chapter of this Volume.

THE PUBLISHER.

CONTENTS

CONTENTS.

8 CONTENTS.

CONTENTS. 9

THE CONCLAVE[196]

OR

CELESTIAL CITY

Containing an epitome of the twelve degrees of the Philosophic Chamber of the Ancient and Accepted Rite.

The twelve degrees preceding the Rose Croix are, as we have shown, associated with the twelve signs of the Zodiac.

From these fixed signs, the Rite passes to the Sun, Moon and the Planets.

From these the Rite looks to the four elements or four components of man, etc., and from these it considers the spirit and matter, or infinite and finite of the Universe and of man.

In the Rose Croix Degree, we have seen the son of masonry and heard the promise of universal peace and joy. Now let us proceed to seek the methods of realization, and learn how to restore the lost Eden and re-edify the Celestial City.

Note 196.—"Conclave. Commanderies of Knights Templars in England and Canada are called Conclaves, and the Grand Encampment the Grand Conclave. The word is also applied to the meetings in some other of the high degrees. The word is derived from the Latin con, 'with,' and clavis, 'a key,' to denote the idea of being locked up in seclusion, and in this sense was first applied to the apartment in which the cardinals are literally locked up when met to elect a pope."—Mackey's Encyclopaedia of Freemasonry, Article Conclave.

CHAPTER XXXIII

NINETEENTH DEGREE OR GRAND PONTIFF.[197]

MERCURY. ☿

DECORATIONS:—The hangings are blue sprinkled with stars of gold; the whole Chapter is lighted by one large Spherical Transparency behind the Master's seat in the East.

In the East is a throne, and over it is a blue canopy. Around the room are twelve columns as follows: One on each side of the Master, one on each side of the Warden in the West, four in the North and four in the South of the Chapter; on the Capitals of these Columns are the initials of the names of the twelve tribes,[198] in the following order, beginning on the column on the right hand of the Master, and going round by the North, West and South, viz:

Ephraim,	Benjamin,	Issachar,
Naphtali,	Asher,	Dan,
Manassah,	Zebulon,	Reuben,
Simeon,	and	Gad.

Under these in the same order, are the zodiacal signs.

Note 197.—"Grand Pontiff. The 19th degree of the Ancient and Accepted rite. The degree is founded on the mysteries of the Apocalypse, relating to the new Jerusalem, as set forth in the Revelation of St. John. xxi. and xxii., which it illustrates and endeavors to explain. The assembly is styled a chapter; two apartments are required. The presiding officer is styled Thrice Puissant Grand Pontiff. The members are called Faithful Brothers."—Macoy's Encyclopaedia and Dictionary of Freemasonry,. Article Grand Pontiff.

Note 198.—"Tribes of Israel. All the twelve tribes of Israel were engaged in the construction of the first Temple. But long before its destruction, ten of them revolted, and formed the nation of Israel; while the remaining two, the tribes of Judah and Benjamin, retained possession of the Temple and of Jerusalem under the name of the kingdom of Judah. To these two tribes alone, after the return from the captivity, was intrusted the building of the second Temple. Hence in the high degrees. which, of course, are connected for the most part with the Temple of Zerubbabel. or with events that occurred subsequent to the destruction of that of Solomon. the tribes of Judah and Benjamin only are referred to. But in the primary degrees. which are based on the first Temple, the Masonic references always are to the twelve tribes. Hence in the old lectures the twelve original points are explained by a reference to the twelve tribes."—Mackoy's Encyclopaedia of Freemasonry, Article Tribes of Israel.

♉ · ♊ ♋ ♌ ♍ ♎ ♏ ♐ ♑ ♒ ♓ ♈

On the base of each column is the initial in the same order of the name of one of the Apostles of Christ, viz:

John,	Peter,	Andrew,	James,
Philip,	Bartholomew,	Thomas,	Matthew,
James,	Lebbeus,	Simon, and	Matthias.

DRAFT:—The tracing board has a mountain in the foreground. A four-square city appears descending from the sky; below is a representation of Jerusalem,'" overturned and in ruins. There are twelve gates of pearl, three on each side; a great glory in the center gives it light. Beneath the ruins of the city lies a serpent with three heads bound in chains; on one side of the draft is a high mountain.

TITLES:—The Master is styled Thrice Puissant and is seated on a throne in the East, and holds a sceptre in his hand, on his breast is the High Priest's Breast Plate. There is but one Warden seated in the West with a golden staff in his hand.

There is also an Orator, two Deacons and a Master of Ceremonies, and Tyler. The brethren are styled Faithful and True Brethren.

DRESS:—The brethren are clothed in white linen robes, each with a blue fillet of satin round his head with twelve gold stars on it.

ORDER:—A broad crimson ribbon, with twelve gold stars in front, worn from right to left.

JEWEL:—A gold medal or square plate, on one side of which is engraved the word Alpha, and on the other Omega.

BATTERY:—Is twelve equal strokes.

Note 199.—"The eastern portion of Jerusalem, known as Mt. Moriah, with which, as masons, we are particularly concerned, is fully described under that head; as are the clefts of rocks, the hill west of Mt. Moriah, the Valley of Jehoshaphat, the value of Shaveh and other neighboring places under their respective titles. The history of this memorable city partakes in its misfortunes of the exaggerations of romance. Levelled again and again to the ground; pillaged, burned; made the spoil of every nation of antiquity, it has yet resisted every attempt to blot it from existence and stands, at the present day, with a population of 125,000, insignificant in comparison with its former grandeur, yet representing the grandest and most important scenes recorded in the pages of history, human and divine. In 1809 a lodge was established here under the title of the Royal Solomon Mother Lodge."—Morris's Masonic Dictionary, Article Jerusalem.

OPENING CEREMONIES

DEGREE OF GRAND PONTIFF.[***]

Thrice Puissant—Faithful and true brethren Grand Pontiff, I propose to open this Chapter; aid me to do so. Brother Junior Deacon, see that we are properly tyled.

Junior Deacon—(Knocks twelve on the door, opens it and says:) Faithful and true brother, this Chapter of Grand Pontiffs is about to be opened, take due notice and govern yourself accordingly. (Then shuts the door.) Thrice Puissant, we are properly tyled.

Thrice Puissant—How?

Junior Deacon—By a faithful and true brother without, armed and vigilant.

Thrice Puissant—Faithful and true brother Warden, what is the hour?

Warden—The time is foretold to all nations, the Sun of Truth has risen over the desert, the last struggle between good and evil, light and darkness commences, the Cube Stone has become a mystic Rose and the lost word is recovered.

Thrice Puissant—Be grateful to God, my brethren. and let us proceed to open this Chapter, that we may

---

Note 200.—"Grand Pontiff. (Grand Pontife ou Sublime Ecossais.) The nineteenth degree of the Ancient and Accepted Scottish Rite. The degree is occupied in an examination of the Apocalyptic mysteries of the New Jerusalem. Its officers are a Thrice Puissant and one Warden. The Thrice Puissant is seated in the east on a throne canopied with blue, and wears a white satin robe. The Warden is in the west, and holds a staff of gold. The members are clothed in white, with blue fillets embroidered with twelve stars of gold, and are called True and Faithful Brothers. The decorations of the Lodge are blue sprinkled with gold stars."—**Mackey's Encyclopaedia of Freemasonry**. Article Grand Pontiff.

labor together for his glory and the improvement of mankind. Together my brethren, (all give the sign.)

Thrice Puissant—(Strikes one; 0.)

Warden—(Strikes one; 0, and so on alternately to twelve.)

All—(Clap twelve with their hands, and cry three times;) Hoshea.**'

Thrice Puissant—The Sun is up and this Chapter is open.

Thrice Puissant—(Strikes one; 0.) Be seated, faithful and true brethren.

Note 201.—"Hoshea. The word of acclamation used by the French Masons of the Scottish Rite. In some of the Cahiers it is spelled Osee. It is, I think, a corruption of the word huzza, which is used by the English and American Masons of the same Rite."—Mackey's Encyclopaedia of Freemasonry, Article Hoshea.

CHAPTER XXXIV

Nineteenth Degree or Grand Pontiff.[202]

INITIATION.

[Master of Ceremony retires and prepares the candidate as a Knight Rose Croix, conducts him to the door, knocks six and one.]

Junior Deacon—(Knocks six and one, opens the door and says:) Who hails?

Master of Ceremonies—A Knight Rose Croix, who desires to attain the degree of Grand Pontiff.

Junior Deacon—How long hath he served?

Master of Ceremonies—Three years.

Junior Deacon—Where?

Master of Ceremonies—In the ranks of Truth.

Junior Deacon—How armed?

Master of Ceremonies—With Charity, Hope and Faith.

Junior Deacon—Against what enemies?

Master of Ceremonies—Intolerance and oppression.

Note 202.—"Grand Pontiff." [Scotch Masonry.]—The first degree conferred in the Consistory of Princes of the Royal Secret, Scotch Masonry, and the 19th upon the catalogue of that system. Its officers are a Thrice Puissant Grand Pontiff and a Warden. The members are termed True and Faithful Brothers. The historical lessons are drawn from the Book of Revelations. The assembly is styled a Chapter. The hangings are blue, sprinkled with gold stars. The members are clothed in white linen with blue fillets, embroidered with 12 golden stars. Jewel, a square plate of gold having on one side the word Alpha, on the other the word Omega. Hours, from the hour foretold to the hour accomplished. The draft of the lodge represents a square city with 12 gates, three on a side; in the midst a tree bearing twelve manner of fruits."
—Morris's Masonic Dictionary, Article Grand Pontiff.

Junior Deacon—Why doth he now desire to attain the degree of Grand Pontiff?

Master of Ceremonies—That he may be better qualified to serve the cause of truth and light.

Junior Deacon—What other weapons does he need than Charity, Hope and Faith?

Junior Deacon—Then let him take his first lesson now, and wait with patience until the Thrice Puissant is informed of his request, and his will ascertained. [Junior Deacon shuts the door, goes to the Thrice Puissant, and the same questions and answers are given, except the last to be patient and wait.]

Thrice Puissant—Since his desires are commendable, faithful and true brother Junior Deacon, let him enter. [Junior Deacon opens the door, the candidate enters with the Master of Ceremonies who conducts him twelve times round the Chapter, halting at one of the columns at each circuit. At the fourth column.]

Master of Ceremonies—Judah*** shall return again to his first estate, when the empire of evil ends; Light and not darkness is eternal; Truth and not error is immortal. (At the third column.)

Master of Ceremonies—Issachar shall once more be free, when sin and suffering are known no longer; far in the future unto us, that day of light is now with God. Time is a succession of points, each in the center of eternity; evil lasts only during time. The reign of God is measured by eternity. (At the ninth column.)

Master of Ceremonies—Zebulon, shall find peace, as ships that come out of great storms, and furl their sails and let drop their anchors in quiet harbors. **For peace.** shall be the universal law to all the children of a common father. (At the tenth column.)

Master of Ceremonies—Reuben, like all mankind, has wandered far into the darkness, the steps of the ages ring in their stately march down no long slopes of time, and ever the dawn draws nearer. Men are God's instruments to accelerate its coming work, then my brother, be patient, wait. (At the eleventh column.)

Master of Ceremonies—Simeon, shall be reconciled to God, when intolerance no longer persecutes and bigotry no longer hates; when man, brother of man shall no longer be his torturer, his death, his fate. The waves of eternity roll ever nearer to us, on the narrow sands of life, that crumble under our weary feet. Those on whose ears the roar of the same surges smite, and whom the next wave will engulf together, should have in their hearts a prayer to God, and not hatred for their brother. (At the twelfth column.)

Master of Ceremonies—Gad, shall overcome at last, though a troop of evils long overcame him, as they overcome us all. The serpent is still unchained. The giants still assail the battlements of Heaven and scarce recoil before its lightnings. (At the first column.)

Master of Ceremonies—Ephraim. has strayed from home, he shall return in tears and penitence and find eternal rest. From God all souls have emanated and to him all return. (At the eighth column.)

Master of Ceremonies—Manasseh, shall be restored to sight; We are all blind swimmers in the currents of a mighty sea that hath no shore. We see as in a dream the effects and not the causes. The simplest things are miracles to us. We do not see the flower that is within the seed, nor the towering oak enveloped in the acorn; nor the odors and colors in the tasteless, colorless, invisible air and limpid water and rank dark earth, from which the seed extracts them by its mysterious chemistry. When the divine light cometh we shall see and know. (At the second column.)

Master of Ceremonies—Benjamin, shall be redeemed and come back from exile and captivity, for they, like pain, poverty and sorrow are blessings. Without them there would be scant excellence in human nature, neither fortitude nor self-denial, industry nor patience, charity nor tolerance, magnanimity nor generosity, heroism nor gratitude. (At the seventh column.)

Master of Ceremonies—Dan, shall obey the new law; the law of love. He prayeth best who loveth best, all things both great and small; for the great God that loveth us, he made and loveth all. (At the sixth column.)

Master of Ceremonies—Asher, shall pluck the fruit of the tree of life, that towers above the golden spires and overlooks the Jasper walls of the New Jerusalem. (At the fifth column.)

Master of Ceremonies—Napthali, believes hopes, waits and is patient; believes that all death is new life, all destruction and dissolution re-combination and re-production, and all evil and affliction, but the modes of this great genesis that shall not be eternal. Hopes for the time when this incessant flux and change shall cease, and the new law of love and light rule in all spheres and over all existence. and waits with patience the fulfillment of the inviolable promises of God. [At this moment a thick veil is thrown over the candidate and he is hurried into a small dark room, so he can take the cloth off when he chooses. They make him sit on the floor in the middle, and then retire. This room should be black, with no furniture. Apertures must be made so that without admitting any one, the voice of one speaking outside may be heard. It must also be arranged so that flashes of lighting may be produced. The candidate is left there for about five minutes, when a brother says in his hearing:]

First Brother—All who will not worship the Beast with seven heads and ten horns, and upon his horns ten crowns, and the mysterious name upon his forehead shall be slain, all men, the high and low, the rich and poor, freeman and slave shall receive upon their right hand or on their forehead, his mark, his name, and the number[204] of his name which is 666, or they shall neither buy nor sell; for his is power, dominion and authority of the Great Dragon. Man, helpless and in darkness, wilt thou receive his mark that thou mayest emerge to light.

Second Brother—Fear God, and give glory to him, for the hour of his judgment is come, and worship him that made Heaven and Earth, and the sea, and the springs of water, for he alone has the true sign. If any man worship the Beast and his image, and receive his

Note 204.—"Numbers. The symbolism which is derived from numbers was common to the Pythagoreans, the Kabbalists, the Gnostics, and all mystical associations. Of all superstitions, it is the oldest and the most generally diffused. Allusions are to be found to it in all systems of religion; the Jewish Scriptures, for instance, abound in it, and the Christian show a share of its influence. It is not, therefore, surprising that the most predominant of all symbolism in Freemasonry is that of numbers.

The doctrine of numbers as symbols is most familiar to us because it formed the fundamental idea of the philosophy of Pythagoras. Yet it was not original with him, since he brought his theories from Egypt and the East, where this numerical symbolism had always prevailed. Jamblichus tells us (Vit Pyth., C. 28), that Pythagoras himself admitted that he had received the doctrine of numbers from Orpheus, who taught that numbers were the most provident beginning of all things in heaven, earth, and the intermediate space, and the root of the perpetuity of divine beings, of the gods and of demons."—Mackey's Encyclopaedia of Freemasonry, Article Numbers.

mark on his forehead or in his hand, he shall drink the wine of God's indignation and be banished from the presence of the Holy Angels and of the World, that is the Redeemer. Remorse shall torture them, and they shall have no rest, who worship the beast and his image and receive the marks of his name.

Third Brother—Have patience, Oh! thou, who though in darkness art still our brother; keep the commandments of God, and this faith in his justice and infinite goodness. [There is silence for a little while.]

First Brother—The first Angel hath poured his vial on the earth and a foul and horrid plague hath fallen on all who wear the mark of the Beast and have worshipped his image. [Light flashes in the room.]

Second Brother—The second Angel hath poured his vial on the Sea, and it hath become like the blood of a dead man, and everything therein hath died. [Another flash.]

Third Brother—The third Angel hath poured his vial upon the rivers and the living springs, and they have become blood. [Another flash.]

Thou art just and righteous Oh God; the infinite and eternal in all thy judgments. For thou hast given them blood to drink, who have persecuted their brethren for their faith and usurped the power and prerogative of judgment, and shed the blood of the virtuous and good.

First Brother—The fourth Angel hath poured his vial upon the Sun, and the wicked are scorched with great heat and yet will not repent. [Another flash.]

Second Brother—The fifth Angel hath poured his vial upon those who worship the Beast, his kingdom is shrouded in darkness and his followers howl from pain and terror and blaspheme, and still do not repent. [Another flash.]

Third Brother.—The sixth Angel hath poured out his vial upon the great rivers of the Orient, and they are dried up and the spirits of falsehood, fraud and evil marshall their armies for the great battle to be fought on the great day of the Almighty God. Unexpectedly, before men see it dawn, that day will come; see that ye be not found unprepared, but wear evermore the armor of Charity, Hope and Faith, lest it come suddenly and find you naked and defenceless. [Another flash.]

First Brother—The seventh Angel hath poured his vial into the Air. It is done. (Upon this thunder is heard without, and frequent flashes light the cell, then there are loud noises, voices, etc., and a crash representing a city destroyed by an earthquake.)

First Brother—The Cities of the nations have fallen and intolerance, that great Babylon*** is no more. The chains imposed by fraud upon the human mind, the manacles and fetters fastened by force upon free thought have fallen. The towers and battlements the bastions and the ramparts, that power and fraud, and falsehood though impregnable have fallen, and they no longer shall be drunk with the blood of the saints and martyrs of the Truth.

Second Brother—Salvation, Glory, Honor and Power to the eternal God and Infinite Father. True and righteous are his judgments. Let all his creatures and the great voice of the ocean and his thunders cry rejoicingly. "The Lord omnipotent reigneth, and sin and evil are dethroned. Blessed are they that obey his law and trust in his goodness, that they may have right to the

Note 205.—"Babylon. The ancient capital of Chaldea, situated on both sides of the Euphrates, and once the most magnificent city of the ancient world. It was here that upon the destruction of Solomon's Temple by Nebuchadnezzar in the year of the world, 3394, the Jews of the tribe of Judah and Benjamin, who were the inhabitants of Jerusalem, were conveyed and detained in captivity for seventy-two years, until Cyrus, king of Persia, issued a decree for restoring them, and permitting them to rebuild their temple, under the superintendence of Zerubbabel, the Prince of the Captivity, and with the assistance of Joshua the High Priest and Haggai the Scribe.

Babylon the Great, as the prophet Daniel calls it, was situated four hundred and seventy-five miles in a nearly due east direction from Jerusalem"—Mackey's Encyclopaedia of Freemasonry, Article Babylon.

Tree of Life, and may enter through the gates into the city."

Brother who art in darkness, wilt thou obey that law and trust in that infinite goodness and be patient, though the appointed time may seem to draw no nearer during thy life, nor thy labors and exertions to produce any fruit?

Candidate—I will. .

Second Brother—Wilt thou be neither weary nor discouraged; satisfied to sow the seed and that those who come after thee may reap, if God so wills it?

Candidate—I will.

First Brother—Come then with us to the abode of light. (The door is opened and the candidate received by several brethren and conducted into the Chapter. The draft is seen, displayed, and after he enters the officers read as follows:)

Orator—I saw a new Heaven and a new Earth, for the first Heaven and first Earth were passed away, and there was no more Sea. I saw the Holy City, the new Jerusalem coming down from God out of Heaven. Henceforth he will dwell with men and be their father, and they his obedient and loving children. He will wipe the tears from all eyes, and there shall be no more death, nor fraud, nor falsehood; there shall be no more sin and shame, no remorse and affliction, sickness nor death any more, for the ancient wrong and evil have passed away forever.

Warden—He that sits upon the throne saith, "I make all things new, write, for these words are true. To him that thirsteth I give freely the waters of the Spring of Life. He that overcometh shall inherit all things, I will be his father and will love my child."

Thrice Puissant—In the Heavenly City there shall be no temple, for the Lord God Almighty and the Redeemer are its temple; nor Sun, nor Moon shall be needed there, for the primitive light shall shine therein and give it light. In that light shall all nations walk, and there shall all the splendor of the universe have their spring and centre. Therein shall be no night, wickedness nor falsehood; but the light and everlasting life and truth of God shall reign there forever. He is Alpha and Omega[206] the beginning and the end, the first and the last, from whom all things come, and to whom all return. My brother if you believe in these promises, go now to the holy altar and there assume the obligation of this degree. (Candidate kneels at the altar, places his hands upon the Bible and takes the following obligation:)

OBLIGATION DEGREE OF GRAND PONTIFF.

I———in the presence of the Almighty God, and believing in justice and mercy, do hereby and hereon most solemnly and sincerely promise and swear, that I will never reveal any of the secrets of this degree to any person in the world, except to him or them to whom the same may lawfully belong, and then only when I am duly authorized and empowered so to do.

I furthermore promise and swear that I will obey the by-laws, rules and regulations of any Chapter of this degree to which I may belong; and the edicts, laws and mandates of the Grand Consistory[207] of Sublime Princes and Commanders of the Royal Secret, under whose jurisdiction it may be holden, as well as those of the

Note 206.—"Alpha and Omega. The first and last letters of the Greek language, referred to in the Royal Master and some of the higher degrees. They are explained by this passage in Revelations ch. xxii., v. 13. 'I am Alpha and Omega, the beginning and the end, the first and the last.' Alpha and Omega is, therefore, one of the appellations of God, equivalent to the beginning and the end of all things, and so referred to in Isaiah xli. 4, 'I am Jehovah, the first and the last.' " —Mackey's Encyclopaedia of Freemasonry, Article Alpha and Omega.

Note 207.—"Grand Consistory. The governing body over a State of the Ancient and Accepted Scottish Rite; subject, however, to the superior jurisdiction of the Supreme Council of the Thirty-third. The members of the Grand Consistory are required to he in possession of the thirty-second degree."—Mackey's Encyclopaedia of Freemasonry, Article Grand Consistory.

Supreme Council of the 33rd degree, within whose
jurisdiction I may reside, so far as the same may come
to my knowledge.

I furthermore promise and swear that I will devote
myself, my heart, my hand, my speech and my intellect
to the cause of justice, truth and toleration[208] and will
endeavor to do something for the benefit of my country
and the world that shall live after I am dead; and that
I will henceforth consider only what is right and just,
and noble, and generous for me to do, and not whether
any benefit to myself or mine will result therefrom, or
whether I shall receive therefor thanks or ingratitude.
All of which I do most solemnly and sincerely promise
and swear, binding myself under no less a penalty[209]
than that of being held false Knight and faithless soldier by every true Knight and honest man in Christendom. So help me God.

Thrice Puissant—Melchizedek, King of Salem, whose
name signifies just and equitable King, was the Priest
of the Most High God; he met Abram returning from
the slaughter of the Kings and blessed him, and Abram

Notes 208.—"The same old Charges say, 'No private piques or quarrels
must be brought within the door of the Lodge, far less any quarrels
about religion, or nations, or state policy, we being only, as Masons,
of the Catholic religion above mentioned; we are also of all nations,
tongues, kindreds, and languages, and are resolved against all politics,
as what never yet conduced to the welfare of the Lodge, nor ever
will.'"—**Mackey's Encyclopaedia of Freemasonry, Article Toleration.**

Note 209.—The words 'So help me God,' refer exclusively to the
withdrawal of divine aid and assistance from the jurator in the case of
his proving false, and not to the human punishment which society would
inflict.
  In like manner, we may say of what are called Masonic penalties,
that they refer in no case to any kind of human punishment; that is
to say, to any kind of punishment which is to be inflicted by human
hand or instrumentality. The true punishments of Masonry affect neither
life nor limb. They are expulsion and suspension only. But those
persons are wrong, be they mistaken friends or malignant enemies, who
suppose or assert that there is any other sort of penalty which a Mason
recreant to his vows is subjected to by the laws of the Order, or that
it is either the right or duty of any Mason to inflict such penalty on
an offending brother. The obsecration of a Mason simply means that
if he violates his vows or betrays his trust he is worthy of such penalty,
and that if such penalty were inflicted on him it would be but just
and proper. 'May I die,' said the ancient, 'if this be not true, or if
I keep not this vow.' Not may any man put me to death, nor is any
man required to put me to death, but only, if I so act, then would
I be worthy of death. The ritual penalties of Masonry, supposing such
to be, are in the hands not of man, but of God, and are to he inflicted
by God, and not by man."—**Mackey's Encyclopædia of Freemasonry,
Article Penalty.**

gave unto him the tenth of the spoils. (He anoints him with a little oil on the crown of his head and says:)

Be thou a Priest forever, after the order of Melchizedek, virtuous, sincere, equitable, true; minister of justice and priest of toleration, be faithful to God, thy duty and thyself, and thus deserve the title of Sublime Pontiff or Scottish Mason, which you are henceforward entitled to wear. Rise now my brother, and receive the sign, token and words of this degree.

SIGN.

Extend horizontally the right arm; the hand is also extended, bring down the three last fingers perpendicularly.

Sign, Grand Pontiff Degree,

TOKEN.

Each places the palm of his right hand on the other's forehead; one says, Alleluia, the other answers Praise the Lord; the first then says, Emanuel, the other, God speed you. Both say Amen.

Token, Grand Pontiff.

BATTERY :—Twelve equi-timed strokes.

TO OPEN :—It is the predicted hour.

TO CLOSE :—The hour is accomplished.

PASS WORD :—Emanuel.

SACRED WORD :—Alleluia. (Every brother now advances in turn to the candidate and gives him the token.)

Thrice Puissant—(Invests him with Insignia, saying:)

This Robe of white linen, with which I now invest you, is emblematical of that equality and purity which should characterize one who is consecrated to the service of truth and remind us also of the vesture of the 144,-000 who refused to wear the mark of the beast upon their foreheads.

This Cordon of Crimson, bordered with white, teaches you that the zeal and ardor of a Knight and Pontiff ought to be set off by the greatest purity of morals and perfect charity and beneficence. The twelve stars upon it and upon the fillet allude to the twelve gates of the new city, and the twelve signs of the zodiac, the twelve fruits of the tree of life, the twelve tribes of Israel and the twelve Apostles, the initials of whose names appear upon the gates and foundation of the new city, and on the twelve columns of the Chapter.

This Fillet, is the peculiar emblem of your Pontificate, and as the slightest contact with earth will soil its spotless purity, remember that so the least indiscretion will soil the exalted character that you have now volun-

tarily assumed. Receive this jewel, and let the letters
upon it and the Cordon, the first and last of the Hebrew
and Greek alphabet, ever remind you of the love and
veneration which you owe to that great being; the
source of all existence, the Alpha and Omega, the first
and the last, on whose promises we rely with perfect
confidence, in whose mercy and goodness we implicitly
trust, and for the fulfillment of whose wise purposes we
are content to wait. (Warden shows candidate the
draft.)

Thrice Puissant—My brother, after the ceremonies of
this degree, this painting needs but little explanation.

The Serpent[210] writhing in chains has to us a peculiar
signification; it was promised that the offspring of the
woman should bruise the serpent's head, fulfill thou the
prophecy. (The candidate is caused to step on the three
heads of the serpent.)

Thrice Puissant—So shall the foot of truth crush
error! So honesty and honor tramples on falsehood,
so charity treads in the dust intolerance. Go now my
brother, and listen to the lecture of this degree. (The
Master of Ceremonies presents him to the Orator who
delivers [assisted by the Master of Ceremonies] the
lecture.

Note 210.—"Serpent. As a symbol, the serpent obtained a prominent
place in all the ancient initiations and religious. Among the Egyptians
it was the symbol of Divine Wisdom when extended at length. and the
serpent with his tail in his mouth was an emblem of eternity. The
winged globe and serpent symbolized their triune deity. In the ritual
of Zoroaster, the serpent was a symbol of the universe. In China, the
ring between two serpents was the symbol of the world governed by
the power and wisdom of the Creator. The same device is several times
repeated on the Isiac table. Higgins (Anacal., i. 521), says that, from
the faculty which the serpent possessed of renewing itself, without the
process of generation as to outward appearance, by annually casting
its skin. it became, like the Phoenix, the emblem of eternity; but he
denies that it ever represented. even in Genesis, the evil principle.
Faber's theory of the symbolism of the serpent, as set forth in his work
on the Origin of Pagan Idolatry, is ingenious. He says that the
ancients in part derived their idea of the serpent from the first tempter.
and hence it was a hieroglyphic of the evil principle. But as the deluge
was thought to have emanated from the evil principle, the serpent
became a symbol of the deluge. He also represented the good principle:
the idea being borrowed from the winged seraphim which was blended
with the cherubim who guarded the tree of life.—the seraphim and
cherubim being sometimes considered as identical."—Mackey's Encyclopaedia of Freemasonry, Article Serpent.

LECTURE DEGREE OF GRAND PONTIFF OR DOCTRINE OF GRAND PONTIFF.

Query—What are you?

Answer—I am a Sublime Grand Pontiff.

Query—Where did you receive this degree?

Answer—In a place that wants neither sun nor moon to light it.

Query—Explain this to me?

Answer—As the Grand Pontiffs never wanted any artificial lights to light them, in same manner the faithful and true brothers, the Sublime Grand Pontiffs want neither riches nor titles to be admitted into this sublime Chapter, as they prove themselves in their attachment to masonry, and faithfulness in their obligations and true friendship to their brethren.

Query—What represents the Draft of this Chapter?

Answer—A square city of four equal sides, with three gates on each side, in the middle of which is a tree bearing twelve different kinds of fruit; said city is suspended as on clouds, below is a representation of Jerusalem overturned and in ruins. There are twelve gates of pearl, three on each side; a great glory in the center gives it light, beneath the ruins of the city lies a serpent with three heads, bound in chains, on one side of the draft is a high mountain.

Query—Explain this to me?

Answer—The square city represents ancient masonry, under the title of Grand Pontiff, that comes down from Heaven to replace the ancient destruction (say the temple) when the Grand Pontiffs make it appear as 'tis represented by the ruins and the chained serpent with three heads.

Query—How comes masonry fallen to ruins, as we are so bound together by our obligations?

Answer—It was so decreed in olden times, as we learn by St. John, who we understand was the first mason that held a Perfect Chapter.

Query—Where does St. John say this?

Answer—In his revelation'''' where he talks of Babylon, and the celestial Jerusalem.

Query—What signifies the tree with twelve different kinds of fruit in the center of the city?

Answer—It is the tree of life which is placed there to make us understand where the sweets of life are to be found, and the twelve different kinds of fruit that we meet every month to instruct ourselves and sustain one another against our enemies.

Query—What signifies the fillet or veil that the candidate is blinded with?

Answer—It procures him entrance into our Chapter as it did procure entrance into the celestial Jerusalem to those that wore it; thus hath St. John'''' explained him-

Note 211.—"Apocalypse, Masonry of the.. The adoption of St. John the Evangelist as one of the patrons of our Lodges, has given rise, among the writers on Freemasonry, to a variety of theories as to the original cause of his being thus connected with the Institution. Several traditions have been handed down from remote periods, which claim him as a brother, among which the Masonic student will be familiar with that which represents him as having assumed the government of the Craft, as Grand Master, after the demise of John the Baptist. I confess that I am not willing to place implicit confidence in the correctness of this legend, and I candidly subscribe to the prudence of Dalcho's remark, that 'it is unwise to assert more than we can prove, and to argue against probability.' There must have been, however, in some way, a connection more or less direct between the Evangelist and the institution of Freemasonry, or he would not from the earliest times have been so universally claimed as one of its patrons. If it was simply a Christian feeling—a religious veneration—which gave rise to this general homage, I see no reason why St. Matthew, St. Mark, or St. Luke might not as readily and appropriately have been selected as one of the 'lines parallel.' But the fact is that there is something both in the life and in the writings of St. John the Evangelist, which closely connects him with our mystic Institution. He may not have been a Freemason in the sense in which we now use the term; but it will be sufficient, if it can be shown that he was familiar with other mystical institutions, which are themselves generally admitted to have been more or less intimately connected with Freemasonry by deriving their existence from a common origin."—Mackey's Encyclopaedia of Freemasonry, Article Apocalypse, Masonry of the.

self?

Query—What signifies the twelve golden stars on the Fillet?

Answer—They represent the twelve angels who watched the twelve gates of the celestial city of Jerusalem, the twelve signs of the zodiac, the twelve fruits of the tree of life, the twelve tribes of Israel, and the twelve apostles, the initials of whose names appear upon the gates and foundation of the new city and on the twelve columns of the Chapter.

Query—What signifies the blue hangings of the Chapter and the gold stars thereon?

Answer—The blue is the symbol of Lenity, Fidelity, and Sweetness, which ought to be the character of all faithful and true brothers; and the stars represent those

Note 212.—"'The whole machinery of the Apocalypse says Mr Faber, 'from beginning to end, seems to me very plainly to have been borrowed from the machinery of the Ancient Mysteries; and this, if we consider the nature of the subject, was done with the very strictest attention to poetical decorum.

'St. John himself is made to personate an aspirant about to be initiated; and, accordingly, the images presented to his mind's eye closely resemble the pageants of the Mysteries both in nature and in order of succession.'

'The prophet first beholds a door opened in the magnificent temple of heaven; and into this he is invited to enter by the voice of one who plays the hierophant. Here he witnesses the unsealing of a sacred book, and forthwith he is appalled by a troop of ghastly apparitions, which flit in horrid succession before his eyes. Among these are preeminently conspicuous a vast serpent, the well known symbol of the great father; and two portentous wild beasts, which severally come up out of the sea and out of the earth. Such hideous figures correspond with the canine phantoms of the Orgies, which seem to rise out of the ground, and with the polymorphic images of the hero god who was universally deemed the offspring of the sea.

'Passing these terrific monsters in safety, the prophet, constantly attended by his angel hierophant, who acts the part of an interpreter, is conducted into the presence of a female, who is described as closely resembling the great mother of Pagan theology. Like Isis emerging from the sea and exhibiting herself to the aspirant Apuleius, this female divinity, upborne upon the marine wild beast, appears to float upon the surface of many waters. She is said to be an open and systematical harlot, just as the great mother was the declared female principle of fecundity; and as she was always propitiated by literal fornication reduced to a religious system, and as the initiated were made to drink a prepared liquor out of a sacred goblet, so this harlot is represented as intoxicating the kings of the earth with the golden cup of her prostitution. On her forehead the very name of Mystery is inscribed; and the label teaches us that, in point of character, she is the great universal mother of idolatry.' "—Mackey's Encyclopaedia of Freemasonry, Article Apocalypse, Masonry of the.

masons who have given proof of their attachment to the statutes and rules of the order, which in the end will make them deserving of entering the celestial Jerusalem."[212]

Query—What is your name?

Answer—Faithful and True brother.

Note 212.—"All that is venerable, all that is universa., all that is worth preserving in Masonry, dates from Jerusalem, the Golden City, 'The City of the Great King.' There is no locality in the world so worthy of a mason's study as this, and, thanks to the researches of travelers, there is no city of ancient renown that has been so thoroughly explored and opened out to public view."—Morris's Masonic Dictionary.

CLOSING CEREMONIES

Degree of Grand Pontiff.

Thrice Puissant—Brother Warden, what is the hour?

Warden—Thrice Puissant, the hour is accomplished.

Thrice Puissant—What then remains to be done?

Warden—To work, to wait and be patient.

Thrice Puissant—Work then my brethren while it is yet day, for the night cometh in which no man can work. For what do we wait, brother Warden?

Warden—For the light of noon-day.

Thrice Puissant—Let us then close this Chapter and be patient brother Warden; inform the Knights and Pontiffs that I am about to close this Chapter if they consent in order that each may go forth into the world and do his duty as soldier and priest of Truth, Light and Toleration.

Warden—Brothers Knights and Pontiffs, the Thrice Puissant Master is about to close this Chapter if you consent that we may each go forth into the world and labor to elevate and enoble humanity as true soldier and priest of Light, Truth and Toleration. If you consent give me the sign. (All give the sign.)

Thrice Puissant—Raps as in opening.

Warden—Raps as in opening.

All—Clap twelve and cry three times, Hoshea.

Thrice Puissant—The sun climbs toward the Zenith and this Chapter is closed.

PHILOSOPHICAL ANALYSIS

NINETEENTH DEGREE, OR GRAND PONTIFF.

Idolatry the Parent of all Sin—The Lodge Master Personates Christ—The Purpose to Inspire Awe and Horror—Masonry the Image of the Romish Beast—Character of Dr. Dalcho.

"What is the matter with a little by-play of idolatry?" _Ans._—The matter is just this:—From kissing one s hand to the moon, in the days of the Patriarch Job. (_c. 31, 27,_) to Sun-worship by solemn circumambulation in a Masonic lodge; every act of idolatry, however trivial or contemptible, is an expedient to un-God our globe, by getting rid of Christ. When the Eternal Father brought forth his Son into the world, and said: _"Let all the Angels of God worship him;"_ (_Heb. 1, 6,_) one angel refused, and became chief of the devils. And all "Gentile" or Christless worship is paid to that fallen angel, or to some of his legions, (_1, Cor. 10:20._) To dispense with Christ, is to leave our ruined race with no means or mediator, by whom to reach God and Heaven. And the lodge dispenses with Christ, by dropping his name and person, to take in his enemies; Jews, pagans and others; or, by insulting him with false, spurious worships. When Aaron told Israel to worship Jehovah, by dancing naked around a calf, (_Ex. 32:18,_) he attempted to add a heathen ritual to an orthodox creed: and three thousand men that day paid for their idolatry with their lives. The sins of men are numberless. Idolatry is the one parent of them all; and lodge worship is idolatry. And, of all idolarty, the most daring and damning, is *when sinners imitate and copy the approaches of God to men.* And this is what is done in this 19th degree.

The lodge master is *"Thrice Puissant;"* personating Christ, who has *"all power."* The master is "seated on a throne and holds a Sceptre," with the blue canopy of the heavens over him. This is Christ's rival, the usurping *"god of this world."* The degree itself, says Mackey, (*Note 197,*) "is founded on the mysteries of the Apocalypse," which is "the Revelation of Jesus Christ," (*Rev. 1, 1.*) And his lodge members are "clothed in white linen robes," like attending Angels; (*Rev. 15:6.*) And on the jewel is engraved *"Alpha and Omega,"* which is the title of Christ. And in opening, the Warden says: "the Sun of Truth has risen." "Christ is the Sun of Righteousness." And ' *The Truth and Life."* And, as in a preceding degree, the grim mockery of opening the seals and sounding the trumpets (p. 451,) was gone through with, so here follow the vials poured out, and the dwelling place of God, the New Jerusalem, comes down to men. And after these superlatively impudent mockeries are gone through with, the candidate is made to kneel down and swear to conceal them from all but Masons of this degree; after which the candidate is solemnly anointed into the priesthood of Christ, who is "a priest forever after the order of Melchizedek." There is nothing more revoltingly blasphemous in the Mormon Endowment House, where Brigam Young used, as *El Shaddai,* to personate Almighty God! And when this horrible fanfaronade is gone through with, by men such as are found in ordinary Masonic lodges, the wretched dupe is told that he is 'henceforward entitled to wear the sublime title of Scottish Mason.' It is noticeable that in this blasphemous recitative, there are no ascriptions of glory to Christ. The ritual runs; (p. 22.)

"Salvation, Glory, Honor and Power to the Eternal God and Infinite Father."

The Bible ascription is;—"Every creature which is in Heaven and on the Earth; and under the Earth, and such as are in the Sea, and all that are in them, heard I saying; blessing and honor and glory and power be unto him that sitteth upon the throne, *and unto the Lamb,* forever and ever."

While the book itself is *"the Revelation of Jesus Christ,"* this Rite mutilates it by leaving him out of such passages as the above and compliments him only with a half contemptuous allusion to him as "the Master of Nazareth;" and a wooden image of a lamb, lying on a book with seven seals; with a further allusion to him as "the Word."

But the most extraordinary part of this 19th degree is its bold allusion to "the Beast and His image."

The candidate is being led twelve times around the lodge, he is jerked into a small dark room and seated on the floor; sitting there he hears a brother say: "All who will not worship the Beast with seven heads and ten horns, shall be slain;" all men, the high and low, the rich and the poor, freeman and slave shall receive upon their right hand, or on their forehead his mark, etc., or they shall neither buy nor sell." And a second brother takes up the strain and adds:—"Remorse shall torture them and they shall have no rest who worship the beast and his image;" and here the matter is dropped. The purpose would seem to be to inspire awe and horror in the candidate, and leave his mind in absolute emptiness and confusion.

Now the secret lodge system of which this Rite is the ruling part, is the image of the Romish beast, which was, and is the secret despotism of the world. That the seven-headed beast with his harlot rider is Rome, the book itself teaches, (*Rev. 17, 18.*) *"The woman which thou sawest is that great city which ruleth over the Kings of the Earth."* There can be no mistaking this. No other city on earth ever claimed and exercised jurisdiction over Kings. Pagan Rome was the Beast, and Popery the religious harlot rider.   In this, without exception Protestant commentators agree.

And the lodge net-work which now covers the Globe, differs from Rome in two particulars: It has neither fixed government, church or nationality like Rome: but lodges are made "by *them that dwell on the Earth*," (*Rev.* 13, 14,) promiscuously; neither visible government nationality or church, yet controls business and religion! 2nd.—It is flitting as a shadowy image; changing its shapes endlessly, but keeping its diabolical priest nature. And the beast and his image are one, murderous and false as their master and god Satan, who was "liar and murderer from the beginning and the father of it." (*Jno.* 8, 44.)   And the last we hear of them; Beast, False Prophet, Image and their worshipers, they are cast into a *lake of fire burning with brimstone, (Rev.* 19, 20.)   And whoever comforts himself in the fact that the fire and brimstone are not literal, will doubtless find the reality as fearful as its symbols.

One would suppose that a scripture like this would be the last woven into a Masonic rite, by men supposed to be educated and attentive to their own interests. The only explanation which can be suggested is that these degrees are the work of semi-apostate priests, like those swept into the French Revolution of 1789, manufactured at the Jesuits' College of Clermont in 1754-8:—That they were sent to this country in 1761 by an ex-Jew, *Morin,* whose religion was money, as the Rite of Perfection:—that *Morin* appointed sixteen "Inspectors General" with himself, of whom thirteen were Jews also. Dr. Dalcho, the son of a Prussian, born in London, a soldier, settled in Charleston, S. C.; a Physician,

afterwards a priest in the Prot. Episcopal Church:—A
Sovereign Inspector of the Scottish Rite:—helped form
the first Supreme Council:—A successful Masonic writer; became involved in Masonic disputes, and quit Masonry in disgust and died out of connection with the
Order.

Such were the minds that formed the present Ruling
Rite of the world. They took the old Rite of Perfection and the swarms of side degrees which had over run
Europe, combined, modified and revised:—added eight
more to make the present Rite of 33°, which fears not
God nor regards man. Such men could dabble with
"The beast and his image, as snake-fanciers play with
snakes; conscious of no motive but to make an impression, not knowing they were dabbling with their own
doom!

In the closing lecture of this degree we have the key
to the motive of the contrivers:—*Query.*—"What signifies the tree with twelve different kinds of fruit in the
centre of the City," (p. 30.)

"*Answer*—It is the tree of life which is placed there
to make us understand where the sweets of life are, and
the twelve different kinds of fruit that we meet every
month to instruct ourselves, and sustain one another
against our enemies." Thus from the creation until
now, the Globe has stood and trees and fruits have grown
ripened and fallen for a Masonic lodge! It is difficult
to determine whether stupidity, cunning, swindling or
superstition predominates in this vile compound. And
though one can understand how sorcerers and jugglers
can deal with such trash; the minister of Christ, who
has ever known the truth, and yet deals in it must surely incur "*wrath to the uttermost.*"

CHAPTER XXXV

Twentieth Degree; Grand Master of all Symbolic Lodges or Associate Master ad Vitam.

[Past Master] also called Grand Master of Wisdom.

VENUS OR ADONIS. ♀ ***

DECORATIONS:—The hangings are blue and gold. In the east is a throne which you ascend by nine steps, under a canopy, before it is an altar on which are an open

Note 214.—"Adonis, Mysteries of. An investigation of the mysteries of Adonis peculiarly claims the attention of the Masonic student: first, because, in their symbolism and in their esoteric doctrine, the religious object for which they were instituted, and the mode in which that object is attained, they bear a nearer analogical resemblance to the Institution of Freemasonry than do any of the other mysteries or systems of initiation of the ancient world; and, secondly, because their chief locality brings them into a very close connection with the early history and reputed origin of Freemasonry. For they were principally celebrated at Byblos, a city of Phoenicia, whose scriptural name was Gebal, and whose inhabitants were the Giblites or Giblemites, who are referred to in the 1st Book of Kings (chap. v. 18) as being the stone-squarers employed by King Solomon in building the Temple. Hence there must have evidently been a very intimate connection, or at least certainly a very frequent intercommunication, between the workmen of the first Temple and the inhabitants of Byblos, the seat of the Adonisian mysteries, and the place whence the worshipers of that rite were disseminated over other regions of country.

These historical circumstances invite us to an examination of the system of initiation which was practised at Byblos, because we may find in it something that was probably suggestive of the symbolic system of instruction which was subsequently so prominent a feature in the system of Freemasonry.

Let us first examine the myth on which the Adonisiac initiation was founded. The mythological legend of Adonis is, that he was the son of Myrrha and Cinyras, King of Cyprus. Adonis was possessed of such surpassing beauty, that Venus became enamored with him, and adopted him as her favorite. Subsequently Adonis, who was a great hunter, died from a wound inflicted by a wild boar on Mount Lebanon. Venus flew to the succor of her favorite, but she came too late. Adonis was dead. On his descent to the infernal regions, Proserpine became, like Venus, so attracted by his beauty, that, notwithstanding the entreaties of the goddess of love, she refused to restore him to earth. At length the prayers of the desponding Venus were listened to with favor by Jupiter, who reconciled the dispute between the two goddesses, and by whose decree Proserpine was compelled to consent that Adonis should spend six months of each year alternately with herself and Venus."—Mackey's Encyclopaedia of Freemasonry, Article Adonis, Mysteries of.

Bible, square and compass, sword, mallet, etc., etc., as in a Symbolic lodge. The lodge is lighted by nine[215] lights of three triangles one within the other, in a candlestick with nine branches between the altar and the west on the tracing board. Over the Venerable Master in the East is a glory surrounding a triangle, in the centre of which are the words Fiat Lux.[216] In the middle of the room surrounding the altar, in the form of a triangle are three columns on which are these words: On that in the East, Truth, on that in the West, Justice, on that in the South, Toleration. The lodge cannot be opened unless nine members be present. Besides the nine lights mentioned above, there may be others used in different parts of the lodge; but should be arranged in squares and triangles. The nine great lights should be of yellow[217] wax.

OFFICERS:—The officers are as in a Symbolic lodge; the Orator sits in the North and the Pursuivant guards the door within. All wear their hats.

SASH:—The sash is yellow and sky blue, or two, one of each color, crossing each other.

APRON:—The apron is yellow, lined and bordered with sky blue. Upon it in the centre are three equilateral triangles one within the other, with the initial letters of the nine great lights in the corners; thus in the corners of the outer one at the apex, C.·.; at the

Note 215.—"Nine. This is one the sacred Numbers. It possesses remarkable powers of reproduction, and in the Pythagorean philosophy was made the subject of much mysterious dissertation."—Morris's Masonic Dictionary, Article Nine.

Note 216.—"Lux Fiat et Lux Fit, Latin. 'Let there be light, and there was light.' A motto sometimes prefixed to Masonic documents."—Mackey's Encyclopaedia of Freemasonry, Article Lux Fiat et Lux Fit.

Note 217.—"The natural sun was the symbol of the spiritual sun. Gold represented the natural sun, and yellow was the emblem of gold. But it is evident that yellow derives all its significance as a symbolic color from its connection with the hue of the rays of the sun and the metal gold.
  Among the ancients, the divine light or wisdom was represented by yellow, as the divine heat or power was by red. And this appears to be about the whole of the ancient symbolism of this color."—Mackey's Encyclopaedia of Freemasonry, Article Yellow.

right hand corner G.·.; at the left V.·.; middle triangle, at the apex, H.·.; at the right P.·.; at the left H.·.; inner one, at the apex T.·.; at the right T.·.; at the left Z.·.. In the centre of the inner one in the tetragrammaton[218] and across it from below upwards, the words *Fiat Lux.*

TRACING BOARD:—The tracing board is an octagon with a square raised on each of five sides, and an equilateral triangle on each of the three others, with the initials of the twenty-nine virtues of a mason in the corners of the squares and triangles. In the centre of the octagon are the nine great lights.

JEWEL:—The jewel is gold, like the triangle on the apron, with the same words and letters, or like the tracing board.

BATTERY:—Is one and two; 0 00.

Note 218. "Tetragrammaton. In Greek. It signifies a word of four letters. It is the title given by the Talmudists to the name of God Jehovah, which in the original Hebrew consists of four letters."— Mackey's Encyclopaedia of Freemasonry, Article Tetragrammaton.

OPENING CEREMONIES

Grand Master of all Symbolic Lodges.[219]

Venerable Master—(Knocks one.) Grand Master and brethren, the hour has come for this Grand Lodge to convene, be pleased to clothe yourselves and repair to your stations.

Venerable Master—Brother Junior Deacon, see that the doors are well tyled. (He obeys.)

Junior Deacon—Venerable Grand Master, the doors are duly tyled.

Venerable Master—Brother Senior Grand Warden, ascertain whether all present are Grand Masters. (Senior Warden goes around, receives the word from each brother and returns to his station.)

Senior Warden—Venerable Grand Master, all present have proved themselves Grand Masters.

Venerable Master—Brother Junior Grand Deacon, what compose the first masonic square?

Note 819.—"Grand Master of all Symbolic Lodges. The 20th degree of the Ancient and Accepted rite. This degree affords a thorough exemplification of the philosophical spirit of the system of Freemasonry. Philosophy and Masonry, being one and the same principle, have the same object and mission to attain—the worship of the Great Architect of the universe, and the disenthralment of mankind. Here the candidate is charged with the responsible duties of instructor of the great truths of the universality of Masonry, inspired by an upright and enlightened reason, a firm and rational judgment, and an affectionate and liberal philanthropy. This degree bears the same relation to Ineffable Masonry that the Past Master's degree does to the symbolic degrees. Veneration, Charity, Generosity, Heroism, Honor, Patriotism, Justice, Toleration, and Truth are inculcated. The body is called a Lodge; the hangings are blue and gold. The presiding officer is styled Venerable Grand Master, and is seated in the East. A Lodge cannot be opened with less than nine members. In the East is a throne, ascended by nine steps, and surmounted by a canopy; the Lodge is lighted by nine lights of yellow wax. The apron is yellow, bordered and lined with blue; the sash is of broad yellow and blue ribbon, passing from the left shoulder to the right hip; the jewel is a triangle, of gold, on which is engraved the initials of the sacred words."—Macoy's Encyclopaedia and Dictionary of Freemasonry, Article Grand Master of all Symbolic Lodges.

Junior Deacon—Prudence, Temperance, Chastity and Sobriety.

Venerable Master—Brother Senior Grand Deacon, what compose the second masonic square?

Senior Deacon—Heroism, Firmness, Equanimity and Patience.

Venerable Master—Brother Grand Secretary, what compose the third masonic square?

Grand Secretary—Purity, Honor, Fidelity and Punctuality.

Venerable Master—Brother Grand Treasurer, what compose the fourth masonic square?

Grand Treasurer—Charity, Kindness, Generosity and Liberality.

Venerable Master—Brother Grand Orator, what compose the fifth masonic square?

Grand Orator—Disinterestedness, Mercy, Forgiveness and Forbearance.

Venerable Master—Brother Junior Grand Warden, what is the first great masonic triangle?

Junior Warden—Veneration, Devotedness, and Patriotism.

Venerable Master—Brother Senior Grand Warden, what is the second great masonic triangle?

Senior Warden—Gratitude to God, Love of mankind, and confidence in human nature.

Venerable Master—And the third great masonic triangle, composed of Truth which includes Frankness, Plain Dealing and Sincerity; Justice which includes Equity and Impartiality; and Toleration.

Venerable Master—(One rap,) Brethren in the South, what seek ye to attain in masonry?

Junior Deacon—Light, the light of Knowledge, Science and Philosophy.

Venerable Master—Brethren in the North, what seek

ye to attain in masonry?

Grand Orator—Light, the light of liberty, free thought, free speech for all mankind, free conscience, free action, within law, the same for all.

Venerable Master—Brethren in the West, what seek ye to attain in masonry?

Senior Warden—Light, the great light of God's divine truth, eternal as himself; and of virtue, immortal as the soul.

Venerable Master—Aid me then my brethren to open this lodge, that we may seek the true masonic light. Together brethren.

All—(Give the sign.)

Venerable Master—My brethren, let the great lights of the lodge shine.

Pursuivant—(Advances, lights one of the great lights and returns.) Let veneration for the deity burn in this lodge as its first great light.

Senior Deacon—(Lighting another light.) Let the light of generosity be lifted up in this lodge.

Grand Orator—(Lighting another.) Let the light of heroism blaze like the day among us.

Grand Treasurer—(Lighting another.) Let the light of honor ever direct our footsteps.

Grand Secretary—(Lighting another.) Let the light of patriotism shine in our souls as in the lodge.

Junior Warden—(Lighting another.) Let the great light of justice burn steadily upon our altars.

Senior Warden—(Lighting another.) Let the great light of toleration dim the fires of persecution.

Venerable Master—Let the great light of truth, (lights it) illumine our souls and complete the great triangles of perfection.

Venerable Master—Together brethren.

All—(Clap one and two; 0 00.) Fiat Lux.

Venerable Master—Brethren the nine great lights are burning in our lodge and it is duly open; be seated.

CHAPTER XXXVI

Twentieth Degree; Grand Master of all Symbolic
Lodges or Associate Grand Master
Ad vitam.[220]

[Past Master] also called Grand Master of Wisdom[221]

INITIATION.

[The nine great lights having been extinguished, the
Senior Deacon retires, invests the candidate with the
collar and jewel of a Grand Pontiff and the jewel of a
Rose Croix and leads him to the door.]

Senior Deacon—(Knocks one and two; 0 00.)

Junior Deacon—(From within knocks three, 0 00;
and opens the door.) Who seeks admission?

Senior Deacon—A mason, who having attained the

Note 220.—"Ad Vitam. [Scotch Masonry.]—The principle of life-
office (ad vitam, for life) has been adopted to a limited extent in
American Grand Lodges by giving to Past Grand Masters. Past Masters
of Lodges, life-membership with restricted suffrage. But in Scotch
Masonry ad vitam has its broadest scope; in some countries the highest
officer in the institution holding his office for life."—Morris's Masonic
Dictionary, Article Ad Vitam.

Note 221.—"King Solomon has been adopted in Speculative Masonry
as the type or representative of wisdom, in accordance with the character which has been given to him in the First Book of Kings (iv. 30-32:)
'Solomon's wisdom exceeded the wisdom of all the children of the east
country, and all the wisdom of Egypt. For he was wiser than all men;
than Ethan the Ezrahite, and Heman and Chalcol and Darda, the sons
of Mahol; and his fame was in all the nations round about.'

In all the Oriental philosophies a conspicuous place has been given
to wisdom. In the book called the Wisdom of Solomon, (vii. 7, 8). but
supposed to be the production of a Hellenistic Jew, it is said: 'I called
upon God, and the spirit of wisdom came to me. I preferred her before
sceptres and thrones, and esteemed riches nothing in comparison of her.'
And farther on in the same book, (vii. 25-27,) she is described as 'the
breath of the power of God, and a pure influence [emanation] flowing
from the glory of the Almighty..... the brightness of the everlasting
light, the unspotted mirror of the power of God, and the image of his
goodness.'"—Mackey's Encyclopaedia of Freemasonry, Article Wisdom.

nineteenth degree desires to be here qualified to preside over all symbolic lodges that he may still further advance in masonry.

Junior Deacon—Is it not through mere idle curiosity, or for the sake of distinction among his fellows that he makes this request?

Senior Deacon—It is not.

Junior Deacon—Is he of that number of masons who, having attained this degree, repose thereafter in contented indolence, indifferent to the evils that demand to be redressed?

Senior Deacon—He is not.

Junior Deacon—Is he of that class of masons who utter beautiful sentiments and press on others the performance of masonic duty, and with that remain content?

Senior Deacon—He is not.

Junior Deacon—Is he of that class of masons who spare their own purse and levy liberal contributions on those of others, for works of charity and the welfare of the order?

Senior Deacon—He is not.

Junior Deacon—If he be one of these let him speedily withdraw; for such we have here no room, no need, no use; do you vouch for him that he is none of these?

Senior Deacon—I do.

Junior Deacon—Then let him wait with patience until the Venerable Grand Master is informed of his request, and his answer returned. (Junior Deacon closes the door, goes to the Grand Master, knocks three; 0 00, and the same questions are asked and the like answers returned as before, except the last.)

Venerable Master—Let the candidate be admitted.

Junior Deacon—(Having returned and opened the door.) It is the order of the Venerable Grand Master, that the candidate be admitted. (Senior Deacon enters with him and places him in the centre of the triangle formed by the three columns surrounding the altar and leaves him.)

Venerable Master—My brother you have often knelt before the altar of masonry, and you now stand before it again, enclosed in a great triangle formed by three great columns which support this lodge. What name do you read upon the column in the South?

Candidate—Toleration.

Venerable Master—No man has the right to dictate to another in matters of belief or faith; no man can say that he has possession of truth as he has of a chattel. When man persecutes for opinion's sake, he usurps the prerogative of God. Do you admit the truth of these principles?

Candidate—I do.

Venerable Master—What name do you read upon the column in the West?

Candidate—Justice.[222]

Venerable Master—Man should judge others as he judges himself; believe others honest and sincere as he believes himself; find for their actions the excuses that he readily finds for his own, and look always for a good rather than a bad motive. God made them common to all, and he who denies justice to his brother or wrongs him in any manner is unfit to live. Do you recognize the truth of these principles?

Candidate—I do.

Venerable Master—What name do you read on the

Note 222.—"Justice. One of the four cardinal virties, the practice of which is inculcated in the first degree. The mason who remembers how emphatically he has been charged to preserve an upright position in all his dealings with mankind, should never fail to act justly to himself, to his brethren, and to the world. This is the corner-stone on which alone he can expect to erect a superstructure alike honorable to himself and to the Fraternity. In iconology, Justice is usually represented as a matron with bandaged eyes, holding in one hand a sword and in the other a pair of scales at equipoise. But in Masonry the true symbol of Justice, as illustrated in the first degree, is the feet firmly planted on the ground, and the body upright."—Mackey's Encyclopaedia of Freemasonry, Article Justice.

column in the East?

Candidate—Truth."""

Venerable Master—He who lies is a coward; no falsehood can be other than evil. To lie expressly, or by implication, is base and dishonorable; without truth there can be no virtue, and he who professes an opinion he does not entertain, originates a falsehood and is a slanderer and deserves to be branded as such. Do you recognize the truth of these principles?

Candidate—I do.

Venerable Master—Will you make them hereafter the rule of your life, conduct and conversation, letting no inducement however stringent persuade you to swerve from them?

Candidate—I will.

Venerable Master—Kneel then at the altar and assume the obligation of this degree. (The candidate kneels and contracts the following obligation.)

OBLIGATION GRAND MASTER OF ALL SYMBOLIC LODGES."""

I......of my own free will and accord, in the presence of the Great Architect of the Universe, do hereby and hereon solemnly and sincerely swear, and to each

Note 223.—"Truth. Truth is a divine attribute, and the foundation of every virtue. To be good and true, is the first lesson we are taught in Masonry. On this theme we contemplate, and by its dictates endeavor to regulate our conduct; influenced by this principle, hypocrisy and deceit are unknown in the lodge; sincerity and plain dealing distinguish us, while the heart and tongue join in promoting the general welfare, and rejoicing in each other's prosperity.—Preston."—Macoy's Encyclopaedia and Dictionary of Freemasonry, Article Truth.

Note 224.—"Grand Master of all Symbolic Lodges. (Venerable Maitre de toutes les Loges. The twentieth degree in the Ancient and Accepted Scottish Rite. The presiding officer is styled Venerable Grand Master, and is assisted by two Wardens in the west. The decorations of the Lodge are blue and yellow. The old ritual contains some interesting instructions respecting the first and second Temple.

Among the traditions preserved by the possessors of this degree, is one which states that after the third Temple was destroyed by Titus, the son of Vespasian, the Christian Freemasons who were then in the Holy Land, being filled with sorrow, departed from home with the determination of building a fourth, and that, dividing themselves into several bodies, they dispersed over the various parts of Europe. The greater number went to Scotland, and repaired to the town of Kilwinning, where they established a Lodge and built an abbey, and where the records of the Order were deposited. This tradition preserved in the original rituals, is a very strong presumptive evidence that the degree owed its existence to the Templar system of Ramsay."—Mackey's Encyclopaedia of Freemasonry, Article Grand Master of all Symbolic Lodges.

Grand Master here present, promise and vow that I will never reveal any of the secrets of this degree to any person or persons, except to one duly authorized to receive them.

I do furthermore promise and swear that I will hereafter make these virtues, which compose the five masonic squares and three masonic triangles of this lodge, the rule and guide of my life, conduct and conversation, and will endeavor to extend and increase the practice of them among men; and particularly that my steps shall ever be guided and directed by the nine great lights of a Grand Master, as I shall hereafter be informed.

I furthermore promise and swear that I will not rule and govern my lodge in a haughty manner, but will use my best endeavors to preserve peace and order and harmony among the members. To all these and those, I do most solemnly and sincerely promise and swear, binding myself under no less a penalty than that of being dishonored and despised by all masons. So help me God.

Venerable Master—Arise my brother and receive the signs, grips and words of this degree. (Candidate rises and receives the following:)

FIRST SIGN.

Form four squares; first by placing the right hand on the heart, the fingers close together, the thumb separate, which makes two squares; second by placing the left hand on the lips, the thumb separate, which makes a third square; third by bringing the heels together, the feet open on a square.

SECOND SIGN.

Kneel down, place the elbows on the floor, the head downwards and a little inclined to the left.

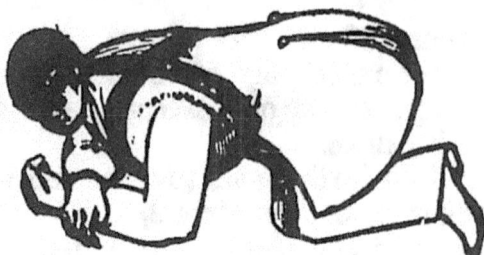

Second Sign, 20th Degree.

THIRD SIGN.

Cross the arms on the breast, the right arm over the left, the fingers extended and close together, the thumb forming a square, heels touching, which makes **five** squares.

Third Sign, 20th Degree.

N. B.—In some rituals only one sign is given instead of the first two, and this is to kneel on the right knee, the left hand being raised, which forms two squares; then place the left elbow on the left knee, fingers extended and closed, the thumb forming the square, the head downwards, somewhat inclined to the left.

SIGN OF INTRODUCTION.

The sword elevated, or if no sword is worn, the right arm raised before the head as if to ward off a stroke. In coming together, cross swords and form the arch of steel.

TOKEN.

Take one the other's right elbow, with the right hand; press it four times; then slide the hand along the forearm down to the wrist; lastly, press the wrist-joint with the first finger only.

Token, 20th Degree.

Token of Introduction.

TOKEN OF INTRODUCTION.

[Given after the sign of introduction.]

Take each other's right hand, the first finger on the wrist joint; then as you retire slide the hand along the other's hand down to the tip of the fingers.

N. B.—Some in the last token squeeze on the other's wrist, each drawing the other nine times alternately, and repeating each time the word Cyrus.

BATTERY:—The battery is three strokes, by one and two; 0 00.

MARCH:—Nine steps, each forming a square.

PASS WORD:—Jekson.[225]

ANSWER:—Stolkin.

SACRED WORD:—Razah-belsijah,

Venerable Master—(Investing him with the collar, jewel and apron.) My brother, as the presiding officer

Note 225.—"Jekson. This word is found in the French Cahiers of the high degrees. It is undoubtedly a corruption of Jacquesson, and this a mongrel word compounded of the French Jacques and the English son, and means the son of James, that is, James II. It refers to Charles Edward the Pretender, who was the son, of that abdicated and exiled monarch. It is a significant relic of the system attempted to be introduced by the adherents of the house of Stuart, and by which they expected to enlist Masonry as an instrument to effect the restoration of the Pretender to the throne of England. For this purpose they had altered the legend of the third degree, making it applicable to Charles II., who, being the son of Henrietta Maria, the widow of Charles I., was designated as 'the widow's son.' "—Mackey's Encyclopaedia of Freemasonry, Article Jekson.

of a lodge, it will be your duty to dispense light and knowledge to the brethren. That duty is not performed, nor is that which the old charges require, that at opening and closing the Master shall give a lecture or portion thereof for the instruction of the brethren. On the contrary that duty is far higher and more important, and it behooves the Master to be prepared to perform it; nor should any one accept the office of Master, until by acquaintance and familiarity with the history, morals and philosophy of masonry, he is fitted to enlighten and instruct his brethren. That you may ever remember that duty, you will now proceed symbolically to perform it by restoring to us the splendor of our nine great lights in masonry.

Brother Senior Grand Warden, let the great light of veneration shine in our lodge. (The Master now goes to the East and the Senior Warden conducts the candidate once around the lodge, walking over the crossswords, which lay on the floor between the columns of justice and the tracing board, and by the altar of incense up to the north-west light of the triangle, which the candidate lights. He is then conducted up to and facing the altar of obligation.)

Venerable Master—The light shines, let us applaud my brethren.

All—(Clap three; 0 00.) Lux Est.

Venerable Master—(To candidate.) Say after me my brother: So let the light of Veneration shine in me.

Candidate—(Repeats.)

Venerable Master—Brother Senior Grand Warden, let the great light of Charity*** shine in our lodge

Note 226.—"However freemasons may fall short of their profession in other things, the most severe criticism cannot deny their proficiency in charity."—Morris's Masonic Dictionary, Article Charity.

(Senior Warden conducts candidate as before, and he lights that light and is conducted back.)

Venerable Master—The light shines, let us applaud my brethren.

All—(Clap three; 0 00.)

Venerable Master—Say after me my brother: So let the light of Charity shine in me.

Candidate—(Repeats.)

Venerable Master—Brother Senior Grand Warden, let the great light of Generosity shine in our lodge. (Senior Warden conducts candidate as before and causes him to light the third light.)

Venerable Master—The light shines, let us applaud my brethren.

All—(Clap three; 0 00.)

Venerable Master—Say after me my brother: So let the great light of Generosity shine in me.

Candidate—(Repeats.)

Venerable Master—Brother Senior Grand Warden, let the great light of Heroism shine in our lodge. (Senior Warden conducts him and causes him to light the fourth light.)

Venerable Master—The light shines, let us applaud my brethren.

All—(Clap three; 0 00.)

Venerable Master—Say after me my brother· So may the light of Heroism shine in me.

Candidate—(Repeats.)

Venerable Master—Brother Senior Grand Warden, let the great light of Honor shine in our lodge. (Senior Warden causes him to light the fifth light.)

Venerable Master—The light shines, let us applaud my brethren.

All—(Clap three; 0 00.)

Venerable Master—Say after me. my brother: So may the light of Honor shine in me.

Candidate—(Repeats.)

Venerable Master—Brother Senior Grand Warden, let the great light of Patriotism shine in our lodge. (Senior Warden conducts and causes him to light the sixth light.)

Venerable Master—The light shines, let us applaud my brethren.

All—(Clap three · 0 00.)

Venerable Master—Say after me my brother: So may the light of Patriotism shine in me.

Candidate—(Repeats.)

Venerable Master—Brother Senior Grand Warden, let the great light of Justice shine in our lodge. (Senior Warden causes him to light the seventh light.)

Venerable Master—The light shines, let us applaud my brethren.

All—(Clap three; 0 00.)

Venerable Master—Say after me my brother: So may the light of Justice shine in me.

Candidate—(Repeats.)

Venerable Master—Brother Senior Grand Warden, let the great light of Toleration shine in our lodge. (Senior Warden conducts and causes him to light the eighth light.)

Venerable Master—The light shines, let us applaud my brethren.

All—(Clap three; 0 00.)

Venerable Master—Say after me my brother: So may the light of Toleration shine in me.

Candidate—(Repeats.)

Venerable Master—Brother Senior Grand Warden,

let the great light of Truth"" shine in our lodge. (Senior Warden causes him to light the ninth light.)

Venerable Master—The light shines, let us applaud my brethren.

All—(Clap three; 0 00.)

Venerable Master—Say after me my brother: So may the Divine light of Truth shine in me.

Candidate—(Repeats.)

Venerable Master—Seal now, and perfect your obligation as Grand Master of all Symbolic Lodges; repeat after me: (Candidate repeats as follows:)

Venerable Master—And when these great lights cease to illumine my soul, direct my conduct and guide my footsteps, may I, false mason and faithless man, cease to exist and be remembered only to be despised. So help me God.

Venerable Master—Brother Senior Grand Warden, you will now give the candidate an explanation of the tracing-board."" (Senior Warden conducts him to tracing-board."")

Senior Warden—My brother, behold the five great

Note 227.—"To be good and true is the first lesson we are taught in Masonry. On this theme we contemplate, and by its dictates endeavor to regulate our conduct. Hence, while influenced by this principle, hypocrisy and deceit are unknown among us, sincerity and plain dealing distinguish us, and the heart and tongue join in promoting each other's welfare and rejoicing in each other's prosperity."—Morris's Masonic Dictionary, Article Truth.

Note 228.—"Tracing-Board. The same as a Floor-Cloth, which see." —Mackey's Encyclopaedia of Freemasonry, Article Tracing-Board.

Note 229.—"Floor-Cloth. A frame-work of board or canvas, on which the emblems of any particular degree are inscribed, for the assistance of the Master in giving a lecture. It is so called because formerly it was the custom to inscribe these designs on the floor of the Lodge room in chalk, which was wiped out when the Lodge was closed. It is the same as the 'Carpet,' or 'Tracing-Board.' "—Mackey's Encyclopaedia of Freemasonry, Article Floor-Cloth.

squares, and three great triangles[210] of masonry composed as follows:

The Square[211] at the bottom of the Octagon that surrounds the Ineffable name, and the seven letters of the words with which he created light; of Prudence, Temperance,[212] Chastity and Sobriety.

First Square on the right; of Heroism, Firmness, Equanimity and Patience.

First Square on the left; of Probity, Honor, Fidelity[213] and Punctuality.

Note 230.—"Triangle. There is no symbol more important in its significance, more various in its application, or more generally diffused throughout the whole system of Freemasonry, than the triangle. An examination of it, therefore, cannot fail to be interesting to the Masonic student.

The equilateral triangle appears to have been adopted by nearly all the nations of antiquity as a symbol of the Deity, in some of his forms or emanations, and hence, probably, the prevailing influence of this symbol was carried into the Jewish system, where the yod within the triangle was made to represent the Tetragrammaton, or sacred name of God.

'The equilateral triangle,' says Bro. D. W. Nash (Freem. Mag., iv. 294,) 'viewed in the light of the doctrines of those who gave it currency as a divine symbol, represents the Great First Cause, the creator and container of all things, as one and indivisible, manifesting himself in an infinity of forms and attributes in this visible universe.'

Among the Egyptians, the darkness through which the candidate for initiation was made to pass was symbolized by the trowel, an important Masonic implement, which in their system of hieroglyphics has the form of a triangle. The equilateral triangle they considered as the most perfect of figures, and a representative of the great principle of animated existence, each of its sides referring to one of the three departments of creation, the animal, vegetable, and mineral."—Mackey's Encyclopaedia of Freemasonry, Article Triangle.

Note 231.—"In the very earliest catechism of the last century, of the date of 1725, we find the answer to the question, How many make a Lodge? is 'God and the Square, with five or seven right or perfect Masons.' God and the Square, religion and morality, must be present in every Lodge as governing principles. Signs at that early period were to be made by squares, and the furniture of the Lodge was declared to be the Bible, Compass and Square.

In all rites and in all languages where Masonry has penetrated, the square has preserved its primitive signification as a symbol of morality.—Mackey's Encyclopaedia of Freemasonry, Article Square.

Note 232.—"The Worshipful Master is required publicly to declare, in the ceremony of his installation, that he will 'guard against intemperance and excess.' The Junior Warden is charged to see that the brethren 'do not convert the purposes of refreshment into intemperance and excess.' Finally, this vice is made a prominent subject of masonic penalties."—Morris's Masonic Dictionary, Article Temperance.

Note 233.—"Noel (Dict. Fab.) says that there was an ancient marble at Rome consecrated to the god Fidius, on which was depicted two figures clasping each other's hands as the representatives of Honor and Truth, without which there can be no fidelity nor truth among men. Masonry borrowing its ideas from the ancient poets, also makes the right hand the symbol of Fidelity."—Mackey's Encyclopaedia of Freemasonry, Article Fides.

Upper Square on the right; of Disinterestedness, Mercy, Forgiveness and Forbearance.

Upper Square on the left; of Charity, Kindness, Generosity and Liberality.

Triangle on the right; of Gratitude to God, love of mankind, and confidence in human nature.

Triangle on the left; of Veneration, devotedness and patriotism; Veneration of God, Devotedness to God, family and friend and ardent love for our country.

Triangle at the top; of Truth, which includes Frankness, Plain dealing and sincerity; Justice which includes Equity and Impartiality and Toleration.

Venerable Master—Brother Senior Grand Warden you will now conduct the candidate to the post of Honor. (Senior Warden seats him on the right of the master.)

Venerable Master—Brother Grand Orator, you have the floor.

DISCOURSE BY GRAND ORATOR.

My brother, as Grand Master of all Symbolic Lodges, it is your especial duty to aid in restoring masonry to its primitive purity. You have become an instructor. Masonry long wandered in error. Instead of improving it degenerated from its primitive simplicity and retrograded toward a system, distorted by stupidity and ignorance, which, unable to construct a beautiful machine made a complicated one. Less than two hundred years ago its organization was simple and altogether moral; its emblems, allegories and ceremonies easy to be understood, and their person and object readily to be seen. It was then confined to a very small number of degrees.

Innovators and inventors overturned that primitive simplicity. Ignorance engaged in the work of making degrees and trifles and gewgaws; and pretended mysteries, absurd or hideous, usurped the place of masonic truth.

The picture of a horrid vengeance,[234] the poniard and the bloody head appeared in the peaceful temple of masonry without sufficient explanation of their symbolic meaning. Oaths[235] out of all proportion with their object shocked the candidate and then became ridiculous, and were wholly disregarded.

The rituals, even of the respectable degrees, copied and mutilated by ignorant men, became nonsensical and trivial, and the words so corrupted that it has hitherto been found impossible to recover many of them at all. Candidates were made to degrade themselves and to submit to insults not tolerable to a man of spirit and honor. Hence it was that practically the largest portion of the degrees claimed by the Ancient and Accepted Rite, and the Rites of Perfection and Misraim[236] fell into disuse, were merely communicated, and their rituals became jejune and insignificant.

Note 234.—"The word is used symbolically to express the universally recognized doctrine that crime will inevitably be followed by its penal consequences. It is the dogma of all true religions; for if virtue and vice entailed the same result, there would be no incentive to the one and no restraint from the other."—Mackey's Encyclopaedia of Freemasonry, Article Vengeance.

Note 235.—"The engagements of masonry, commonly styled obligations or vows, are of a nature scarcely to be distinguished from the definition of an oath, although the word oath does not occur in the Blue Lodge ritual."—Morris's Masonic Dictionary, Article Oath.

Note 236.—"Misraim, Rite of. This rite was introduced into France near the commencement of the present century. It made considerable progress, and, in 1817 application was made on the part of its friends to the Grand Orient, to accept it as a legitimate branch of Masonry. The application was denied, partly on the ground that the antiquity of the rite had not been proved, and partly because of the 90 degrees which its ritual comprised 68 were already included in the French system. The rite of Misraim is interesting and instructive, but many of its degrees are too abstruse to be popular. The initiation is a reproduction of the ancient rite of Isis, and represents the contests of Osiris and Typhon, the death, resurrection, and triumph of the former, and the destruction of the latter. There are 90 degrees, divided into four series—symbolic, philosophical, mystical and cabalistic and again divided into seventeen classes.

The traditions of this system are full of anachronisms, historical events and characters, separated by hundreds of years, being made to figure on the same scene, at the same time. The work entitled 'De l' Ordre Maconnique de Misraim,' published at Paris, in 1835, by Mons. Marc Bedarride, purporting to give the history of the Order, is a mere romance, and full of puerilities. Nevertheless, many of the degrees are highly interesting and instructive."—Macoy's Encyclopaedia and Dictionary of Freemasonry, Article Misraim, Rite of,

Lofty titles, arbitrarily assumed, and to which the inventors had not condescended to attach any explanation that should acquit them of the folly of assuming temporal rank, power and titles of nobility, made the world laugh and the initiates feel ashamed. Some of the titles we still retain, but they have, with us, meanings entirely consistent with that spirit of equality which is the foundation and peremptory law of its being; of all masonry.

The Knight, with us, is he who devotes his hand, his heart, and his brain to the science of masonry, and professes himself the sworn soldier of truth. The Prince[237] is he who aims to be chief, first, leader, among his equals, in virtue and good deeds.

The Sovereign[238] is he who, one of an order whose members are all Sovereigns, is supreme only because the law and constitutions are so which he administers, and by which he, like every brother, is governed.

The titles Puissant, Potent, Wise and Venerable, indicate that power of virtue, intelligence and wisdom, which those ought to strive to attain who are placed in

Note 237.—"Prince. The word Prince is not attached as a title to any Masonic office, but is prefixed as a part of the name to several degrees, as Prince of the Royal Secret, Prince of Rose Croix, and Prince of Jerusalem. In all of these instances it seems to convey some idea of sovereignty inherent in the character of the degree. Thus the Prince of the Royal Secret was the ultimate and, of course, controlling degree of the Rite of Perfection, whence, shorn, however, of its sovereignty, it has been transferred to the Ancient and Accepted Scottish Rite. The Prince of Rose Croix, although holding in some Rites a subordinate position, was originally an independent degree, and the representative of Rosicrucian Masonry. It is still at the head of the French Rite."—Mackey's Encyclopaedia of Freemasonry, Article Prince.

Note 238.—"Sovereign. An epithet applied to certain degrees which were invested with supreme power over inferior ones; as Sovereign Prince of Rose Croix, which is the highest degree of the French Rite and of some other Rites, and Sovereign Inspector-General, which is the controlling degree of the Ancient and Accepted Rite. Some degrees, originally Sovereign in the Rites in which they were first established, in being transferred to other Rites, have lost their sovereign character, but still improperly retain the name. Thus the Rose Croix degree of the Scottish Rite, which is there only the eighteenth, and subordinate to the thirty-third or Supreme Council, still retains everywhere, except in the Southern Jurisdiction of the United States, the title of Sovereign Prince of Rose Croix."—Mackey's Encyclopaedia of Freemasonry, Article Sovereign.

high office by the suffrage of their brethren, and all other titles and designations have an esoteric meaning, consistent with modesty and equality, and which those who receive them should fully understand.

As Master of a lodge, it is your duty to instruct your brethren that they are all so many constant lessons, touching the lofty qualifications which are required of those who claim them, and not merely idle gew-gaws worn in ridiculous imitation of the times when the Nobles and the Priests were masters and the people slaves, and that in all true masonry, the Knight, the Pontiff,[239] the Prince, and the Sovereign, are but the first among their equals, and the Cordon,[240] the clothing and the jewel but symbols and emblems of the virtues required of all good masons. The Mason kneels no longer to present his petition for admittance, or to receive the answer; no longer to a man as his superior, who is but his brother, but to his God, to whom he appeals for the rectitude of his intentions, and whose aid he asks to enable him to keep his vows. No one is de-

Note 239.—"What is the meaning of 'pontiff'? 'Pontiff' means bridge maker, bridge builder. Why are they called in that way? Here is the explanation of the fact: In the very first years of the existence of Rome, at a time of which we have a very fabulous history and but few existing monuments, the little town of Rome, not built on seven hills, as is generally supposed—there are eleven of them now; then there were within the town less than seven, even—that little town had a great deal to fear from an enemy which should take one of the hills that were out of town—the Janiculum—because the Janiculum is higher than the others, and from that hill an enemy could very easily throw stones, fire, or any means of destruction into the town. The Janiculum was separated from the town by the Tiber. Then the first necessity for the defence of that little town of Rome was to have a bridge. They had built a wooden bridge over the Tiber, and a great point of interest to the town was, that this bridge should be kept always in good order, so that at any moment troops could pass over. Then, with the special genius of the Romans, of which we have other instances, they ordained, curiously enough, that the men who were a corporation to take care of that bridge should be sacred; that their function, necessary to the defence of the town, should be considered holy; that they should be priests; and the highest of them was called 'the high bridge maker.' So it happened that there was in Rome a corporation of bridge makers —pontifices—of whom the head was the most sacred of all Romans; because in those days his life and the life of his companions was deemed necessary to the safety of the town.'

And thus it is that the title of Pontifex Maximus, assumed by the Pope of Rome, literally means the Grand Bridge Builder."—Mackey's Encyclopaedia of Freemasonry, Article Pontiff.

Note 240.—"Cordon. The Masonic decoration, which in English is called the collar, is styled by the French Masons the cordon."—Mackey's Encyclopaedia of Freemasonry, Article Cordon.

graded by bending his knee to God at the altar, or to receive the honor of knighthood as Bayard and Du Quesclin knelt. To kneel for other purposes, masonry does not require.

As Master of a lodge, you will therefore be exceedingly careful that no candidate in any degree be required to submit to any degradation whatever, as has been too much the custom in some of the degrees, and take it as a certain and inflexible rule to which there is no exception, that masonry requires of no man, anything to which a Knight and gentleman cannot honorably and without feeling outraged or humiliated, submit.

As Master, you will teach those who are under you, and to whom you will owe your office, that the decorations of many of the degrees are to be dispensed with, whenever the expense would interfere with the duties of Charity, Relief and Benevolence; and to be indulged in only by wealthy bodies that will thereby do no wrong to those entitled to their assistance. The essentials of all the degrees may be procured at slight expenses, and it is at the option of every brother to procure or not to procure, as he pleases, the dress, decorations and jewels of any degree other than the 14°, 18°, 30° and 32°.

As Master of a lodge, Council or Chapter, it will be your duty to impress upon the minds of your brethren all views of the general plan and separate parts of the Ancient and Accepted Rite;[241] of its spirit and design, its harmony and regularity of the duties of the officers and members; and of the particular lessons intended to be taught by each degree; especially you are not to allow any assembly of the body over which you may preside to close without recalling to the mind of the breth-

Note 241.—"The Scotch Rite, during a few years past has experienced a vast expansion through this country. Consistories of the 32d grade have been established in several States; books of Constitutions have been published; Rituals have been prepared by the leading minds of the society and men of high political and social distinction placed in prominent positions."—Morris's Masonic Dictionary, Article Scotch Masonry.

ren the masonic virtues and duties which are represented upon the tracing-board of this degree; that is an imperative duty.

Urge upon your brethren the teaching and the unostentatious practice of the morality of the lodge without regard to times, places, religions, or peoples.

Urge them to love one another, to be devoted to one another, to be faithful to the country, the government and the laws, to serve the country is to pay a dear and sacred debt.

To respect all forms of worship, to tolerate all political'' and religious opinions, not to blame, still less to condemn the religion of others, to fraternize with all men, to assist all who are unfortunate; and to cheerfully postpone their own interests to that of the order. To make it the constant rule of their lives, to think well, to speak well, and to act well. To place the sage above the soldier, the noble or the Prince; and to take the wise and good as their models. To see that their profession and practice, their teachings and conduct do always agree. To make this also their motto, "Do that which thou ought to do, let the result be what it will."

Such, my brother, are some of the duties of that office which you have sought to be qualified to exercise; may you perform them well, and in so doing gain honor for yourself and advance the great cause of masonry, humanity and progress.

Note 242.—"Politics. There is no charge more frequently made against Freemasonry than that of its tendency to revolution, and conspiracy, and to political organisations which may affect the peace of society or interfere with the rights of governments. It was the substance of all Barruel's and Robison's accusations, that the Jacobinism of France and Germany was nurtured in the Lodges of those countries; it was the theme of all the denunciations of the anti-Masons of our own land, that the Order was seeking a political ascendancy and an undue influence over the government; it has been the unjust accusation of every enemy of the institution in all times past, that its object and aim is the possession of power and control in the affairs of state. It is in vain that history records no instance of this unlawful connection between Freemasonry and politics; it is in vain that the libeller is directed to the Ancient Constitutions of the Order, which expressly forbid such connection; the libel is still written, and Masonry is again and again condemned as a political club."—Mackey's Encyclopaedia of Freemasonry, Article Politics.

CLOSING CEREMONIES

Grand Master of all Symbolic Lodges.[243]

Venerable Master—Brother Senior Grand Warden, have you anything in the West to offer before this lodge of Grand Masters?

Senior Warden—Nothing, Venerable Master.

Venerable Master—Brother Junior Grand Warden, have you anything in the South to offer before this lodge of Grand Masters?

Junior Warden—Nothing, Venerable Master.

Venerable Master—Brother Orator, have you anything in the North to offer before this lodge of Grand Masters?

Orator—Nothing, Venerable[244] Master.

Venerable Master—Has any Grand Master anything to offer to this degree for the benefit of a brother mason? (No answer.)

Note 243.—"Grand Master Ad-Vitam or Grand Master of all Symbolic Lodges. [Scotch Masonry.]—The second degree conferred in the Consistory of Princes of the Royal Secret, Scotch Masonry, and the 20th upon the catalogue of that system. The presiding officer is styled Grand Master and represents Cyrus Artaxerxes; there are two Wardens. The hangings of the Lodge are Blue and Yellow. The historical instructions relate to the construction of the three temples of Solomon, Zerubbabel and Herod, with the establishment of a fourth, or spiritual structure, which will outlast the ravages of time. The lights are nine. Jewel, a triangular plate of gold showing the word Secret."—Morris's Masonic Dictionary, Article Grand Master Ad-Vitam or Grand Master of all Symbolic Lodges.

Note 244.—"Venerable Grand Master of all Symbolic Lodges. The twentieth degree of the Ancient and Accepted Scottish Rite. See Grand Master of all Symbolic Lodges. The Dictionnaire Maconnique says that this degree was formerly conferred on those brethren in France who, in receiving it, obtained the right to organize Lodges, and to act as Masters or Venerables for life, an abuse that was subsequently abolished by the Grand Orient. Ragon and Vassal both make the same statement. It may be true, but they furnish no documentary evidence of the fact. And examination of an old MS. French ritual of the degree, when it formed part of the Rite of Perfection, which is in my possession, shows nothing in the catechism that renders this theory of its origin improbable."—Mackey's Encyclopaedia of Freemasonry, Article Venerable Grand Master of all Symbolic Lodges.

Venerable Master—Brother Senior Grand Warden, what is the hour?

Senior Warden—The world waits for the light, Venerable Master.

Venerable Master—Then it is time to close, that the great light of this lodge may be borne into and illumine the world. Together brethren.

All—(Give the first sign.)

Venerable Master—(Knocks three; 0 00.)

Senior Warden—(Knocks three; 0 00.)

Junior Warden—(Knocks three; 0 00.)

All—(Clap three; 0 00.) Lux Est.

Venerable Master—Wherever the nine great lights are, there is this lodge. Let the great light of Veneration go forth and shine in the lodge. (Pursuivant takes that light and retires.)

Venerable Master—Let the great light of Charity go forth into and inspire the world. (Junior Deacon takes that light and retires.)

Venerable Master—Let the great light of Generosity go forth into and ennoble the world. (Senior Deacon takes that light and retires.)

Venerable Master—Let the great light of Heroism go forth into and burn in the spirits of men. (Secretary takes that light and retires.)

Venerable Master—Let the great light of Honor go forth into the world and baseness skulk and hide from its presence. (Treasurer takes that light and retires.)

Venerable Master—Let the great light of Patriotism go forth and shine in the world. (Orator takes that light and retires.)

Venerable Master—Let the great light of Justice go forth and blaze upon the altars of all men's hearts. (Junior Warden takes that light and retires.)

Venerable Master—Let the great light of Toleration go forth and dim the fires of persecution. (Senior Warden takes one of the lights and retires.)

Venerable Master—I bear the light of Truth into the world to overcome falsehood and error, and this lodge is closed until the light returns. (He retires with the light and the remaining brethren follow, which closes the lodge.)

CHAPTER XXXVII

TWENTY-FIRST DEGREE; NOACHITE OR PRUSSIAN KNIGHT.[446]

ORIGIN.

The most ancient order of Noachite[446] known, are

Note 245.—"Noachite, or Prussian Knight. (Noachite ou Chevalier Prussien.) 1. The twenty-first degree of the Ancient and accepted Scottish Rite. The history as well as the character of this degree is a very singular one. It is totally unconnected with the series of Masonic degrees which are founded upon the Temple of Solomon, and is traced to the tower of Babel. Hence the Prussian Knights call themselves Noachites, or Disciples of Noah, while they designate all other Masons as Hiramites, or Disciples of Hiram. The early French rituals state that the degree was translated in 1757 from the German by. M. de Beraye. Knight of Eloquence in the Lodge of the Count St. Gelaire. Inspector General of Prussian Lodges in France. Lenning gives no credit to this statement, but admits that the origin of the degree must be attributed to the year above named. The destruction of the tower of Babel constitutes the legend of the degree, whose mythical founder is said to have been Peleg, the chief builder of that edifice. A singular regulation is that there shall be no artificial light in the Lodge room, and that the meetings shall be held on the night of the full moon of each month.

The degree was adopted by the Council of Emperors of the East and West, and in that way became subsequently a part of the system of the Scottish Rite. But it is misplaced in any series of degrees supposed to emanate from the Solomonic Temple. It is, as an unfitting link, an unsightly interruption of the chain of legendary symbolism substituting Noah for Solomon, and Peleg for Hiram Abiff. The Supreme Council for the Southern Jurisdiction has abandoned the original ritual and made the degree a representation of the Vehmgericht or Westphalian Franc Judges. But this by no means relieves the degree of the objection of Masonic incompatibility. That it was ever adopted into the Masonic system is only to be attributed to the passion for high degrees which prevailed in France in the middle of the last century."—Mackey's Encyclopædia of Freemasonry, Article Noachite, or Prussian Knight.

Note 246.—"The legend of the degree describes the travels of Peleg from Babel to the north of Europe, and ends with the following narrative: 'In trenching the rubbish of the salt-mines of Prussia was found in A. D. 553, at a depth of fifteen cubits, the appearance of a triangular building in which was a column of white marble, on which was written in Hebrew the whole history of the Noachites. At the side of this column was a tomb of freestone on which was a piece of agate inscribed with the following epitaph: Here rest the ashes of Peleg, our Grand Architect of the tower of Babel. The Almighty had pity on him because he became humble.'

This legend, although wholly untenable on historic grounds, is not absolutely puerile. The dispersion of the human race in the time of Peleg had always been a topic of discussion among the learned. Long dissertations had been written to show that all the nations of the world, even America, had been peopled by the three sons of Noah and their descendants. The object of the legend seems, then, to have been to impress the idea of the thorough dispersion. The fundamental idea of the degree is, under the symbol of Peleg, to teach the crime of assumption and the virtue of humility.

2. The degree was also adopted into the Rite of Mizraim, where it is the thirty-fifth."—Mackey's Encyclopædia of Freemasonry, Article Noachite, or Prussian Knight.

now called Prussian Knight Servants of the White and
Black Eagle, which we gather from the German trans-
lation by Berage, Knight of Eloquence and Lieutenant
Commander of the Council of Noachite in France, and
Grand Master General Commander. The Most Illustrious Frederick [247] of Brunswick, King of Prussia was
a patron of the order, as also his ancestors for 300 years.
This degree was established by the Prussians in order to
commemorate the discovery of the ancient trophies
while digging for salt mines, and to perpetuate the
building of the tower of Babel by the descendants of
Noah. The Ark [248] and Dove illustrate the mercy of
the Lord in the preservation of Noah and his family,

Note 247.—"Frederick the Great was certainly a Mason. But Carlyle,
in his usual sarcastic vein, adds: 'The Crown Prince prosecuted his
Masonry at Reinsberg or elsewhere, occasionally, for a year or two, but
was never ardent in it, and very soon after his accession left off altogether....A Royal Lodge was established at Berlin, of which the new
king consented to be patron; but he never once entered the palace, and
only his portrait (a welcomely good one, still to be found there) presided
over the mysteries of that establishment.'
    Now how much of truth with the sarcasm, and how much of sarcasm
without the truth, there is in this remark of Carlyle, is just what the
Masonic world is bound to discover. Until further light is thrown upon
the subject by documentary evidence from the Prussian Lodges, the
question cannot be definitely answered. But what is the now known
further Masonic history of Frederick?
    Bielfeld tells us that the zeal of the Prince for the Fraternity induced
him to invite the Baron Von Oberg and himself to Reinsberg, where, in
1739, they founded a Lodge, into which Keyserling, Jordan, Moolendorf,
Queis, and Fredersdorf (Frederick's valet) were admitted.
    Bielfeld is again our authority for stating that on the 20th of June,
1740, King Frederick—for he had then ascended the throne—held a
Lodge at Charlottenburg, and, as Master in the chair, initiated Prince
William of Prussia, his brother, the Margrave Charles of Brandenburg,
and Frederick William, Duke of Holstein. The Duke of Holstein was
seven years afterwards elected Adjutant Grand Master of the Grand
Lodge of the Three Globes at Berlin.
    We hear no more of Frederick's Masonry in the printed records until
the 16th of July, 1774, when he granted his protection to the National
Grand Lodge of Germany, and officially approved of the treaty with the
Grand Lodge of England, by which the National Grand Lodge was established"—Mackey's Encyclopaedia of Freemasonry, Article Frederick the
Great.

    248.—"Ark of Noah. One of the three Sacred Structures; it was
made of cypress or pine (gopher) wood. The planks, after being put
together, were protected by a coating of pitch, laid inside and outside,
to make it water-tight. The Ark consisted of a number of small com-
partments arranged in three stories. A window, 18 inches broad, was
made in the roof, extending, perhaps, its whole length. There was a
door in the side. The whole structure was 450 long, 75 feet broad, and
45 high. The Temple of Solomon was the same height as the Ark, but
only one-fifth as long."—Morris's Masonic Dictionary, Article Ark of
Noah.

when all the rest of mankind were destroyed. The pagans called this degree by the name of Pilaus, the name of their Deity; but the Knights of our day acknowledge no other God but the Great Architect of the Universe, and find it their chief happiness to worship him and keep his commandments. In the times of the crusades the Knights of the different orders were initiated into this degree by the Christian Princes in order to conquer the Holy Land which was invaded by the infidels. Those masons that were descended from Solomon were most attached to the Noachites'''' and were initiated into their order and admitted Prussian Knights, and according to the mysteries of masonry, since which time none are admitted to this degree unless they have received all the degrees of Ancient Craft Masonry.

DECORATIONS:—A Grand Chapter must be held in a retired place, on the night of the full moon. The place is lighted by a large window or opening so arranged as to admit the rays of the moon, which is the only light allowed, at as early an hour of the night as practicable. The presiding officer sits facing the moonlight, and the Knights in front of him and on either hand, in no particular place or order.

OFFICERS'''—There are seven officers, viz:

First—Knight Lieutenant Commander.

Second—Knight Official or Grand Inspector.

Note 249.—"This name is applied to freemasons as the successors, in piety and virtue, of that eminent 'preacher of righteousness,' Noah."—Morris's Masonic Dictionary, Article Noachidae.

Note 250.—"In the modern ritual the meetings are called Grand Chapters. The officers are a Lieutenant Commander, two Wardens, an Orator, Treasurer, Secretary, Master of Ceremonies, Warder, and Standard Bearer. The apron is yellow, inscribed with an arm holding a sword and the Egyptian figure of silence. The order is black, and the jewel a full moon or a triangle traversed by an arrow. In the original ritual there is a coat of arms belonging to the degree, which is thus emblasoned: Party per fees; in chief, asure, seme of stars, or a full moon, argent; in base, sable, an equilateral triangle, having an arrow suspended from its upper point, barb downwards."—Mackey's Encyclopaedia of Freemasonry, Article Noachite, or Prussian Knight.

Third—Knight Introductor.

Fourth—Knight Orator.

Fifth—Knight of Chancery or Grand Secretary.

Sixth—Knight of Finance or Grand Treasurer.

Seventh—Knight Captain of the Guards.

The members are called Prussian Knights.

DRESS:—Black, with swords, spurs and black masks. All the officers wear the jewel of the order, fastened to the button hole of the waist coat.

SASH:—Black, worn from right to left.

JEWEL:—Silver moon, full, or a golden triangle traversed by an arrow, point downwards, suspended from a collar; on the jewel is an arm upraised holding a naked sword and around it the motto, *Fiat Justitia, Ruat Coelum.*

APRON AND GLOVES:—Yellow; on the upper part of the apron is a naked arm upraised, holding a naked sword, and under it a human figure erect with wings, with the forefinger of the right hand upon his lips, and the other hand hanging by his side holding a key, being the Egyptian figure of silence.³¹¹

Note 251.—"Secrecy and Silence. These virtues constitute the very essence of all Masonic character; they are the safeguard of the Institution, giving to it all its security and perpetuity, and are enforced by frequent admonitions in all the degrees, from the lowest to the highest. The Entered Apprentice begins his Masonic career by learning the duty of secrecy, and silence. Hence it is appropriate that in that degree which is the consummation of Initiation, in which the whole cycle of Masonic science is completed, the abstruse machinery of symbolism should be employed to impress the same important virtues on the mind of the neophyte.

The same principles of secrecy and silence existed in all the ancient mysteries and systems of worship. When Aristotle was asked what thing appeared to him to be most difficult of performance, he replied, 'To be secret and silent.'

'If we turn our eyes back to antiquity,' says Calcott, 'we shall find that the old Egyptians had so great a regard for silence and secrecy in the mysteries of their religion, that they set up the god Harpocrates, to whom they paid peculiar honor and veneration, who was represented with right hand placed near the heart, and the left down by his side, covered with a skin before, full of eyes.'

Apuleius, who was an initiate in the mysteries of Isis, says: 'By no peril will I ever be compelled to disclose to the uninitiated the things that I have had intrusted to me on condition of silence.'

Lobeck, in his Aglaophamus, has collected several examples of the reluctance with which the ancients approached a mystical subject, and the manner in which they shrank from divulging any explanation or fable which had been related to them at the mysteries, under the seal of secrecy and silence."—**Mackey's Encyclopaedia of Freemasonry, Article Secrecy and Silence.**

DRAFT:—Represents the firmament with full moon and stars, on which the eye may rest. There are nine wax candles, in three rows in front of the altar, but not lighted. In the West is a representation of Noah's Ark, with a dove holding an olive leaf in his beak flying to the window whence it was let out. In one part of the Chapter is an Urn made of an agate stone, and in another part a representation of the Tower of Babel and near it a coffin with a human figure in it.

BATTERY:—Three equi-timed strokes (0 0 0).

ARMORIAL BEARINGS:—*First*—Blue, with silver moon surrounded with gold stars.

Second—Black, with the triangle and the gold dart.

OPENING CEREMONIES

TWENTY-FIRST DEGREE; NOACHITE OR PRUSSIAN KNIGHT.

Lieutenant Commander—Knight Official, the full moon is midway between the horizon and the zenith, and the hour for this Grand Chapter to convene has arrived, let the Knight Captain of the Guards post the Sentinels that no spy may gain admission among us.

Knight Official—Knight Captain of the Guards, you will see that the Sentinels are posted, that no spy may gain admission among us. (Captain of the Guards retires for a short time and returns.)

Captain of Guards—Sir Knight Official, the Sentinels are posted, and we are in security.

Knight Official—Illustrious Lieutenant Commander, the Sentinels are posted, and we are in security.

Lieutenant Commander—Sir Knight Official, you will now examine every Knight present and receive from each the pass-word, that we may know that all present are Prussian Knights. (Knight Official receives the pass-word from each Knight.)

Knight Official—Illustrious Lieutenant Commander, all have the pass-word. None but true Knights are present.

Lieutenant Commander—Sir Knight Official, are you a Prussian Knight?

Knight Official—I am.

Lieutenant Commander—How were you received a Puissant Knight?

Knight Official—By the light of the full moon, like our ancient brethren initiated in the temple of Belus.

Knight Commander—Do you know the names of the sons of Noah?

Knight Official—I know three of them.

Lieutenant Commander—What are they?

Knight Official—Shem, Ham and Japheth.

Lieutanant Commander—Give me the sign?

Knight Official—(Gives it.)

Lieutenant Commander—Give me the pass-word.

Knight Official—(Gives it.)

Lieutenant Commander—(Three knocks; 000.) All rise. Together, Sir Knights.

All—(Raise their arms toward Heaven, sword in the right hand turn towards the moon, then drop their arms and face the Lieutenant Commander.)

Lieutenant Commander—1 declare this Grand Chapter open. Be seated, Sir Knights.

CHAPTER XXXVIII

INITIATION.

[The Knight of Introduction after preparing the candidate with a white apron and white gloves leads him to the door and knocks three equal strokes.]

Captain of Guards—(From within knocks one and opens the door.) Who desires to enter this Grand Chapter?

Introductor—The Knight Introductor, with a Master Mason of Hiram; and who has received the degree of Grand Master of all Symbolic lodges.

Captain of Guard—Give me the sign, grip and pass-word of that degree.

Candidate—(Gives the sign, pass grip and pass-word, Tubal Cain.)

Captain of Guard—The sign, grip and word are correct. You will wait a time with patience and I will inform the Illustrious Lieutenant Commander of your request. (Shuts the door, goes to the Knight Official and knocks three.)

Captain of Guard—Sir Knight official, there is in the ante-room the Knight Introductor with a Master Mason, descendant from Hiram, and Grand Master of all Symbolic lodges, clothed in white apron and white gloves who desires to enter.

Knight Official—(Announces the same to the Lieutenant Commander. Order is obeyed.)

Lieutenant Commander—What does he desire Sir Knight Captain of the Guards?

Captain of Guard—To be advanced to the degree of Noachite or Prussian Knight.

Lieutenant Commander—Sir Knights, a Perfect Mason of Hiram is desirous of becoming a Prussian Knight; do you consent that he shall be received among us?

All—(Rise, draw their swords and come to a present.)

Lieutenant Commander—Sir Knight, Captain of the Guards, let this Perfect Mason of Hiram be admitted. (Captain of the Guards opens the door, the Introductor enters with candidate and conducts him up to the tower of Babel in the North.)

Lieutenant Commander—My brother, behold the remains of Peleg the Projector of the tower of Babel.[252] He forgot that he was mortal and therefore also forgot what was due to future generations. He built to gratify his own vanity and vain glory, without regard to the common welfare and popular will, and therefore his work remained unfinished, for the confusion of opinions arose.

Peleg was overpowered, fled to the desert, and died repenting, while his divided people were scattered over the face of the earth to form dissimilar nations of various tongues; may his example profit you. Sir Knight of Introduction, you will now conduct the candidate to the altar. (Introductor conducts him to the altar, where he

Note 252.—"It is the name of that celebrated tower attempted to be built on the plains of Shinar, A. M. 1775, about one hundred and forty years after the deluge, and which, Scripture informs us, was destroyed by the special interposition of the Almighty. The Noachite Masons date the commencement of their order from this destruction, and much traditionary information on this subject is preserved in the degree of 'Patriarch Noachite.' At Babel, Oliver says that what has been called Spurious Freemasonry took its origin. That is to say, the people there abandoned the worship of the true God, and by their dispersion lost all knowledge of his existence, and the principles of truth upon which Masonry is founded. Hence it is that the rituals speak of the lofty tower of Babel as the place where language was confounded and Masonry lost."—Mackey's Encyclopaedia of Freemasonry, Article Babel.

makes three genuflections and kneels upon his left knee, when the Lieutenant Commander leaves the throne, approaches the candidate and extends to him the hilt of his sword which he takes in his right hand, the Lieutenant Commander holding the blade.)

Lieutenant Commander—Do you promise and agree that you will be just and righteous, and in all things strive to emulate and equal that Patriarch from whom we take the name of Noachite?

Candidate—I do.

Lieutenant Commander—Do you promise to avoid idleness, to live honestly, to deal fairly by all men, and discourage strife and contention?

Candidate—I do.

Lieutenant Commander—Do you promise that you will be neither haughty nor vain-glorious, nor obsequious to the great, nor insolent to your inferiors?

Candidate—I do.

Lieutenant Commander—Do you promise that you will be humble and contrite before the Deity, and ever bear in mind the fate of Peleg and his followers, who endeavored to build a tower, whereby they might climb beyond the reach of another deluge and defy the omnipotence of God?

Candidate—I do.

Lieutenant Commander—Repeat after me then the solemn obligation of a Patriarch Noachite or Prussian Knight.

OBLIGATION PATRIARCH NOACHITE.

I......upon the sacred word of a Master Mason and Knight of Rose Croix, do most solemnly promise and vow, that I will faithfully keep the secrets of this degree, and will reveal them to no person in the world, unless to one who shall be legally authorized to receive them. So help me God.

Lieutenant Commander—Arise my brother and receive the sign, token and words of this degree.

SIGN OF ORDER.

Raise the arms to heaven, the face toward the East, where the moon rises.

Sign of Order, Noachite Degree.

SIGN OF INTRODUCTION.

One raises three fingers of the right hand, the other seizes those fingers with his right hand, a n d says, Frederick the Second. He then presents his three fingers, which the first one seizes in the same manner, saying Noah.

Sign of Introduction, Noachite Degree.

Second Sign of Introduction.

SECOND SIGN.

Seize one the first finger of the other s right hand and press it with the thumb and first finger, saying Shem.

The other gives the same token, saying Ham, then the first gives the same token, saying Japheth.

BATTERY :—Three slow strokes ; 0 0 0.

MARCH :—Three steps of a Master.

PASS WORD :—Peleg, Peleg, Peleg.

SACRED WORD :—Shem, Ham, Japheth.

Lieutenant Commander—(Invests him with the apron, collar and jewel, causes him to kneel on both knees when he strikes him on the right and left shoulder, and on the head with the flat of his sword, saying:)

By virtue of the authority vested in me, by this grand Chapter, I do constitute and create you a Mason Noachite, and Prussian Knight, and devote you hence-forward to the cause of every one who hath been wronged by the great, or oppressed by the powerful; of the widow, the orphan, the poor, the distressed and the destitute. Arise Sir Knight, and soldier of suffering humanity and be armed for the combats that await you. (Raises him up, the Knight Official buckles on his spurs, and the Lieutenant Commander hands him a sword.)

Lieutenant Commander—You are now prepared to do

the duties of a true Knight. (Knight Official seats him and the Lieutenant Commander takes his station.)

Lieutenant Commander—Sir Knight Orator, you have the floor.

DISCOURSE BY ORATOR.

My brother, we read that the descendants of Noah resolved to build a tower so high as to prevent the Almighty from again destroying the world by a flood and to get themselves a name in the world. They chose for their purpose the plains of Shinar, in Asia. Ten years after the foundation was laid, the Lord looking down upon earth and beholding the pride and audacious attempt of the people, He descended to confound their project by causing a confusion of languages among the workmen so that they could not understand one another; whence it was called Babel. Sometime after, Nimrod⁣'''' established a distinction among men, and founded a city, and called it Babylon. Tradition says, the dedication was at the full of the moon so the festivals of this degree are held in the month of March, at the full of the moon. Tradition further informs us that after the languages were confounded at the building of the tower of Babel, the workmen separated and dispersed into different countries. The architect of the tower traveled into Germany where he arrived after a long and tedious journey, living upon roots and other vegetables. He

Note 553.—"Nimrod. The legend of the Craft in the Old Constitutions refers to Nimrod as one of the founders of Masonry. Thus in the York Manuscript we read: 'At ye making of ye Toure of Babell there was Masonrie first much esteemed of, and the King of Babilon yt was called Nimrod was A mason himselfe and loved well Masons.' And the Cooke Manuscript thus repeats the story: 'And this same Nembruth began the tower of babilen and he taught to his werkemen the craft of Masonrie, and he had with him many Masons more than forty thousand. And he loved and cherished them well.' The idea no doubt sprang out of the Scriptural teaching that Nimrod was the architect of many cities; a statement not so well expressed in the authorized version, as it is in the improved one of Borhart, which says: 'From that land Nimrod went forth to Asshur, and builded Nineveh, and Rehoboth city, and Calah, and Resen between Nineveh and Calah, that is the great city.'"— Mackey's Encyclopaedia of Freemasonry, Article Nimrod.

fixed his residence in that part now called Prussia, where he erected a dwelling to shelter himself from the inclemency of the weather, and where he also erected many monuments.

In the year 1553, in digging for salt mines, the workmen found the ruins of a triangular edifice 15 cubits deep. In the centre of this edifice they found many trophies of antiquity: An urn of agate, and many marble columns with hieroglyphics engraven thereon.

The origin of this order, my brother, was long before the era of Hiram or Solomonian Masonry; as every one knows that the tower of Babel was built long before the temple of Solomon, and in former times it was not necessary that a candidate should be a Master Mason to be qualified to receive this; for in the times of the crusades the Knights of the different orders in Europe were initiated into this degree by the Christian Princes to conquer the Holy Land which was invaded by the Infidels, as were also the masons descendant from Hiram.

You are especially charged in this degree, to be modest and humble, and not vain-glorious nor filled with self-conceit. Be not wiser in your own opinion than the Deity, nor find fault with his works, nor endeavor to improve upon what he has done.

Be modest also in your intercourse with your fellows, and slow to entertain evil thoughts of them, and reluctant to ascribe to them evil intentions.

When a mason hears of any man who hath fallen into public disgrace, he should have a mind to commiserate his mishap and not to make him more disconsolate. To envenom a name by libels that already is openly tainted is to add stripes with an iron rod to one that is flayed with whipping, and to every well tempered mind will seem most inhuman and diabolical.

Even the man who does wrong and commits errors, often has a quiet home, a fireside of his own, a gentle loving wife, and innocent children who, perhaps do not know of his past errors and lapses, past and long repented of, or if they do, do love him the better, because being mortal, he hath erred, and being in the image of God, he hath repented.

That every blow at this husband and father, strikes full upon the pure and tender bosoms of the wife and those daughters is a consideration that doth not concern or stay the hand of the base and brutal informer.

My brother, if men weighed the imperfections of humanity, they would breathe less condemnation. Ignorance gives disparagement a louder tongue than knowledge does; wise men had rather know than tell. If we even do know vices in men we can scarce show ourselves in a nobler virtue than in the charity of concealing them. if that be not a flattery, persuading to continuance and it is the basest office man can fall into, to make his tongue the defamer of the worthy man.

There is but one rule for a mason in this matter: If there be virtues, and he is called upon to speak of him who knows them, let him tell them forth impartially, and if there be vices mixed with them let him be content the world shall know them by some other tongue than his; for if the evil doer deserves no pity, his wife, his parents or his children, or other innocent persons who love him, may.

Where we want experience, charity bids us think the best and leave what we know not to the searcher of hearts. For mistakes, suspicions and envy often injure a clear fame; and there is least danger in a charitable construction.

And finally the mason should be humble and honest and modest toward the Great Architect of the Universe, and not impugn his wisdom nor set up his own imperfect sense of right against His providence and dispensations, nor attempt too rashly to explore the mysteries of God's infinite essence and inscrutable plans and of that great nature which we are not made capable to understand.

Let him not spend his time in building a new tower of Babel; in attempting to change that which is fixed by an inflexible law of God's enactment, but let him, yielding to the Superior Wisdom of Providence, be content to believe that the march of events is rightly ordered by an infinite wisdom, and leads, though we cannot see it, to a great and perfect result.

Let him my brother be satisfied to follow the path pointed out by that providence, and to labor for the good of the human race in that mode in which God has chosen to enact that that good shall be effected. And above all, let him build no tower of Babel under the belief that, by ascending he will mount so high that God will disappear, or be superseded by a great monstrous aggregation of material forces, or a mere glittering logical formula; but evermore standing humbly and reverently upon the Earth, and looking with awe and confidence toward Heaven, let him be satisfied that there is a real God, a person and not a formula, a father and a protector, who loves and sympathizes and compassionates; and that the eternal ways by which He rules the world are infinitely wise no matter how far they may be above the feeble comprehension and limited vision of man.

CLOSING CEREMONIES

NOACHITE OR PRUSSIAN KNIGHT.

Lieutenant Commander—(Three knocks; 000.) Sir Knight Official, the moon is passing from us, the hour for this Grand Chapter to close has arrived, give notice to the Sir Knights that our labors are about to end.

Knight Official—(One knock; 0.) Brethren and Knights, prepare to close this Grand Chapter; the light by which we work is about to be obscured. Let us go forth to imitate in our conduct and conversation the righteous Patriarch, and thus become true Noachites.

Lieutenant Commander—True brethren, let us go forth and perform these duties. Sir Knight Official give notice to the Knights that this Grand Chapter is darkened.

Knight Official—Knights and Brethren, this Grand Chapter is darkened and its labors ended.

Lieutenant Commander—Together, Sir Knights.

All—(Give the sign.) Peleg, Peleg, Peleg.

Lieutenant Commander—The light has departed, farewell.

CHAPTER XXXIX

Twenty-Second Degree; Knight of the Royal Axe or Prince of Libanus.[254]

MARS.♂

ORIGIN:—This degree was established, and added thereto, on different occasions. When the cedars of Lebanon were cut down for holy purposes, the Sidonians were zealous for all holy enterprises. The descendants of Japhet cut the cedars for all the holy purposes of the temple of Solomon. They were furnished under the direction of Prince Herodim.[255] The same nation floated the timbers by sea to Joppa, for the temple and other buildings at Jerusalem. Solomon was so pleased with the fidelity of the Sidonians that he built him a house

Note 254.—"Knight of the Royal Axe, or Prince of Libanus. The 22d degree of the Ancient and Accepted rite. The legend of this degree informs us that it was instituted to record the memorable services rendered to Masonry by the mighty cedars of Lebanon, as the Sidonian architects cut down the cedars for the construction of Noah's ark. Our ancient brethren do not tell us how the Israelites had the wood conveyed to them from the land of promise to the mountains in the wilderness. They say, however, that the descendants of the Sidonians were employed in the same place, in obtaining materials for the construction of the ark of the covenant; and also, in later years, for building Solomon's Temple; and, lastly, that Zerubbabel employed laborers of the same people in cutting cedars of Lebanon for the use of the second temple. The tradition adds that the Sidonians formed colleges on Mount Libanus, and always adored the G. A. O. T. U."—Macoy's Encyclopaedia and Dictionary of Freemasonry, Article Knight of the Royal Axe.

Note 255.—"Heredom. In what are called the 'high degrees of the continental Rites' there is nothing more puzzling than the etymology of this word. We have the Royal Order of Heredom, given as the ne plus ultra of Masonry in Scotland, and in almost all the Rites the Rose Croix of Heredom, but the true meaning of the word is apparently unknown. Ragon, in his Orthodoxie Maçonnique, (p. 91,) asserts that it has a political signification, and that it was invented between the years 1740 and 1745, by the adherents of Charles Edward the Pretender, at the Court of St. Germain, which was the residence, during that period, of the unfortunate prince, and that in their letters to England, dated from Heredom, they mean to denote St. Germain."—Mackey's Encyclopaedia of Freemasonry, Article Heredom.

of cedar at Lebanon, whither he used to repair yearly to visit Prince Herodim. The descendants of the zealous craftsmen furnished timber from the same mountains for the construction of the second temple; by order of Cyrus, Darius and Xerxes under the guidance of Zerubbabel.

This celebrated nation formed in the earliest days a college for instructing the people and worshipped the Great Architect of the Universe. We are indebted to these patriarchs for much knowledge we possess of the mysteries of this degree.

DECORATIONS:—Bodies of this degree are styled colleges.''' There are two apartments. The first is a plain room without any fixed number of lights and represents a carpenter's workshop on Mount Lebanon. The second is hung with red and lighted by 36 lights, arranged by sixes, and each six by twos. It represents the Council room of the round table. In the center of the room is a round table around which the brethren sit. On the altar is an open Bible, square and compass and an axe.

OFFICER:—Are a Chief Prince, styled Thrice Puissant, a Senior and Junior Warden, and a Senior and Junior Deacon.

ORDER:—Broad, rainbow colored ribbon, worn as a collar; it may be worn as a sash from right to left, and lined with purple.

JEWEL:—A golden hatchet, on the top of it a golden crown. On the top or end of the handle are the letters N.·. and S.·. initials of Noah and Solomon. On one side of the handle the letter L.·. initial of Lebanon; and on

Note 256.—"The places of meeting in this degree are called 'Colleges. This degree is especially interesting to the Masonic scholar in consequence of its evident reference to the mystical association of the Druses, whose connection with the Templars at the time of the Crusades forms a yet to be investigated episode in the history of Freemasonry."—Mackey's Encyclopaedia of Freemasonry, Article Knight of the Royal Axe.

that side of the blade, the letters A.∴C.∴D.∴Z.∴N.∴ and E.∴ initials of Adoniram, Cyrus, Darius, Zerubbabel, Nehemiah and Ezra.

On the other side of the handle the letter S.∴ initial of Sidonias, and on that side of the blade the letters S.∴ H.∴J.∴M.∴A.∴ and B.∴ initials of Shem, Ham, Japhet, Moses, Aholiab'''' and Bezaleel.

APRON:—White, lined and bordered with purple, on the middle a round table is embroidered on which are mathematical instruments and plans enrolled; on the flap is a serpent with three heads.

TRACING BOARD:—View of the mountains and forests of Lebanon;'''' the summit of the mountains covered with snow and of the temple erected of its cedars and pines.

WORKSHOP:—The Senior Warden presides and is styled Master Carpenter, he and all the brethren wear frocks or blouses and aprons.

BATTERY:—Is two; 00. No particular one in the workshop.

Note 257.—"Aholiab was associated with Moses and Bezaleel in the construction of the Tabernacle in the wilderness. While Bezaleel designed and executed the works of art required, Aholiab attended to the textile fabrics. He was a Danite of great skill as a weaver and embroiderer. Exodus xxv. It is a curious coincidence that both Aholiab and Hiram Abif were of the tribe of Dan."—Morris's Masonic Dictionary, Article Aholiab.

Note 258.—"The forests of the Lebanon mountains only could supply the timber for the Temple. Such of these forests as lay nearest the sea were in the possession of the Phoenicians, among whom timber was in such constant demand, that they had acquired great and acknowledged skill in the felling and transportation thereof; and hence it was of such importance that Hiram consented to employ large bodies of men in Lebanon to hew timber, as well as others to perform the service of bringing it down to the seaside, whence it was to be taken along the coast in floats to the port of Joppa, from which place it could be easily taken across the country to Jerusalem.

The ancient and Accepted Scottish Rite has dedicated to this mountain its twenty-second degree, or Prince of Lebanon. The Druses now inhabit Mount Lebanon, and still preserve there a secret organization."
—Mackey's Encyclopaedia of Freemasonry, Article Lebanon.

OPENING CEREMONIES

KNIGHTS OF THE ROYAL AXE OR PRINCE OF LIBANUS.[*]

Chief Prince—(Knocks one; 0.) My brethren the day star is risen in the East. It is time to arouse the workmen that they may prepare for their labors. Brother Senior Grand Warden, are all the Princes present?

Senior Warden—Thrice Puissant, they are.

Chief Prince—Announce to them by brother, through the Junior Grand Warden, that I am about to open this College, that directions may be given to the workmen.

Senior Warden—Brother Junior Grand Warden, the Thrice Puissant is about to open this College that directions may be given to the workmen.

Junior Warden—Brethren, you will please take notice that the Thrice Puissant is about to open this College that direction may be given to the workmen.

Chief Prince—Brother Junior Grand Warden, arouse the workmen by the usual alarm.

Junior Warden—(Sounds the bell twice; 00.)

Senior Warden—(Sounds the bell twice; 00.)

Chief Prince—(Sounds the bell twice; 00.) Together brethren.

All—(Give the sign.)

Chief Prince—The cedars upon Mount Lebanon wait to be fitted and this College is open.

Note 259.—"Prince of Lebanus, or Knight of the Royal Axe. [Scotch Masonry.]—The fourth degree conferred in the Consistory of Princes of the Royal Secret. Scotch Masonry, and the twenty-second upon the catalogue of that system. Its historical lectures relate to the Cedars of Lebanon, which formed so important a part of the materials for constructing the temples of Solomon and Zerubbabel. (See Cedars.) The presiding officer is styled Most Wise. The apron is white. It displays a round-table, on which appears various architectural instruments and drawings. The jewel is a gold axe, surmounted by a gold crown. On one side of the handle are the letters A. B. D. C. D. X. Z. A., and on the blade L. S. On the other side of the handle are the letters S. N. S. C. I. M. B. E., and on the blade S."—Morris's Masonic Dictionary, Article Prince of Lebanus, or Knight of the Royal Axe.

CHAPTER XL

Twenty-Second Degree; Knight of the Royal Axe or Prince of Libanus.'''

INITIATION.

[The candidate is prepared by the Senior Deacon as a Prussian Knight or Rose Croix, with sword, etc., and brought to the door of the second apartment in which the officers and brethren are seated round the table, on which are plans and mathematical instruments and knocks two; 00.]

Junior Deacon—(Opening the door.) Who comes here?

Senior Deacon—A Worthy Prussian Knight and Knight of the Rose Croix, who desires to obtain the degree of Prince of Libanus.

Junior Deacon—Has he received all the preceding degrees?

Senior Deacon—He has.

Junior Deacon—Has he proved himself a true Knight?

Senior Deacon—He has.

Note 260.—"Knight of the Royal Axe. (Chevalier de la royale Hache.) The twenty-second degree of the Ancient and Accepted Scottish Rite, called also Prince of Libanus, or Lebanon. It was instituted to record the memorable services rendered to Masonry by the 'mighty cedars of Lebanon.' The legend of the degree informs us that the Sidonians were employed in cutting cedars on Mount Libanus or Lebanon for the construction of Noah's ark. Their descendants subsequently cut cedars from the same place for the ark of the covenant; and the descendants of these were again employed in the same offices, and in the same place, in obtaining materials for building Solomon's Temple. Lastly, Zerubbabel employed them in cutting the cedars of Lebanon for the use of the second Temple. This celebrated nation formed colleges on Mount Lebanon, and in their labors always adored the Great Architect of the Universe. I have no doubt that this last sentence refers to the Druses, that secret sect of Theists who still reside upon Mount Lebanon and in the adjacent parts of Syria and Palestine, and whose mysterious ceremonies have attracted so much of the curiosity of Eastern travellers."—Mackey's Encyclopaedia of Freemasonry, Article Knight of the Royal Axe.

Junior Deacon—What further claims has he to this privilege?

Senior Deacon—The claim of birth and rank in Masonry.

Junior Deacon—Let him wait a time with patience until the College is informed of his request. (Junior Deacon shuts the door.)

Chief Prince—Brother Junior Deacon, who seeks admission to the College?

Junior Deacon—A Worthy Prussian Knight and Knight of the Rose Croix, who desires to obtain the degree of Prince of Libanus.

Chief Prince—Has he received all the preceding degrees?

Junior Deacon—He has.

Chief Prince—Has he approved himself a true Knight?

Junior Deacon—He has.

Chief Prince—What further claims has he to this privilege?

Junior Deacon—The claim of birth and rank in Masonry.

Chief Prince—The claim is not sufficient, but let him be admitted. (Junior Deacon opens the door and the Senior Deacon conducts candidate to the table.)

Chief Prince—Is it your desire my brother, to obtain the degree of Prince of Libanus?

Candidate—It is.

Chief Prince—We know the ground on which you claim it, but birth is not regarded here, and rank in Masonry does not of itself suffice. We are all workmen in our several vocations. You see us now engaged in preparing plans for the laborers and studying the calculations of astronomy. None can by our constitutions, be admitted to the high privileges of this degree unless he hath first wrought one year in the workshop, and obtained the unanimous suffrages of the workmen.

Is your desire for this degree sufficient to induce you to lay aside your insignia, your sword and jewels for a time and join the sons of labor?

Candidate—It is.

Chief Prince—Go then my brother, obtain their suf-frages and return to us. (Candidate withdraws with the Senior Deacon and goes to the door of the first apart-ment and gives three or four knocks, the door is opened and théy enter. The workmen are hewing, sawing, planing, etc., and the master workmen copying designs, from a tracing board. As the candidate enters he gives one loud rap and the workmen all stop.)

Master Carpenter—Whom have you there brother Senior Deacon?

Senior Deacon—A Knight of Rose Croix and Prussian Knight, who desires your suffrages that he may obtain the degree of Prince of Libanus.

Master Carpenter—Our suffrages are given to those who work. Hath he yet learned to work?

Senior Deacon—He has not, but desires to do so, and for that came hither.

Master Carpenter—Doth he acknowledge the dignity of labor; and that it is no curse but a privilege for man to be allowed to earn his sustenance by the exercise of his strong arms and sturdy muscles?

Senior Deacon—He does.

Master Carpenter—Does he admit that the honest laboring man, upright and independent is in nature's heraldry the peer of kings, and that no labor, but idle-ness, is disgraceful?

Senior Deacon—He does.

Master Carpenter—Art thou willing to eat only what thou earnest, patiently to receive instructions and to recognize and treat these humble workmen as your brethren and equals?

Candidate—I am.

Master Carpenter—Then as you were divested of your outer apparel upon your first entry into a Masonic lodge, divest yourself now of your insignia and jewels, and put on the apron of a workman. (Candidate puts off his regalia, rolls up his shirt sleeves, puts on a cap penter's apron and proceeds, as directed, to saw a long plank in two, lengthwise.)

Master Carpenter—My brother, the saw, the plane and the hewing axe, (showing them) are the working tools of a Prince of Libanus.

THE SAW symbolizes that steady patience and persevering determination by which the resolute man makes his way to the object of his endeavors, through all obstacles and teaches us that Masons laboring for the improvement of the world and the great cause of human progress, must be content to advance, certainly, though never so painfully and slowly, toward success and as

THE PLANE cuts down the inequalities of surface, it is symbolical of Masonry which cuts off the prejudices of ignorance and the absurdities of superstition, and aids to polish and civilize mankind.

THE AXE is a great agent of civilization and improvement. It is the troops armed with that weapon that have conquered barbarism. Under its blows the primeval forests disappear and the husbandman displaces the hunter. Settled society and laws, and all the arts that refine and elevate mankind, succeed the rude barbarism of early ages. The axe is nobler than the sword my brother. (He is then made to use the plane, and a brother brings him a piece of dry bread and a cup of water.)

Master Carpenter—Eat my brother of the laborer's food, it is thine own, for thou hast earned it and no one suffers because thou dost eat. (He is then made to use the axe.)

Master Carpenter—Brethren, this Knight by his ready acquiescence to our customs, has shown a true appreciation of the dignity of labor and has cheerfully conformed to our customs.

We may require him to toil with us a year, or, at our option, we may at once give him our suffrages. If no one wishes otherwise, we will proceed to vote upon his request to be admitted among the Princes of Libanus. (The vote is taken by ballot and declared clear.)

Master Carpenter—My brother, you have been duly elected to receive this degree. Brother Senior Deacon, you will now invest the brother with his insignia and jewels and conduct him to the second apartment. (Senior Deacon invests him and conducts him to the door of the second apartment. Meanwhile the brethren retire and dress themselves with the insignia and jewels of this degree.)

Senior Deacon—(Two knocks; 00.)

Junior Deacon—(Opening the door.) Who comes here?

Senior Deacon—A Knight of the Rose Croix and Prussian Knight who, having wrought cheerfully in the workshop and learned the use of the saw, the plane and the axe, has received the suffrages of the workmen and demands to be received a Prince of Libanus. (Junior Deacon shuts the door and says:)

Junior Deacon—Thrice Puissant, it is a Knight of Rose Croix and Prussian Knight, who, having wrought cheerfully in the workshop and learned the use of the saw, the plane and axe, has received the suffrages of the workmen and demands to be received a Prince of Libanus.

Chief Prince—Let him be admitted. (The three principal officers now take their stations; the Junior Deacon opens the door and the Senior Deacon enters with the candidate and conducts him to the altar.)

Senior Deacon—Thrice Puissant I present to you a Knight Rose Croix, who has toiled in the workshop and received the unanimous suffrages of his brethren.

Chief Prince—My brother do you still persist in your desire to enter this association of laborers?

Candidate—I do.

Chief Prince—Are you not deterred by the hazard of such toil and fare as you experienced in the workshop?

Candidate—I am not.

Chief Prince—Kneel then at this altar and contract your obligation. (Candidate kneels on both knees with his hands upon the axe and Bible and takes the following obligation.)

OBLIGATION KNIGHT OF THE ROYAL AXE.

I....of my own free will and accord, in the presence of the Grand Architect of the Universe, and this Illustrious College of Princes of Libanus, do hereby and hereon most solemnly and sincerely promise and swear that I will never communicate the secrets of this degree to any person or persons unless it be to one lawfully entitled to receive the same.

I furthermore promise and swear that I will ever hereafter use my best endeavors to elevate the character of the laboring classes and improve their condition, to disseminate the blessings of education among their children and to give to themselves their due and proper social and political weight. All of which I promise and swear under the penalty of exposure on the highest pinnacle of Mount Libanus, there miserably to perish in its perpetual snows. So help me God.

(Chief Prince raises him and invests him with the following signs:)

SIGN.

Make the motion of lifting an axe with both hands, and striking as if to fell a tree.

ANSWER.

Raise both hands to the height of the forehead, the fingers extended, and then let the hands fall, thus indicating the fall of a tree.

Sign, Prince of Libanus.

Answer to Sign, Prince of Libanus.

TOKEN.

Seize each other's hands and cross the fingers as a sign of good faith.

BATTERY:—Two equi-timed strokes; 00.

MARCH:—Three cross steps.

PASS WORDS:—Japhet, Aholiab, Lebanon.

SACRED WORDS:—Noah, Bezaleel, Sadonias.

Chief Prince—(Invests him with the collar, apron and jewel; explains the initials upon the jewel, and says:) The serpent with three heads upon the flap of the apron is Idleness, the body from which issue the three vices symbolized by the heads; *Drunkeness, Impurity* and *Gaming,* by which so many youths have been lost and so many great nations have sunk into ignoble imbecility and shameful bondage.

Chief Prince—Brother Senior Deacon, you will now conduct the candidate to the post of honor. (Senior Deacon seats him on the right of the Thrice Puissant who delivers the history.)

HISTORY.

My brother, sympathy for the great laboring classes, respect for labor itself and resolution to some good work in our day and generation, these are the lessons of this degree, and they are purely masonic.

Masonry has made a working man and his associates
the heroes of her principal legend and herself the companion of Kings. The idea is as simple and true as it
is sublime; from first and last masonry is work. It
venerates the Great Architect of the Universe. It commemorates the building of a temple. Its principal emblems are the working tools of masons and artisans.
It preserves the name of the first worker in brass and
iron as one of its pass-words. The master is the over-
seer who sets the craft to work and gives them proper
instructions.

Masonry is the apotheosis of work. It is the hands
of brave, forgotten men that have made this great popu-
lous, cultivated world a world for us. It is all work and
forgotten work.

The real conquerers, creators and eternal proprietors
of every great and civilized land are all the heroic souls
that ever were in it, each in his degree. All men that
ever felled a forest tree or drained a marsh, or contrived
a wise scheme, or did or said a true or valiant thing
therein. Genuine work alone, done faithfully, that is
eternal, even as the Almighty founder and world-builder
himself.

All work is noble. A life of ease is not for any man,
nor for any God. The Almighty Maker is not like one
who in old, immemorial ages, having made his machine
of a universe, sits ever since and sees it go.

Man's highest destiny is not to be happy, to love
pleasant things and find them.

His only true unhappiness should be that he cannot
work and get his destiny as a man fulfilled. The day
passes swiftly over and the night cometh wherein no
man can work. That night once come, our happiness
and unhappiness are vanished and become as things that

never were. But our work is not abolished and has not vanished. It remains, or the want of it remains for endless times and eternities. It is in our influences after death that we are immortal. Labor is the truest emblem of God, the Architect and Eternal Maker; noble labor which is yet to be the King of this Earth, and sit on the highest throne. Men without duties to do are like trees planted on precipices from the roots of which all the earth has crumbled.

Nature owns no man who is not also a martyr. She scorns the man who sits screened from all work, from want, danger, hardship, the victory over which is work, and has all this work and battling done by other men.

And yet there are men who pride themselves that they and theirs have done no work, time out of mind.

The chief of men is he who stands in the van of men, fronting the peril which frightens back all others, and if not vanquished would devour them.

Hercules was worshipped for twelve labors. The Czar of Russia became a toiling shipwright and worked with his axe in the docks of Saardam, and something came of that. Cromwell worked, and Napoleon and effected somewhat. There is perennial nobleness and even sacredness in work. Be he never so benighted and forgetful of his high calling, there is always hope in a man that actually and earnestly works. In idleness alone is their perpetual despair. Man perfects himself by working. Jungles are cleared away, fair seed-fields rise instead, and stately cities, and withal, the man himself first ceases to be a foul unwholesome jungle and desert thereby. Even in the meanest sort of labor the whole soul of man is composed into a kind of real harmony the moment he begins to work. Labor is life; from the inmost heart of the worker rises his God-given force, the sacred celestial life-essence breathed into him by Almighty God and awakens him to all nobleness as soon as work fitly begins.

By it, man learns patience, courage, perseverance, openness to light, readiness to own himself mistaken, resolution to do better and improve. Only by labor will man continually learn the virtues.

Let him who toils complain not, nor feel humiliated. Let him look up and see his fellow workmen there in God's Eternity; they alone surviving there. Even in the weak human memory they long survive, as saints, as heroes, and as gods they alone survive, and people the unmeasured solitudes of time. It was well to give the earth to man as a dark mass, whereon to labor. It was well to provide rude and unsightly materials in the ore bed and the forests for him to fashion into splendor and beauty.

It was well, not because of that splendor and beauty, but because the act creating them is better than the things themselves. Because exertion is nobler than enjoyment, because the laborer is greater and more worthy of honor than the idler, masonry stands up for the nobility of labor. It is Heaven's great ordinance for human improvement. It has been broken down for ages and masonry desires to build it up again. It has been broken down because men toiled only because they must, submitting to it as in some sort, a degrading necessity and desiring nothing so much on earth as to escape from it. They fulfill the great law of labor in the letter; but break it in the spirit, they fulfill it with the muscles, but break it with the mind.

Masonry teaches that every idler ought to hasten to some field of labor, manual or mental, as a chosen and coveted theater of improvement, but he is not impelled to do so under the teachings of an imperfect civilization. On the contrary he sits down, folds his hands, and blesses and glorifies himself in his idleness. It is time that this opprobrium of toil were done away. To be ashamed of toil, of the dingy workshop and dusty labor-field, of the hard hand, stained with service more honorable than that of war; of the soiled and weather-stained garments on which mother nature has stamped, midst sun and rain, midst fire and steam, her own heraldic honors; to be ashamed of these tokens and titles, and envious of the flaunting robes of imbecile idleness and vanity is treason to nature, impiety to Heaven, a breach of heaven's great ordinance. Toil of brain, heart or hand is the only true manhood and genuine nobility. Labor is man's great function, his peculiar distinction and his privilege. From being an animal that eats and drinks only, to become a worker, and with the hand of ingenuity to pour his own thoughts into the moulds of nature, fashioning them into forms of grace and fabrics of convenience and converting them to purposes of improvement and happiness, is the greatest possible step in privilege.

What is there glorious in the world that is not the product of labor? What is history but its record? What are the treasuries of genius and art but its work? What are cultivated fields but its toils? The busy marts, the rising cities, the enriched empires of the world are but the great treasure-houses of labour. The pyramids of Egypt, the castles, and towers and temples of Europe, the buried cities of Italy and Mexico, the canals and railroads of Christendom are but tracks all round the world of the mighty footsteps of labor. Without it antiquity would not have been; without it there would be no memory of the past and no hope for the future.

Even utter indolence reposes on treasures that labor at some time gained and gathered.

He who does nothing, and yet does not starve, has still his significance, for he is a standing proof that somebody has at some time worked. But not to such does masonry do honor. It honors the worker, the toiler, him who produces and not alone consumes, him who puts forth his hand to add to the treasury of human comforts and not alone to take away. It honors him who goes forth amid the struggling elements to fight his battle and who shrinks not, with cowardly effeminacy, behind pillows of ease. It honors the strong muscle and the manly nerve, and the resolute and brave heart, the sweating brow, and toiling brain.

It honors the great and beautiful offices of humanity, manhood's toil and woman's task, fraternal industry and maternal watching and weariness, wisdom teaching and patience learning; the brow of care that presides over the state and many handed labor that toils in workshop, field and study, beneath its mild and beneficent sway.

To aid in securing to all labor, permanent employment and its just reward; to help to hasten the coming of that time when no one shall suffer from hunger or destitution, because, though willing and able to work, he can find no employment, or because he has been overtaken by sickness in the midst of his labor is one part of your duties as a Knight of the Royal Axe, and if we can succeed in making some small nook of God's creation more fruitful and cheerful, a little better and more worthy of Him, or in making some one or two human hearts a little wiser, more manly, hopeful and happy, we shall have done work worthy of masons, and acceptable to our Father in Heaven.

CLOSING CEREMONIES

KNIGHT OF THE ROYAL AXE OR PRINCE OF LIBANUS.

Chief Prince—(Knocks one.) Brother Senior Grand Warden, what is the hour?

Senior Warden—Thrice Puissant, the sun has set.

Chief Prince—It is time then to call the workmen from their labors that they may rest; announce to the Princes that this College is about to be closed.

Senior Warden—Brother Junior Grand Warden, the Thrice Puissant is about to close this College of Princes of Libanus. You will communicate the same to the brethren.

Junior Warden—Brethren, the Thrice Puissant is about to close this College of Princes of Libanus.

Chief Prince—Brother Junior Grand Warden, you will call the workmen from their labors by the usual alarm.

Junior Warden—(Sounds the bell twice.)

Senior Warden—(Sounds the bell twice.)

Chief Prince—(Sounds the bell twice.) Together brethren.

All—(Give the sign and answer.)

Chief Prince—The cedars of Mount Lebanon are felled and this College is closed.

HISTORICAL AND PHILOSOPHICAL ANALYSIS
TWENTIETH, TWENTY-FIRST AND TWENTY-SECOND DEGREES.

Freemasonry a Universal Religion—Satan the Masonic God Puerilities of the Mass, the Pagoda and Lodge—Hum Drum Platitudes on Labor

THE TWENTIETH DEGREE; GRAND MASTER OF ALL SYMBOLIC LODGES; OR ASSOCIATE MASTER AD VITAM

Is another of the Philosophical degrees.

"Philosophy and Masonry being one and the same principle, have the same object and mission to attain— the worship of the Great Architect of the Universe, and the disenthrallment of mankind." *Mackey.* (See Note 219.)

Dr. Mackey has no superior, if equal, in the thousands of Masonic writers. And no one can read him without believing him sincere. In his article *"Puerility of Freemasonry"* (*Encyc. p.* 618,) he evinces candor, strength and learning. He says:—"Is it possible that scholars of unquestioned strength of intellect and depth of science, who have devoted themselves to the study of Masonry and given the result of their learning in thousands of volumes, have been altogether mistaken: (*Encyc. p.* 618.)

Let every reader who wishes to know accurately what Masonry is memorize and ponder *Dr. Mackey's* words above given. Its object and mission are *"the worship of the Great Architect of the Universe."* Masonry is, and claims to be received as a *Universal Religion,* and in this all Masonic writers worth quoting, agree. And Mackey, and the rest, scout "Oliver's theory" that "Christ is that Great Architect," as *"the narrowest Sectarian view,"* (*Encyc. p.* 547.)

The proofs afforded by this degree that it belongs to the Satanic and not to the Christian religion are:

1st. It is throughout. like a Shaker's dance. Mormon Endowment or Popish Mass; a simple human invention or contrivance.

2nd. The long catalogue of moral virtues are simple sham pretences. *Benedict Arnold and Aaron Burr were*

not only Masons, but Masons who were never censured
by the craft in any lodge. Yet they were profligate in
morals, and "concerning every good work, reprobate."

3nd. This twentieth degree is one compact mass of falsehood and false pretences. Its password, *"Jeckson,"* or *"Jaq-
ucsson,* (French for the "Son of James") Mackey admits
(Note 225,) to be proof that *Ramsay* invented it, to over-
turn the Protestant throne of *William and Mary,* and restore the Stuarts who were Papists, who held that Kings
were not bound to keep their word ("Patriotism and
Truth,") and that killing Protestant rulers by assassina-
tion was a virtue. This was attempted by intelligent and
capable Papists in the Gunpowder Plot and vindicated by the
doctrine of the Douay.

4th. This degree was modified by *Mitchell, Dalcho,* and
others, as the *Orator's* speech shows, to explain away and
actually declare previous degrees, which still stand in the
33° *Rite,* to be "trifles, gew gaws and absurd or hideous
mysteries," (read page 58,) to accommodate them to a
democratic country and taste.

But remember and `read over and again, (Note 219.)
Mackey's authoritative declaration that the *"object and mission"* of the whole thing is the worship of *the Grand Architect
of the Universe;* a religion whose God is the devil, "the God of
this world," who is pronounced by Christ *"a liar from the beginning, and the father of it."*

TWENTY-FIRST DEGREE; NOACHITE OR PRUSSIAN KNIGHT.

"The history as well as character of this degree is a
very singular one." (*Mackey in Note* 245.) Language
needs stronger words than "Puerile" and "contemptible" to characterize it. Masons themselves despise it.
Mackey says, in the above note, "that it was ever admitted into the Masonic system is only attributable to the
passion for high degrees which prevailed in France."
* * "This degree was adopted into the Rite of Misraim, where it is the thirty-fifth." Which Rite of
Misraim *Bedarride* (Note 236,) quoted approvingly by
Macoy, says:—*"is full of puerilities,"* and even *Mackey,*
with every earthly motive to praise it, says: *"It is not
absolutely puerile."* (Note 246.)

Whoever runs his eye over its ritual and the *notes*
will see that its name is derived from Noah, and its

substance from the tower of Babel, ages later. It was said to be dug up out of salt mines, A. D. 1553; and the early French writers admit that it originated in 1757. (*Note 245.*) *Carlyle,* whose great popularity rested largely on his known and wonderful fidelity to fact, says that Frederick the Great of Prussia, from whom the degree is called *"Prussian Knight,"* while Crown Prince was in a lodge a year or two, and "socn left off altogether," and that his picture alone ever presided in a lodge. (*Note 247.*) But Frederick, and Voltaire, who lived at his court, hated the Bible, and the only conceivable motive for writing such a degree, was to make the Bible history contemptible, by its twaddling legend of the Tower of Babel and the travels of *Peleg.* which so nearly resemble the travels of Nephi in the *Book of Mormon.*

But if we constantly recur to the authentic utterance of *Dr. Mackey,* that *"the* mission and object of Masonry is the worship of the *Great Architect of the Universe,"* or *"God of this world,"* and then consider for a moment the nature of the worships now paid to him around our globe; we shall see that the endless *"puerilities"* of those worships, so far from being an objection, are a double advantage and help to the end sought. The frivolity of Masonry keeps sensible but uninformed men from fearing it, and brings thousands under its devilish magnetism, who think it must be a harmless thing, and so venture into it for worldly advantage; while others believe in its mysterious power because its legends and forms are contemptible! The mightiest powers on earth to manage mind, are in the contemptible "puerilities" of the mass, the pagoda and the lodge. How insane then the talk of the little secrecy of temperance lodges. Poison enough can be injected through the capillary tube of a rattlesnake's tooth, to break down the blood of a giant. Who can analyze or measure the invisible, intangible essence, by which contagious disease is transmitted, or by which the eye of a snake charms birds, and even men? And yet does anyone doubt their reality or power? The man who enters a secret organization, where the foot of Christ never trod, enters on ground which devils inhabit, and which angels of light shrink from, and from that instant his moral sight grows dim, and his conscience grows weak, and he *worships he knows not what.*

TWENTY-SECOND DEGREE; KNIGHT OF THE ROYAL AXE OR PRINCE OF LIBANUS.

The notes show that the Masonic writers are stumped and puzzled by this degree. It has no mark of French or European origin, and is probably one of the eight which the Jew, Morin and his Inspectors added to the twenty-five of the Rite of Perfection, which Morin brought over to Charleston; and, as Americans were generally laborers at that day, this degree was fashioned to flatter them, and increase the sale of the 33° Rite. Indeed, the bulk of the degree consists of an average piece of stump-oratory, made up of the hum drum platitudes on labor, written by men who knew only the theory of toil.

But the degree is steady to the one *"mission and object"* (*Mackey*) of Masonry, "the worship of the god of this world." No matter what subject is handled, or romance invented, this is never forgotten or omitted. Hence we are told (p. 88,) that the Sidonians "worshiped the Great Architect of the Universe." And the candidate, who at last is allowed a short oath, is made to swear, "in the presence of the Great Architect of the Universe," that "he will never communicate the secrets of this degree," which consist mainly of an average stump-speech on labor, *So help him God!* Thus binding himself by the oath of God to conceal this worship of the devil. The only possible explanation, why the eyes of Americans are not opened by such paltering, is, that the god of this world blinds the mind of those who practice his worship; as the serpent blinds the eyes of charmed animals to all objects but itself. .(*2 Cor. 3; 14 and 4, 4.*)

CHAPTER XLI

JUPITER. ♃

DECORATIONS:—Lodges in this degree are styled Hie-
rarchies. The hangings are white, supported by red and
black columns, by twos, placed here and there according
to taste. In the eastern part of the room, a sanctuary is
separated from the rest of the room by a balustrade and
a crimson curtain in front of the balustrade looped on
each side. In the East of the Sanctuary is a throne, to
which you ascend by seven steps. Before the throne is
a table covered with a crimson cloth; on it is a roll of
the book of the law, and by that a poniard. Above the
throne is a representation of the ark of the covenant,
crowned with a glory, in the center whereof is the
Tetragrammaton in Hebrew characters, and on either
side of the ark are the sun and the moon. To the right
of the first table, and more to the West, is the horned
altar of sacrifices. To the left, and more to the West,
the altar of perfumes. In the West are two chandeliers,
each with five branches, and in the East, one with two

Note 361.—"Chief of the Tabernacle.. The twenty-third degree in the
Ancient and Accepted Scottish Rite. It commemorates the institution of
the order of the priesthood in Aaron and his sons Eleazar and Ithamar.
Its principal officers are three, a Sovereign Sacrificer and two High
Priests, now called by the Supreme Councils of America the Most Excellent High Priest and Excellent priests, and the members of the 'Hierarchy' or 'Court' as the Lodge is now styled, are called Levites. The
apron is white, lined with deep scarlet and bordered with red, blue, and
purple ribbon. A golden chandelier of seven branches is painted or
embroidered on the centre of the apron. The jewel, which is a thurible,
is worn from a broad yellow, purple, blue, and scarlet sash from the
left shoulder to the right hip."—Mackey's Encyclopaedia of Freemasonry,
Article Chief of the Tabernacle.

branches. During an initiation, there is a dark apartment with an altar in the centre of it, near which are placed a light and three skulls. In front of the altar is a human skeleton.

OFFICERS:—The presiding officer sits upon the throne. He represents Aaron[1] the High Priest or Sovereign Grand Sacrificator. The Wardens sit in front of the altar and represent his two sons, Eleazar and Ithamar. They are styled Excellent Priests and all the other members, Worthy Levites. There are also two Deacons and a Captain of the Guards.

CLOTHING:—The High Priest wears a large red tunic, over which is placed a shorter one of white without sleeves; on his head is a close mitre of cloth of gold, on the front of which is painted or embroidered a Delta enclosing the Ineffable name in Hebrew characters. Over the dress he wears a black sash with silver fringe from which hangs by a red rosette a dagger; the sash is worn from left to right. Suspended on his breast is the Breast Plate.

The Wardens have the same dress except the Delta, on the mitre, and the Breast Plate. The Deacons, Captain of the Guards and the Levites wear a white Tunic, cinctured with a red belt fringed with gold. From this belt, by a black rosette, is suspended a censer of silver, which is the jewel of this degree.

High Priest. Chief of Tabernacle Degree.

APRON:—White, lined with deep scarlet and bordered with red, blue and purple ribbon. In the middle is the seven-branch candlestick, and on the flap a myrtle tree of violet color.

BATTERY:—Seven, by 00 00 00 0.

Note 262.—"In the degree of 'Chief of the Tabernacle,' which is the 23d of the Ancient and Accepted Rite, the presiding officer represents Aaron, and is styled 'Most Excellent High Priest.' In the 24th degree of the same Rite, or 'Prince of the Tabernacle,' the second officer or Senior Warden also personates Aaron."—Mackey's Encyclopaedia of Freemasonry, Article Aaron.

OPENING CEREMONIES

High Priest—(Knocks two and says:) Eleazar, my son, what is the hour?

Eleazar—My father, it is the hour to replenish the fire that burns continually upon the altar of burnt offering, and to prepare for the morning sacrifices.

High Priest—Brother Junior Deacon, what is the first care of the Chiefs of the Tabernacle when about to convene?

Junior Deacon—To see that the Tabernacle is duly guarded, that none may approach thereto, save those to whom its care and services are entrusted.

High Priest—Attend to that duty and inform the Captain of the Guards that we are about to open this assembly, to carry forth the ashes from the altar, and to prepare for the morning sacrifice, and instruct him to see that none approach save those appointed for that service lest they die. (Junior Deacon attends to order.)

Junior Deacon—Most Excellent High Priest, the Tabernacle is duly guarded and none can approach but those who have the proper pass-word.

High Priest—Eleazar, my son, are all present Chiefs of the Tabernacle?

Eleazar—My father, all present have been initiated in the first degree, and know the sacred name of the God of Israel of which the letters only can be pronounced.

High Priest—What is that name?

Eleazar—The ineffable, at which the fallen angels

tremble.

High Priest—Will you give it to me?

Eleazar—I cannot, it is forbidden to pronounce it, except once each year by the High Priests, and in conformity to the ancient usage.

High Priest—Pronounce the letters then with Ithamar.

Eleazar—Yod.*"

Ithamar—He.

Eleazar—Vau.

Ithamar—He.

High Priest—Great is Adonai. Ithamar, my son, give notice to the Levites that I am about to open this assembly, that they may prepare to discharge the duties for which they have been set apart.

Ithamar—(As Junior Warden.) My brethren, the Most Excellent High Priest is about to open this assembly of Chiefs of the Tabernacle. You will take due notice and prepare to discharge your appropriate duties.

High Priest—Together brethren.

All—(Give the sign.)

High Priest—(Two knocks; 0 0.)

Eleazar—(Two knocks; 0 0.)

Ithamar—(Two knocks; 0 0.)

High Priest—(One knock; 0.) I declare this assembly open.

Note 268.—"Basnage, (lib., iii., c. 13.) while treating of the mysteries of the name Jehovah among the Jews, says of this letter. "The yod in Jehovah is one of those things which eye hath not seen, but which has been concealed from all mankind. Its essence and matter are incomprehensible; it is not lawful so much as to meditate upon it. Man may lawfully revolve his thoughts from one end of the heavens to the other, but he cannot approach that inaccessible light, that primitive existence, contained in the letter yod; and indeed the masters call the letter thought or idea, and prescribe no bounds to its efficacy. It was this letter which, flowing from the primitive light, gave being to emanations."—Mackey's Encyclopaedia of Freemasonry, Article Yod.

CHAPTER XLII

INITIATION.

[The candidate represents Eliasaph, the son of Lael, the son of Levi. The Senior Deacon, who represents Moses, prepares him, by bandaging his eyes, and leads him to the door and knocks seven; 00 00 00 0.]

Junior Deacon—[Representing Joshua, opens the door and says:] who comes there?

Senior Deacon—Eliasaph, the son of Lael, the son of Levi, who desires to be prepared to the service of the people of the Lord in the Tabernacle of the congregation and to make an atonement for the children of Israel.

Junior Deacon—Is this an act of his own free will and accord?

Senior Deacon—It is.

Junior Deacon—Is he duly prepared and worthy to receive so great an honor?

Senior Deacon—He is.

Junior Deacon—By what further right does he ex-

Note 864.—"Chief of the Tabernacle. The 23d degree of the An-
Ancient and Accepted rite. This is the first of a series of three degrees
giving a full description of the setting up of the Tabernacle in the
wilderness, its form, materials, furniture, etc., the sacredotal and sacri-
ficial ceremonies performed by the Priests in their worship of the Deity,
as described in the instructions delivered to Moses in Exodus xxix and xl.
The Ceremonies of this degree commemorate the institution of the order of
the High-Priesthood in Aaron and his sons Eleazar and Ithamar."—
Macoy's Encyclopaedia and Dictionary of Freemasonry, Article Chief of
the Tabernacle.

pect to obtain so great a privilege?

Senior Deacon—Because the Lord has given him and those numbered with him, as a gift to Aaron and his sons from among the children of Israel; and he and his brethren have been taken by the Lord instead of all the first-born among the children of Israel.

Junior Deacon—Let him wait a time with patience until the Most-Excellent High Priest is informed of his request and his answer returned. (Junior Deacon closes the door, goes to the East, knocks six and one, the High Priest answers them and the same questions are asked, and the like answers returned as before.)

High Priest—Since he comes endowed with these necessary qualifications, let him be conducted to the cell of probation and purification. (Junior Deacon goes to the door, opens it and repeats this order and the Senior Deacon conducts him to the darkchamber and seats him on the floor in front of the altar and skeleton.

Senior Deacon—My brother, I leave you for a while, and after I retire remove the bandage from your eyes and await with patience and fortitude whatever shall befall you. (He then retires and the candidate removes the bandage. After a little while *a loud crash of thunder* is heard near the door of the apartment followed by a profound silence and then in the profound stillness, one cries with a loud voice:)

First Voice—Korah, Dathan*** and Abiram*** and their company have put fires in their censers and laid

Note 265.—"Dathan.. A Reubenite who, with Korah and Abiram, revolted against Moses and unlawfully sought the priesthood. In the first chapter of the Book of Numbers, where the whole account is given. It is said that as a punishment the earth opened and swallowed them up. The incident is referred to in the Order of High Priesthood, an honorary degree of the American Rite, which is conferred upon the installed High Priests of Royal Arch Chapters."—**Mackey's Encyclopaedia of Freemasonry**, Article Dathan.

Note 266.—"Abiram.. The names of Korah, Dathan and Abiram are introduced into High Priest Masonry. Abiram was a Reubenite, the son of Eliab, who, with Dathan and On, men of the same tribe, and Korah, a Levite, organized a conspiracy against Moses and Aaron, terminating in their swift ruin: Numbers xv and xxvi."—**Morris's Masonic Dictionary**, Article Abiram.

incense thereon and stood in the door of the Tabernacle, before the Lord, and the Lord hath done a new thing, for the earth hath opened her mouth and hath swallowed them up, for their presumption, with all that appertained to them and they have gone down alive into the chasm and the earth has closed upon them and they have perished from among the congregation. (Another crash of thunder.)

Second Voice—Flee children of Israel, for there hath come a fire from the Lord and consumed the two hundred and fifty men who offered incense. (Another crash of thunder.)

Third Voice—The children of Israel have murmured against the Lord, and against Moses and Aaron for the death of Korah and his company, and he hath sent the plague upon them and many thousands have died thereof; and the whole people is about to be destroyed. (After a profound silence, a light is silently introduced into the room, at the bottom of the door, and closed again, and a *gong* is sounded loudly by the door, then *another crash of thunder,* when chains are rattled together and dashed on the floor, and *groans* and *cries* are heard as of persons in great agony; then the wicket is opened.)

First Voice—Hast thou repented of thy sins?

Candidate—I have.

Second Voice—Pray then to the God of Israel for mercy and forgiveness, lest he consume thee with fire as he hath consumed Nadab and Abihu, the sons of Aaron the High Priest.

Third Voice—(After a few minutes.) Hast thou bowed thee to the earth and prayed? (If not answered in the affirmative, he is ordered to do so. Then the Senior Deacon enters.)

Senior Deacon—My brother, hast thou heard of the awful punishment with which God has visited those who not being duly qualified have presumptuously intermeddled with holy things? Take heed that thou

do not so likewise, for as God has said that no stranger
not of the seed of Aaron shall approach to offer incense
before the Lord that he be not dealt with as Korah and
his companion, even so, if thou approach our mysteries,
except with a pure heart, thy sins repented of and the
sincere desire to serve God and thy fellow man, will
their fate or a worse overtake thee.   Dost thou now dare
to proceed?

Candidate—I do.   (Senior Deacon sprinkles him
with water and cuts off a lock of his hair.)

Senior Deacon—I sprinkle thee with pure water in
token of that purity of heart and blamelessness of life
which must hereafter characterize thee as a Levite[257]
without guile, and as I sever from thy head this lock
of hair, even so must thou divest thyself of every selfish
and sordid feeling and devote thyself hereafter to the
service of God and the welfare, happiness
and improvement of mankind.   (He then
clothes him in a white tunic and white
drawers, puts sandals on his feet and a
white cloth over his head, covering his eyes
so as to prevent him from seeing, and leads
him to the door of the assembly and
knocks seven; 00 00 00 0.   The door is
opened, he is admitted, the Junior Warden meets him, opens his tunic and makes
the sign of the cross upon his breast.)

Junior Warden—Upon thy entrance into this holy place, thou art marked with
the sign of the cross, which, pointing to
the four quarters of the compass, is a sym-

Preparation of Can-
didate, Chief of the
Tabernacle Degree.

bol of the Universe of which God is the soul, and it teaches you how insignificant is man, and how continually he should humble himself in the presence of that great being who knows his inmost thoughts. (The Senior Deacon now conducts him three times around the room, keeping the altar on his right, while the High Priest reads:)

High Priest—O mighty and inscrutable being, we bow down before Thee as the primitive creator, that with a thought didst from thyself utter all the worlds! Eternal Father, of whose thoughts the Universe is but a mode; infinite in attributes, of which each is infinite, incorruptible, coeval with time and co-extensive with space, the ancient, absolute and sole original existence; whose laws of harmony guide the motions of the sun and stars. Thou art the all, and in Thee all things exist. (At the end of the third circuit, the Senior Deacon halts with him in the East.)

High Priest—Whom do you bring hither, brother Senior Deacon?

Senior Deacon—Eliasaph, the son of Lael, whom God has given as a gift to thee, and to thy sons from among the children of Israel to do the service of the children of Israel in the Tabernacle of the congregation and to make atonement for the children of Israel.

High Priest—Hath he prayed in the silence and darkness of the cell of probation and purification?

Senior Deacon—He has.

High Priest—Hath he heard the thunder of the Lord; the roar of the earthquake, and repented of his sins?

Senior Deacon—He has.

High Priest—Hath he been sprinkled with the water of purification, and passed through the other necessary ceremonies to prepare him to receive the mysteries?

Senior Deacon—He has.

High Priest—Hast thou been warned that thou must enter here and seek to know our mysteries with a pure heart and a sincere desire to serve God and thy fellow-men?

Candidate—I have.

High Priest—Art thou willing henceforward to devote thyself to that service?

Candidate—I am.

High Priest—Brother Senior Deacon, you will now conduct the candidate to the West and cause him to approach the altar by seven steps, where he will kneel with his wrists crossed upon the bible, square and compass. (Senior Deacon does so and the members surround him with their arms crossed on their breasts, when he contracts the following obligation:

OBLIGATION CHIEF OF THE TABERNACLE.

I....promise and swear never to reveal the secrets of this degree to any person or persons except he has received all the preceding degrees, and not unto him or them unless lawfully entitled to receive the same.

To all of which I do most solemnly swear, binding myself under no less a penalty than that of having the earth open under my feet and being swallowed up alive, like Korah, Dathan and Abiram. So help me God.

High Priest—My brother, what now dost thou desire?

Candidate—Light.

High Priest—Light is the gift of God, and common to all men. Brother Senior Deacon, bring this brother to light. (Senior Deacon removes the cloth.)

High Priest—Be thou henceforth a son of light. Arise my brother and receive the signs, tokens and words.

SIGN.

Advance the left foot; make with the right hand the motion of taking the Censer, which is supposed to be in the left hand.

Sign, Chief of the Tabernacle.

TOKEN.

Seize each other by the left elbow with the right hand, bending the arm so as to form a kind of circle.

Token, Chief of Tabernacle.

BATTERY:—Seven strokes, by six and one, or thus; 00 00 00 0.

PASS WORD:—Uriel.***

Note 266.—" An archangel, mentioned only in 2 Esdras. Michael Glycas, the Byzantine historian, says that his post is in the sun, and that he came down to Seth and Enoch, and instructed them in the length of the years and the variations of the seasons. The book of Enoch describes him as the angel of thunder and lightning. In some of the Hermetic degrees of Masonry, the name, as representing the angel of fire becomes a significant word."—Mackey's Encyclopædia of Freemasonry, Article Uriel.

ANSWER:—The Tabernacle of revealed truth.

SACRED WORD:—*Jehovah*; never pronounced but spelled.

High Priest—I accept and receive you my brother, as a Levite and Chief of the Tabernacle''' and consecrate and devote you henceforth to the service of the children of light, and I now invest you with the tunic and belt, the jewel and apron of this degree.

The jewel or censer of silver is ever to remind you to offer up unceasingly to God, the incense of good deeds and charitable actions, dictated by a pure and upright heart. The three colors, crimson, blue and purple, with which the white apron is bordered are symbols:

Red, of the splendor and glory of God, Blue of his infinite perfection, and the Purple of his infinite majesty and power.

The seven branch candlestick, upon the apron, represents what were anciently known as the seven planets or principal heavenly bodies, viz: Saturn, Jupiter, Mars, the Sun, Moon, Venus, Mercury and the Seven Angels, that the Hebrews assigned to their government, viz:

```
To Saturn..................Michael.
To Mars....................Awriel.
To Moon....................Saphiel.
To Jupiter.............. .Gabriel.
To Sun................ ..Zerachiel.
To Venus...................Hamaliel.
```

The myrtle tree of violet color, embroidered on the flap of the apron is a symbol of the immortality of the soul.

High Priest—Brother Senior Deacon, you will now seat the brother among the Levites.

Note 269.—"Chief of the Tabernacle. [Scotch Masonry.]—The fifth degree conferred in the consistory of Princes of the Royal Secret, Scotch Masonry, and the twenty-third upon the catalogue of that system. The hangings are white. The historical lectures relate to the establishment of the priesthood in the family of Aaron. The officers are three in number, a Sovereign Sacrificer and two High Priests. The members are styled Levites. The assembly is termed a hierarchy. The apron is white, lined with scarlet and trimmed with a ribbon of crimson, blue and purple. It displays a golden seven branched candlestick; on the movable part is a violet-colored myrtle. The jewel is a pot of incense. Opening hour, the instant of coming to the sacrifice; closing, the consummation of the sacrifice."—Morris's Masonic Dictionary, Article Chief of the Tabernacle.

CLOSING CEREMONIES

CHIEF OF THE TABERNACLE.

High Priest—Eleazar, my son, what is the hour?

Eleazar—The sacrifices are concluded, and the fire burns brightly upon the altar of burnt offering.

High Priest—What now remains to be done?

Eleazar—To mediate in silence and prepare for the duties of the morrow.

High Priest—That we may retire and do so, let this Hierarchy be now closed. Together brethren.

All—(Give the Sign and Battery as at opening.)

High Priest—I declare this Hierarchy closed.

PHILOSOPHICAL ANALYSIS

Twenty-Third Degree, or Chief of the Tabernacle.

Lands Men in Pagan Worship—Finite Man and the Infinite God—Satan Both Imitates and Resists Christ.

In this and the two following degrees, we are taken back to the Old Testament, where Ramsay, Jesuits, and Jews were at home; and the stupendous realities and truth of God redeemed the *Rite* from contempt and disgust, even though used as Simon the sorcerer wished to use the Holy Ghost, for gain. For there is sublimity in the name and works of God, even when used in blasphemy and sacrilege. Nadab and Abihu fall dead by the fiery eye flash of God, while using God's instituted worship, as these Masons use his word for worldly advantage, and we see here acted over what impressed us so solemnly in our childhood when we read and saw pictured in the old *"New England Primer"*

"Proud Korah's troop"
"Was swallowed up."

And we can endure the home made earth-quakes and manufactured thunder of this degree, for the sake of some glintings of Bible history, which show the fearful doom which awaits all impudent cozeners with the word and worship of God. The reader need only glance at the *Ritual and Notes* to get the whole drift of the degree, which, on page 116, lands us in the pagan worship of the heavenly bodies by the "branch candlestick which is God's symbol of a church of Christ. (*Rev. 1, 20.*)

But let us glance at the philosophy of this degree.

A priest, which word first meant an aged and venerable man, or father, came to be the man who was a day's man or intercessor between the family or tribe and God. When our race had run down so that "the earth was filled with violence," like the South before our slavery war, and had become so corrupt that a Universal Deluge did not cleanse it; then God instituted a pictorial and pantomime worship suited to the ignorance of grown-up babes, with the strength and passions of men.

But sin and corruption was not all that kept men from God. God was infinite and men infinitesimal. The blind worm beneath the sod knows as much of the solar system, and the infinity beyond as a finite sinner knows of the Infinite God. "Touching the Almighty we cannot find him out," (Job, 37, 23,) is literal verity. But Christ was and is "God manifest" to man, or *more humano.* He *"spake,"* and the worlds came. He *"spake"* to Adam and Eve. Without ceasing to be God, he became man, our Prophet, Priest, and King: and we know, and can know of God, only what we are taught by Christ. And as sin is certain ruin and law has no mercy in itself, however "holy, and just and good;" Christ, being the same yesterday, to-day and forever;" "Eternity, past, present and to come," he could and did become our *Wisdom, Righteousness, Sanctification and Redemption.* How sin came we know not; God if He will may explain that to us in Eternity. But we very well know there is sin. And the Bible being true, (and if it is not, Masons insult us by quoting it,) we know there are devils, and their chief is Christ's adversary, rival and antagonist. And he is as Christ called him the usurping "Prince of this world": and the God of its false worships. And God gave by Moses, a law which any one can see is perfect; because that supreme love to God and equal love to man would and will perfect our globe, is just as

plain as that two halves of an apple make the whole of
it. And He gave by Moses, not only a perfect law, but
a perfect Gospel in every lamb on their altars. And
he gave a human priesthood to apply that law, and explain that Gospel. And every one of those priests was
a fingerpost pointing to Christ. And when they became corrupt, Christ Himself came in person. And
when we crucified Him, He sent "another Comforter,"
a sweet and Holy Presence or Spirit, whom we could
not, can not kill; and the chart of the world shows what
that Holy Spirit has done, and is doing among *the
nations.*

Now this devil has followed, copied, imitated and resisted Christ from Eden until now! He was a serpent in Eden and he has crawled after Christ ever
since, aping and imitating his methods. He turned
rods to serpents in Egypt. He has inspired prophets,
sometimes hundreds to Christ's one! And since He is
now come, and "hath an unchanging priesthood," we
need no priest but Him, since He is ready to come at
call, and the Holy Spirit will show him to us. So
since Christ there are no priests but usurpers. Every
Masonic priest is a devil's counterfeit. When Christ
began to exercise divine power here, the devil met
Him and claimed through Him the world's worship.
That he has been at ever since, and Freemasonry and
its spawn are the last hope of the devil. He shifts his
forms, he hides under aliases and changes the fashions
of his worships. And as *Mackey* says: "The mission
and object of Masonry is *"worship,"* and it is not the
worship of Christ. The "Gentiles" (nations without
Christ) all worship devils. (1 Cor. 10, 20.) The issue is now joined, and when Christianity throws off the
worship of Satan the Gospel will subdue the world,
and

"Attending Angels, shout for Joy:
"And the bright armies sing
"Mortals, behold the sacred seal
"Of your descending King.
        Glory to God!

CHAPTER XLIII

TWENTY-FOURTH DEGREE; OR PRINCE OF THE TABERNACLE.[270]

INITIATION.

SATURN.

DECORATIONS:—This lodge is styled a Hierarchy, and consists of two apartments.

FIRST APARTMENT:—Proceeds directly into the second and is called the vestibule, where the brethren clothe themselves; it is furnished at all points like a Master's lodge, but instead of a Bible a roll of parchment representing the book of the law lies on the altar. The Hebrew letter ר in the east instead of the G.

SECOND APARTMENT:—Is circular, made so by hangings. The decorations of this vary as will be stated hereafter, according to the three points of reception. In the centre is a candlestick with seven branches, each holding seven lights.

DRESS:—Blue silk tunic, the collar of which is decorated with rays of gold representing a glory, and the

Note 270.—"Prince of the Tabernacle. (Prince du Tabernacle.)—The twenty-fourth degree of the Ancient and Accepted Scottish Rite. In the old rituals the degree was intended to illustrate the directions given for the building of the tabernacle, the particulars of which are recorded in the twenty-fifth chapter of Exodus. The Lodge is called a Hierarchy, and its officers are a Most Powerful Chief Prince, representing Moses, and three Wardens, whose style is Powerful, and who respectively represent Aaron, Bezaleel, and Aholiab. In the modern rituals of the United States, the three principal officers are called the Leader, the High Priest, and the Priest, and respectively represent Moses, Aaron, and Ithamar, his son. The ritual is greatly enlarged, and while the main idea of the degree is retained, the ceremonies represent the initiation into the mysteries of the Mosaic tabernacle.

The jewel is the letter A, in gold, suspended from a broad crimson ribbon. The apron is white, lined with scarlet and bordered with green. The flap is sky-blue. On the apron is depicted a representation of the tabernacle.

This degree appears to be peculiar to the Scottish Rite and its modifications. I have not met with it in any of the other Rites."—Mackey's Encyclopædia of Freemasonry, Article Prince of the Tabernacle.

body of it is sprinkled with stars of gold. Upon the head is a close crown, encircled with stars and surmounted by a Delta.

SASH :—Watered scarlet, worn as a collar; if a sash, from left to right.

APRON :—White, lined with deep scarlet and bordered with green, the flap sky blue. In the middle of the apron is a representation of the first tabernacle built by Moses.

JEWEL :—Is the letter   or the letter A. . in gold, worn from a collar of crimson ribbon..

TITLES :—The Master is styled Thrice Puissant and represents Moses. There are three Wardens styled Puissant. First Warden represents Aaron, the High Priest, and sits in the West; the Second Warden represents Bezaleel, and sits in the South; the Third Warden represents Aholiab, and sits in the North; the candidate represents Eleazar, son of Aaron. There are besides these two Deacons.

OPENING CEREMONIES

PRINCE OF THE TABERNACLE.[271]

Thrice Puissant—Puissant Warden in the North, I am about to open this Hierarchy of Princes of the Tabernacle, that we may take council for the welfare of the order. Are we well quartered so that none save those who are entitled to do so can approach the Tabernacle?

Aholiab—Thrice Puissant, the Tabernacle is guarded on all sides, and we are in security.

Thrice Puissant—Puissant Warden in the West, are all present Princes of the Tabernacle?

Aaron—All are Princes of the Tabernacle, Thrice Puissant, and have seen the perfection of the holy mysteries of the Hebrews.

Thrice Puissant—What are the duties of a Prince of the Tabernacle?

Aaron—To labor incessantly for the glory of God, the honour of his country and the happiness of his brethren.

Thrice Puissant—Puissant Warden in the North, whom do you represent?

Note 271.—"The presiding officer represents Moses, and is called Most Puissant Leader. The second officer represents Eleazar, the High-Priset, the son of Aaron. The candidate represents Phinehas, the son of Eleazar the High-Priest. Two apartments are required when conferring the degree. The hangings are red and black. The jewel is the letter א, suspended from a violet colored watered ribbon. This degree is most intimately connected with, and should be considered a continuation of, that of the Chief of the Tabernacle. The especial duties of a Prince of the Tabernacle are to labor incessantly for the glory of God, the honor of his country, and the happiness of his brethren; to offer up thanks and prayers to the Deity in lieu of sacrifices of flesh and blood."—Macoy's Encyclopaedia and Dictionary of Freemasonry, Article Prince of the Tabernacle.

Aholiab—I represent Aholiab, who aided in the building of the first Tabernacle.

Thrice Puissant—How did he labor upon the Tabernacle of the Lord?

Aholiab—As an engraver, beautifying the vessels thereof, and as an embroiderer in blue and purple, and scarlet and fine linen.

Thrice Puissant—What does his occupation teach you in morals?

Aholiab—To engrave upon my heart and ever recollect the laws of God and the statutes of righteousness, virtue and truth, and to make my life beautiful with the embroidery of good actions.

Thrice Puissant—Puissant Warden in the South, whom do you represent?

Bezaleel—I represent Bezaleel, who aided in the building of the first Tabernacle.

Thrice Puissant—How did he labor upon the Tabernacle of the Lord?

Bezaleel—In gold, silver and brass, in the cutting of stones and in carving wood.

Thrice Puissant—What does his occupation teach you in morals?

Bezaleel—Ever to strive to attain perfection, and to be patient and persevering in every good work.

Thrice Puissant—Puissant Warden in the West, Most Excellent High Priest, what is your duty in the Tabernacle?

Aaron—To offer up prayers and thanks to the Deity, in lieu of sacrifices, and to aid you with my counsel and advice.

Thrice Puissant—It is time to proceed to discharge our duties; aid me Princes to open this Hierarchy. Together.

All—(Give the second sign.)

Thrice Puissant—(Seven knocks; 00 00 00 0.)

Aaron—(Seven knocks; 00 00 00 0.)

Bezalecl—(Seven knocks; 00 00 00 0.)

Aholiab—(Seven knocks; 00 00 00 0.)

Thrice Puissant—I declare this Hierarchy opened.

CHAPTER XLIV

Twenty-Fourth Degree; or Prince of the Tabernacle.[*]

INITIATION.

[The candidate is prepared by the Senior Deacon in a white tunic without ornaments or insignia, and conducted into the vestibule and up to the altar, without ceremony.]

Senior Deacon—Brother Eleazar, thou hast been chosen to be anointed, consecrated and sanctified to minister unto the Lord in the Priest's office. But before thou canst enter upon the mysteries of consecration, thou must in the most solemn manner give assurances that no unworthy motive prompts thee to seek to know those ancient mysteries which were instituted among the Patriarchs and the knowledge of which is indispensable to him who would become a Priest in Israel. Kneel therefore and place thy hand on the book of the law, and make true answers to such questions as shall be asked thee. (Candidate obeys.)

Note 272.—"Prince of the Tabernacle. [Scotch Masonry.]—The sixth degree conferred in the Consistory of Princes of the Royal Secret. Scotch Masonry, and the twenty-fourth upon the catalogue of that system. The historical instructions refer to the building of the tabernacle. The assembly is termed a hierarchy. The officers are, a Most Powerful Chief Prince, representing Moses, and three Wardens, entitled Powerful, representing Aaron, Aholiab and Besaleel. The apron is white, lined with crimson—the movable part sky-blue. It displays, in red, a view of the tabernacle. The jewel is the letter A, of gold, suspended from a crimson ribbon. Hours of work, from the first hour of the organisation of the hierarchy to the last hour of life."—Morris's Masonic Dictionary, Article Prince of the Tabernacle.

First—Dost thou now, representing Eleazar, the son of Aaron, solemnly declare that in seeking to know the hidden ancient mysteries, thou art not actuated by any spirit of idle curiosity or the pride of knowledge, but by a sincere desire thereby to be the better able to serve God, your country and your brethren, and more effectually to labor for the reformation of mankind?

Candidate—I do.

Second—In the character of a Chief of the Tabernacle, hast thou earnestly striven to discharge all the duties required of thee, and to live worthily, act justly and fear God?

Candidate—I have.

Third—Hast thou, while a Chief of the Tabernacle, done wrong to any one without making reparation as far as in thy power?

Candidate—I have not.

Fourth—Dost thou solemnly swear, upon the holy book of the law,''' and with thy heart open before God, and all its thoughts legible to him, that these answers are true and sincere, without equivocation or mental reservation? If thou dost; say, I swear and kiss the book of the law.

Candidate—(Kissing the book.) I swear. (Senior Deacon raises him and orders him to wash himself in the brazen sea, after which he gives him an explanation of the furniture of the lodge.)

Senior Deacon—I am charged my brother, to explain to you the meaning of the several symbols with which you are now surrounded.

Note 272.—"Masonically, the Book of the Law is that sacred book which is believed by the Mason of any particular religion to contain the revealed will of God; although, technically, among the Jews the Torah, or Book of the Law, means only the Pentateuch, or five books of Moses. Thus, to the Christian Mason, the Book of the Law is the Old and New Testaments; to the Jew, the Old Testament; to the Mussulman, the Kuran; to the Brahman, the Vedas; and to the Parsee, the Zendavesta." —Mackey's Encyclopædia of Freemasonry, Article Book of the Law.

The Triangle.

THE TRIANGLE:—With the letter Yod in the center, suspended in the East, is an emblem of the Deity and of equity, because its sides are equal and it is the first perfect figure that can be formed with straight lines.

THE SQUARE."'ᵛ

Upon the altar is an emblem of rectitude of intention and action, and obedience to constituted authority.

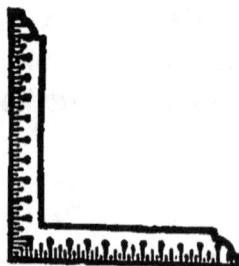

Square.

The Compasses.

THE COMPASSES:"'ᶜ

Of command of the motion of the heavenly bodies, of harmony and of eternity.

Note 274.—"With great propriety, therefore, is the square put into the hands of the Worshipful Master, in order that he may keep the brethren within the square of the ancient charges of Freemasonry. This symbol must at all times, and in all places, be regarded as a great light, and th genuine Freemason is not only reminded by this light to do his duty to his brethren, but to all mankind.—Gadicke."—Macoy's Encyclopædia and Dictionary of Freemasonry, Article Square.

Note 275.—"One of the most prominent objects used as emblems in Masonry. It lies on the Open Word that surmounts the altar in the center of the lodge. Its points being towards the West. Its position is made to represent a gradation. Its lesson is limiting or circumscribing the passions—a sublime inculcation. In the third degree it plays a still more prominent part. It teaches to the Worshipful Master at his installation 'that he should limit his desires to his station, that rising to eminence by merit, he may live respected and die regretted.'"—Morris's Masonic Dictionary, Article Compass.

THE THREE LIGHTS:[116]—On the East, West and South of the altar, represent the summer solstice, and the vernal and autumnal equinoxes.

THE TWO COLUMNS:—Represent those erected by Enoch to perpetuate the history of the times before the flood.

Plumb.

THE PLUMB.[117]

Is a symbol of decision, firmness and independence; of truth and straightforward simplicity.

Note 876.—"Three. Everywhere among the ancients the number three was deemed the most sacred of numbers. A reverence for its mystical virtues is to be found even among the Chinese, who say that numbers begin at one and are made perfect at three, and hence they denote the multiplicity of any object by repeating the character which stands for it three times. In the philosophy of Plato, it was the image of the Supreme Being, because it includes in itself the properties of the two first numbers, and because, as Aristotle says, it contains within itself a beginning, a middle, and an end. The Pythagoreans called it perfect harmony. So sacred was this number deemed by the ancients that we find it designating some of the attributes of almost all the gods. The thunder-bolt of Jove was three-forked; the sceptre of Neptune was a trident; Cerberbus, the dog of Pluto, was three-headed; there were three Fates and three Furies; the sun had three names, Apollo, Sol, and Liber; and the moon three also, Diana, Luna, and Hecate. In all incantations three was a favorite number, for, as Virgil says, 'numero Deus impari gaudet.' God delights in an odd number."—Mackey's Encyclopædia of Freemasonry, Article Three.

Note 877.—"In the scriptures the Plumb-Line is emblematic of regular rule; hence, to destroy by line and plummet, as in Amos vii., is understood, a regular and systematic destruction. Such had nearly been the fate of the Masonic institution in the United States, consequent upon political anti-Masonry, 1826-1836."—Morris's Masonic Dictionary, Article Plumb-Line.

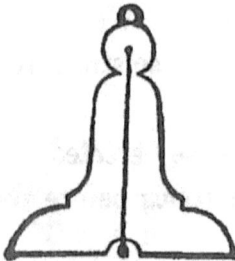

Level.

THE LEVEL.[278]

Is a symbol of equality and equanimity and teaches us that all men are equal in the sight of God and in the mysteries.

THE BLAZING STAR.[279]

The Blazing Star.

Represents Sirius, the dog star, announcing the approach of the inundation of the Nile, to the fore-fathers of the Hebrews when

THE ROUGH STONE.[280]

Represents the profane, who are ignorant of its mysteries.

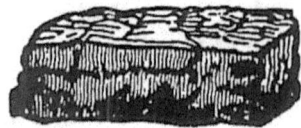

The Rough Stone.

Note 278.—"Level. In Freemasonry the level is a symbol of equality; not of that social equality, which would destroy all distinctions of rank and position and beget confusion. Insubordination and anarchy, but of that fraternal equality which, recognizing the fatherhood of God, admits as a necessary corollary, the brotherhood of man. It, therefore, teaches us that, in the sight of the Grand Architect of the Universe, his creatures, who are at an immeasurable distance from him, move upon the same plane; as the far-moving stars, which though millions of miles apart, yet seem to shine upon the same canopy of the sky. In this view, the level teaches us that all men are equal, subject to the same infirmities, hastening to the same goal, and preparing to be judged by the same immutable law."—Mackey's Encyclopædia of Freemasonry, Article Level.

Note 279.—"Blazing Star. The blazing star must not be considered merely as the creature which heralded the appearance of T. G. A. O. T. U., but the expressive symbol of that Great Being himself, who is described by the magnificent appellations of the Day Spring, or Rising Sun; the Day Star; the Morning Star, and the Bright, or Blazing Star. This, then, is the supernal reference of the Blazing Star of Masonry, attached to a science which, like the religion it embodies, is universal and applicable to all times and seasons, and to every people that ever did or ever will exist on our ephemeral globe of earth."—Macoy's Encyclopædia and Dictionary of Freemasonry, Article Blazing Star.

Note 280.—"In Speculative Masonry we adopt the ashlar in two different states, as symbols in the Apprentice's degree. The Rough Ashlar, or stone, in its rude and unpolished condition, is emblematic of man in his natural state—ignorant, uncultivated, and vicious."—Mackey's Encyclopædia of Freemasonry, Article Ashlar.

THE PERFECT CUBE.[281]

The Perfect Cube.

Is a symbol of the enlightened, to whom they are known. (Senior Deacon now blinds him and leads him to the door of the second apartment, which is now hung with scarlet; and around in front of the hangings are twelve columns, each having painted on it in brilliant letters, one of the signs of the zodiac, which follow each other in regular order as follows:)

Thrice Puissant—As Moses in the East, clothed with all the insignia, between the columns, on which are the signs Taurus♉ and Aries.♈

Aaron—In the West, between the columns on which are the signs Libra♎ and Scorpio.♏

Bazaleel—In the South, between the columns on which are the signs Capricornus♑ and Aquarius.♒

Aholiab—In the North, between the columns on which are the signs Cancer♋ and Leo.♌ In the centre of the room, by the chandelier, is a triangular altar, to which candidate is now led when the Senior Deacon knocks seven; 00 00 00 0.

Junior Deacon—(Opening the door.) Who seeks admission to this inner chamber of the mysteries?

Senior Deacon—Eleazar, the son of Aaron, who having been appointed to minister unto God in the Priest's office, desires first to know the mysteries and receive the indispensable degree of Prince of the Tabernacle.

Junior Deacon—Has he attained the degree of Chief of the Tabernacle?

Senior Deacon—He has.

Junior Deacon—In that character has he earnestly

Note 281.—"Cube. The cube is a symbol of truth, of wisdom, of moral perfection. The New Jerusalem promised by the Apocalypse is equal in length, breadth, and height."—Macoy's Encyclopædia and Dictionary of Freemasonry, Article Cube.

striven to discharge all the duties required of him, and to live worthily, act justly, and fear God?

Senior Deacon—He has.

Junior Deacon—Has he, while such, done wrong to any one, without afterwards making reparation as far as has been in his power?

Senior Deacon—He has not.

Junior Deacon—Eleazar, art thou actuated in seeking to know the mysteries by a sincere desire to be thereby better able to serve God, your country and your brethren, and more efficiently to labor for the great good of man?

Candidate—I am.

Junior Deacon—Art thou not induced to come hither through idle curiosity, or the pride of knowledge and a desire to become superior to thy brethren and fellows?

Candidate—I am not.

Junior Deacon—Brother Senior Deacon, by what further right does he expect to gain admission here?

Senior Deacon—By the sacred word.

Junior Deacon—Has he the sacred word?

Senior Deacon—He has.

Junior Deacon—Let him give it.

Senior Deacon—He cannot, except with our assistance.

Junior Deacon—Let him begin then.

Candidate—Yod.

Senior Deacon—He.

Junior Deacon—Vau.

Candidate—He.

Junior Deacon—The word is right, let him wait until the Thrice Puissant is informed of his request. (Junior Deacon closes the door, goes to the center of the circle and gives the battery. The Thrice Puissant answers it and the same questions are asked and the like answers returned, as at the door.)

Thrice Puissant—Brother Junior Deacon, has the candidate the sacred word?

Junior Deacon—He has, Thrice Puissant.

Thrice Puissant—You will retire and let him enter and be received in due form. (Junior Deacon goes to and opens the door.)

Junior Deacon—It is the order of the Thrice Puissant, that he enter and be received in due form. (Senior Deacon enters with him and conducts him within the circle, then the Junior Deacon stops him, bares his right arm, holds a lighted candle near enough to it to cause him to feel the heat, and says:)

Junior Deacon—I test thee by fire'" and let this present pain ever remind you that he who rashly assumes to perform office for which he is unfit, deserves the fate of Nadab and Abihu, who were consumed by fire from heaven when they offered strange fire before the Lord in the wilderness of Sinai. (Senior Deacon then conducts him slowly three times around the room.)

Thrice Puissant—And the Lord spake unto Moses, saying: Bring the tribe of Levi near and present them before Aaron the Priest, that they may minister unto him, and they shall keep his charge and the charge of the whole congregation before the Tabernacle of the congregation, to do the service of the Tabernacle. And

Note 282.—"The purifying power of fire is naturally deduced from this symbol of the holiness of the element. And in the high degrees of Masonry, as in the ancient institutions, there is a purification by fire, coming down to us insensibly and unconsciously from the old Magian cultus. In the Mediæval ages there was a sect of 'fire philosophers'—philosophi per ignem—who were a branch or offshoot of Rosicrucianism, with which Freemasonry has so much in common. These fire philosophers kept up the veneration for fire, and cultivated the 'fire-secret,' not as an idolatrous belief, but modified by their hermetic notions. They were also called 'theosophists,' and through them, or in reference to them, we find the theosophic degrees of Masonry, which sprang up in the eighteenth century. As fire and light are identical, so the fire, which was to the Zoroastrians the symbol of the Divine Being, is to the Mason, under the equivalent idea of light, the symbol of Divine Truth, or of the Grand Architect."—*Mackey's Encyclopædia of Freemasonry, Article Fire-Worship.*

they shall keep all the instruments of the Tabernacle of the congregation, and the charge of the children of Israel, to do the service of the Tabernacle. And thou shalt give the Levites unto Aaron, and to his sons; they are wholly given unto him, out of the children of Israel. And thou shalt appoint Aaron and his sons; and they shall wait on their Priest's office, and the stranger that cometh nigh shall be put to death. (Candidate halts in the South in front of Bezaleel, who pours a small quantity of water on his head.)

Bezaleel—Thou hast reached the South, I test thee with water, the second test. Let it ever remind thee that none but the pure of heart can be admitted to the Holy Tabernacle in the heavens. (Senior Deacon conducts him slowly three times around the room.)

Aaron—At the door of the Tabernacle of the congregation, I will meet with the children of Israel and I will sanctify the Tabernacle of the congregation and the altar; I will sanctify also both Aaron and his sons to minister to me in the Priest's office, and I will dwell among the children of Israel and I will be their God, and they shall know that I am the Lord their God that brought them forth out of the land of Egypt, that I might dwell among them, I the Lord their God. (Candidate halts in the West in front of Aaron, who causes him to kneel on some sand and gravel.)

Aaron—Thou hast reached the West, I test thee with earth. It is the common mother, and to it, our frail bodies return. It is well to kneel upon its bosom when we implore the mercy and forgiveness of God. Let the beneficence of the earth, which produceth liberally and generously, even for the unworthy, teach thee generosity and that the open hand is a fit companion of the pure heart. (Senior Deacon then conducts him slowly three times around the room.)

Bezaleel—Ye shall do no unrighteousness in judgment. Thou shalt not respect the person of the poor, nor honor the person of the mighty. In righteousness shalt thou judge thy neighbor. Thou shalt not hate thy brother in thy heart. Thou shalt not seek revenge, nor bear ill-will against the children of thy people, but thou shalt love thy neighbor as thyself. (Candidate halts in the East at the station of the Thrice Puissant. The members with fans make a wind about him while he is thus addressed:)

Thrice Puissant—Thou hast reached the East; I test thee with air,''' the life of all men; the free inestimable gift of God. Like him, it is mighty, but invisible; like him it blesses us ever. Be thou liberal and generous as the air, for it God freely gives thee light and air, and asks in return nothing but gratitude and whispered thanks, thou mayest well afford to share thy plenty with thy destitute, afflicted and unfortunate brethren.

Thrice Puissant—Brother Senior Deacon, whence come you?

Senior Deacon—Out of darkness.

Thrice Puissant—And whither go you?

Note 263.—"Elements. It was the doctrine of the old philosophies, sustained by the authority of Aristotle, that there were four principles of matter—fire, air, earth, and water—which they called elements. Modern science has shown the fallacy of the theory. But it was also taught by the Kabbalists, and afterwards by the Rosicrucians, who, according to the Abbe de Villars (Le Comte de Gabalis), peopled them with supernatural beings called, in the fire, Salamanders; in the air, Sylphs; in the earth, Gnomes; and in the water, Undines. From the Rosicrucians and the Kabbalists, the doctrine passed over into some of the high degrees of Masonry, and is especially referred to it the Ecossais or Scottish Knight of St. Andrew, originally invented by the Chevalier Ramsay. In this degree we find the four angels of the four elements described as Ardarel, the angel of fire; Casmaran, of air; Talliasd, of water; and Furlac, of earth; and the signs refer to the same elements."—Mackey's Encyclopedia of Freemasonry, Article Elements.

Senior Deacon—To the East, the place of light and cradle of the mysteries.***

Thrice Puissant—Thou art already there, what is thy desire?

Senior Deacon—That this candidate may go the way that we have gone before him.

Thrice Puissant—The soul is immortal, but for the body, life comes only out of death.*** If he would see the light, conduct him to the holy altar and let him there assume the obligation. Senior Deacon conducts him to the West and causes him to advance by six (6) equal and one (1) long step, when he kneels and with his hands upon the book of the law, contracts the following obligation.

OBLIGATION PRINCE OF THE TABERNACLE.

I....do solemnly promise and swear, never to reveal the secrets of this degree to any person or persons, except he has received all the preceding degrees, and not unto him or them unless lawfully entitled to receive the same.

I furthermore promise and swear that I will stand to and abide by the laws, statutes and regulations of this

Note 284.—"Mysteries, Ancient. Each of the Pagan gods, says Warburton (Div. Leg., I., ii. 4), had, besides the public and open, a secret worship paid to him, to which none were admitted but those who had been selected by preparatory ceremonies called Initiation. This secret worship was termed the Mysteries. And this is supported by Strabo (lib. x., cap. 3), who says that it was common, both to the Greeks and the Barbarians, to perform their religious ceremonies with the observance of a festival, and that they are sometimes celebrated publicly and sometimes in mysterious privacy. Noel (Dict. de la Fable) thus defines them: Secret ceremonies which were practiced in honor of certain gods, and whose secret was known to the initiates alone, who were admitted only after long and painful trials which it was more than their life was worth to reveal."—Mackey's Encyclopædia of Freemasonry, Article Mysteries, Ancient.

Note 285.—"The ceremonies of initiation were all funereal in their character. They celebrated the death and the resurrection of some cherished being, either the object of esteem as a hero, or of devotion as a god. Subordination of degrees was instituted, and the candidate was subjected to probations, varying in their character and severity; the rites were practiced in the darkness of night, and often amid the gloom of impenetrable forests or subterranean caverns; and the full fruition of knowledge, for which so much labor was endured, and so much danger incurred, was not attained until the aspirant, well tried and thoroughly purified, had reached the place of wisdom and of light."—Mackey's Encyclopædia of Freemasonry, Article Mysteries, Ancient.

Hierarchy of Princes of the Tabernacle, also the statutes and regulations of the Supreme Council and Sovereign Grand Consistory of the United States of America, their territories and dependencies and of the Grand Consistory of the State of........so long as I remain within its jurisdiction.

To all of which I do most solemnly swear, binding myself under no less a penalty that to be consumed with fire from heaven, like Nadab and Abihu and that my ashes should be flung into the air and blown to the four corners of the earth by the wind. So help me God. (After the obligation he is brought to light and the Thrice Puissant takes in his left hand a small vessel of perfumed oil and says:)

Thrice Puissant—I will sanctify the Tabernacle of the congregation and the altar, I will sanctify also both Aaron and his sons to minister to me in the Priest's office. In the Tabernacle of the congregation, without the veil, which is before the testimony, Aaron and his sons shall order it from evening to morning before the Lord. It shall be a statute forever unto their generations on behalf of the children of Israel, and thou shalt anoint Aaron and his sons and consecrate them that they may minister unto me in the Priest's office. (He then pours oil on his head, saying:)

Thrice Puissant—Eleazar, son of Aaron, I do anoint thee and consecrate thee to the service of truth and virtue, which is the service of the Lord, to minister unto him and unto thy fellow men in this world, which is his truest tabernacle and temple. (He then takes a small vessel filled with red liquid, and with a small brush saying:)

Thrice Puissant—With the blood of a ram slain for a burnt offering, I touch the tip of thy right ear, (touching it) the thumb of thy right hand, (touching it) and the great toe of thy right foot, (touching it) and with the same blood I sprinkle thy garments, (sprinkling them) and do sanctify thee and them. Thine ear is hereafter to be ever open to the cry of distress, the prayer of want, the moan of suffering, the supplication of the penitent and the call of duty. Thy hand is henceforth to be opened wide in charity and ready to labor in every good work. And thy feet are to stand firmly wherever duty places thee, however dangerous the post; nor ever to slide upon the slippery paths of temptation. Arise my brother Eleazar. (Candidate rises and the Thrice Puissant invests him with the following signs, grip and words, and with the insignia and jewel.)

SIGN OF RECOGNITION.

Place the right hand open over the eyes, as if to protect them from a strong light, the left hand on the breast, then raise the right hand to the left shoulder, and bring it down diagonally to the right side. This is called the sign of the scarf.

Sign of Recognition,
Prince of the Tabernacle

Grand Sign, Prince
of the Tabernacle.

GRAND SIGN.

Place both hands open upon the head, join the two thumbs and the two forefingers by their extremities so as to form a triangle.

N. B.—The token, battery and word, are the same as in the preceding degree.

MARCH :—Six equal steps and one longer, total seven steps.

Thrice Puissant—Brethren, behold a new Prince of the Tabernacle, to be instructed and prepared to fulfill all his duties as a Prince of well doers in this Tabernacle of clay, that he may be raised on the great day of account, a shining monument of God's glory in the tabernacle, not made with hands, eternal in the heavens. (Thrice Puissant resumes his station and if there is no business, closes the Hierachy.)

CLOSING CEREMONIES

PRINCE OF THE TABERNACLE.

Thrice Puissant—Puissant Warden in the West, what is the hour?

Aaron—Thrice Puissant, it is time for the evening sacrifices.

Thrice Puissant—If so, it is time to close this Hierarchy. Together Princes.

All—(Give the Grand Sign.)

Thrice Puissant—Knocks seven; (00 00 00 0.)

Aaron—(Knocks seven; 00 00 00 0.)

Bezaleel—(Knocks seven; 00 00 00 0.)

Aholiab—(Knocks seven; 00 00 00 0.)

Thrice Puissant—I declare this Hierarchy of Princes of the Tabernacle closed.

SIGNS HIEROGLYPHIQUES, PRINCES DU TABERNACLE

A Λ ⋀ ⋀ ⋀ A V V V V V
a   b   c   d   e   f   g   h   i   k   l

A A ⋀ ⋀ ⋀ ⋀ A V V V V
m   n   o   p   q   r   s   t   u   v   z

V V
y   z

PHILOSOPHICAL ANALYSIS

Zodiacal Signs a Heathen Invention—Masonic Baptsim a Heathen Rite—
Freemasonry Simple Heathenism—governed by the Terrors of a Secret
Clan.

*Proofs afforded by this degree that Freemasonry is
vulgar, debased heathenism:*

Proof First. Its oath (which makes the Mason) is
sworn on the "Holy Book of the Law," which, Mackey
says, "Masonically," means the Sacred Book of any and
every religion on earth. (See Note 273.) This includes not only the Books of Curious Arts (Acts 19, 19)
and the "Book of Mormon," which sanctions polygamy
and despotism, but the Gree Gree-Ritual, sworn upon
in African lodges, which practice whoredom, human
sacrifice and cannibalism.

Proof Second. The second apartment of the lodge-
room of this degree is surrounded with twelve pillars, on
which are painted the twelve signs of the Zodiac, with
an officer stationed between two signs; as Moses between Taurus and Aries; the Bull and the Ram, and
so on. And these signs, used in consecrating a priest
of all the religions of the world, have a religious, net
an astronomical, significance. These signs were invented by Egyptian priests who practiced brute-worship
and brutalized Egypt till it became, as the Bible predicted: "the basest of the kingdoms" (Ezek. 29, 15),
as it is at this day. The Egyptians worshiped the ani-

mals whose names they gave to the twelve signs of the
Zodiac, and transferred them to the heavens, and worshipped them still. *McClenachan's book of the Ancient
and Accepted Scottish Rite,* page 558, says: "This
rite (Baptism) has come to us by legitimate transmis-
sion * * * in the simple sense in which it was
used in the land watered by the Nile, before the building of the Pyramids." And "The Ceremony of Baptism" occupies twenty-one pages in this "Book of the
Rite." If this does not identify Masonic baptism with
the religion of Egyptian brute-worship, language has no
meaning.

Proof Third. Commenting on *The Three Lights,*
(*Ritual, p. 129, Note 276*) Mackey says: "The sun
has three names, and the moon three also. And in all
incantations, three was a favorite number." Incantation was raising devils by magic. And seeking knowledge and power from' devils is worshiping them. If
Dr. Mackey intended to identify Masonry with sun,
moon and demon worship, the above is the language he
would use.

Proof Fourth. Macoy (Note 279) .gives Christ's
appellations: "Morning Star," "Rising Sun," "Day
Star," etc., to Satan, the God of all Gentile or heathen
worships: under the title of the *G. A. O. T. U.,* who is
neither Father, Son, nor Holy Ghost, but the "prince,"
and "god of this world."

Proof Fifth. And Mackey, the lexicographer, and
jurisconsult of Masonry, expressly declares it to be mag-
ical or heathen worship, thus: "In the high degrees
of Masonry, as in the ancient institutions, there is a
purification by fire coming down to us insensibly and
unconsciously from the old Magian cultus." (Note
282.) "Cultus" is the Latin for *worship.* These
proofs might be extended indefinitely. And if they do
not establish, by Masonic authorities, that Freemasonry

is "vulgar, debased heathenism," then Egyptian brute-worship, sun and moon-worship, fire-worship and all the rest, are not heathenism. To call it "philosophy" is to insult civilization, reason and religion.

The uniform, universal declaration of Masonic writers that *"Masonry is the religion in which all mankind agree,"* and that dictum of *Dr. Mackey,* that *"The mission and object of Masonry is the worship of the Great Architect,"* etc., who is neither FATHER, SON nor HOLY GHOST, settles it: if authority can settle anything; that Freemasonry is simple heathenism. And "A heathen man," by Christ's word, was to be an outcast from the church *(Matt. 18, 17),* and reason, observation and common sense affirm the same.

Hence this twenty-fourth degree employs the names of the men of God, and the terms of the Bible, to consecrate priests for the devil! And as there are no human priests since Christ, "who hath an unchangeable priesthood" *(Heb. 7, 24),* to make a priest of any one religion, is to make a counterfeit. But this degree makes a universal priest! A priest of all the religions on earth! And if this degree has done its full work in him, his heart contains all the priestly depravity from *Cain* in Eden to the *Mormon* at Salt Lake. And history as well as theory proves it. And when Aaron Burr browbeat into a duel and shot the friend of Washington; and Benedict Arnold burnt and pillaged towns and villages which, as an American officer, he had sworn to protect with his own life, they both showed what moral monsters Masonry can make of men. And the sole reason why the Episcopalian, Baptist and Methodist clergymen of Chicago who are high Masons, sworn full of oaths, are not *Burrs* and *Arnolds* in religion, is, that they do not understand the system to which they belong, and are held back by the influence of surrounding Christianity. In our mills and workshops there are plenty of honest, sworn dupes, like the assassins of *Morgan*, who believe it right to murder when they are ordered to do so!

This "Prince of the Tabernacle," who and what is he? He is a man whose conscience is so full of oaths, that, like the liver of a calomel patient, which no medicine can affect, no sacred obligation can bind him; and so leaves him to be lured by the interest, or governed by the terrors of his secret clan! If we would know the true nature of priestism, we must look in Africa, where the lodges reduce their theory to practice.

But our high priest is in the heavens, at the right hand of God, "*wherefore he is able to save them to the uttermost who come unto God by Him, seeing He ever liveth to make intercession for them.*" (*Heb. 7, 25.*) "Thanks be to God for His unspeakable gift."(*2 Cor. 9, 15.*)

CHAPTER XLV

TWENTY-FIFTH DEGREE; OR KNIGHTS OF THE BRAZEN SERPENT.[***]

NORTH OR WINTER.

.. DECORATIONS :—This lodge is styled the Court of Sinai. The hangings are red and blue. Over the throne in the east is a transparency, on which is painted a burning bush, and in the centre the word יְהֹוָה. The lodge is illuminated by seven lights extending from East to West, the centre a burning bush, one being a large globular light representing the Sun. Over these lights are suspended the signs of Saturn, Jupiter, Mars, the Sun, Venus, Mercury, the Moon. Around the lodge are twelve columns, each having on its capital one of the zodiacal signs, commencing in the East with Taurus and going round by the North, West and South in regular order. In the North is a painting representing Mount Sinai, with the tents of the Israelites in the foreground. Over the

Note 256.—'Knight of the Brazen Serpent. The 25th degree of the Ancient and Accepted Rite. The history of this degree is founded upon the events described in the Book of Numbers xxi. 6-9. The body is styled the Council, and represents the camp of the Israelites in the wilderness, after the death of Aaron. The camp, standards, and tabernacle, with its court, are arranged as in the 23d and 24th degrees. In the East is a transparency on which is painted a cross, with a serpent coiled round it and over the arms. The teaching and moral of the degree is Faith. The presiding officer represents Moses, and is styled 'Most Puissant Leader.' The candidate is called 'A Traveler.' The hangings of the council are red and blue. The jewel is a tau cross, of gold, surmounted by a circle—the Crux Ansata—round which a serpent is entwined, suspended by a red ribbon. The legend states that this degree was founded during the time of the crusades in the Holy Land, as a military and monastic order, and gave it the name it bears, in allusion to the healing and saving virtues of the brazen serpent among the Israelites in the wilderness—it being part of the obligation of the Knights to receive and gratuitously nurse sick travelers, protect them against the attacks of the infidels, and escort them safely through Palestine.''—Macoy's Encyclopædia and Dictionary of Freemasonry, Article Knight of the Brazen Serpent.

seat of the presiding officer is a winged globe, encircled by a serpent. On each side of him is a short column on which is a serpent, his body coiled in folds and his head and neck erect above the folds.

TITLES :—The presiding officer represents Moses[287] and is styled Most Powerful Grand Master. He sits in the East. The Senior Warden represents Joshua[288] and sits on his right and is styled Commander of the Host. The Junior Warden represents Aaron, and sits in the West and is styled Lieutenant Commander. The Orator represents Eleazar, sits in the North and is styled High Priest. The Secretary is styled Registrar; sits on the right of Joshua. The Treasurer sits on the left of the presiding officer. There are also a Senior and Junior Deacon. The brethren are styled Knights. The candidate represents a Traveller.[289]

Note 287.—"He proved himself therein a man of marvelous gifts, raised up by Divine Providence for a special purpose, and received into a closer communion with the invisible world than was vouchsafed to any other in the Old Testament. He confronted Pharaoh, and by a series of ten plagues finally conquered his obdurate heart. Then he led forth Israel as a flock, two millions strong, passing through the Red Sea and on to Mount Sinai. Remaining there for a year, he received the Commandments, constructed the Ark, the Tabernacle and the sacred furniture and established order and method amongst the mighty host under his charge. Oppressed with two prime difficulties, the reluctance of the people to submit to his guidance and the impracticable character of the country to be traversed, he bore their murmurs patiently, only inflicting penalties when absolutely needed, and through forty years of journeyings brought them at last to the dividing river in full view of the Promised Land. There, upon the top of Mount Nebo, he satiated his gaze with a lingering view of the country he should never tread and then, B. C. 1451, was taken to his reward at the age of 120 years."—Morris's Masonic Dictionary, Article Moses.

Note 288.—"Joshua. The high priest who, with Zerubbabel, the Prince of Judah, superintended the rebuilding of the Temple after the Babylonian captivity. He was the high priest by lineal descent from the pontifical family, for he was the son of Josadek, who was the son of Seraiah, who was the high priest when the Temple was destroyed by the Chaldeans. He was distinguished for the zeal with which he prosecuted the work of rebuilding, and opposed the interference of the Samaritans."—Mackey's Encyclopædia of Freemasonry, Article Joshua.

Note 289.—"Travel. In the symbolic language of Masonry, a Mason always travels from west to east in search of light—he travels from the lofty tower of Babel, where language was confounded and Masonry lost, to the threshing-floor of Ornan, the Jebusite, where language was restored and Masonry found."—Mackey's Encyclopædia of Freemasonry, Article Travel.

sash:—Crimson ribbon, worn from right to left with the words virtue and valor painted or embroidered thereon where it crosses the breast.

jewel:—A tau cross[300] of gold surmounted by a circle round which is a serpent entwined, with the ineffable name engraved on it. Worn suspended from a white ribbon.

apron:—White, bordered with black and sprinkled with black tears; on the flap, a triangle in a glory, in the centre the Hebrew letter ה

battery:—Is nine, five (5) slow, three (3) quick and one (1) by itself.

Note 300.—"Being placed in the center of a triangle and circle, both emblems of the Deity, it would appear that it was originally intended to typify the sacred name, as the author probably of eternal life; being tripled in the Christian system, because the life to come, according to the light of revelation, is superior to the elysium of the heathen; or perhaps in allusion to the three heavens mentioned by St. Paul. It has been referred to the three great lights of Masonry, expressive of the creative, preserving, and destroying power of God."—Macoy's Encyclopedia and Dictionary of Freemasonry, Article Tau Cross.

OPENING CEREMONIES

KNIGHTS OF THE BRAZEN SERPENT.[291]

Most Powerful Grand Master—Brother Princes of the Tabernacle and Knights of the Brazen Serpent, if the day and the hour have arrived, I propose to open here a Court of Sinai.[292] Be clothed and await, each in his station, the customary order. (The brethren are clothed and the officers take their stations.)

Most Powerful Grand Master—Brother Junior Deacon, it is our first duty to see that we are secure from

Note 291.—"Knight of the Brazen Serpent. (Chevalier du Serpent d' Airain.) The twenty-fifth degree of the Ancient and Accepted Scottish Rite. The history of this degree is founded upon the circumstances related in Numbers ch. xxi., ver. 6-9: 'And the Lord sent fiery serpents among the people, and they bit the people; and much people of Israel died. Therefore the people came to Moses, and said, We have sinned; for we have spoken against the Lord, and against thee: pray unto the Lord that he take away the serpents from us. And Moses prayed for the people. And the Lord said unto Moses, Make thee a fiery serpent, and set it upon a pole: and it shall come to pass, that every one that is bitten, when he looketh upon it shall live. And Moses made a serpent of brass, and put it upon a pole; and it came to pass, that if a serpent had bitten any man, when he beheld the serpent of brass, he lived.' In the old rituals the Lodge was called the Court of Sinai; the presiding officer was styled Most Puissant Grand Master, and represented Moses; while the two Wardens, or Ministers, represented Aaron and Joshua. The Orator was called Pontiff; the Secretary, Grand Graver; and the candidate a Traveler. In the modern ritual, adopted in this country, the Council represents the camp of the Israelites. The first three officers represent Moses, Joshua, and Caleb, and are respectively styled Most Puissant Leader, Valiant Captain of the Host, and Illustrious Chief of the Ten Tribes. The Orator represents Eleazar; the Secretary, Ithamar; the Treasurer, Phinehas; and the candidate an intercessor for the people. The jewel is a crux ansata, with a serpent entwined around it."— Mackey's Encyclopædia of Freemasonry, Article Knight of the Brazen Serpent.

Note 292.—"Sinai. A mountain of Arabia between the horns of the Red Sea. It is the place where Moses received the Law from Jehovah, and where he was directed to construct the tabernacle. Hence, says Linning, the Scottish Masons make Mt. Sinai a symbol of truth. Of the high degrees the twenty-third and twenty-fourth of the Ancient and Accepted Rite, of the Chief and the Prince of the Tabernacle, refer in their rituals to this mountain and the Tabernacle there constructed."— Mackey's Encyclopædia of Freemasonry, Article Sinai.

intrusion. See that the Guards are set, and inform them that we are about to open this Court, and allow none who are not entitled to approach. (Junior Deacon retires, enters again, gives the alarm, which is answered from without, and says:)

Junior Deacon—Most Powerful Grand Master, the Guards are posted and duly instructed; we are secure against intrusion.

Grand Master—Brother Lieutenant Commander, are all present Knights of the Brazen Serpent?

Lieutenant Commander—All present are Knights of the Brazen Serpent, Most Powerful.

Grand Master—Brother Commander of the Host, what is the hour?

Commander of Host—Most Powerful Grand Master, it is the break of day.

Grand Master—If that be the hour it is time to open this Court. You will please inform the Lieutenant Commander and he the Knights, that all may have due notice thereof.

Commander of Host—Lieutenant Commander, it is the pleasure of the Most Powerful Grand Master that this Court of Sinai be now opened. You will please inform the Knights, that, having due notice thereof, they may assist in opening the same.

Lieutenant Commander—(Three knocks.) Knights and Masons, you will please take notice that the Most Powerful Grand Master is about to open this Court of Sinai. You will please take due notice thereof and aid him in so doing.

Grand Master—Let the seven mystic lights dispel the darkness of this Court.

Lieutenant Commander—(Lighting the first light nearest him.) The *Moon* shines in our Court and over it presides the arch-angel *Saphael*, the messenger of God. (Lights the next one.)

Mercury shines in our Court and over it presides the arch-angel *Raphael*, the healing influence of God. (Lights the next one.)

Venus shines in our Court and over it presides the arch-angel *Hamaliel*, the merciful kindness of God. (He then takes his station and the Commander of the Host lights the light nearest the East, saying:)

Commander of Host—Saturn shines in our Court and over it presides the arch-angel *Michael*, the semblance and image of God. (Lights the next one.)

Jupiter shines in our Court and over it presides the arch-angel *Gabriel*, the strength and mightiness of God. (Lights the next one.)

Mars shines in our Court and over it presides the arch-angel *Auriel*, the light and fire of God. (The Grand Master advances and lights the center one, saying:)

The Sun, type of the principle of good, and light, and feeble, and imperfect image of the Deity shines in our Court and over it presides the arch-angel *Zerachiel*, the rising of God, the sun of righteousness. (Then takes his station.)

Grand Master—Together, brethren.

All—(Give the sign.)

Grand Master—(Knocks five (5), three (3) and one; 00000 000 0.)

Commander of Host—(Knocks five (5), three (3) and one; 00000 000 0.)

Lieutenant Commander—(Knocks five (5), three (3) and one; 00000 000 0.)

Grand Master—I declare this Court of Sinai duly opened.

CHAPTER XLVI

Twenty-Fifth Degree; or Knight of the Brazen Serpent.[298]

INITIATION.

[The candidate represents a traveller and is dressed in plain clothes without insignia. He is loaded with chains by the Senior Deacon, who conducts him to the door, knocks five slow, three quick and one.]

Junior Deacon—(Opening the door.) Who comes here?

Senior Deacon—One of the people of Israel, to announce to the Most Powerful Grand Master a great misfortune that has befallen the people and to implore at his hands relief and assistance.

Junior Deacon—Who is this applicant, and by what right does he claim admission here?

Senior Deacon—He is one of the tribe of Reuben, loaded with chains in token of the penitence of the people who flee in terror before the venomous serpents

Note 298.—"Knight of the Brazen Serpent. [Scotch Masonry.]—The eighth degree conferred in the Consistory of Princes of the Royal Secret, Scotch Masonry, and the twenty-sixth upon the catalogue of that system. The historical instructions are, the use of the Brazen Serpent erected by Moses in the camp of Israel, that whoever had been bitten and looked thereon might live.—Numbers xxi. The assembly is termed the Court of Sinai. The hangings are red and blue. There is one light. The officers are Most Powerful Grand Master, representing Moses; two Wardens, entitled Ministers, represent Aaron and Joshua; an Orator, termed Pontiff; the Secretary, called Grand Graver; and an Examiner. A transparency, representing the Burning Bush, and the Sacred Name of four letters, is in the east; a conical mount, representing Sinai, in the center. Jewel, a golden serpent twined about a triple tau cross, standing upon a triangle, with the sacred name; it is suspended from a white ribbon. Apron, white, strewed with black tears; on the movable part, a triangle in a glory; within it, the Hebrew letter H. Hours of work, open at one, close at seven."—Morris's Masonic Dictionary, Article Knight of the Brazen Serpent.

that Adonai hath sent to punish them.

Junior Deacon—Wait a time with patience until the Most Powerful Grand Master is informed of his request and his answer returned. (Junior Deacon closes the door, goes to the altar, knocks five, three and one; Grand Master answers it and the same questions are asked and like answers returned as at the door.

Grand Master—Let him be admitted. (Junior Deacon opens the door, Senior Deacon enters with him, conducts him in front of the Grand Master and causes him to kneel.)

Grand Master—Brother Senior Deacon, whom do you bring hither thus loaded with chains?

Senior Deacon—One of the tribe of Reuben, sent in behalf of the people, who dare not come before you, Adonai being angered with them.

Grand Master—Disobedient race; have they again tempted his anger?

Senior Deacon—Most Powerful Grand Master, the soul of the people was much discouraged because of their journeying in the wilderness, and they spake against Adonai, calling him the power of evil and against you, saying, why hath Moses brought us up out of Egypt to die in the wilderness? There is no bread nor any water, and our souls loathe this unsubstantial manna. We go to and fro, lo now almost these forty years, and as Aaron hath died in the desert, so also shall we all die here. Let us trust in Adonai no longer. Let us call on the great gods to deliver us from this bondage of misery, and as they cried aloud unto these gods, lo Adonai sent venomous serpents among them, who darted among the people, curling round and biting them, and by their venom many of the people of Israel hath already died, and those that remain have repented and say we have sinned, for we have spoken against Adonai and his servant Moses. And they said unto me, put heavy chains upon thy neck in token of our penitence, and go for us unto Moses our leader, and beseech him to pray unto Adonai that he take away the serpents from us, and I have done as they desired.

Grand Master—Hast thou (to candidate) also murmured and called upon the false gods.

Senior Deacon—(For candidate.) I have not, but because I refused and withstood the people, and rebuked them in the name of Adonai, they sought to slay me, but repenting they sent me hither because I had not sinned like them.

Grand Master—Thou has done well. Arise! Relieve him of his chains and give him a seat of honor, for that  he hath not forgotten his duty to his God. I will now retire and pray unto the God of Israel again to forgive and save his people that he hath chosen. (He retires and the Senior Deacon relieves the candidate of his chains and gives him a seat. After a while the Grand Master enters, bringing with him a serpent of brass entwined round a tau cross with his head elevated above it, and after taking his seat says:)

Serpent and Cross.

Grand Master—I have prayed for the people, and Adonai hath said unto me; make thee an image of a venomous serpent and set it upon a pole and it shall come to pass that every one that is bitten, when he looketh upon it shall live. Take thou, therefore, Eleazar the High Priest, this serpent*** and cross and place it upon a pole and set it in the middle of the camp; and

Note 294.—"In the Templar and in the Philosophic degrees—such as the Knight of the Brazen Serpent, where the serpent is combined with the cross—it is evidently a symbol of Christ; and thus the symbolism of these degrees is closely connected with that of the Rose Croix."— Mackay's Encyclopædia of Freemasonry, Article Serpent.

make proclamation that those who look upon it, confess-
ing their sins and having faith in the Most High God,
though they have been bitten by the venomous serpents,
shall not die, but live, for Adonai is the God of mercy.
(Eleazar takes the serpent and retires, and after a time
returns and says:)

Orator—(As Eleazar.)   Most Powerful Grand Master, great is Adonai, the God of mercy, for he hath had
mercy on his people, Israel and every one that hath beheld the serpent, owning his sin and doing homage to
the Most High is healed and liveth, and the plague of
the serpent is stayed.

Grand Master—Praise ye the Lord, Adonai, my children, the supporter of the heavens and the earth, for
he is great and his mercy endureth forever, and he hath
forgiven his people Israel.

Lieutenant Commander—Most Powerful Grand Master, what shall be done with the brazen image of the
serpent and the cross which thou didst cause to be set
up before the people?

Grand Master—I give it you, my brother, that it may
be evermore a symbol of faith, repentance and mercy,
which are the great mysteries of man's destiny, and lest
the knowledge of its true symbolic meaning should be
lost, let us kneel and swear, in the presence of the Most
High God, faithfully to keep the secrets of this degree.
(All kneel, including the candidate, and take the following obligation:)

OBLIGATION KNIGHTS OF THE BRAZEN SERPENT.

I......do solemnly promise and swear, before the
Most High God, that I will never reveal the secrets of
this degree of Knights of the Brazen Serpent to any
person or persons, unless he shall have taken all the
preceding degrees in a regular and constitutional manner.

To all of which I do most solemnly swear, binding myself under no less a penalty than that of having my heart eaten by the most venomous of serpents and left thus to perish most miserably, from which may the Almighty Creator of the Universe guide and defend me. Amen. (All rise and are seated.)

Grand Master—My brother, approach and receive the signs, tokens and words of this degree.

SIGN OF ORDER.

Incline the head downwards, and point to the ground with the forefinger of right hand.

Sign of Order, Knignu of the Brazen Serpent.

SIGN OF RECOGNITION.

Form a cross upon yourself.

Sign of Recognition. Knights of Brazen Serpent.

KNIGHT OF THE BRAZEN SERPENT.

TOKEN.

Place yourself on the right of the brother, and take his left wrist with your left hand.

ANSWER.

He then takes your right wrist with his right hand.

Token Knights of the Brazen Serpent.

BATTERY :—Nine strokes, five slow, three hurried, and one by itself; 00000 000 0.

MARCH :—Nine serpentine steps.

HOURS OF LABOR :—The Court is opened at one o'clock and closed at four o'clock.

PASS WORD :—I∴N∴R∴I∴*** lettered only.

COVERED WORD :—Johannes Ralp.

SACRED WORD :—*Moses;* this word must be spelled. (Moses died 1451 B∴C∴) (Grand Master now invests him with the apron, collar and jewel of the degree.)

Grand Master—I now accept and receive you a Knight of the Brazen Serpent, and invest you with the apron, collar and jewel of the degree. You will now be conducted to our brother orator, who will deliver the history. (Grand Master takes his station and the Senior Deacon conducts the candidate to the Orator, who may either read the twenty-first chapter of Numbers, from which the degree is taken, or make such comments thereon as he thinks proper.)

Note 285.—"I. N. R. I., i. e., Jesus Nazarenus Rex Iudaeorum. Jesus of Nazareth, King of the Jews, the inscription which was placed upon the cross of the Savior. In the Philosophical Lodge they represent Fire, Salt, Sulphur, and Mercury. In the system of the Rosicrucians they have a similar use. 'Igne Natura Renovatur Integra'—'by fire nature is perfectly renewed.' This idea is also found in the degree of 'Knights Adepts of the Eagle or the Sun.' '''—Macoy's Encyclopædia and Dictionary of Freemasonry, Article I. N. R. I.

CLOSING CEREMONIES

Grand Master—Brother Lieutenant Commander, what is the hour?

Lieutenant Commander—Most Powerful Grand Master, the twilight, after sunset.

Grand Master—Then it is time to close this Court, Brother Commander of the Host, give notice that this Court of Sinai is about to be closed, in order that the brethren may rest from their labors.

Commander of Host — Brother Lieutenant Commander, inform the brethren that the Most Powerful Grand Master is about to close this Court of Sinai, that the brethren may rest from their labors.

Lieutenant Commander—Brethren, the Most Powerful Grand Master is about to close this Court of Sinai, that you may rest from your labors.

Grand Master—Knocks five, three and one; 00000 000 0.)

Commander of Host—(Knocks five, three and one; 00000 000 0.)

Lieutenant Commander—(Knocks five, three and one; 00000 000 0.)

Grand Master—Together, brethren.

All—(Give the sign.)

Grand Master—I declare this Court of Sinai closed.

PHILOSOPHICAL ANALYSIS

The Goodness and Severity of God—False Lights on the Coast of Christendom—"Satan's Ignes Fatui, to Swamp Men Eternally"—Quotes the Bible as Satan Did to Deceive Men—All Religion but Holiness and Justice.

In discussing these degrees, why use harshness and severity? The wisdom from above is "pure," "peaceable," "gentle," "full of mercy." Paul himself was "gentle," as a nurse among children. And Moses, but especially Christ, was "meek." *Ans.*: In dealing with teachers of false religion, and corrupters of the true, the severity of Christ, the prophets and apostles knew no bounds but the limits of language. Thus Peter: "Thy money perish with thee!" Paul: "Thou child of the devil!" John: "Serpents, and the seed of serpents!" Christ uttered the same words. And Moses, who was ruler and law-giver, as well as teacher, said of a dealer in "wonders" and false mysteries: Though thine own brother, son, daughter or "wife of thy bosom," whoever should entice into man-made religious rites, like this Scottish Rite: "thou shalt surely kill him; thine hand shall be first upon him to put him to death; and, afterwards, the hand of all the people." (*Deut. 13, 1-9.*) And though in warring against demon-worships, the Christians' weapons are "not carnal, but spiritual," the treatment of sorcerers by Paul and Peter, and the fate of Ananias and Sapphira, show what estimate God puts on Ramsay and his Jesuits, Morin and his Jews, and their abettors, who framed this 33° degree rite, for money and worldly advantage. A high Masonic authority says: "If history speaks correctly, *Morin* and his coadjutors found the manufacturing of Masonic degrees and the sale of Masonic dignities a very profitable and lucrative undertaking. They pursued it diligently, making all the money they could from the traffic." (*Folger's Ancient and Accepted Scottish Rite, p. 38.*) This is high Masonic testimony concerning the founding of this *Rite*, which now rules the Masonic world. And there is nothing like it in the catalogue of human crimes and sins. The guilt of wreckers and sea-thieves who hold out false lights to lure ships on rocks, to drown passengers in order to get their goods, is slight, compared with that of the inventors and sellers of these Masonic degrees. Christ is come a light into the world. And here are thirty-three false lights hung out along the whole coast of Christendom, by men whose fathers sold Christ for thirty pieces of silver, to lure men on the "slippery rocks" of perdition. Let none say this is exaggeration. *Dr. Mackey,* in his "Ritualist," the authoritative liturgy of the lodges, says that the Entered Apprentice is "seeking the new birth, and asking that light which restores fallen man to his Maker;" which light, he says, "the lodge alone can give!" And he refers to the same thing in *Note 289* of this degree. "A Mason always travels from west to east *in search of light.*" "The shock of entrance is the symbol of 'The New Birth,'" which, he says, the Apprentice "appears before our portals seeking." Every time the blinder falls, which is thirty-three times in these degrees, this same thing is repeated. The blinded and bewildered candidate is brought to the "light," discovers the "*word,*" etc., both which are Satan, as an angel of light, personifying or symbolizing Christ, who only is the true "Light" and the true "Word," who "was with God and who was God." (*John 1, 1.*) And we do not slander the framers of these 33 degrees in saying they made them for money. *Folger* is good Masonic authority, and *he says it.* See his book of this *rite*, p. 38, already cited. Were these Jews framing degrees to bring men to Christ? No! A thousand times No! Then these degrees are Satan's ignes fatui, to swamp men eternally in hell. And it is of such false worshipers of whom the Psalmist says: "Surely thou didst set them in slippery places." (*Ps. 73, 18.*) And these degrees are those places into which these false coast lights are drawing life's voyagers. The only escape from this dire conclusion is to suppose that the Holy Ghost goes into the lodges, as *Dr. Oliver* supposed, and takes the names of Christ which the ritual uses, and converts men to Christ. But whoever heard of a Christian revival in a lodge? Or of village lodges joining in a village revival? No: Voltaire, who was a Mason, did not lead prayer-meetings, nor do lodge-masters love and worship Christ.

This very twenty-fifth degree, which makes "*Knights of the Brazen Serpent,*" the lodge uses for purposes of idolatry, as the children of Israel did, who burnt incense to it (*2 Kings 18, 4*), and which Hezekiah destroyed. Read on page 157 the finishing touches, when this "*Knight of the Brazen Serpent*" is made. Nine strokes; five slow, three hurried, and one by itself, are struck with mallets. Nine steps are taken like the waving motions of a snake, and the pass-word given him is *I. N. R. I.*. which are the initials in Latin of: Jesus of Nazareth, King of the Jews, and this, ages before there was any Latin tongue. And he who cannot see in this conjuring, every mark and feature of devil-worship, has already been blinded by idolatry.

But why do these degree-makers, grade after grade, follow and employ the Sacred Scriptures? The answer is: for the same purpose for which the *Book of Mormon* does the same thing. That foul imposition contains whole chapters of the Bible; sometimes quoted literally and sometimes as in these degrees, mixed with Mormon gibberish. They quote the Bible as Satan did to Christ, to deceive men. They quote it while they hate it, and would destroy it if they could. Did Aaron Burr and the traitor Arnold love the Bible? Does Albert Pike love it? Some ten years ago the Grand Orient lodge of France, as is well known, erased from their ritual the name of God and *the immortality of man,* and though some of the lodges went through the farce of excommunicating that lodge and its adherents, others did not. And Masonic prints now declare the standing of those atheist Masons good!

And why should they not? The standard Masonic authorities, cited in the *notes* of the preceding degrees, boast their origin from the heathen mysteries; from astrology; from "incantations," and all that the Bible calls demon-worship. The lower degrees drop the name of Christ from Scriptures used in their lodge lectures, to invite and draw in the Jews and Christ-hating classes. And the higher degrees only admit Him when the lodge-dupes have become hardened by their idolatries and mockeries; and then only admit Him on a level with heathen teachers; and worship, or rather insult him, by the use of human skulls, cross-bones, and crossed swords, hoodwinks oaths, blasphemies and sworn secrecy, and concealed ceremonies which His Word and example forbid! And then, having established and set abroad a system of known antagonism and contempt towards Christ and the Christian religion, they then follow the holy solemnities and sublimities of the Bible, as wolves follow lambs to destroy them and eat them; to save their "cunningly devised fables" and "doctrines of devils" from the world's loathing and contempt.

Let the authoritative teaching of *Dr. Mackey* be continually borne in mind, that: *"the mission and object of Masonry is the worship of the Great Architect of the Universe."* It follows that the lodges must have something for their dupes to do, called worship. And what could wicked men and devils invent craftier or better suited to deceive the simple, than this very scheme of *"the Ancient Scottish Rite,"* which now rules the *rites* of the world. It seizes and appropriates all of religion but its holiness and justice; and all of Christ but his truth and his atonement. It mixes things sacred with things profane, till the whole compound is profanity; and quoting the Bible as if it believed it true, which notoriou ly it does not, it has furnished a dark system, which angels flee from and which devils inhabit. It keeps its initiates under the power and mesmerism of Satan, and by nightly worships and military drills, it is preparing them for the war and bloodshed which are yet to precede the binding of Satan for the prophetic thousand years. But let it be remembered: "Our help is in the name of the Lord which made heaven and earth" (*Ps. 124, 8*) and that He is mightier than Satan, stronger than "the strong man armed." (*Luke 11, 21, 22.*)

CHAPTER XLVII

WEST OR SPRING.

DECORATIONS:—Lodges of this degree are called Chapters. The hangings are green, supported by nine columns, alternately white and red, upon each of which is a chandelier holding nine lights. The canopy over the throne is green, white and red. Before the throne is a table covered with cloth of the same color. Instead of a gavel, the presiding officer uses an arrow, the plume of which is red on one side and green on the other. The spear is white; the point gilded. Before the altar is a statue representing Truth, clad in the same colors. It is the palladium of the order. The altar in the center is of a triangular shape, the top being a gilded plate in

Note 296.—"Prince of Mercy. (Prince du Merci.)—The twenty-sixth degree of the Ancient and Accepted Scottish Rite, called also Scottish Trinitarian or Ecossais Trinitaire. It is one of the eight degrees which were added on the organization of the Scottish Rite to the original twenty-five of the Rite of Perfection.

It is a Christian degree in its construction, and treats of the triple covenant of mercy which God made with man; first with Abraham by by circumcision; next with the Israelites in the wilderness, by the intermediation of Moses; and lastly, with all mankind, by the death and sufferings of Jesus Christ. It is in allusion to these three acts of mercy that the degree derives its two names of Scottish Trinitarian and Prince of Mercy, and not, as Ragon supposes, from any reference to the Fathers of Mercy, a religious society formerly engaged in the ransoming of Christian captives at Algiers. Chemin Dupontes (Mem. Sur l' Ecoss, p. 378), says that the Scottish rituals of the degree are too full of the Hermetic philosophy. an error from which the French Cahiers are exempt; and he condemns much of its doctrines as 'hyperbolique plaisanterie.' But the modern rituals as now practiced are obnoxious to no such objection. The symbolic development of the number three of course constitutes a large part of its lecture, but the real dogma of the degree is the importance of Truth, and to this all its ceremonies are directed."—Mackey's Encyclopædia of Freemasonry, Article Prince of Mercy.

the shape of a Delta on which in glittering stones is the ineffable name יהוה.

OFFICERS:—The officers are a Chief Prince, styled Most Excellent. Two Wardens, styled Excellent. Two Deacons, a Sacrificer and Guard of the Palladium. The other members are styled Princes.

DRESS:—The Chief Prince wears a tri-colored tunic, green, white and red, and a crown surmounted with nine points. The other members wear a white tunic.

ORDER:—All wear the order, which is a broad tri-colored collar, green, white and red.

APRON:—Red, with a white border. In the middle of it is an equilateral triangle, embroidered with gold, in the center of which is the jewel; the flap sky blue.

JEWEL:—An equilateral triangle of gold, in the center of which is a heart of gold, on the heart are engraved the letters יה.

BATTERY:—Fifteen, by three, five and seven; 000 00000 0000000.

MARCH:—Three equal steps, commencing with the left foot.

AGE:—Eighty-one years.

TESSERA OR MARK:'''—Given to the candidate, is a small fish of silver or ivory, on one side of which is the word יהוה and on the other, in the Rose Croix cipher, the pass-word of the degree

Note 297.—"It was the custom, says the Scholiast, when a guest had been entertained, to break a die in two parts, one of which parts was retained by the guest, so that if at any future period he required assistance, on exhibiting the broken pieces of the die to each other, the friendship was renewed. Plautus, in one of his comedies, gives us an exemplification of the manner in which these tesserae or pledges of friendship were used at Rome, whence it appears that the privileges of this friendship were extended to the descendants of the contracting parties. Pœnulus is introduced, inquiring for Agorastocles, with whose family he had formerly exchanged the tessera."—Mackey's Encyclopædia of Freemasonry, Article Mark.

OPENING CEREMONIES

PRINCE OF MERCY.[***]

Most Excellent—Excellent Senior Warden, I am about to open a Chapter of Princes of Mercy. Are all present entitled to remain?

Senior Warden—Most Excellent, all present are of the faithful.

Most Excellent—Brother Junior Deacon, the first duty of a Chapter of Princes of Mercy, when assembled?

Junior Deacon—To see that the Chapter is duly guarded, Most Excellent.

Most Excellent—Attend to that part of your duty and inform the Sentinel that we are about to open this Chapter of Princes of Mercy and direct him to tyle accordingly. (Junior Deacon retires, returns again, closes the door, gives the alarm, which is answered from without, then takes his station.)

Junior Deacon—Most Excellent, the Sentinel is at his post and duly instructed.

Most Excellent—Brother Senior Warden, you will please inform our brother Junior Warden and he the

Note 283.—'Prince of Mercy, or Scotch Trinitarian. The 26th degree of the Ancient and Accepted Rite. It is a highly philosophical degree and its ritual very impressive; its title clearly designates its character and intention. The body is styled a Chapter. The hangings are grn b. supported by 9 columns, alternately white and red, upon each of which is a chandelier, holding 9 lights. Near the altar is a statute of white marble, the figure of a virgin, covered with thin gauze. This represents Truth, and the palladium of the Order of the Princes of Mercy. The presiding officer is styled Most Excellent Chief Prince. The jewel is an equilateral triangle of bars of gold, with a flaming heart, of gold, in the center. On the heart are the letters I. H. S., and on the respective sides of the triangle. W. on the right, F. on the left, and H. on the bottom.''—Macoy's Encyclopædia and Dictionary of Freemasonry, Article Prince of Mercy.

Princes, that this Chapter is about to be opened, that they may take due notice thereof and govern themselves accordingly.

Senior Warden—Brother Junior Warden, you will please take notice and inform the Princes that this Chapter is about to be opened, that they may take due notice thereof and govern themselves accordingly.

Junior Warden—Princes, this Chapter is about to be opened; you will take due notice thereof and govern yourselves accordingly.

Most Excellent—Together, Princes.

All—(Give the sign.)

Junior Warden—(Knocks three; 000.)

Senior Warden—(Knocks five; 00000.)

Most Excellent—(Knocks seven; 0000000.)

All—(Clap hands three, five and seven.)

Most Excellent—I declare this Chapter duly opened

CHAPTER XLVIII

TWENTY-SIXTH DEGREE; OR PRINCE OF MERCY.***

INITIATION.

(The candidate is prepared by the Senior Deacon in a plain white robe, reaching from the neck to the feet, barefooted, hoodwinked so as to prevent his seeing, with a rope passed three times around his body. He then leads him to the door of the Chapter and knocks three.)

Guard of Palladium—(From within, knocks five.)

Senior Deacon—(From without, knocks seven.)

Guard of Palladium—(Opening the door.) Who comes here?

Preparation of Candidate. Prince of Mercy Degree.

Senior Deacon—A brother who wishes to receive the degree of Prince of Mercy.

Guard of Palladium—Has he passed the regular

Note 239.—"The seventh degree conferred in the Consistory of Princes of the Royal Secret, Scotch Masonry, and the twenty-fifth upon the catalogue of that system. Its historical allusions are to the three covenants of mercy, made by God with man, viz.: those with Abraham, Moses and Jesus Christ; hence the name. The assembly is termed a Chapter. The hangings are green. The officers are, a Chief Prince, whose title is Most Excellent, representing Moses; the Senior Warden, representing Aaron; the Junior Warden, Eleazar; the Sacrificer and Guard of the Palladium. The apron is red, trimmed with white fringe; it displays two crossed arrows. Jewel, an equilateral triangle of gold, a golden heart in the center, inscribed with the Hebrew letter H. Hour of work, evening. Age, 9x9. The lights are eighty-one."—Morris's Masonic Dictionary, Article Prince of Mercy, or Scotch Trinitarian.

terms of probation[300] and undergone the necessary tests and trials?

Senior Deacon—He has.

Guard of Palladium—Let him wait a time with patience, until his request is made known to the Most Excellent Chapter of Princes of Mercy. (Guard of the Palladium closes the door, goes to the East, where the same questions are asked and like answers received as at the door.)

Most Excellent—Is he duly and truly prepared to receive this degree?

Guard of Palladium—He is.

Most Excellent—You will retire and let him be admitted after he shall have washed[301] his hands in pure water. (Guard retires to preparation room.)

Guard of Palladium—It is the order of the Most Excellent that he be admitted, after he shall have washed

Note 300.—Probation. "The interval between the reception of one degree and the succeeding one is called the probation of the candidate, because it is during this period that he is to prove his qualification for advancement. In England and in this country the time of probation between the reception of degrees is four weeks, to which is generally added the further safeguard of an open examination in the preceding degree. In France and Germany the probation is extended to one year. The time is greatly extended in the Ancient and Accepted Scottish Rite. The statutes of the Southern Supreme Council require an interval of two years to be passed between the reception of the fourteenth and the thirty-second degrees. An extraordinary rule prevailed in the constitutions of 1762, by which the Rite of Perfection was governed. According to this rule, a candidate was required to pass a probation from the time of his application as an Entered Apprentice until his reception of the twenty-fifth or ultimate degree of the Rite, of no less than six years and nine months. But as all the separate times of probation depended on symbolic numbers, it is not to be presumed that this regulation was ever practically enforced."—Mackey's Encyclopædia of Freemasonry, Article Probation.

Note 301.—"Lustration. A religious rite practiced by the ancients and which was performed before any act of devotion. It consisted in washing the hands, and sometimes the whole body, in lustral or consecrated water. It was intended as a symbol of the internal purification of the heart. It was a ceremony preparatory to initiation in all the Ancient Mysteries.. The ceremony is practised with the same symbolic import in some of the high degrees of Masonry. So strong was the idea of a connection between lustration and initiation, that in the low Latin of the Middle Ages lustrare meant to initiate. Thus Du Cange (Glossarium) cites the expression 'lustrare religione Christianorum' as signifying 'to initiate into the Christian religion.'"—Mackey's Encyclopædia of Freemasonry, Article Lustration.

his hands in pure water. (Senior Deacon causes him to wash his hands in pure water, leads him in and conducts him nine times around the Chapter while the Most Excellent reads:)

First Round—Thus saith the holy book, there is but cne Supreme God, the single, imperishable, infinite, omnipotent, excellent, perfect, invisible God; omnipresent the universal substance and soul of the world.

Second Round—Jesus of Nazareth, born of a Virgin without sin, was chaste and holy. He descended into Hell, he arose again and ascended to Heaven, he charged his disciples to teach his pure doctrines and gave them the gift of miracles. He will appear again at the end of the world and a new creation and a new age of innocence shall commence.

Third Round—The stars shall salute him at his nativity, the running waters shall become clear as crystal, the winds breathe softly and the sky be pure and serene, the tortures of the wicked shall be suspended, all venomous reptiles and beasts of prey disappear, the sick and infirm shall become well and strong, and all mankind unite in orisons of glory.

Fourth Round—The mountains shall melt and torrents of metal flow from their bosoms, through which all souls shall pass, that thus parting with the defilement of their sins, they may be fitted for the bliss that awaits them. A new earth, more beautiful, more fertile, more delicious than the first, shall become the home of restored mankind.

Fifth Round—He is love. King of the living and dead; the supremely pure, holy and wise, he is three and one, for his essence illuminates, warms and makes fruitful at once. Seated in the middle chamber,["] between light and darkness he presides over initiates, crowned with the sun of truth and justice, and bearing the gavel of gold, eternal, living, victorious and intelligent.

Sixth Round—The fields shall produce bountifully without labor; calamity be unknown and a vast golden palace more brilliant than the sun receive and be the home of the just forever. Then the Supreme Being shall come from his dwelling on high, administer divine justice, pronounce his decrees and establish his immortal laws.

Seventh Round—The actions of each shall be weighed in the unerring scales and final sentence pronounced on each, according to his deserts. The irreclaimable depart to the lower hemisphere of darkness, remorse and pain. The just return to the bosom of the Deity to enjoy eternal happiness in the realm of light and love.

Eighth Round—Thus was it promised unto Judah: "The Sceptre shall not depart from Judah, nor a law giver from between his feet until Shiloh come, and unto him shall the gathering of the people be.

"Unto us a child is born, unto us a son is given, and the government shall be upon his shoulders, and his name shall be Wonderful, Counselor, the Mighty God, the Everlasting Father, the Prince of Peace."

Ninth Round—"In the beginning was the Word, and the Word was with God, and the Word was God. All

Note 302.—"The door for the middle chamber was in the right side of the house, and they went up with winding stairs into the middle chamber, and out of the middle into the third.

These chambers, after the Temple was completed, served for the accommodation of the priests when upon duty; in them they deposited their vestments and the sacred vessels. But the knowledge of the purpose to which the middle chamber was appropriated while the Temple was in the course of construction, is only preserved in Masonic tradition. This tradition is, however, altogether mythical and symbolical in its character, and belongs to the symbolism of the Winding Stairs."— Mackey's Encyclopædia of Freemasonry, Article Middle Chamber.

things were made by him. In him was life, and that life was the light of mankind; the true light, which lighteth every man that cometh into the world. And the Word became incarnate and dwelt among men, and they beheld his glory; and the glory of the first born of the father, full of benevolence and truth." (After this round he halts in front of the Junior Warden.)

Junior Warden—Brother Senior Deacon, whom have you here?

Senior Deacon—A brother, who, having passed through the necessary terms of probation and undergone the tests and trials, now anxiously desires to see the great light and to be received among the Princes of Mercy.

Junior Warden—Brother Senior Deacon, dost thou vouch for him, that he will devote himself to the teachings of this degree?

Senior Deacon—I do.

Junior Warden—Since thou art his security, let him see to it that he bring no shame upon thee by making false thy pledge in his behalf. You will now conduct him to our brother Senior Warden. (Order is obeyed and same questions are asked by Senior Warden, who, after same answers had been given, orders him conducted to Most Excellent; who asks the same questions and receives the same answers when he continues:)

Most Excellent—Brother Senior Deacon, you will now conduct the candidate to our Senior Warden, who will place him near the great light by the proper steps. (He conducts him to the Senior Warden, who causes him to advance to the altar by three steps, commencing with the left foot, where he kneels and contracts the following obligation:)

OBLIGATION PRINCE OF MERCY.

I......do promise and swear, in the presence of the Great Architect of the Universe, that I will never reveal the secrets of this degree to any person or persons whatever, unless he shall have taken all the preceding degrees in a regular and constitutional manner.

I do furthermore promise and swear that I will never confer or assist in conferring this degree upon any person unless by virtue of a Patent or warrant of constitution emanating from a Sovereign or Deputy Grand Inspector General or a regular constituted consistory of Princes of the Royal Secret, 32nd degree, to whose constitutions and regulations I now swear fealty and allegiance, and then only after I shall have been informed of the pure life and irreproachable manner and morals of the candidate.

And should I violate this, my obligation, I consent to be condemned, cast out and despised by the whole universe, and may the Supreme Architect of the Universe guide, guard and protect me to fulfil the same. Amen.

Most Excellent—My brother, what now dost thou desire?

Candidate—Light.'''

Most Excellent—My brother, Senior Deacon, bring this new brother to light. (Senior Deacon removes the bandage.)

Most Excellent—My brother, behold the darkness is passed and the true light now shineth. You have before this been brought to light in masonry. When

Note 303.—"Light. Light is a symbol of knowledge. May every Mason strive incessantly for light, and especially for the light eternal! When a society is assembled anywhere to do good, they require an influential person to communicate the light of experience, instruct them, and point out the way they should go, or bring light to them. This may be done, symbolically, by suddenly lighting up a dark room with torches. He who thus introduces the light into the lodge must be a worthy man and experienced in the craft."—Mackey's Encyclopædia and Dictionary of Freemasonry, Article Light.

the Worshipful Master, with the aid of the brethren, first made you a mason, and your attention was directed to the three great lights upon the altar. On being brought to light in this degree, you see before you the luminous Delta with three equal sides, in all ages the representative of Deity, the trinity of wisdom, power and harmony. You will now approach the East and be invested with the signs, token and words of this degree. (All are now seated; the Senior Deacon conducts him to the East and he is invested with the following signs.)

Sign of Entrance, Prince of Mercy.

SIGN OF ENTRANCE.

Place the right hand open, so as to form a triangle above the eyes as if to be protected against a strong light.

Sign of Character Prince of Mercy.

SIGN OF CHARACTER.

Form a triangle with the two thumbs, and the two forefingers; join them by the extremities, place the hands in front of, and touching the body.

Sign of Help.
Prince of Mercy.

SIGN OF HELP.

Cross both arms above the head, the hands open, palms outwards and say: To me, the children of Truth.

SIGN OF ORDER.

Stand up, the right hand resting on the. hip.

Sign of Order.
Prince of Mercy.

TOKEN.

Place both hands, each on the other's shoulders, press them slightly thrice and say, Gomel.

BATTERY:—Fifteen strokes, by three, five and seven.

MARCH:—Three equal steps, commencing with the left foot.

AGE:—Eighty-one years.

PASS WORD:—Gomel.

COMMON WORDS:—Ghiblim[•••] and Gabaon.

SACRED WORDS:—Jehovah, Jachin.

SUBLIME WORD:—Ednl-pen-cagu, that is, do as you would be done by. (After he is invested with the above he is seated in front of the table facing the East, and listens to the following lecture:)

LECTURE PRINCE OF MERCY.

Most Excellent—Brother Senior Warden, are you a Prince of Mercy?

Senior Warden—I have seen the Delta, and the holy name upon it, and an Ameth[•••] like yourself, in the triple covenant of which we bear the mark.

Note 304.—"Ghiblim. The form in which Dr. Anderson spells Giblim. In the Book of Constitution. ed. 1738, page 70, it is stated that in 1850, 'John de Spoulee, call'd Master of the Ghiblim,' rebuilt St. George's Chapel."—Mackey's Enclopaedia of Freemasonry, Article Ghiblim.

Note 305.—"Ameth. Properly, Emeth, which see." [See Note 99.]—Mackey's Encyclopædia of Freemasonry, Article Ameth.

Most Excellent—What is the first of the three covenants of which we bear the mark?

Senior Warden—That which God made with Noah, when he said, I will not again curse the earth any more for man's sake, neither will I smite any more everything living, as I have done. While the earth remaineth, seed time and harvest, and cold and heat, winter and summer, and day and night shall not cease. I will establish my covenant with you, and with your seed after you, and with every living creature. All mankind shall no more be cut off by the waters of a flood, nor shall there any more be a flood to destroy the earth. This is the token of my covenant; I do set my bow in the clouds and it shall be for a token of a covenant between me and every living creature on the earth.

Most Excellent—What is the second of the three covenants?

Senior Warden—That which God made with Abraham when he said, I am the absolute, uncreated God. I will make my covenant between me and thee, and thou shalt be the father of many nations, and kings shall come from thy loins. I will establish my covenant between me and thee, and thy descendants after thee, to the remotest generations for an everlasting covenant, and I will be thy God and their God, and will give thee the land of Canaan for an everlasting possession.

Most Excellent—What is the third covenant?

Senior Warden—That which God made with all men by his prophets, when he said, I will gather all nations and tongues, and they shall come and see my glory. I will create a new heavens and a new earth, and the former shall not be remembered nor come into mind. The sun shall no more shine by day, nor the moon by night, but the Lord shall be an everlasting light and splendor. His spirit and his word shall remain with men forever.

Most Excellent—What is the symbol of the triple covenant?

Senior Warden—The triple triangle.

Most Excellent—What are the symbols of the purification necessary to make us perfect masons?

Senior Warden—Lavation, with pure water, because to cleanse the body is emblematical of purifying the soul. Unction, or anointing with oil, because thereby we are set apart and dedicated to the service and priesthood of the beautiful, the true and the good. And robes of white, emblems of candor, purity and truth.

Most Excellent—My brethren and Princes, let us purify this our newly adopted brother and devote him to the service of God and virtue. (Most Excellent knocks three, all rise and form a circle round the candidate at the altar, and the Senior Deacon brings a cup of pure water, when the Most Excellent pours a small quantity upon the head of the candidate.)

Most Excellent—I pour this water upon thy head as a symbol of the purification of the soul by suffering and sorrow, by which parting with the stains of sin and the sordidness of vice it becomes fit to return to its eternal home in the bosom of the Father who loveth all the children he hath made. (Senior Deacon brings perfumed oil in a cup, and the Most Excellent, dipping his finger in it, makes with it a *tau-cross* upon the forehead of the candidate.)

Most Excellent—By this sign I do devote thee henceforward to the cause of Truth. (Senior Deacon unveils the statue of Truth.)

Most Excellent—Behold the Palladium of this order, an emblem of purity and truth. Truth which here we worship, truth, the antagonist of error, fraud and false-hood, and of which you are now the servant. (Senior Deacon now clothes him in a white tunic and invests him with the apron, collar and jewel.)

Most Excellent—(Continuing.) My brother, the colors of this degree are green, white and red; the green is an emblem of the immortality of God, the soul and virtue; the white of sincerity, candor and purity; the red of zeal, fervour and courage.

By the holy name upon the Delta, I charge thee to be true, sincere, merciful and tolerant; and as I press the point of this arrow against thy heart, so may eter-nal truth there penetrate and enter and abide forever; and as the arrow flies straight to its mark, so be thou ever frank, honest and straightforward in all thou sayest and doest, remembering that in this world thou art being prepared for that which is to come. And so I receive thee as one of the faithful and a Prince of Mercy, and I present thee with this *tessera* or *mark,* which thou wilt hereafter wear in evidence that thou art entitled to the privileges and honors of this degree. (Most Excel-lent returns to his station and all are seated.)

CLOSING CEREMONIES

PRINCE OF MERCY.

Most Excellent—Brother Senior Warden, what is the hour?

Senior Warden—Past midnight, Most Excellent.

Most Excellent—Since it is past midnight, the hour of rest has arrived. Brother Junior Warden, what of the night?

Junior Warden—Most Excellent, the clouds have broken, and the stars begin to appear.

Most Excellent—Brother Senior Warden, what remains for us to do?

Senior Warden—To watch and pray, Most Excellent.

Most Excellent—Since that alone remains, it is my pleasure that this Chapter be now closed. This you will please communicate to the Junior Warden, and he to the brethren, that they may have due notice thereof and govern themselves accordingly.

Senior Warden—Brother Junior Warden, it is the pleasure of the Most Excellent that this Chapter be now closed. You will please communicate the same to the brethren, that they may have due notice thereof and govern themselves accordingly.

Junior Warden—Brethren, it is the pleasure of the Most Excellent that this Chapter be now closed. You will please take due notice thereof and govern yourselves accordingly.

Most Excellent—(Knocks seven; 0000000.)

Senior Warden—(Knocks five; 00000.)

Junior Warden—(Knocks three; 000.)

Most Excellent—I declare this Chapter closed.

PHILOSOPHICAL ANALYSIS

TWENTY-SIXTH DEGREE; OR PRINCE OF MERCY.

**Usurps the Prerogatives of Christ—"Liars Have Need of Good Memories"
—Renewing the Plagues of Egypt on American Soil.**

To be able to comprehend the nature and power of these degrees, we should keep steadily in mind their "object and mission," which is to break down the worship of Christ, and establish that of Satan. The very title of the degree does this. The word "Prince" (Latin: *princeps*) means: chief, supreme, the first, or highest one. Christ is the only one who ever exercised divine power on earth. Therefore He only is *First*, or Prince. Christ gave His life a ransom for sinners, and *"Greater love hath no man than this."* (*John 15, 13.*) Therefore He is "Prince of Mercy," and the only one. There cannot be many *firsts*. An earthly prince is first in his realm. So our *chief* magistrate is the highest, or first officer. Christ told Pilate that He came into this world to be its king, not an earthly sovereign, yet a born king. (*Jno. 18, 37.*) And as Savior, or procurer of pardon, He is *"Prince of Mercy," "that in all things He might have the pre-eminence."* (*Col. 1, 18.*)

Now the Senior Warden says: "I am about to open a Chapter of Princes of Mercy." (*P. 166.*) This is solecism, absurdity and blasphemy, and each in the highest degree. It is gross impropriety of language; inconsistent with obvious truth; and indignity offered to God. As night-meeting societies, which should, in sober earnest, elect and inaugurate Presidents of the United States, and attempt to clothe them with presidential power and prerogative, would be guilty of ribald nonsense, mockery towards the President, and swindling imposition on taxed candidates.

This 26th degree therefore is a direct insult to and

assault upon Christ; doubtless stimulated and set on by
the devil, who asked Jesus to worship him, as His
superior or equal! We can well believe Dr. Mackey,
who says (*Note 296*): "It is one of the eight degrees
which were added, on the organization of the Scottish
Rite, to the original twenty-five of the Rite of Perfection." Not, like the Knight of the Axe, which is an
American stump speech, injected into the body of the
rite, to please laborers and get their money; but selected from several thousands invented by Jesuits in
France to protect Romish priest-power, and called "a
Christian degree." (See *Note 266, by Mackey*.)

But as if absurdity and contradiction were to prove
bottomless, look at the following: In the above Note,
Mackey says: "This degree treats of the triple covenant of mercy made by God with Abraham, Moses and
Jesus Christ." Now turn forward to page 176, and
read the answers of the *Senior Warden to the Most
Excellent*, which declare the three covenants of this
degree to be made by God with Noah, Abraham and "all
men by His prophets." "Liars have need of good
memories," but these writers' memories are bad and
their morals worse.

Now turn back to page 167, and look at the candidate
in this 26th degree, hoodwinked and still searching for
"Light," into which he has been brought over and
again, and then say, with our Bible in hand, that "the
god of this world blinds minds." Is it irrational to
suppose that, while that man's eyes were being blind-
folded, the devil was blinding his mind, so that Masons
do not, *cannot* see the contradictions and absurdities of
these degrees? When, in all time, and where, in all
the world, is this blinding done, which the Bible im-
putes to Satan, unless it is done *then* and *there?* It
will not do for them to meet us with denials of the
truth of the Bible: If the Bible is composed of lies,
why do they quote it from beginning to end of this
Scottish Rite? And if the Bible tells the truth when

it says that Satan blinds minds; what minds, if not
those of his worshipers? And do we not see in this
how it can be that Masons of apparent candor can say,
and say truly, they *can see nothing* in lodgery which
conflicts with the Christian religion?

Isaiah (9, 26), predicting Christ's coming, says:
*"The people that walked in darkness have seen a great
light."* Who were those people "walking in darkness"
but those very men whose hill-top worships Masons
truly call "lodges," and the worshipers themselves, "our
ancient brethren," and who, as Masons have today, had
counterfeit "Princes of Mercy" of their own make?

Read on page 169 the lying promises of this dark
degree. "A new earth, more beautiful and more fertile,
shall become the home of mankind!" These blind
guides, not looking, as Paul did, at "the things not
seen," promise none but a heaven on earth with good
crops, etc., etc.; while the Word of God, and the history of Palestine, nay, our own history also, show that
just in proportion as lodge-worships supplant the
worship of Christ; drought, grasshoppers, potato-rot
and bugs, with swarms of invisible pests, such as desolated Egypt and sunk the inhabitants to cattle-worship-
ing slaves, whose country is mortgaged to a handful of
London merchants, are slowly renewing the "plagues of
Egypt" on our own soil; while Charleston, the city
where this Scottish Rite was planted, and from which
it has spread over America and Europe, has plucked
down wrath on our Continent in the shape of treason,
secession and bloodshed.

Instead of the heaven of fine soil and good crops
promised to the "Princes of Mercy," we seem to be in
great danger of renewing on our prairies the sterility of
once fertile, but now impoverished, monk-worshiping
Palestine; until earthquakes rend the earth under us,
and cyclones lay bare its surface; and in the vigorous
words of the old hymn

"Earth trembles beneath till her mountains give way,
"And hell shakes her fetters with fear!

CHAPTER XLIX

Twenty-Seventh Degree, or Commander of the Temple.[***]

SOUTH OR SUMMER.

DECORATIONS:—This lodge is styled a Court. The hangings are red, ornamented here and there with black columns, upon each of which is placed a branch holding a light. The canopy and throne are red, sprinkled with black tears. In the centre of the lodge, which is circular in its shape, is a chandelier with three rows of lights one above the other; in the lower circle twelve, in the next nine, and in the upper one six; making twenty-seven in all. Twenty-seven other lights are placed upon a round table, around which the Knights are seated when the Court is open.

OFFICERS:—The presiding officer is styled Most Potent Grand Commander, and sits in the East. The Wardens are styled Most Sovereign Commanders, and the Knights Sovereign Commanders. There is a Senior and Junior Deacon.

DRESS:—The Grand Commander wears a white tunic

Note 306.—"Commander of the Temple. [Scotch Masonry.]—The ninth degree conferred in the Consistory of Princes of the Royal Secret, Scotch Masonry, and the twenty-seventh in the catalogue of that system. The assembly is termed a Court. The hangings are red. The lights are twenty-seven. The presiding officer is styled Most Potent, and the two Wardens, Most Sovereign Commanders. The title of the members is Sovereign Commanders. The apron is flesh-colored, lined and edged with black; on it is a key; the movable part displays a Teutonic cross en circled by a wreath of laurel. The scarf is red, edged with black and sustains a Teutonic cross in enameled gold. Jewel, a golden triangle, displaying the sacred four-lettered name; it is suspended from a white collar, edged with red and embroidered with four Teutonic crosses. Hours of work, open at 10, close at 4."—Morris's Masonic Dictionary, Article Commander of the Temple.

and over it a knight mantle of red, lined with ermine; on his head he wears a ducal-coronet.

APRON :—Flesh colored, lined and edged with black, on the flap is a Teutonic cross, (which is also the jewel of the order) encircled by a laurel wreath, and beneath it, on the apron a key. The cross, wreath and key are all black.

GLOVES :—White, lined and bordered with black. The scabbard and belt of the sword are black.

SASH :—White, edged with red, worn as a collar, and the jewel suspended from it. On each side of the collar are two black Teutonic crosses, there is also a sash, red, bordered with black; worn from right to left, from which hangs a gold enameled tau cross.

JEWEL:—The principal jewel is a triangle of gold, on which is engraved the sacred name יְהֹוָה

OPENING CEREMONIES

COMMANDER OF THE TEMPLE.

Grand Commander—(Three knocks; 000.) Attention Commanders. I pray you to assist me to open this Sublime Court of Grand Commanders of the Masonic Temple. (All rise in their stations, draw swords, salute the Grand Commander and stand at a carry.)

Grand Commander—Brother Junior Deacon, see that the doors of this Court are duly guarded and inform the Sentinel that we are about to open this Court, that none may enter without the words and signs.

Junior Deacon—(Having obeyed orders and returned.) Most Potent Grand Commander, the Sentinels are posted and we are in security.

Grand Commander—Most Sovereign Commander in the West. What are the duties of a Commander of the Temple?

Senior Warden—To guard the temple and city of Jerusalem, to succor and assist the helpless and feeble and to defend the innocent.

Grand Commander—Assemble round the altar Sovereign Commanders, that we may Open this Court of Commanders of the temple of Jerusalem. (All form a circle round the altar, hold the horizontal point of the sword inwards, and repeat after the Grand Commander:)

All—As these swords point to one common centre, so we here, renewing our vows, do devote our swords to the cause of God and the cross; our hearts to the glory of God and the welfare of man and our hands to assist the sick, the suffering and the destitute. So help us God.

Grand Commander—Let us pray. (All recover and return swords, and kneel on the left knee and the Grand Commander repeats the following prayer:)

OPENING PRAYER COMMANDER OF THE TEMPLE.

Father and creator of the Universe, we implore thy beneficence, deign to receive our prayers, and diffuse on the members of this order thy precious gifts. We who do not cease in our prayers to ask of thee that celestial mark that thou didst bestow upon thy people, and which thou dost still continue to diffuse daily on those who follow thy precepts. We are assembled here in thy name to offer thee our hearts and our vows, and thank thee for thy favors, praying for a continuation of the same goodness until the last generation. Amen. (All rise and take their stations.)

Junior Warden—(Three knocks; 000.)

Senior Warden—(Twelve knocks; 000000000000.)

Grand Commander—(Twelve knocks; 000000000000.) Sovereign Commanders, I declare this Court of Commanders of the Temple duly opened.

CHAPTER L

INITIATION.

Senior Deacon, prepares the candidate in a white mantle with a large black Teutonic cross upon the left breast, he then hoodwinks him and conducts him to a small room, seats him on a chair in front of a table on which are a light, and a skull and cross-bones, bible square and compasses; he then says:

Senior Deacon—My brother, you desire to receive the degree of Commander of the Temple. Before you can do so, you are required to answer certain questions which you will find in writing on the table before you. I shall leave you alone, and when you hear three distinct knocks, you will remove the bandage from your eyes and annex your answers to those questions in writing, and sign your name at the bottom. Consider the questions well;

Note 307.—"Sovereign Commander of the Temple. (Sovereign Commandeur du Temple.) Styled in the more recent rituals of the Southern Supreme Council 'Knight Commander of the Temple.' This is the twenty-seventh degree of the Ancient and Accepted Scottish Rite. The presiding officer is styled 'Most Illustrious and Most Valiant,' the Wardens are called 'Most Sovereign Commanders,' and the Knights 'Sovereign Commanders.' The place of meeting is called a 'Court.' The apron is flesh-colored, lined and edged with black, with a Teutonic cross encircled by a wreath of laurel and a key beneath, all inscribed in black upon the flap. The scarf is red bordered with black, hanging from the right shoulder to the left hip, and suspending a Teutonic cross in enameled gold. The jewel is a triangle of gold, on which is engraved the Ineffable Name in Hebrew. It is suspended from a white collar, bound with red and embroidered with four Teutonic crosses."—Mackey's Encyclopædia of Freemasonry, Article Sovereign Commander of the Temple.

let what you will see upon the table before you, remind you that you will answer them in the hearing of the Deity who knows your thoughts. When you shall have answered the questions you will give three distinct knocks upon the table and I will return. (He then retires and closes the door and gives three knocks. The candidate removes the bandage and reads the following questions which he answers in writing:)

First—Have you ever violated any masonic obligation without atoning for it by repentance and reformation?

Second—Are you willing to aid, assist and comfort the sick, the needy and the destitute, to watch with them and minister to their wants, and to help to feed, to clothe and to protect the widow and the orphan?

Third—Have you any enmity toward any one that you would not readily abandon if you found him sincerely willing to be reconciled to you?

Fourth—Would you, if called upon, draw your sword in defence of truth, of human freedom and the rights of conscience; against falsehood, tyranny and usurped power and can you rather choose to die than desert your post of duty? (Candidate writes answers as he thinks proper, signs his name and gives three knocks on the table. Senior Deacon enters, takes the paper, conducts him to the door and knocks twelve.)

Junior Deacon—(From within knocks twelve; 00000 0000000.)

Senior Deacon—(From without knocks three; 000.)

Junior Deacon—(Opening the door.) What do you wish my brother?

Senior Deacon—To participate in your deliberations.

Junior Deacon—Are your words agreeable to your thoughts?

Senior Deacon—The request of an Elect Mason is most sincere.

Junior Deacon—Brother Senior Deacon, has he subscribed to the necessary questions?

Senior Deacon—He has. (Presenting him the paper.)

Junior Deacon—You will wait a time with patience until the pleasure of the Most Potent Grand Commander be made known. (Junior Deacon then shuts the door, goes to the Most Potent Grand Commander and hands him the paper which he reads.)

Grand Commander—Let this brother be admitted. (Junior Deacon goes to the door and opens it, when the Senior Deacon enters with candidate and advances to the East, in front of, and facing the Grand Commander.)

Grand Commander—My brother, are these your answers?

Candidate—They are.

Grand Commander—Are you an Elu*** and Grand Elect Perfect and Sublime Mason?

Candidate—I am.

Grand Commander—Dost thou desire to obtain the degree of Knight Commander of the Temple?

Candidate—I do.

Grand Commander—Knowest thou that thou wouldst thus embrace a life of toil and hardship, of self-denial and of danger?

Candidate—I do.

Grand Commander—And dost thou not hesitate and falter at the prospect?

Note 808.—'Elus. The French word elu means elected; and the degrees, whose object is to detail the detection and punishment of the actors in the crime traditionally related in the third degree, are called Elus, or the degrees of the Elected, because they referred to those of the Craft who were chosen or elected to make the discovery, and to inflict the punishment. They form a particular system of Masonry, and are to be found in every Rite, if not in name, at least in principle. In the York and American Rites, the Elu is incorporated in the Master's degree; in the French Rite it constitutes an independent degree; and in the Scottish Rite it consists of three degrees, the ninth, tenth and eleventh. Ragon counts the five preceding degrees among the Elus, but they more properly belong to the Order of Masters. The symbolism of these Elu degrees has been greatly mistaken and perverted by anti-Masonic writers, who have thus attributed to Masonry a spirit of vengeance, which is not its characteristic. They must be looked upon as conveying only a symbolic meaning."—Mackey's Encyclopædia of Freemasonry, Article Elus.

Candidate—I do not.

Grand Commander—Go then, with our brother Senior Deacon to the altar and there assume the obligation of this degree. (Senior Deacon conducts him to the altar, causes him to kneel on both knees, with his hands upon the blades of the swords of three of the Knights who hold them crossed before him upon the bible, in which position he contracts the following obligation:)

TWENTY-SEVENTH DEGREE, OR COMMANDER OF THE TEMPLE.

Candidate taking Obligation, Commander of the Temple Degree.

OBLIGATION COMMANDER OF THE TEMPLE.

I........on my word of honor, in quality of a Grand Elect, Perfect and Sublime Mason, do promise and swear in the presence of the Great Architect of the Universe and of this respectable Court, to keep the secrets of this degree which are about to be communicated to me, and that I will never be present and assist in conferring of this degree on any person except it be in a regular Court of Commanders of the Temple, or by virtue of a Patent from a Supreme Council or from a Sovereign or Deputy Grand Inspector General. And in case of perjury, may

I be an object of horror to all men and to myself. So help me God. (Grand Commander raises him and invests him with the following signs:)

Sign of Recognition
Commander of the
Temple.

SIGN OF RECOGNITION.

Form on your forehead a cross, with the thumb of your right hand, the fingers clinched.

ANSWER.

Kiss the place where the cross was made. (This sign is used in the Court only.)

ANSWER.

(Out of Court.) Place first two fingers of the right hand on the mouth, the other fingers closed the palm of the hand turned outward.

Answer.

SIGN OF ORDER.

(In the Court.) Extend your right hand on the round table, thumb separate so as to form a square. When standing, place the right hand on the body below the breast, forming also a square.

Sign of Order, Commander of the Temple.

TOKEN.

Give three light blows with right hand on the other's left shoulder.

ANSWER.

He takes your right hand and gives it three light shakes.

Token, Commander of the Temple.

BATTERY:—Twenty-seven strokes with the flat of the sword, by twelve, twelve and by three.

PASS WORD:—Solomon.

SACRED WORD:—I∴N∴R∴I∴ lettered. (Grand Commander now causes him to kneel, and with the blade of his sword gives him twelve strokes on the right shoulder, twelve on the left and three on the right, saying)

Grand Commander—By authority and power in me vested, I hereby constitute, create and dub thee a Knight Commander of the Temple of Jerusalem, be true, be devout, be brave. (Grand Commander takes his station, the members are seated and the Senior Deacon conducts the candidate up to the East.)

Grand Commander—My brother, these trophies which the Court yields to you, and particularly this one (showing Crown of Laurel) is to crown the acts and benefits you have made to the order, to the Court, and to the Commanders. We entreat your perserverance, (puts it on his head.)

Grand Commander—This trophy, (showing a palm ornamented with five crosses) announces to you the antiquity of the order, and the faith you must have in the Great Architect of the Universe and toward the decrees of masonry. (Invests him with it.)

Grand Commander—This trophy, (showing the apron) denotes to you the beneficence and union of the members of this Court; to succor the unfortunate found among them. This day my brother, you are to enjoy the delights of stopping the tears of the wretched. (Invests him with apron.)

Grand Commander—This trophy, (showing gloves etc.,) gives you the force to sustain the rights of masonry and of men. (Invests him with the gloves, etc.)

Grand Commander—This expressive trophy, (showing triangular jewel and collar) of the Court merits your attention and will direct you in the course of your life, your movements, your words and actions. It is an ocular witness of every thing you promised us, and that the remembrance of your vows will be the consolatiou of your last days, is the sincere wish of the members of this Court. (Invests him with them.)

Grand Commander—Attention Commanders! Join me in applauding our newly admitted Commander among us. (All give the battery when Grand Commander takes his seat.)

Grand Commander—Brother Senior Deacon, you will now conduct the Commander to the post of honor. (Senior Deacon seats him on the right of the Grand Commander who delivers the following:)

HISTORY.[309]

When the St. Jean D'Acre, the ancient Ptolemais, on the south side of which was Mount Carmel, was besieged by the Christian forces for nearly two years under Guy of Lusignan, King of Jerusalem, Conrad, Marquis of Mont Ferrat, and other princes and leaders from every country in Europe, and especially by Henry Sixth of Germany, son of Frederic Barbarossa, joined, near the end of the siege, by Philip Augustus of France, and Richard Coeur de Leon of England, they were long afflicted with famine until they ate the flesh of horses with joy. Men of high rank and the sons of great men greedily devoured the grass; the starving fought together like dogs for the little bread baked at the ovens; they gnawed the bones that had already been gnawed by the dogs, and noblemen, ashamed to beg, were known to steal bread. Constant rains added to their miseries and Saladin, Sultan of the Saracens, encamped near them

Note 309.—"Vassal, Ragon, and Clavel are all wrong in connecting this degree with the Knights Templars, with which Order its own ritual declares that it is not to be confounded. It is without a lecture. Vassal expresses the following opinion of this degree:

"'The twenty-seventh degree does not deserve to be classed in the Scottish Rite as a degree, since it contains neither symbols nor allegories that connect it with initiation. It deserves still less to be ranked among the philosophic degrees. I imagine that it has been intercalated only to supply an hiatus, and as a memorial of an Order once justly celebrated.'" Mackey's Encyclopædia of Freemasonry, Article Sovereign Commander of the Temple.

with a vast army from every portion of his dominions, and all the Great Emirs of Islamism harassed them with constant attacks. Sickness also, caused by the rains and the intense heat, decimated the Christian forces. The wounded German soldiers, whom none of the others understood, could not make known their sickness nor their necessities.

Certain German Nobles from the cities of Bremen and Lubec, who had arrived at Acre by sea, moved by miseries of their countrymen, took the sails of their ships and made of them a large tent, in which for a time they placed the wounded Germans and tended them with great kindness. Forty nobles of the same nation united with them and established a kind of hospital in the midst of the camp, and this noble and charitable institution and association, like the Knights of the Temple and of St. John of Jerusalem, soon and incessably, became a new hospitaller and military order. This was in the year 1191.

In 1192 Pope Celestin Third, at the request of the Emperor Henry Sixth, solemnly approved of the order by his Bull of the 23rd of February. He prescribed as regulations for the new Knights, those of St. Augustine, and for special statutes, in all that regarded the poor and the sick, those of the hospitallers of St. John; in regard to military discipline the regulations of the Templars. This noble order, exclusively composed of Germans, was styled the order of Teutonic Knights of the House of St. Mary of Jerusalem.

After the destruction of the Templars, they were also known as Commanders of the Temple.

The first name was given them because while the city of Jerusalem was under the government of the Latin Christians, a German had erected there, at his own expense, a Hospital and Oratory for the sick of that nation, under the protection of, and dedicated to the Holy Virgin.

Their dress was a white mantle with a black cross, and they, like the Hospitallers, were required to take three solemn vows. Before assuming the habit, they were required to swear that they were Germans of noble extraction and birth, and to bind themselves for a whole life to serve the poor and sick and defend the holy places. Ever to adhere to truth, to attend and nurse the sick and wounded, and never to recede before the enemy were their three solemn vows.

Truth is the first masonic duty, To leave the path of duty is to recede before the enemy, and therefore you have taken the three vows of the Teutonic Knights'" and Hospitallers in a still more noble and enlarged spirit. The Teutonic Knights soon became one of the Most Illustrious of the military and religious orders. The three were the chief strength of the army before Acre, but the siege advanced slowly where there were neither absolute chiefs nor discipline.

On the 13th of July, 1191, it surrendered. In the year 1226, most of the Teutonic Knights went from the Holy Land to Prussia, the people of which were still Idolaters, waging war against their Christian neighbors, murdering

Note 310.—"Teutonic Knights. The origin of this Order was an humble but a pious one. During the Crusades, a wealthy gentleman of Germany, who resided at Jerusalem, commiserating the condition of his countrymen who came there as pilgrims, made his house their receptacle, and afterwards built a hospital, to which, by the permission of the Patriarch of Jerusalem, he added an oratory dedicated to the Virgin Mary. Other Germans coming from Lubeck and Bremen contributed to the extension of his charity, and erected at Acre, during the third Crusade, a sumptuous hospital and assumed the title of Teutonic Knights, or Brethren of the Hospital of Our Lady of the Germans of Jerusalem. They elected Henry Walpott their first Master, and adopted for their government a Rule closely approximating to that both of the Templars and the Hospitallers, with an additional one that none but Germans should be admitted into the Order. Their dress consisted of a white mantle, with a black cross, embroidered in gold."—Mackey's Encyclopædia of Freemasonry, Article Teutonic Knights.

Priests at the foot of the altar and employing the sacred vessels for profane use.

Conrad, Duke of Masovia, called in the Teutonic Knights to his assistance and gave them, as a commencement for their establishment there, the whole Territory of Culm, with all lands they should conquer from the Infidels. De Daltza, the Grand Master, sent thither a Knight called Conrad dé Lansburg, who concluded the treaty which was signed by three Bishops of that country. The Knights then entered these northern countries and by continued wars acquired in time the entire sovereignty of Royal and Ducal Prussia, Livonia and the Duchies of Cowrland and Semigal; all vast Provinces and capable of forming a great kingdom. And when in 1291, the Sultan stormed and took St. Jean D'Acre, the Teutonic Knights'" that survived returned to Europe and joined their brethren in Prussia and Livonia. Times change and circumstances, but virtue and duty remain the same. The evils to be warred against but take another shape and are developed in a different form.

There is the same need now of truth and loyalty as in the days of Frederic Barbarossa. The characters religious and military, attention to the sick and wounded in the Hospital and war against the Infidel in the field, are no longer blended, but the same duties to be performed in another shape, continue to exist and to environ us all.

The innocent virgin is no longer at the mercy of the brutal Baron or licentious man-at-arms, but purity and

Note 311.—"Teutonic Order. A religious order of Knights, founded in 1190, by Frederick, Duke of Suabia, during a crusade in the Holy Land, at the time of the siege of Acre, and intended to be confined to Germans of noble rank; hence its name. The rule of the order was similar to that of the Templars. The original object of the association was to defend the Christian religion against the infidels, and to take care of the sick in the Holy Land. As the Order was dedicated to the Virgin Mary the Knights called themselves also 'Brethren of the German House of Our Lady of Jerusalem.' The dress of the members was black, with a white cloak, upon which was worn a black cross with a silver edging. The Grand Master lived first at Jerusalem, but afterward, when the Holy Land fell again under the power of the Turks, at Venice, and, from 1207, at Marburg. The order was abolished by Napoleon, April 24, 1809. The Teutonic cross forms a part of the decorations of the 27th degree of the Ancient Scotch Rite.'—Macoy's Encyclopædia and Dictionary of Freemasonry, Article Teutonic Order.

innocence still need protectors. To purity and innocence everywhere, the Knights Commanders owe protection as of old, against bold violence or those more
guilty, the murderers who by art and treachery seek to
slay the soul; and against that grim want and gaunt,
and haggard destitution that drive too many to sell their
honor and their innocence for food. In no age of the
world has man had better opportunity than now, to display those lofty virtues and that noble heroism that so
distinguished the three great military and religious orders in their youth, before they became corrupt and
vitiated by prosperity and power. When a fearful
epidemic ravages a city, and death is inhaled with the
air men breathe; when the living scarcely suffice to bury
the dead, most men flee in abject terror, to return and
live respectable and influential when the danger has
passed away.

But the old Knightly spirit of devotion and disinterestedness and contempt of death, still lives, and is not
extinct in the human heart. Everywhere a few are found
to stand firmly and inflinchingly at their posts, to front
and defy the danger, not for money, or to be honored
for it, or to protect their own household, but from mere
humanity and to obey the unerring dictates of duty.
They nurse the sick, breathing the pestilential atmosphere of the hospital. They explore the abodes of want
and misery. They perform the last sad offices to the
dead, and they seek no other reward than the approval
of their own conscience. These are the true Knights of
the present age. To the performance of acts of heroism
like these, you have devoted yourself, my brother, by
becoming a Knight Commander of the Temple.

Soldier of the truth and of loyalty, protector of purity and innocence, defier of plague and pestilence, nurser
of the sick and burier of the dead; Knight preferring
death to the abandonment of the post of duty, welcome
to the bosom of this order.

CLOSING CEREMONIES

COMMANDER OF THE TEMPLE.[312]

Grand Commander—(Knocks three; 000.) All rise, draw swords and bring them to a carry.)

Grand Commander—Most Sovereign Commander in the West, what is the hour?

Senior Warden—It is four in the afternoon, Most Potent Grand Commander.

Grand Commander—Since the sun is declining in the West, it is time that we should close this Court; that we may not omit, even for one day, our duties in the world. Sovereign Commanders, let us assemble around the altar that we may close this Court. (All form as in opening ceremonies.)

Grand Commander—Let us be one, Sovereign Commanders, now and hence forward, and let our swords, our arms, our hearts, be devoted to the great cause of truth, humanity and duty. Let us pray. (All kneel and the same prayer is said as at opening, after which all rise and take their stations.)

Grand Commander—(Knocks three; 000.)

Senior Warden—(Knocks twelve; 000000000000.)

Junior Warden—(Knocks twelve; 000000000000.)

Grand Commander—Attention Commanders! As this is the hour in which we terminate our operations, I declare this Court of Grand Commanders of the Temple of Jerusalem closed.

Note 312.—"Vassal expresses the following opinion of the degree: "The 27th degree does not deserve to be classed in the Scotch Rite as a degree, since it contains neither symbols nor allegories that connect it with initiation. It deserves still less to be ranked among the philosophical degrees. I imagine that it has been intercalated only to supply an hiatus, and as a memorial of an Order once justly celebrated."— Macoy's Encyclopædia and Dictionary of Freemasonry, Article Sovereign Commander of the Temple.

PHILOSOPHICAL ANALYSIS

TWENTY-SEVENTH DEGREE: OR, COMMANDER OF THE TEMPLE.

Masonic Contempt for This Degree—Napoleon and the Roman Inquisition.
—Vile Enough for the Scottish Rite.

"This degree does not deserve to be classed, in the Scottish Rite, as a degree. * * * I imagine that it has been interpolated only to supply a hiatus;" i. e., fill a gap. (*Mackey*, in *Note 309.*) The same contempt for this 27th degree is expressed in stronger terms by *Macoy*, (*Note 312.*) Its origin is this. the *Teutons* were aboriginal Germans. When Europe was swept into the craze of the Crusades, Germans, in the siege of Acre, A. D. 1190, formed a German-speaking, Teutonic order of military monks, or priests. They were mendicants, and like those orders everywhere gained wealth and power, as Popish orders still do by the gifts of the ignorant and superstitious, who are fascinated by their dazzling uniform and sanctimonious pretensions. The military spirit is not the spirit of Christ, and monasteries of monks have ever been remarkable for cunning, idleness, gluttony, and the most loathsome and detestable vices. Napoleon abolished this Teutonic order, or lodge, when he overran Germany in 1809; and gave their lands to the princes of the German territories, which they had so overspread that its annual revenue had become 800,000 marks; as the secret orders of this country, now, as a spiritual empire, draw more money from the people than the government. *This 27th degree is that old Teutonic, secret order revived!* And these

"*Commanders of the Temple,*" here in the United States, as you read on page 198, profess to protect American girls from seduction, and destitution, and "selling their honor for food." They are, in short, if we take their professions for genuine, a secret lodge, organized to purify society and abate the social evil; whereas, military monks have ever been vampires of lust to the purity of the sex.

Col. Lemanowski, who followed Napoleon from a captain of a private company to the fall of the Kremlin and the retreat from Russia, was detailed by him to blow up the Inquisition at Madrid, during the Peninsular campaign. The priests met the Colonel with sanctity and suavity and opened the doors for their admission, where they found nothing amiss, till soldiers poured buckets of water on the mosaic marble floor of the main hall, when it ran down the crevices in the tessellated pavement. Their bayonets opened a passage below, where they found men and women, old and young, prisoners in the Inquisition. They brought them out to the crowd of their friends outside. "And," said the Colonel, "old mustaches, whom I had seen sit down on the corpse of a comrade, after a battle, and drink from the dead man's canteen, wept like little children at the scene there presented: parents clasping to their bosoms sons and daughters, whom they had given up for dead; and old prisoners looking for husbands and wives in vain among the crowd, who had died or left the country, during the long years of their incarceration in the prison of a secret order!

Such experiences of *Napoleon* prepared him to abolish the secret Teutonic order of Knighted Priests in 1809; which is now renewed as an armed secret order of Freemasons, consisting of men, sworn, with their hands on sword-blades, to conceal the proceedings of their order, *So help them God!* (See page 190.)

But we shall be told, and it is true, that both *Mackey* and *Macoy*, leading Masonic authorities, dislike and scout this 27th degree, as un-Masonic. Well, what is the reason of their dislike? They themselves tell us, in Notes 309 and 312; because it lacks *"symbols," "allegories,"* and *"philosophy."* Now the next, or 28th degree, both these authorities hail as the "most important, interesting," and "by far the most philosophical." (Note 314.) Turn forward and read the Analysis of the 28th degree, and you will see what they mean by allegory, symbol, and philosophy: they mean the symbols and allegories of Masonry, which alone give the true "knowledge of God!!" (Note 319.) Philosophy which worships God not in His church on earth, but "in deep solitudes and sequestered forests," (page 210) along with Goths and Druids. (Note 325.) And that Masonry is "the purest philosophy," and "the basis of all religions," Christianity of course included!

And because this 27th degree does not put Christ on a level with Joseph Smith, and Christianity with Mormonism; because, in short, it does not, as the 28th degree does, throughout, put the rabble of pagan gods above the God of heaven, and the worship of devils above the worship of Christ, Mackey and Macoy deem it unworthy to belong to Masonry.

But surely, surely, this Teutonic degree, with its secret signs, tokens, and impudent traffic in the name *Jehovah* on its jewels (page 184) and its prayers, from lips used to blasphemy; surely this grand swindle of the young men of America, dubbing them Knights for money is vile enough to belong to the *Ancient and Accepted Scottish Rite;* which was manufactured by Jesuits, remodeled and sold by Jews.

CHAPTER LI

EAST OR AUTUMN.

DECORATIONS:[314]—No particular hangings are prescribed. There may be painted on the walls of the lodge, landscapes of mountains and forests, designated to represent nature both in the rude and natural, and the refined and cultivated state. The lodge is illuminated by a Sun placed above the head of the Master, in

Note 313.—"Of all the high degrees it is, perhaps, the most important and the most interesting to the scholar who desires to investigate the true secret of the Order. Its old catechisms, now unfortunately too much neglected, are full of suggestive thoughts, and in its modern ritual, for which we are indebted to the inventive genius of Brother Albert Pike, it is by far the most learned and philosophical of the Scottish degrees."—Mackey's Encyclopædia of Freemasonry, Article Knight of the Sun.

Note 314.—"The walls should be painted to represent the open country, mountains, plains, forests and fields. The chamber is lighted by a single light, a great globe of ground glass, in the South; this represents the Sun. The only additional light is from the transparencies. In the East is suspended a transparency, displaying the sign of the Macrocosm, or of the seal of King Solomon—the interlaced triangles; one white and the other black. In the West is suspended a transparency displaying the sign of microcosm, or the pentagram traced on a pure white ground with lines of vermilion, and with a single point upward. Many other transparencies, symbolising objects of great importance, are appropriately arranged around the chamber, particularly the accompanying figures, which are placed in the North. On the right hand of the presiding officer, in the East, on a gilt pedestal, is a Caduceus, gilded, the upper part of it a cross, surmounted by a globe, and with two serpents twining around it, their heads rising above the cross. The ceiling should represent the heavens, with the crescent moon in the West, the principal planets, and the stars, in the constellations Taurus and Orion and those near the polar star. The presiding officer is styled Father Adam. The Warden sits in the West, and is called Brother Truth; there are seven other officers, who are styled Brothers Gabriel, Auriel, Michael, Camaliel, Raphael, Zaphiel and Zarakhiel. The collar is a broad white watered ribbon: on the right side is painted or embroidered an eye, in gold. The apron is of pure white lambskin, with no edging or ornament, except the pentagram, which is traced on the middle of it with vermilion. The jewel is a medal of gold, on one side a full sun, on the other a globe. When the degree is conferred no jewel or apron is worn."—Macoy's Encyclopædia and Dictionary of Freemasonry, Article Knight of the Sun.

the centre of a triangle inscribed in a circle. In each angle of the triangle is the letter S, abbreviations of *Stella, Sedet, Science; Wisdom, Morality.*

DRESS:—Adam wears a yellow covered robe. His head is covered. In his right hand is a sceptre, on the top of which is a golden globe. The handle or extremity of the sceptre is gilt. He wears a Sun suspended by a chain of gold. No jewel or apron is worn when candidate is being initiated. Brother Truth holds a sceptre with a golden eye on the end of it in his hand. The cherubim wear the order.

ORDER:—White watered ribbon, worn across the body, at the bottom of which is painted or embroidered an eye.

JEWEL:—A golden triangle with rays, and in the centre an eye. It is suspended from the bottom of the sash. No aprons are worn. The Sylphs wear a short habit or tunic, a brown apron and a blue cap, tied with a yellow ribbon.

TITLES:—The Master is styled Father Adam. There is but one Warden. He acts as Introducer and preparer when there is a reception [initiation] and is called brother Truth. The other members of the Council are named Cherubim[315] and there can be only seven cherubim in a Council. If more than that number are present, the additional brethren, to the number of five, are called Sylphs.

The fixed number of cherubim correspond with the

Note 315.—"Josephus says that they resemble no known creature but that Moses made them in the form in which he saw them about the throne of God; others, deriving their ideas from what is said of them by Ezekiel, Isaiah, and St. John, describe them as having the face and breast of a man, the wings of an eagle, the belly of a lion, and the legs and feet of an ox, which three animals, with man, are the symbols of strength and wisdom. But all agree in this, that they had wings, and that these wings were extended. The cherubim were purely symbolic. But although there is great diversity of opinion as to their exact signification, yet there is a very general agreement that they allude to and symbolize the protecting and overshadowing power of the Deity Mackey's Encyclopædia of Freemasonry, Article Cherubim.

number of angels who governed the number of planets known to the ancients, viz: *Michael, Gabriel, Auriel, Hamaliel, Raphael, Zarachiel and Saphael,* which were supposed to preside over and govern the planets *Saturn, Jupiter, Mars, Venus, Mercury;* the *Sun* and *Moon.*

BATTERY:—Six equi-timed strokes; OOOOOO.

OPENING CEREMONIES

KNIGHTS OF THE SUN.'''

Father Adam—Brother Truth, what time is it on earth?

Brother Truth—Father Adam, it is midnight among the profane or cowans, but the Sun''' is in its meridian in this lodge.

Father Adam—My children, profit by the favor of this austere, luminary at present showing its light to us,

Note 316.—"Knight of the Sun, or Prince Adept. Sometimes known by the names 'The Philosophical Lodge,' 'Prince of the Sun,' 'Key to Masonry.' It is the 28th degree of the Ancient and Accepted Rite, and is strictly philosophical and scientific. The ceremonies and lecture, which are of great length, furnish a history of all the preceding degrees and explain in the fullest manner the various Masonic emblems. The great object of the degree is to inspire men with the knowledge of Heavenly Truth, which is the pure source of all perfection, and as this virtue is one of the three great tenets of Masonry it deserves commendation. The body is styled a Council, and consists of not less than ten members."—Macoy's Encyclopædia and Dictionary of Freemasonry, Article Knight of the Sun.

Note 317.—"The Master, therefore, in the East is a symbol of the rising sun; the Junior Warden in the South, of the Meridian Sun; and the Senior Warden in the West, of the Setting Sun. So in the mysteries of India, the chief officers were placed in the east, the west, and the south, respectively, to represent Brahma, or the rising; Vishnu, or the setting; and Siva, or the meridan sun. And in the Druidical rites, the Archdruid, seated in the east, was assisted by two other officers—the one in the west representing the moon, and the other, in the south, representing the meridian sun.

This triple division of the government of a Lodge by three officers, representatives of the sun in his three manifestations in the east, south, and west, will remind us of similar ideas in the symbolism of antiquity. In the Orphic mysteries, it was taught that the sun generated from an egg, burst forth with power to triplicate himself by his own unassisted energy. Supreme power seems always to have been associated in the ancient mind with a threefold division. Thus the sign of authority was indicated by the three-forked lightning of Jove, the trident of Neptune, and three-headed Cerberus of Pluto. The government of the Universe was divided between these three sons of Saturn. The chaste goddess ruled the earth as Diana, the heavens as Luna, and the infernal regions as Hecate, whence her rites were only performed in a place where three roads met.

The sun is then presented to us in Masonry first as a symbol of light, but then more emphatically as a symbol of sovereign authority."—Mackey's Encyclopædia of Freemasonry, Article Sun.

which will conduct us in the path of virtue and to follow that law which is eternally to be engraved on our hearts, and the only law by which we cannot fail to come to the knowledge of pure truth. My children, let us pray. (All kneel on the right knee, raise the right hand, and Father Adam repeats the following prayer:)

OPENING PRAYER KNIGHTS OF THE SUN.

Bless, O our Father, those of us who are now here assembled, by giving us those most inestimable of all blessings, far above honors and dignities, the priceless jewels of charity, friendship, love, justice and truth. Aid us in the keeping a perfect observance of all the duties which we have in any wise assumed to perform. Enable us to abide by the promises which we have made to one another, and to thee Eternal, omnipotent and merciful Deity, and to thy ineffable name be all praise for ever more. Amen. (All rise.)

Father Adam—(Gives the sign:)

SIGN.

Place the right hand flat upon the heart, the thumb separate, so as to form a square.

All—(Give the answer:)

ANSWER.

Raise the right hand, and with the index, point to heaven.

Sign. Knights of the Sun.

Answer.

Father Adam—I declare this Council of Knights of the Sun opened.

CHAPTER LII

TWENTY-EIGHTH DEGREE, OF KNIGHTS OF THE SUN.[818]

INITIATION.

(Brother Truth retires and prepares the candidate as follows. A bandage over his eyes, a sword in his right hand; invests him with a ragged and bloody robe, puts a mask on his face, fetters binding his arms, a crown on his head, a purse in his left hand, etc. He then knocks six: 000-000, is admitted and stands at the door of the lodge.)

Candidate

Father Adam—Brother Truth, whom do you conduct?

Brother Truth—A Commander of the Temple, who desires to go out of darkness and to see the true light, and to know the true light in all its purity, and to ask tidings of the times that are promised to man.

Note 818.—"Knight of the Sun. [Scotch Masonry.]—The tenth degree conferred in the Consistory of Princes of the Royal Secret. Scotch Masonry, and the twenty-eighth upon the catalogue of that system. It is otherwise known as Prince Adept, Prince of the Sun, and Key of Masonry, or Chaos Disentangled. The historical instructions embrace the lectures and emblems of all the preceding degrees; its grand moral is the inculcation of truth. The assembly is termed a Council. Its officers are Thrice Perfect Father Adam and Brother Truth; the inferior officers are named after the seven chief angels. The brethren are termed Sylphs. The lodge has one light, shining through a globe of water. The jewel is a gold triangle, with rays; in the center an eye. Hour to open, midnight on earth."—Morris's Masonic Dictionary, Article Knight of the Sun.

Father Adam—What more dost thou desire?

Brother Truth—(For candidate.) To divest myself of original sin and renounce the juvenile prejudices of error which all men are liable to; namely the desire of all worldly attachments and pride.

Father Adam—Are you prepared to receive instructions with humility?

Brother Truth—(For candidate.) I am.

Father Adam—My son, you now desire to be instructed in the knowledge of pure and holy truth'''[*] and to be brought from darkness to light, and to know the pure light in all its purity, but before we comply with your wishes consult your own heart and mind, and see if you feel satisfied to obey her (holy truth) in all things which she commands. If you, in your heart, feel disposed to do so, I am sure she is ready to comply with your wishes and impart those instructions to you. Mankind are so full of error and falsehood that though they search for happiness, few have knocked at the door of true light, which conducts us to felicity.

The Knights of the Sun are instructed to go among men and to use their best efforts to inspire them with a knowledge of truth, which is the pure source of all perfection. Again, do you feel satisfied to obey her in all things which she commands?

Note 219.—'Truth. The real object of Freemasonry, in a philosophical and religious sense, is the search for truth. This truth is, therefore, symbolized by the Word. From the first entrance of the Apprentice into the Lodge, until his reception of the highest degree, this search is continued. It is not always found, and a substitute must sometimes be provided. Yet whatever be the labors he may perform, whatever the ceremonies through which he may pass, whatever the symbols in which he may be instructed, whatever the reward he may obtain, the true end of all is the attainment of truth. This idea of truth is not the same as that expressed in the lecture of the first degree, where Brotherly Love, Relief, and Truth are there said to be the 'three great tenets of a Mason's profession.' In that connection, truth, which is called a 'divine attribute, the foundation of every virtue,' is synonymous with sincerity, honesty of expression, and plain dealing. The higher idea of truth, which pervades the whole Masonic system, and which is symbolized by the Word, is that which is properly expressed to a knowledge of God.'—Mackey's Encyclopedia of Freemasonry, Article Truth.

Brother Truth—(For candidate.) I do.

Father Adam—Brother Truth, conduct this Commander around our temple of Wisdom to the seven Cherubim, and let them in due succession examine and try him, that we may know and be satisfied that he is fit to dwell among us. (Brother Truth conducts him once around the temple while Raphiel says:)

Raphiel—God is the author of every thing that existeth, the eternal, the supreme, the living and awful being, from whom nothing in the universe is hidden. Make of him no idols and visible images, but rather worship him in the deep solitudes of sequestered forests, for he is invisible and fills the universe as his soul, and liveth not in any temple. (Brother Truth now halts in front of Raphiel.)

Raphiel—Brother Truth, whom do you conduct?

Brother Truth—A Commander of the Temple who desires to go out of darkness and to see the true light, and to know the true light in all its purity, and to ask tidings of the times that are promised to man.

Raphiel—He cannot pass here! behold! he has the bandage of ignorance and prejudice upon his brow.

Brother Truth—Enlightened Raphiel, he is ready to cast it off with your assistance.

Raphiel—(Removes the bandage and exhibits the three lights.) Henceforth, my brother, follow these three lights, indicative of Analysis, Synthesis, Analogy; the instruments of thought and look for knowledge with a clear and fearless eye, and greet truth wheresover you meet her, whether on a throne or in a dungeon, triumphant or proscribed. Prove all things and hold

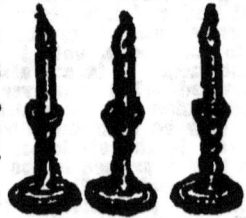

Three Lights.

fast to the good. (Brother Truth conducts him once around the room.)

Gabriel—Light and darkness are the world's eternal ways. God is the principal of everything that exists, and the father of all beings. He is the eternal, immovable and self-existent. There are no bounds to his powers. At one glance he is the past, the present and the future. (Halts in front of Gabriel.''')

Gabriel—Brother Truth, whom do you conduct?

Brother Truth—A Commander of the Temple who desires to go out of darkness and to see the true light, and to know the true light in all its purity, and to ask tidings of the times that are promised to man.

Gabriel—This brother comes with a sword in his hand. He cannot pass till he breaks his weapon under his feet. (Candidate breaks his sword and Gabriel holds up a caduceus.)

Gabriel—In lieu of that sword, in lieu of offensive war bring with you among men the caduceus of peace, and exert yourselves to avert anger and bloodshed; blessed are the peace-makers, for they are the children of God. (Brother Truth, again conducts him once around the room.)

Caduceus.

Auriel—In the beginning man had the word, and that word was from God, and out of the living power which in and by that word was communicated to man came the light of his existence. Let no man speak the word, for by it the Father made light and darkness; the world and living creatures. (Halts in front of Auriel.)

Note 220.—"The name of one of the archangels, referred to in some of the high degrees."—Mackay's Encyclopædia of Freemasonry, Article Gabriel.

Auriel—Brother Truth, whom do you conduct?

Brother Truth—A Commander of the Temple, who desires to go out of darkness and to see the true light, and to know the true light in all its purity, and to ask tidings of the times that are promised to man.

Auriel—What do I see? This Commander you conduct dares to present himself as a fellow laborer and stands clothed in the tattered and impure garb of indolence and vice. Divest him of that garb. (Brother Truth takes off the robe.)

Brother Truth—Glorious Auriel, the aspirant has cast off the disgraceful garb of idleness.

Auriel—'Tis well! His body being relieved from ignominy, his mind may now discover and fulfill the moral meaning of the cone or pyramid; that form of matter from which all other figures may be derived, and which is an emblem of productive truth, varied order and economic utility. It represents the true mason who raises himself by degrees till he reaches heaven, to adore the sacred and unutterable name of the Great Architect of the

Cone or Pyramid. Universe. If any will not work, neither should they eat. (Brother Truth again conducts him once around the room.)

Zarachiel—Man was created pure, and God gave him truth as he gave him light. He has lost the truth and found error. He has wandered far into darkness and round him sin and shame hover evermore. The soul that is impure and sinful and defiled with earthly stains cannot again unite with God, until by long trials and many purifications it is finally delivered from the old calamity, and light overcomes darkness and dethrones it in the soul. (Halts in front of Zarachiel.)

Zarachiel—Brother Truth, whom do you conduct?

Brother Truth—A Commander of the Temple who desires to go out of darkness and to see the true light, and to know the true light in all its purity, and to ask tidings of the times that are promised to man.

Zarachiel—I cannot permit him to pass, for he wears the mask of hypocrisy. (Brother Truth removes the mask.)

Brother Truth—Shining Zarachiel, his mask has fallen and he stands before you, in honesty and innocence.

Zarachiel—'Tis well! He doth stand approved, and may drink of the pure contents of this transparent goblet. Let the perfect purity of its contents be a token of the resolution of this hour, blessed are the pure in heart. (Candidate drinks, when Brother Truth again conducts him once around the room.)

Hamaliel—Before the world grew old, the primitive truth faded out from men's souls. Then man asked himself, what am I and how and whence am I and whither do I go? and the soul looking inward upon itself strove to learn whether that "I" were mere matter; its thought and reason, its passions and affections mere results of material combination or, a material being enveloping an immaterial spirit. (Halts in front of Hamaliel.)

Hamaliel—Brother Truth, whom do you conduct?

Brother Truth—A Commander of the Temple who desires to go out of darkness and to see the true light, and to know the true light in all its purity, and to ask tidings of the times that are promised to man.

Hamaliel—None but the free can enter into the gates of the Eden, for it is the land of liberty. (Brother Truth takes off the chains of the candidate.)

Brother Truth—Hamaliel, he is free.

Hamaliel—Thereafter, my brother, let this globe be an emblem to remind you of true liberty, for though perfectly regular in form, though it measures equally in every direction it has no boundaries or lines of limitation; where the spirit of the Lord is, there is liberty. (Brother Truth again conducts him once around the room.)

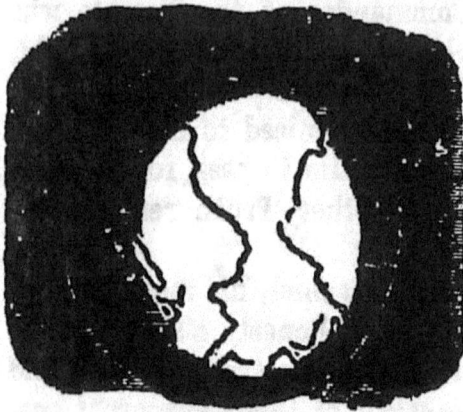

The Globe.

Saphael—God is the first; indestructable, eternal, uncreated, indivisible. Wisdom, justice, truth, mercy, with harmony and love are of his essence, and eternity and infinitude of extension. He is silent, and consents with mind, and is known to soul through mind alone. In him were all things originally contained and from him all things were evolved. (Halts in front of Saphael.)

Saphael—Brother Truth, whom do you conduct?

Brother Truth—A Commander of the Temple who desires to go out of darkness and to see the true light, and to know the true light in all its purity, and to ask tidings of the times that are promised to man.

Saphael—With the haughty crown of vanity and pride upon his forehead, how can he hope to inhabit Eden, where all are equal sons of the Great Architect of the Universe. This arrogant Commander must cast his crown to his feet if he wishes to proceed. (Brother Truth divests him of his crown.)

Brother Truth—Saphael, it is done.

Saphael—Then let him look to this cross. It is the

sign of the sacred dogma of equality, and with it for a monitor we may yet hope for the reign of God on earth. The meek shall inherit the earth. (Brother Truth again conducts him once around the room.)

Cross.

Michael—In the beginning, the universe was one soul. He was the all; alone with time and space, and infinite as they. He had his thoughts: "I create worlds" and lo! the universe and the laws of harmony and motion that rule it; the first of a thought of God, and the bird and beast, and every living thing but man, and light and air, and the mysterious currents, and the dominion of mysterious numbers. (Halts in front of Michael.)

Michael—Brother Truth, whom do you conduct?

Brother Truth—A Commander of the Temple, who desires to go out of darkness and to see the true light, and to know the true light in all its purity, and to ask tidings of the times that are promised to man.

Michael—In vain does this man seek to enjoy the happiness of Eden on earth; for he clutches in his hand the treasure of human avarice. (Brother Truth takes the purse from the candidate and hands it to Michael.)

Brother Truth—Michael,'" he casts it before you to be put into the common treasury.

Note 221.—"Who is like unto God. The chief of the seven arch-angels. He is the leader of the celestial host, as Lucifer is of the in-fernal spirits, and the especial protector of Israel. He is prominently referred to in the twenty-eighth degree of the Ancient and Accepted Scottish Rite, or Knight of the Sun."—Mackey's Encyclopædia of Free-masonry, Article Michael.

Michael—Then let him wear the sign of the ardent dove, to indicate that his soul will ever cherish affection for his fellow-man. (Invests him with it.)

Ardent Dove.

Michael—Brother Truth, you will now conduct the candidate to Father Adam.'" (Order is obeyed.)

Father Adam—My son, dost thou desire to be further instructed in these great primitive truths, which are the treasures of the archives of masonry?

Candidate—I do.

Father Adam—Art thou prepared to give us thy most solemn pledge and promise that thou wilt strenuously endeavor faithfully to practice that pure morality that flows as a result from the great truths that thou hast heard; to repent of, and regret thy short-comings, and thy errors, and to submit patiently to gentle and brotherly rebuke and reprimand if thou shouldest offend?

Candidate—I am.

Father Adam—Go, then, and upon thy bended knees, before the altar of truth and the great light, emblem of the God of the Patriarchs, prepare to receive the solemn obligation of a Knight of the Sun. (Brother Truth

Note 322.—"It is most probably in this collective sense, as the representative of the whole human race, and, therefore, the type of humanity, that the presiding officer in a Council of Knights of the Sun, the 28th degree of the Ancient and Accepted Scottish Rite, is called Father Adam, and is occupied in the investigation of the great truths which so much concern the interests of the race. Adam, in that degree, is man seeking after divine truth. The Kabbalists and Talmudists have invented many things concerning the first Adam, none of which are, however, worthy of preservation. See Knight of the Sun."—Mackey's Encyclopædia of Freemasonry, Article Adam.

conducts him to the altar, and causes him to kneel on both knees.)

OBLIGATION KNIGHTS OF THE SUN.

I........promise and swear, in the presence of the Great Architect of the Universe, and of all the brethren here present, never to take arms against my country, directly or indirectly, in any conspiracy whatever.

I furthermore promise and swear never to reveal any of the secrets of the degree of Knights of the Sun, to any person or persons unless duly qualified to receive the same, and never give my consent to the admission of any one into our mysteries, until after the most scrupulous circumspection and full knowledge of his life and conversation, and who has given at all times full proof of his zeal and fervent attachment for the order, and a submission at all times to the consistory of Princes of the Royal Secret.

I furthermore promise and swear never to confer the degree of Knights of the Sun, without having a permission in writing from the Grand Consistory or from a Grand Inspector or Deputy.

I furthermore promise and swear to redouble my zeal for all my brethren, Knights and Princes, and should I willfully violate this my obligation, may my brethren seize me and thrust my tongue through with a red hot iron, to pluck out my eyes and deprive me of smelling and seeing, to cut off my hands and expose me in that condition in the field to be devoured by the voracious animals, and if none can be found, may the lightning of heaven execute on me the same vengeance. So may God maintain me in righteousness and equity. Amen. (Father Adam then raises him and kisses him on the forehead, invests him with the collar and jewel, and gives him the following:)

SIGN.

Place the right hand flat upon the heart, the thumb separate, so as to form a square.

ANSWER.

Raise the right hand, and
with the index, point to heaven.

Sign, Knights of
the Sun.

Answer.

TOKEN.

Take in your hand, those of the
brother and press them gently; kiss
him on the forehead and say Alpha.
*** He returns the kiss and says,
Omega. But this is not much used.

Token Knights of
the Sun.

BATTERY:—Six equi-timed strokes; 000000.

PASS WORD:—Stibium.

Note 323.—" 'I am Alpha and Omega, the beginning and the end, the
first and the last.' These are respectively the first and the last letters
in the Greek alphabet, corresponding with the English form 'A to Z' or
the Hebrew 'Aleph to Tau.' "—Morris's Masonic Dictionary, Article Alpha
and Omega.

SACRED WORD:—Adonai.

ANSWER:—Abra or Abrag. That is, a king without blot. (After the candidate is invested with the signs, token and words, he is seated in front of Michael (the Orator) who delivers the following history:)

HISTORY.

My brother, in the ancient mysteries,[224] wherever they were practiced, was taught that truth of the primitive revelation, the existence of one great being, infinite and pervading the universe, who was there worshiped without superstition and his marvelous nature, essence and attributes taught to the initiates, while the vulgar attributed his words to secondary gods, personified and isolated from him in fabulous independence. These truths were covered from the common people as with a veil, and the mysteries were carried into every country, that without disturbing the popular beliefs, truth, the arts, and the sciences might be known to those who were capable of understanding them, and maintaining the true doctrine incorruptible, which the people, prone to superstition and idolatry, have in no age been able to do, nor, as many strange aberrations and superstitions of the present day prove, any more now than heretofore. For we need but point to the doctrines of so many sects that degrade the Creator to the rank, and assign to him the passions of humanity, to prove that now as always, the old truths must be committed to a few or they will

Note 224.—"As to their origin, Warburton is probably not wrong in his statement that the first of which we have any account are those of Isis and Osiris in Egypt; for although those of Mithras came into Europe from Persia, they were, it is supposed, carried from Egypt by Zoroaster.

The most important of these mysteries were the Osiric in Egypt, the Mithraic in Persia, the Cabiric in Thrace, the Adonisian in Syria, the Dionysiac and Eleusinian in Greece, the Scandinavian among the Gothic nations, and the Druidical among the Celts.

In all these mysteries we find a singular unity of design, clearly indicating a common origin, and a purity of doctrine as evidently proving that this common origin was not to be sought for in the popular theology of the Pagan world."—Mackey's Encyclopædia of Freemasonry, Article Mysteries, Ancient.

be overlaid with fiction and error, and irretrievably lost.

Though masonry is identical with the ancient mysteries, it is so in this qualified sense, that it presents but an imperfect image of their brilliancy, the ruins only of their grandeur and a system that has experienced progressive alterations, the fruits of social events and political circumstances. Upon leaving Egypt, the mysteries were modified by the habits of the different nations among whom they were introduced. Though originally more moral and political than religious, they soon became the heritage as it were of the priests, and essentially religious, though in reality limiting the sacerdotal power by teaching the intelligent laity the folly of the countries into which they were transplanted. In Greece they were the mysteries of Ceres,[***] in Rome, the good goddess, in Gaul, the school of Mars, in Sicily, the academy of the sciences. Among the Hebrews, they partook of the rights and ceremonies of a religion which placed all the powers of a government and all the knowledge in the hands of the priests and Levites.

The Pagodas of India, the retreats of the Magi of Persia and Chaldea, and the pyramids of Egypt were no longer the sources at which men drank in knowledge. Each people, at all informed, had its mysteries. After a time the temples of Greece and the school of Pythagoras lost their reputation and freemasonry took their place. Masonry, when properly expounded, is at once the interpretation of the great book of nature, the recital of physical and astronomical phenomenon, the purest philosophy and the place of deposit, where, as in a treasury, are kept in safety all the great truths of the primi-

Note 335.—"Ceres. Among the Romans the goddess of agriculture, but among the more poetic Greeks she was worshiped under the name of Demeter, as the symbol of the prolific earth. To her is attributed the institution of the Eleusinian Mysteries in Greece, the most popular of all the ancient initiations."—Mackey's Encyclopædia of Freemasonry, Article Ceres.

tive revelation, that form the basis of all religions. In the modern degrees, three things are to be recognized:

The image of primeval times, the tableau of the efficient causes of the universe, and the book in which are written the morality of all peoples, and the code by which they must govern themselves if they would be prosperous.

The first[326] degree represents man, when he had sunken from his original lofty estate, into what is most improperly styled a state of nature. He represents in that degree the rough ashler, unfit to form a part of the spiritual temple, the pagan who had lost all the great primitive truths of the original revelation. He maintained the same character in the ancient mysteries. He is emphatically a profane,[327] enveloped in darkness, poor and destitute of spiritual knowledge, and emblematically naked.

The material darkness[328] which is produced by the

Note 326.—"Although the Entered Apprentice is but a 'rough ashler,' yet he is of good substance and sound at the core. The statue is in the block, a figure more graceful than human genius can create. The Entered Apprentice has been judged, by men expert in the selection of material, to be 'prepared in heart'; in theory he was a Mason even before he entered at the northwest corner of the Lodge. There is nothing in Masonic science that can do the work of heart-preparation, and those master builders who have attempted, out of inferior materials, to construct the Freemasons' wall, have ever and egregiously erred. Therefore is the Entered Apprentice one already prepared in heart. Nor is this tyro in Masonry altogether ignorant of the principles of the society into which he desires to penetrate; some exoteric knowledge of Masonry he must have had, for, in his petition, he declares that 'he has long entertained a favorable opinion of the ancient and honorable institution.'"—Morris's Masonic Dictionary, Article Entered Apprentice.

Note 327.—"Profane. There is no word whose technical and proper meaning differs more than this. In its ordinary use profane signifies one who is irreligious and irreverent, but in its technical adaptation it is applied to one who is ignorant of sacred rites. The word is compounded of the two Latin words pro and fannum, and literally means before or outside of the temple; and hence a profanus among the ancients was one who was not allowed to enter the temple and behold the mysteries. 'Those,' says Vossius, 'were called profane who were not initiated in the sacred rites, but to whom it was allowed only to stand before the temple—pro fano—not to enter it and take part in the solemnities.'"—Mackey's Encyclopædia of Freemasonry, Article Profane.

Note 328.—"The material darkness which is produced by [the hoodwink] is an emblem of the darkness of his soul. He is deprived of everything that has a value, and wherewith he could purchase food, to indicate his utter destitution of the mental wealth of primitive truth." Pierson's Traditions, Subject Entered Apprentice, page 89.

bandage over his eyes, is an emblem of the darkness of his soul. He is deprived of everything that has a value, and wherewith he could purchase food to indicate his utter destitution of the mental wealth of primitive truth. In this degree he undergoes only physical tests, and receives elementary moral instructions. As yet he takes upon himself no duty but secrecy. He still remains in the dark quarter of the lodge though not in the North,''' but half way towards the East, the place of light. He is not exposed to the fearful trials which await the candidate for initiation into the mysteries. He passes through no gloomy forests or long labyrinthine caves; he meets no hideous spectres; he is stunned and alarmed by no fearful noises, he incurs no danger.

A few solitary moments in reflection and prayer, a short time passed in darkness, a few uncertain steps, a few obstacles to overcome are all; and he enters the temple of truth and virtue. The journeys and trials of the candidate are an emblem of human life. Man enters, feeble and naked, upon a road full of dangers and pitfalls. The ignorance of the fancy, the fiery passions of youth, the troubles and agitations of mature age, the infirmities of old age are so many evils which assail him, and which philosophy alone can aid him against. Defenceless in a world of trouble, what would become of him without the assistance of his brethren?

His obligation is no vulgar oath, such as is administered in the profane world. It is antique and sacred. He repeats it without compulsion. The expressions are

Note 329.—"A candidate in search of Masonic light comes from the West and presses forward to the East, the place of light, by way of the North, 'the place of darkness.' This use of the word North is said, in the lectures of the Blue Lodge, to be derived from the situation of Jerusalem. It was so far north of the Summer Solstice (latitude 31 degrees, 46 minutes, 45 seconds, North, that is more than nine degrees North of the Summer Solstice), that the rays of the meridian sun could never dart into the northern windows of it."—Morris's Masonic Dictionary, Article North.

energetic, because being yet in darkness, he is on the point of passing from barbarism into civilization. It is like those of the ancient mysteries, for violating which, Alcibrades was exiled and devoted to the furies.

When he is brought to light[''''] the allegory is complete. He sees around him a band of brothers bound to protect and defend him.

The obligation he has assumed, they and every mason in the world have assumed toward him. He is one of the brotherhood, bound by its laws and enlisted as a soldier against ignorance and vice. The Master, for the time entitled to respect and veneration, is still but the first among his brethren, who are all his equals. Such is masonic law and usage, and such it has been from the earliest ages. In his journey, imitating that of life, the candidate goes but three times around[''''] the lodge although life has four seasons. This is because his journey also represents the annual revolution of the Sun. Had the mysteries originated in the North or West, in Rome or Greece, the seasons of the year and of life

Note 220.—"Light. Light is an important word in the Masonic system. It conveys a far more recondite meaning than it is believed to possess by the generality of readers. It is in fact the first of all the symbols presented to the neophyte, and continues to be presented to him in various modifications throughout all his future progress in his Masonic career. It does not simply mean, as might be supposed, truth or wisdom, but it contains within itself a far more abstruse allusion to the very essence of Speculative Masonry, and embraces within its capacious signification all the other symbols of the Order. Freemasons are emphatically called the 'sons of light,' because they are, or at least are entitled to be, in possession of the true meaning of the symbol; while the profane or unitiated who has not received this knowledge are, by a parity of expression, said to be in darkness."—Mackey's Encyclopædia of Freemasonry, Article Light.

Note 221.—"Circumambulation is the name given by sacred archæologists to that religious rite in the ancient initiations which consisted in a formal procession around the altar, or other holy and consecrated object. The same Rite exists in Freemasonry.

In ancient Greece, when the priests were engaged in the rite of sacrifice, they and the people always walked three times round the altar while singing a sacred hymn. In making this procession, great care was taken to move in imitation of the course of the sun. For this purpose, they commenced at the east, and passing on by the way of the south to the west and thence by ....e north, they arrived at the east again."—Mackey's Encyclopædia of Freemasonry, Article Circumambulation, Rite of.

would have agreed, and four have been the number instead of three. But in the East, in ancient times there were but three seasons. The three pillars ''' that support the lodge are Wisdom, Strength and Beauty.

The Egyptians and the Hebrews based their civil policy upon the wisdom of the priests, and the power, strength or valor of their civil chiefs who were also military commanders, and the harmony between these (synonymous with beauty among the Egyptians) completed the prosperity of the State. The age of an Apprentice is said to be three years, because in the ancient mysteries three years preparation was required before initiation could commence.

The number three''' belongs in a peculiar manner to this degree. The alarm is three raps. There are three movable and three immovable jewels; three principal officers, three lights, greater and lesser; three journeys are made around the lodge.

In the Fellow Craft degree, the number five succeeds

Note 332.—"Pillars. Every lodge must be supported by three grand shafts, or pillars—Wisdom, Strength, and Beauty. Wisdom constructs the building, Beauty adorns, and Strength supports it; also, Wisdom is ordained to discover, Beauty to ornament, and Strength to bear. He who is wise as a perfect Master will not be easily injured by his own actions."—Macoy's Encyclopædia and Dictionary of Freemasonry, Article Pillars.

Note 333.—"In all the mysteries, from Egypt to Scandinavia, we find a sacred regard for the number three. In the rites of Mithras, the Empyrean was said to be supported by three intelligences, Ormusd, Mithra, and Mithras. In the rites of Hindustan, there was the trinity of Brahma, Vishnu, and Siva. It was, in short, a general character of the mysteries to have three principal officers and three grades of initiation.

In Freemasonry the ternary is the most sacred of all the mystical numbers. Beginning with the old axiom of the Roman Artificers, that tres faciunt collegium, or it requires three to make a college, they have established the rule that not less than three shall congregate to form a Lodge. Then in all the Rites, whatever may be the number of superimposed grades, there lie at the basis the three symbolic degrees. There are in all the degrees three principal officers, three supports, three greater and three lesser lights, three movable and three immovable jewels, three principal tenets, three working-tools of a Fellow Craft, three principal orders of architecture, three chief human senses, three Ancient Grand Masters. In fact, everywhere in the system the number three is presented as a prominent symbol."—Mackey's Encyclopædia of Freemasonry, Article Three.

to three. In this degree the letter G.∴'" represents
Geometry alone. Its deeper meaning is properly reserved for the third. Here the young Fellow Craft is
the representative of the student of the sciences in the
school of Pythagoras; and it was there known that
among the Brahmins, Gannes was the God of numbers
and the patrons of schools and learned societies. With
us, too, the letter is the substitute for the Hebraic Yod,
the initial letter of the Divine name and a monogram
that expressed the uncreated being, principal of all
things, and enclosed in a triangle, the unity of God.

The word of a Fellow Craft has an astronomical
meaning that connects masonry with the primitive times.
Setting the celestial globe for the place where the temple
was built, and the season of the year when it was commenced, the master's station corresponds with the solar
rising. The sun'" has just shown himself above the
horizon. The candidate entering by the west door faces
the day star and is consequently near that star of the
zodiac which sets as the sun rises. It is the star which
blesses the husbandman; that brilliant star which the
Hebrews called Shibboleth, meaning an ear of wheat.

In the Fellow Craft degree, one point of the compass
is raised above the square. The latter is an emblem of
the mechanical world and of obedience. The former

Note 334.—"G. The situation of this letter, when alone, is well
known to all Freemasons. It cannot allude to the name of God alone
in the German lodges, or it could not be found in the situation in
foreign lodges. It has a closer affinity to Geometry, which is so necessary to an Architect, and geometrical certainty and truth is everywhere
necessary.—Gadicke."—Macoy's Encyclopædia and Dictionary of Free
masonry, Article G.

Note 335.—"The heraldic definition of the sun as a bearing fit most
appositely to the symbolism of the sovereignty of the Master. Thus
Gwillim says: 'The sun is the symbol of sovereignty, the hieroglyphic
of royalty; it doth signify absolute authority.' This representation of
the sun as a symbol of authority, while it explains the reference to the
Master, enables us to amplify its meaning, and apply it to the three
sources of authority in the Lodge, and accounts for the respective positions of the officers wielding this authority."—Mackey's Encyclopædia of
Freemasonry, Article Sun.

describes those curves and circles which are figures of
the celestial movements and is an emblem of authority.
Thus the meaning is that the candidate has taken one
step towards celestial knowledge, and from obedience
to command.

The Fellow Craft passes from the perpendicular to
the square, from the column Jachin to the column Boaz;
the perpendicular being a straight line the square two,
forming a right angle.

The third line comes in the Masters degree, to complete the right angled triangle and exhibit the 47th
problem of Euclid and Pythagoras.

The third degree commemorates the murder of
Hiram''' Abiff (whom it styles the Chief Architect of
the Temple and one of our three Ancient Grand Masters) by three perfidious workmen to whom he refused to
give the master's word; the less of that word and the
substitution of another, and hints at the resurrection to
life of the murdered man, though in fact, in the York
rite it relates that he was merely raised to be buried
again. These were events of ordinary occurrence, so far
as the mere murder and the discovery of the body, and
the punishment of the assassins are concerned. Sym-

Note 336.—"Masonic traditions are full of the life, labors and fate
of the 'Widow's son' of Phœnicia. That he was an aged man, devoted
through a long life to architecture and its kindred arts; that he was
a worshiper of the true God in distinction from his countrymen, who
were idolaters; that he entered heartily into the preparations of a moral
system of Masonry, of which the rules, tools and language of practical
building should be the types, the honor of God, and the good of mankind the aim; that as the end of the Temple building drew nigh he
became more endeared to the hearts of his royal patrons and the multitude of builders of all degrees; that he fell a victim to his fidelity a
short time before the completion of that renowned structure, and that
his death, the discovery of his remains and their final disposition were
introduced into Symbolical Masonry, to become constituent portions of its
legends, are admitted as facts by all Masonic historians. The theory
of the learned Dr. Oliver that these facts were adopted by King Solomon
and his royal companion as substitute for the mythological legends then
in use in the Freemasonry of Phœnicia, Hiram taking the place of Osiris
and his death, disappearance and recovery those of parallel traditions in
the Egyptian mysteries will be examined under other heads. The theory
that they are to be considered only as myths is too ill-founded to need
examination at our hands."—Morris's Masonic Dictionary, Article Hiram
the Architect.

bolic Masonry, or the first three degrees, sole heir of the mysteries, does not tell us the true master's word. We are left to discover it in that rite, in other and modern degrees. It is too evident that the degree is corrupted, mutilated and but a poor substitute for the last degree of the great mysteries.

CLOSING CEREMONIES

KNIGHTS OF THE SUN.

Father Adam—Brother Truth, what progress have men made on earth to come to true happiness?

Brother Truth—Men have always fallen. Very few have struggled and less have knocked at the door of this holy place to attain the full light of real truth, which we all ought to acquire.

Father Adam—My dear children, depart and go among men. Endeavor to inspire them with the desire of knowing holy truth; the pure source of all perfection.

Father Adam—(Puts his right hand on his left breast.)

All—(Raise the index finger of the right hand to heaven and clap six; 000000.)

Father Adam—This Council is closed.

PHILOSOPHICAL ANALYSIS

TWENTY-EIGHTH DEGREE: OR, KNIGHTS OF THE SUN.

Invented by the Guerrilla General, Albert Pike—Sets Aside the Bible as Obsolete—Lodges Have Supernatural Power—"But Rather Darkness Visible."

This degree, as here given, was invented by *Albert Pike*, (See Note 313.) *Pike* was the son of a poor shoe-maker, born in Boston, 1809; brought up in Newbury-port; studied a while in Cambridge College; afterwards obtained the honorary A. M. from that institution; went to Mexico, was an editor in Arkansas, and Memphis, Tenn.; became an ultra Southerner, and Mason; obtained, by fraud, from the U. S. Treasury, money appropriated to Indians, for annuities, schools, etc.; initiated some fifty Cherokee and Choctaws in Federal Lodge No. 1, in Washington, D. C.; became a Confederate General, and fought his Indian brigade against Gen. Curtis, at Pea Ridge, where he was defeated by the Union troops. His Indians were said to have scalped and tomahawked Union soldiers. He sold out the *Memphis Appeal*, left civil occupations, and devoted himself to Freemasonry; has translated two volumes of Asiatic pagan religion, one of eight, the other of twelve hundred pages, from which he has taken the doctrines of this 28th degree, which *Mackey* declares to be "perhaps, the most important of all the high degrees."

He has long been the head of the *"Ancient and Accepted Rite."* And though his *Supreme Council* remains in Charleston, whose records and papers for fifty-nine years before the war, were all burnt up, doubtless to conceal treason and crimes committed against the country, and the laws of war, he himself has bought, and resides in the old Blair and Rives building, near the Capitol. If such a man has invented "the most important of the high degrees," what must the others have been!

Of this degree, whose present ritual emanated from such a mind, *Macoy* says: "It is strictly philosophical, and scientific;" whose object is "to inspire men with the knowledge of heavenly truth, which is the pure source of all perfection." (See Note 316.) *The Right Rev. Episcopal Bishop Fallows,* and a *Universalist* Minister, named *Rounseville,* during *Mr. Moody's* first meetings, in Farwell Block in Chicago, spoke at a meeting, called to form a *"Lodge of Intelligence,"* in Oriental Hall in that city. The Bishop delivered an address, and Rounseville a poem on the *"Mission of Masonry."* The speech and poem were published in the *Voice of Masonry;* and their doctrine is identical with that of this degree, as stated by *Macoy,* above, *viz.,* that Masonry is the only perfect revelation of *"heavenly truth,"* and *"source of all perfection!" i. e.,* the only rule of faith and life; thus completely setting aside the Bible as obsolete. To see that this is not misstated, or exaggerated, glance through the degree. Thus we find on page 207: "The *only* law, by which we cannot fail to come to the knowledge of pure truth."

Page 208: "To know the true light in all its purity."

Note 319: "The higher idea of truth, which per- is properly expressed by a knowledge of God;" that is to say, salvation truth. And on page 212: "The true Mason, who raises himself by degrees, till he reaches heaven!!" Again on page 213: The candidate seeks, and this degree is bringing him to "the true light."

Now, Christ is "that true light." (*John, 1, 9.*) He appeared in ineffable brightness in the transfiguration; in "light above the sun's brightness" to Paul at his con- version; so to John throughout the Apocalypse; and in multitudes of instances, at the death-beds of saints, this same supernatural light appears.

Now, this degree recapitulates the substance, and ob- ject of Masonry, up from the Apprentice degree, which is seeking and gaining light in the lodge. But CHRIST is not in a secret lodge. He entered no lodge. He joined none; but abjures, prohibits, denounces them. (*Isaiah 48, 16.*) And we know that the devil hated Him; tempted Him; shrank from Him; fled from Him. We know, too, by simple inspection, that the lodge-god is not *Christ.* Looking at a lodge-procession is enough. And yet we know that Masons profess to get, and lodges to give: "light!" "light!!" "light!!!" And, whatever Masons are, they are not fools. Where do they get their light, and what is it? We know that "the spirits of devils work miracles" (*Rev. 16, 14.*) We see, too, that lodges have supernatural power. Nothing else perpetuates them through centuries. We see, too, that believing Masons have light in their countenances. Not that light with which Moses' face beamed, from intercourse with God; or Stephen's, from a vision of *Christ;* but the baleful beaming light seen in the faces of Mormons, conjurers, spirit-worshipers, and sleight-of-hand men.   As the little child's face draws and reflects the light of the countenance of a godly mother; every Mason, who believingly, worships Satan, transformed into an angel of light, reflects the light that devils see by!

"Yet from those flames, no light
"But rather darkness visible.

Such is Masonry, and such are Masons. May the God of light save us from "fellowship with devils." (*1. Cor. 10, 20.*)

CHAPTER LIII

TWENTY-NINTH DEGREE; KNIGHT OF ST. ANDREW,[897]

OR PATRIARCH OF THE CRUSADES.

ZENITH.

It is the twenty-ninth grade of the Ancient and Accepted Rite, and the eleventh conferred in a Grand Consistory.

INTRODUCTION :—This is supposed to be the first grade

Note 887.—"Grand Scottish Knight of St. Andrew. The 29th degree of the Ancient and Accepted rite. It is also called 'Patriarch of the Crusades,' in allusion to its supposed origin during those wars, and it is also sometimes known by the name of 'Grand Master of Light.' This degree is devoted to toleration and freedom of man in the great moral attributes. It inculcates equality—representing the poor Knight equal to the monarch, and exhibits the requisites of Knighthood; protection to the defenseless and innocent; the possession of virtue, patience, and firmness—and represents the Knight as the exponent of truth, and one alike without fear and without reproach. The assembly is called a chapter. Two apartments are required. In the first apartment the hangings are crimson, supported by white columns. During the reception this room represents the court of Saladin, the great Sultan of Egypt and Syria. The second apartment should be a well-furnished room, decorated in the eastern style. The presiding officer is styled Venerable Grand Master. The Knights are all dressed in crimson robes, with a large white cross of St. Andrew on the breast. The jewel is two interlaced triangles, formed by arcs of large circles, with the concave outward, of gold, and enclosing a pair of compasses open to twenty-five degrees. At the bottom, and to one of the points is suspended a St. Andrew's Cross, of gold, surmounted by a Knight's hemlet; on the centre of the cross is the letter ל, inclosed in an equilateral triangle, and this again in a ring formed by a winged serpent; between the two lower arms of the cross may be suspended a key."—Macoy's Encyclopedia and Dictionary of Freemasonry Article Grand Scottish Knight of St. Andrew.

of Ramsay's''' Rite which was introduced about the year 1728, and was called Eccossais, or Scotch Masonry. It is founded on Chivalric Masonry or the Masonry of the Crusades, and gives a history of the events that led to the union of the Chivalric orders with Freemasonry.

The ceremony of reception [initiation] is brief; the instruction full. This grade is preparatory to the Kadosh and was introduced into the Ancient and Accepted rite by Frederick the Great in 1786.

In this degree my brother, you are admitted into the true Eden or dominion of everlasting truth and fraternity. There you learn what perseverance can do, and in the repose of your heart and mind you find the ultimate result of our Master's doctrine, which for so many, is the text of a thousand vain and false theories. It is for that very same result that Freemasonry has been assailed, both by kingly and priestly usurpers, by Atheists and narrow-minded sectarians. This degree my brother, is usually conferred by communication.

Note 398.—"Ramsay, Andrew, Michael. Commonly called the Chevalier Ramsay. He was born at Ayr, in Scotland, June 9, 1668. His father was a baker, but being a possessor of considerable property was enabled to give his son a liberal education. He was accordingly sent to school in his native burgh, and afterwards to the University of Edinburg, where he was distinguished for his abilities and diligence. In 1709 he was intrusted with the education of the two sons of the Earl of Wemyss. Subsequently, becoming unsettled in his religious opinions, he resigned that employment and went to Holland, residing for some time at Leyden. There he became acquainted with Pierre Poiret, one of the most celebrated teachers of the mystic theology which then prevailed on the continent. From him Ramsay learned the principal tenets of that system; and it is not unreasonable to suppose that he was thus indoctrinated with that love of mystical speculation which he subsequently developed as the inventor of Masonic degrees, and as the founder of a Masonic Rite. In 1710 he visited the celebrated Fenelon, Archbishop of Cambray, of whose mystical tendencies he had heard, and met with a cordial reception. The archbishop invited Ramsay to become his guest, and in six months he was converted to the Catholic faith. Fenelon procured for him the preceptorship of the Duc de Chateau-Thierry and the Prince de Turenne. As a reward for his services in that capacity, he was made a knight of the Order of St. Lazarus, whence he received the title of 'Chevalier,' by which he was usually known. He was subsequently selected by James III., the Pretender, as the tutor of his two sons, Charles Edward and Henry, the former of whom became afterwards the Young Pretender, and the latter the Cardinal York. For this purpose he repaired, in 1724, to Rome. But the political and religious intrigues of that court became distasteful to him, and in a short time he obtained permission to return to France. In 1728 he visited England, and became an inmate of the family of the Duke of Argyle."—Mackey's Encyclopedia of Freemasonry, Article Ramsay, Andrew, Michael.

DECORATIONS:—In this degree, the lodge is hung with red tapestry, supported by white columns. The seats of the Master and of the two Wardens are of red cloth with gold fringe; those of the Knights are blue. At each angle of the hall is a Cross of St. Andrew. In front of each cross are four lights in a line, making sixteen lights. The total number of lights in this lodge is eighty-one, viz.: Two on the altar, seven groups of nine and the first sixteen in front of the crosses.

TITLES:—This lodge is styled *Grand Lodge*. The Master is called *Patriarch* and the Knights, *Respectable Masters*.

CLOTHING:—A red robe. Order a scarf of crimson. At the bottom of the scarf is the jewel, fastened by a rosette of dark green, edged with red. When a collar is worn it must be of green, edged with red. The Knights wear a sash of white silk with gold fringe.

JEWEL:—Is a compass within three triangles, and these within a single triangle. Beneath the grand triangle is a reversed square, a poniard in the angle of the square. When a collar is worn, the jewel is a cross of St. Andrew, surmounted by a closed crown. In the centre and on the crosslet is a pineapple or a J.∴ within a triangle in the middle of a ring. To this ring is suspended a key which hangs between the two inferior branches of the cross. At the extremity of the arms of the cross are the initials B.∴J.∴M.∴N.∴

CHAPTER LIV

TWENTY-NINTH DEGREE; KNIGHTS OF ST. ANDREW, OR PATRIARCH OF THE CRUSADES.[29]

INITIATION.

FIRST SIGN; THAT OF EARTH.

Wipe your forehead with the back of the right hand, the head somewhat inclined forward.

First Sign, Knight of St. Andrew.

FIRST TOKEN.

Seize each successively the first, then the second, and lastly the third joint of the other's index finger of the right hand, each spelling alternately the word of the first degree. (Boaz.)

First Token, Knight of St. Andrew.

Note 339.—"Patriarch of the Crusades. One of the names formerly given to the degree of Grand Scottish Knight of St. Andrew, the twenty-ninth of the Ancient and Accepted Scottish Rite. The legend of that degree connects it with the Crusades and hence the name; which, however, is never used officially, and is retained by regular Supreme Councils only as a synonym."—Mackey's Encyclopædia of Freemasonry, Article Patriarch of the Crusades.

2nd Sign, Water.

SECOND SIGN, THAT OF WATER.

Place the right hand upon the heart; extend it horizontally at the height of the breast; let it fall on the right side, as if to salute with the hand.

SECOND TOKEN.

Seize each successively the first, then the second, and lastly the third joint of the other's middle finger, as indicated for the index in the first token, each spelling the sacred word of the second degree, (Shibboleth.) For mode of giving it see page 184, Freemasonry Illustrated.

THIRD SIGN, THAT OF ASTONISHMENT AND HORROR.

Turn the head to the left, looking downwards; raise both hands clasped to heaven, a little towards the right.

Sign of Horror.

FOURTH SIGN, THAT OF FIRE.

Join both hands, the fingers interlaced and cover the eyes therewith, the palms outwards.

Sign of Fire.

ANSWER.

Give the sign of Air. Extend forward the right arm and hand at the height of the shoulder.

Answer to Sign of Fire.

THIRD TOKEN.

Seize each successively the index finger of the other's right hand by the first joint. Each pronounce alternately one of the three syllables of the sacred word of the third degree. (Mah-hah-bone.)

Sign of Admiration.

FIFTH SIGN, THAT OF ADMIRATION.

Raise the eyes and hands to heaven, the left arm somewhat lower than the right, the heel of the left foot slightly raised, so that the left knee forms a square with the right leg.

SIXTH SIGN, THAT OF THE SUN.

Place the thumb of the right hand upon the right eye; raise the index finger so as to form a square, then bring it on a line, as if to indicate an object in view, saying: "I measure the sun itself."

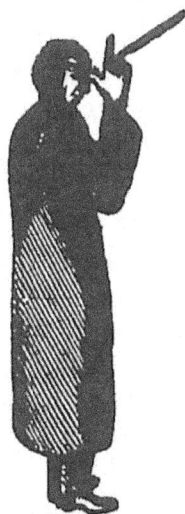

Sign of the Sun.

General Sign, Knight
of St. Andrew.

SEVENTH SIGN ; GENERAL SIGN.

Form, on the breast, a cross of St. Andrew
with the two arms, the hands upwards.

GENERAL TOKEN.

Seize one the last joint of the
index finger of the other's right
hand; the first one says *Ne* the
other *Ka.* Then seize the last
joint of the little finger; the first
one says *Mah,* the other, giving
the whole word, says, *Nekamah.*

General Token, Knight of
St. Andrew.

PASS WORDS.

Ardarel[340] or *Ardriel.*	The Angel of Fire.
Casmaren[341] or	" " " Air.
Talliud or	" " " Water.
Furlac[342] or	" " " Earth.

Note 360.—"Ardarel. A word in the high degrees, used as the name
of the angel of fire. It is a distorted form of Adariel, the splendor
of God."—Mackey's Encyclopædia of Freemasonry, Article Ardarel.

Note 341.—"Casmaran. The angel of air. Referred to in the degree
of Scottish Knight of St. Andrew. The etymology is uncertain."—Mackey's
Encyclopædia of Freemasonry, Article Casmaran.

Note 342.—"Furlac. A word in the high degrees, whose etymology is
uncertain, but probably Arabic. It is said to signify the angel of the
earth."—Mackey's Encyclopædia of Freemasonry, Article Furlac.

SACRED WORD.

Nekamah,''' that of the general token.

MARCH:—Form a cross of Jerusalem, by three steps of an Apprentice, three steps of a Fellow Craft and three steps of a Master.

AGE:—The square of nine; eighty-one years.

BATTERY:—Nine strokes, by two, three and four; 00 000 0000.

TIME TO OPEN:—High twelve.

TO CLOSE:—The beginning of night.

This my brother, ends the twenty-ninth''' degree. You will at once perceive the necessity of erecting a strong wall around our institution and of trusting its guardianship to a certain number of tried and courageous Knights, whose learning and power may at all times defend it against any assault on the part of its enemies, and cause them to tremble on their thrones under their Tiaras in their conventicles and even in the very midst of their revelries. Such will be the duty of our brethren, the Knights of Kadosh, such is the object of the thirtieth degree.

Thrice Puissant Grand Master—To order my brethren! (Candidate rises and puts himself under the general sign of the twenty-ninth degree:)

Note 343.—"Hebrew signifying Vengeance, and, like Nakam, a significant word in the high degrees."—Mackey's Encyclopædia of Freemasonry, Article Nekamah.

Note 344.—"Patriarch of the Crusades, or Knight of St. Andrew. [Scotch Masonry.]—The 11th degree conferred in the consistory of Princes of the Royal Secret. Scotch Masonry, and the 29th upon the catalogue of that system. The assembly is termed a Grand Lodge. The hangings are red. In each corner of the room is a St. Andrew's Cross. The lights are eighty-one. The master is styled Patriarch; the members Respectable Masters. Jewel, a compass within three small triangles, enclosed within a large one, beneath which is a square reversed and a plumb in the angle. When the collar is worn the jewel is a St. Andrew's cross, surmounted by a crown, at the centre of the cross the letter J; on the extremities of the cross the letters B. T. M. N. Hour to open, high twelve; to close, the first hour of the night. Age, 0x0."—Morris's Masonic Dictionary, Article Patriarch of the Crusades. ""-ight of St. Andrew.

Thrice Puissant Grand Master—To the glory of the Grand Architect of the Universe, in the name and under the auspices of the Grand Consistory of Sublime Princes of the Royal Secret, thirty-second degree of the Ancient and Accepted Rite, in and for the Sovereign and Independent State of.........., under the jurisdiction of the Supreme Grand Council of Sovereign Grand Inspectors General of the thirty-third and last degree for the northern jurisdiction of the United States, sitting at New York, State of New York, and by the powers conferred on me by........Council of Kadosh, No..... I do receive and constitute you in all and each of the eleven degrees, the names of which have been to you, and the Philosophy of which has also been briefly explained to you in order that you may receive the degree of Grand Elect Knight Kadosh, for which you have petitioned, and upon the condition that you will swear faithfully to keep the obligations which you have taken in the preceding degrees and which are in the main to love science, to practice virtue, to love your brethren, and to devote yourself to the happiness of mankind, to the best of your knowledge and ability. Do you swear?

Candidate—I do.

Thrice Puissant Grand Master—(Strikes two, three and four; 00 000 0000, with his gavel on his sword, over the head of the candidate.) My brother, I will now leave you to your reflections. In a few moments you will receive the order to appear before the Council. Until then this meeting is called off from labor to refreshment. (The Thrice Puissant Grand Master then withdraws with the other members of the Council, leaving the candidate with the Master of Ceremonies.)

PHILOSOPHICAL ANALYSIS

TWENTY-NINTH DEGREE: KNIGHT OF ST. ANDREW,
OR PATRIARCH OF THE CRUSADES.

Ramsay's Fraud on the French.—Masonic Facts are Falsehoods.

Successful novels are founded on historic truths, and
their writers commonly strive to state those truths accurately. But the novel or novels called Masonry are
founded on falsehoods, intended to pass for truths.
Ramsay (See *Introductionol, V. 1*) as *Professor Robison,* who was familiar with the lodges on the Continent,
states: intended to deceive the French, who thought
the London Tavern degrees too coarse, into the belief
that the first Masons were Crusaders, knights, nobles,
kings, princes and Troubadours. And, although as
Cervantes, in his inimitable, and faithful burlesque,
Don Quixote, has shown, those pretenders called
knights, took for their lady loves such low wenches
as they could pick up at the East Cheap inns, which
Sir Knight *Jack Falstaff* haunted, and though the
Church of *St. Sophia,* Constantinople, was turned into
a huge brothel, by the thousands of Crusaders, who
slept there on the graves of dead Christians, while on
their way to Palestine to rescue the tomb of Christ;
(which Turks still hold). In the face of this general
demoralization of all Europe, when

> "Gaily the Troubadour
> Touched his guitar;
> While he was hastening
> Home from the war."

In the face of these orgies of hell, in the name of
religion; this Scotch falsifier and apostate, Ramsay, followed by Jesuits and Jews, has given us the Templar
Masonry of to-day, with its caps, gauntlets, plumes and
swords, for which industry and Christianity pay the

bills.

We need not requote *Macoy*, (*Cyc. p. 343-4*) who says: "The degrees of this (Scottish) Rite are for the most part elaborated from the system invented by Ramsay, who claimed that he found them in Scotland, where they were planted by Knights of the Temple and of Malta on their return from Palestine. *It is needless to say that these pretensions have no foundation in truth.* Mackey confirms this testimony of *Macoy;* and no Masonic authority dissents from it. And yet Masonry founded on this wholesale, fundamental lying, which equals, if not exceeds that of Mahomet, and the Mormon, is received with open doors by churches called Christian, in the United States of America. The pretended origin in Palestine, furnishes these locusts, originally derived from Egypt, a pretext to pollute the Bible, by their sham legends, to make shallow inventions seem sacred, while they destroy the sacredness of truth.

Mackey, in one place attempts to justify this falsehood. He justifies the Master Masons degree, in saying there were three doors of the temple, when in truth there was but one; by saying it is "symbol," and does "not pretend to historic accuracy." But Masonry does give this stuff for fact, and thousands today believe it! He says: "it is all only symbol, as a lion is a symbol of courage." But suppose there is no lion there; that the promised lion proves only an opossum, porcupine, or skunk?

This is precisely this case. Masonry pretends to be legend, based on facts. But the facts are not facts, but falsehoods. The temple had but one door. Masonry says there were three. Masonry sprung from a London grog-shop; it claims to come from Palestine. It literally "makes lies its refuge," and "hides under falsehood," as did the false religionists in the days of Isaiah. (*28, 15.*) But the hail shall sweep away both the refuge, and them that make it. (*Isaiah, 28, 17.*)

CHAPTER LV

THIRTIETH DEGREE; GRAND ELECT KNIGHT KADOSH[340]
OR KNIGHT OF THE WHITE AND BLACK EAGLE.

TITLES:—In the first two apartments, which are intended only as preparation rooms, the lodge is styled Council. In the third apartment it is called Areopagus, and in the fourth Senate. The President is styled Thrice Puissant Grand Master. The two Wardens, First and Second Lieutenant Grand Masters. The members are called Knights.

STATED MEETINGS:—The stated meetings of all Councils of Kadosh are held on the sixth of January, on Good Friday, or the day of Ascension, and on the second of November in each year. Five Knights Kadosh form a quorum for the dispatch of business.

BANQUETS:—The banquets of the Knights Kadosh are called Agapae, which name indicates that the object is to draw closer the bonds of fraternal love. The word means Love Feast.

CLOTHING:—Not only is the costume in this degree not ridiculously absurd, as in almost all the other degrees,

Note 345.—"As to the history of the Kadosh degree, it is said to have been first invented at Lyons, in France, in 1743, where it appeared under the name of the Petit Elu. This degree, which is said to have been based upon the Templar doctrine heretofore referred to, was afterwards developed into the Kadosh, which we find in 1758 incorporated as the Grand Elect Kadosh into the system of the Council of Emperors of the East and West, which was that year formed at Paris, whence it descended to the Scottish Rite Masons.

Of all the Kadoshes, two only are now important, viz.: the Philosophic Kadosh, which has been adopted by the Grand Orient of France, and the Knight Kadosh, which constitutes the thirtieth degree of the Ancient and Accepted Scottish Rite, this latter being the most generally diffused of the Kadoshes."—Mackey's Encyclopædia of Freemasonry, Article Kadosh.

but besides, it gives to the assembly a grave and impos-
ing aspect. However, as it must be rich and elegant,
and is consequently very costly, it would perhaps be
wiser to wear a black suit of clothes with white gloves,
a black sash with silver fringe and a sword. In this
case the Knights wear a round black hat, a Teutonic
Cross on the heart and a ribbon of the degree from the
left shoulder to the right hip; the poniard suspended
from the end of the ribbon. The officers alone wear
collars with the jewel. On the front of the ribbon are
embroidered in red, two Teutonic crosses, a double
headed eagle and the letters K.∴K.∴H.∴ [Knights Ka-
dosh] embroidered in silver.

In some Councils all the members wear a collar with
the jewel. The collar is black, with a Teutonic cross
embroidered in red on both sides. The ribbon and
collar are edged with silver. The jewel is a Teutonic
cross, enameled with red, in the centre of which are the
three initial letters J.∴B.∴M.∴ On the reverse of the
cross is a death's head, transpierced by a poniard. The
regular costume of the Knights Kadosh is as follows:

A white tunic in the shape of a dalmatic, bordered
with black; on the breast a red Latin cross, a mantle of
black velvet, edged with red, and on the left side another
red Latin cross, a large brimmed black hat with a red
plume, a Knight's tucker with points, a black belt with
a golden buckle, on which are engraved the initials J.∴
B.∴M.∴ tight pantaloons of white cassimere, yellow
morocco boots with a golden spur on the left heel. A
sword with a straight silver guard hangs from the belt
and the poniard from the ribbon. As already stated,
when collars are worn, the poniard is fastened in the
sash, which in this case is red. No apron.

HONORS:—In an inferior body of the Scotch Rite, a

Knight Kadosh visitor shall be received by a deputation of five knights and five swords. But previous to his admission as such, and in order to ascertain whether he is regularly possessed of the thirtieth degree, the following ceremony takes place, provided there are Knights Kadosh present at the time of his visit:

All those who are not possessed of the 30th degree are requested to withdraw. Incense is then burnt. The visitor is introduced and all the Knights surround him, forming over his head the arch of steel, with the sword that they hold in the left hand, while holding in the right a poniard, which they point at the visitor's heart. thereby indicating that they are ready to strike him if he is not really possessed of this degree. The member of the body who possesses the highest dignity then propounds to him the questions which are to be found at the opening of the Council. After he has answered he is requested to give the words, signs and tokens. After which he is seated near the throne, and all the members of the body wherein this ceremony takes place are recalled.

The debates in a Council of Kadosh must be calm and dignified. Harsh words and offensive personalities are strictly forbidden. The Thrice Puissant Grand Master has the privilege, by striking *once* with the pommel of his sword to restore peace; by striking *twice* to impose silence, and by striking *thrice* to close the debate and adjourn the debate to another meeting.

STANDARDS OF THE KNIGHTS KADOSH:—There are two standards of the order. The first is a piece of white silk three and a half feet square with a golden fringe. On the upper part the words, *Dieu Le Veut*"" are embroidered in gold.   In the centre and below these

Note 346.—Dieu le Veut. God wills it. The war-cry of the old Crusaders. and hence adopted as a motto in the degrees of Templarism." Mackay's Encyclopedia of Freemasonry, Article Dieu le Veut.

words is a Teutonic cross, embroidered in gold and red with the number "30" in the middle of the cross . Below and at the extremity of the standard are the words *Ardoab Chao*''' also embroidered in gold. The second is a piece of black silk of the same dimensions as the first standard with silver fringe.

All the embroideries must be of silver. The words *Vincere aut Mori* are embroidered diagonally from the upper corner on the left, to the lower corner on the right. In the upper right corner is a red Teutonic cross; in the lower left corner is an uncrowned double headed eagle with wings open but not spread, and holding a sword in his claws.

OFFICERS OF A COUNCIL OF KADOSH.

Thrice Puissant Grand Master.
First Lieutenant Grand Master.
Second Lieutenant Grand Master.
Orator or Knight of Eloquence.
Chancellor.
Treasurer.
Grand Marshall or Introductor.
Knight Expert.
Master of Ceremonies:
Captain of the Guards.
Tyler.

Note 347.—"Ordo ab Chao. Order out of Chaos. A motto of the 33d degree, and having the same allusion as lux e tenebris, which see. The invention of this motto is to be attributed to the Supreme Council of the Ancient and Accepted Scottish Rite at Charleston, and it is first met with in the Patent of Count de Grasse, dated February 1, 1802. When De Grasse afterwards carried the Rite over to France and established a Supreme Council there, he changed the motto, and, according to Lenning, Ordo ab hoe, was used by him and his Council in all the documents issued by them. If so, it was simply a blunder."—Mackey's Encyclopedia of Freemasonry, Article Ordo ab Chao.

OPENING CEREMONIES

GRAND ELECT KNIGHT KADOSH.[*]

Thrice Puissant Grand Master—(One rap with pommel of sword.) Sir Knight, First Lieutenant Grand Master, are you a Knight Kadosh?

First Lieutenant Grand Master—I am, Thrice Puissant Grand Master.

Thrice Puissant Grand Master—At what hour does the Council open?

First Lieutenant Grand Master—At the beginning of night.

Thrice Puissant Grand Master—What is your age?

First Lieutenant Grand Master—A century and more.

Thrice Puissant Grand Master—Whom do you know?

First Lieutenant Grand Master—Two wretches.

Thrice Puissant Grand Master—Their names?

Note 349.—"Knight Kadosh, or Knight of the White and Black Eagle. The 30th degree of the Ancient and Accepted rite. There are several degrees known as Kadoshes. The French rituals mention seven: 1. That of the Hebrews. 2. That of the first Christians. 3. That of the Crusades. 4. That of the Templars. 5. That of Cromwell, or the Puritans. 6. That of the Jesuits. 7. The Grand Veritable Kadosh, 'apart from every sect, free of all ambition, which opens its arms to all men, and has no enemies other than vice, crime, fanaticism, and superstition.' Its ritual furnishes the history of the destruction of the Templars by the united efforts of Philip of France and Pope Clement V. In this degree, when there is a reception, four apartments are used. In the first and second apartments, the Lodge is termed Council; in the third, Areopagus; in the fourth, the Senate. The presiding officer is styled Most Illustrious Grand Commander. The jewel is a Teutonic cross, and is thus described, in heraldic language: 'A cross potent sable, charged with another cross double potent, or, surcharged with an escutcheon, bearing the letters J. B. M.; the principal cross surmounted by a chief, azure seme of France.' On the reverse, a skull transpierced by a poniard. The stated meetings of all councils of Kadosh are held January 6; on Good Friday; on Ascension day, and on November the 2. in each year. No one of these is ever, on any account, to be omitted."—Macoy's Encyclopædia and Dictionary of Freemasonry, Article Knight Kadosh.

First Lieutenant Grand Master—Philip[249] IV, King of France, called the Fair, and Bertrand de Goth, known as Clement the Fifth, Pope of Rome.

Thrice Puissant Grand Master—What is the object of our assembling?

First Lieutenant Grand Master—The hope of punishing crime.

Thrice Puissant Grand Master—Such being the case, as the darkness of night protects our labors and as we entertain the hope of punishing crime, Sir Knights, First and Second Lieutenant Grand Masters, request the officers and Sir Knights on your respective valleys to be ready to obey my order.

First Lieutenant Grand Master—Officers and Sir Knights on my valley, the Thrice Puissant Grand Master requests you to be ready to obey his orders.

First Lieutenant Grand Master—Thrice Puissant Grand Master, the Knights are all ready to obey your orders.

Thrice Puissant Grand Master—(One rap with the pommel of sword, rising.) Sir Knights, order! (All rise and place themselves under the sign of Order.) To the glory of the Grand Architect of the Universe, in the name and under the auspices of the Grand Consistory of the Ancient and Accepted Rite, in and for the Sovereign and Independent State of........under the jurisdiction of the Supreme Council for the northern jurisdiction of the United States of America, and by virtue of the authority conferred upon me by....Council of Kadosh, No... I declare and pronounce its labors opened. Join

Note 249.—'Philip IV. Surnamed 'le Bel.' or 'the Fair,' who ascended the throne of France in 1285. He is principally distinguished in history on account of his persecution of the Knights Templars. With the aid of his willing instrument, Pope Clement V., he succeeded in accomplishing the overthrow of the Order. He died in 1314, execrated by his subjects, whose hearts he had alienated by the cruelty, avarice and despotism of his administration.''—Mackey's Encyclopædia of Freemasonry, Article Philip IV.

me Sir Knights?

Thrice Puissant Grand Master—(Giving the sign. All join and give both the sign and word.)

Thrice Puissant Grand Master—(Giving the battery; 00 00 00 0.) *Spes mea in Deo est.*[110] (All do the same, and at the same time.)

Thrice Puissant Grand Master—Be seated Sir Knights. Sir Knight Chancellor, is the baluster of our last sitting prepared?

Sir Knight Chancellor—It is, Thrice Puissant.

Thrice Puissant Grand Master—Please read it. (Chancellor reads it.)

Thrice Puissant Grand Master—Sir Knights, First and Second Lieutenant Grand Masters, request the officers and Sir Knights on your respective valleys, to make their observations if any they have, on the baluster of our last sitting.

First Lieutenant Grand Master—Officers and Sir Knights on my valley, the Thrice Puissant Grand Master requests you to make your observations if any you have, on the baluster of our last sitting.

Second Lieutenant Grand Master—Officers and Sir Knights on my valley, the Thrice Puissant Grand Master requests you to make your observations if any you have, on the baluster of our last sitting.

Second Lieutenant Grand Master—Sir Knight, First Lieutenant Grand Master, silence prevails in my valley.

First Lieutenant Grand Master—Thrice Puissant Grand Master, silence prevails.

Thrice Puissant Grand Master—The baluster of our last sitting is approved and adopted. Sir Knight Master of Ceremonies, please have it signed by the officers. (The Master of Ceremonies then takes the minute book

Note 350.—"Spes mea in Deo est. (My hope is in God.) The motto of the thirty-second degree of the Ancient and Accepted Scottish Rite."—Mackey's Encyclopedia of Freemasonry, Article Spes mea in Deo est.

from the Chancellor and carries it successively to the Thrice Puissant Grand Master, the First and Second Lieutenant Grand Masters, and to the Orator. All sign their names, after which the Master of Ceremonies brings back the book to the Chancellor and resumes his seat.)

Thrice Puissant Grand Master—Sir Knight Master of Ceremonies, please ascertain whether there are any Sir Knight visitors in the avenues. (Master of Ceremonies then leaves the Council and visits the avenues, after which he knocks at the door; 00 00 00 0.)

Captain of Guard—(Seven raps; 00 00 00 0.) Sir Knight Second Lieutenant Grand Master, there is an alarm at the door of our Council.

Second Lieutenant Grand Master—Sir Knight First Lieutenant Grand Master, there is an alarm at the door of our Council.

First Lieutenant Grand Master—Thrice Puissant Grand Master, there is an alarm at the door of our Council.

Thrice Puissant Grand Master—Sir Knight First Lieutenant Grand Master, ascertain the cause of it and report accordingly.

First Lieutenant Grand Master—Sir Knight Second Lieutenant Grand Master, ascertain the cause of it and report accordingly.

Second Lieutenant Grand Master—Sir Knight Captain of the Guards, ascertain the cause of it and report accordingly.

Captain of Guard—(Opening the door a little.) Who knocks?

Master of Ceremonies—(From without.) Master of Ceremonies.

Captain of Guard—Sir Knight Second Lieutenant Grand Master, it is the Master of Ceremonies.

Second Lieutenant Grand Master—Sir Knight First Lieutenant Grand Master, it is the Master of Ceremonies.

First Lieutenant Grand Master—Thrice Puissant Grand Master, the alarm is caused by the Master of Ceremonies who asks admission.

Thrice Puissant Grand Master—Sir Knight First Lieutenant Grand Master, permit him to enter.

First Lieutenant Grand Master—Sir Knight Second Lieutenant Grand Master, permit him to enter.

Second Lieutenant Grand Master—Sir Knight Captain of the Guards, permit him to enter. [Captain of the Guards then opens the door and admits the Master of Ceremonies.

Master of Ceremonies—Thrice Puissant Grand Master, there are, (or there are not,) visitors in the avenues.]

Thrice Puissant Grand Master—(If there are visitors) Sir Knight, have you convinced yourself that these visitors are regular Knights Kadosh?

Master of Ceremonies—I have, Thrice Puissant Grand Master.

Thrice Puissant Grand Master—Such being the case, introduce them. (Master of Ceremonies retires and soon after knocks seven; 00 00 00 0, at the door of the Council.)

Captain of Guard—(Knocks seven; 00 00 00 0.) Sir Knight Second Lieutenant Grand Master, there is an alarm at the door of the Council.

Second Lieutenant Grand Master—Sir Knight First Lieutenant Grand Master, there is an alarm at the door of the Council.

First Lieutenant Grand Master—Thrice Puissant Grand Master, there is an alarm at the door of the Council.

Thrice Puissant Grand Master—Sir Knight First Lieutenant Grand Master, ascertain the cause of it and report accordingly.

First Lieutenant Grand Master—Sir Knight Second Lieutenant Grand Master, ascertain the cause of it and report accordingly.

Second Lieutenant Grand Master—Sir Knight Captain of the Guards ascertain the cause of it and report accordingly.

Captain of Guard—(Opening the door a little.) Who knocks?

Master of Ceremonies—Master of Ceremonies with the Knights visitors.

Second Lieutenant Grand Master—Sir Knight First Lieutenant Grand Master, it is the Master of Ceremonies with the Knights visitors.

First Lieutenant Grand Master—Thrice Puissant Grand Master, it is the Master of Ceremonies, with the Knights visitors.

Thrice Puissant Grand Master—(Rising.) Open the door and introduce our brethren. Order Sir Knights! (All rise and place themselves under the sign of "order.")

Master of Ceremonies—(Enters with visitors.)

Thrice Puissant Grand Master—I have the honor to introduce to you the Knights visitors. (On entering, the visitors salute the Thrice Puissant Grand Master, and the First and Second Lieutenant Grand Masters by making the sign, after which they face the East, awaiting the orders of the Thrice Puissant Grand Master.)

Thrice Puissant Grand Master—Sir Knights, we are most happy to receive you this evening and to offer you the hospitality of our Council. Your assistance at this juncture is invaluable, as we have crimes to punish and innocence to protect. Persecution and oppression are raging. The religious and political rulers of the world will not render that justice which they have sworn to render, and we cannot endure their encroachments any longer. In order to live up to the oath we have taken, and to carry out more effectually the plans adopted by the chiefs of the order for the triumph of Liberty, Equality and Fraternity, we have resolved to admit into our Council a few tried and experienced Grand Scotch Knights of St. Andrew, so as to be able by our numbers to secure, without the shedding of a drop of blood, the rights of Gods children, and thereby to fufil the teachings of our beloved Thrice Puissant Grand Master.

Thrice Puissant Grand Master—Join me, Sir Knights!

Thrice Puissant Grand Master—(Strikes seven; 00 00 00 0, with his hands.) All do the same at the same time! (The visitors during this address, remain under the sign of order. But when it is ended, may return thanks and decline repeating the battery, through respect for the Council and the Thrice Puissant Grand Master. Before resuming their seats the Thrice Puissant Grand Master orders the Master of Ceremonies to conduct to the East any Sovereign Grand Inspector General, and the members of the Grand Consistory, if any among the visitors, provided said Sovereign Grand Inspector General and Sublime Princes wear the regalia of their respective degrees. All brethren above the 30th, if clothed accordingly, must be introduced; the members of each degree separately and successively, beginning by the inferior degree up to the highest. In such circumstances, the address of the Thrice Puissant Grand Master is delivered only when all the visitors of the several degrees have been introduced, after which:)

Thrice Puissant Grand Master--Be seated Sir Knights.

Grand Chancellor then presents the Thrice Puissant Grand Master with the "ORDER OF THE DAY."

Which is attended to in the usual manner. At this point the Council shall proceed at once with the business on hand. But in case of reception [initiation] said business may be postponed until after the ceremony.

Then petitions for the eleven intermediate degrees are considered and the brethren state their objections if they have any against the candidate or candidates. If any objection it shall be disposed of previous to the communication. If there is no objection, the Thrice Puissant Grand Master, officers and members of the Council shall proceed into an adjoining room, in order to communicate the intermediate degrees.

CHAPTER LVI

Thirtieth Degree; Grand Elect Knight Kadosh,[**]
or Knight of the White and Black Eagle.

INITIATION.

FIRST APARTMENT:—This apartment is hung with black tapestry. A sepulchral lamp is suspended from the vault. In the middle is a mausoleum, above which is a coffin. In the coffin lies a Knight, wrapped up in a white shroud, his face veiled. On the platform of the mausoleum are three skulls. The middle one, wreathed with laurel and everlasting flowers, rests on a black cushion, the one on the left is surmounted by a Pope's triple crown and the one on the right by a regal crown adorned with flowers-de-luce, but open, as those of the middle ages.

At the west end of the apartment is a large transparency on which are written in flame-colored letters the following words:

"Whoever shall overcome the dread of death, shall emerge from the bosom of the earth, and have a right to be initiated into the greater mysteries."

Beneath are the initials J∴ B∴ M∴

N. B.—The description we here give of each apartment of this degree is that of the real Kadosh.

Note 351.—"The twelfth degree conferred in the consistory of Princes of the Royal Secret, Scotch Rite, and the thirtieth in the catalogue of that system. The historical allusions are to the ancient order of Knights Templar and its downfall. There are five apartments. The officers are Illustrious Grand Commander representing Frederick II. of Prussia, Grand Chancellor, Grand Architect, Grand Master of Ceremonies, Grand Treasurer, Grand Secretary, Grand Captain of the Guards and Expert Brother. There are three banners, the last representing the Beauseant Jewel, a double headed black eagle with gold beaks and claws, holding a golden sword. Hour to open, the hour of secrecy and silence."—Morris's Masonic Dictionary, Article Elected Knight of Kadosh; or, Knight of the White and Black Eagle.

MUSIC.

When all is ready, the Thrice Puissant Grand Master sends a messenger to the Grand Marshal to inform him thereof. The candidate is then introduced with his eyes uncovered. He wears a gray tunic and carries on his right side a poniard suspended from the sword belt with which he has been girded. The Thrice Puissant Grand Master, with his hat over his eyes, makes him sit on a stool opposite the mausoleum. [Music stops.]

Thrice Puissant Grand Master—To candidate. You must not leave that seat, otherwise the greatest dangers await you.

MUSIC.

A few moments after, he points to the three skulls. [Music stops.]

Thrice Puissant Grand Master—I request you to reflect upon the scene before you.

MUSIC.

Another pause for a few minutes. [Music stops.]

Thrice Puissant Grand Master—My brother, these objects conceal a great mystery. Are you prepared to undergo the trials which await you? They are fearful, but there is nothing in them to alarm you if you have understood the degrees through which you have successively passed. I warn you moreover, that you will have to answer very serious questions, and must advise you to confine yourself in all your answers to these words only, "I wish to proceed." You must collect all the powers of your mind, for on yourself alone you will have to depend.

MUSIC.

[Thrice Puissant Grand Master, then retires slowly, leaving candidate for a long time of silence and reflection, when the music stops and the Knight in the coffin raises the lid thereof, sits up and says with a grave and solemn voice.]

Knight in Coffin—Thou who comest hither to disturb my rest fear my wrath. What is thy wish?

Candidate—I wish to procced.

Knight in Coffin—May thy rashness receive its reward. If thy heart is not pure, thy ruin is certain.

Candidate—I wish to proceed.

MUSIC.

[After these words a great noise is heard from without. The door is thrown open with a fearful crash. The Knight in the coffin resumes his position. Thrice Puissant Grand Master enters the room hurriedly with a burning torch in his left hand and a dirk raised in his right. The music stops. He walks up to the candidate and says to him in a threatening voice:]

Thrice Puissant Grand Master—Since your wish is to proceed; since your rashness prompts you to dare the wrath in store for so many centuries, follow me.

Thrice Puissant Grand Master—Walking up majestically to the mausoleum and kneeling before the skull wreathed with the laurel.) Kneel down with me!

Thrice Puissant Grand Master—Hitherto you have seen in masonry nothing but emblems and symbols. Now you must see in it nothing but reality. Are you determined to repudiate all prejudices and to obey, without reserve all that you will be commanded to do for the good of humanity?

Candidate—Most willingly.

Thrice Puissant Grand Master—(Rising) such being the case, I will afford you the means of proving the sincerity of your intentions and the extent of your knowledge. Bend before these illustrious remains and repeat the words of the oath which I will dictate to you. (Thrice Puissant Grand Master, poniard in hand, dictates the following oath which is repeated by the candidate.)

FIRST OATH, KNIGHT KADOSH.

In the presence of God, our Father, and of this noble victim, I.......solemnly promise and swear upon my word of honor, never to reveal the mysteries of the Knights Kadosh, and to obey all the rules and regulations of the order.

I further promise and swear to punish crime and protect innocence.

Thrice Puissant Grand Master—Rise and imitate me. (He then stabs the skull crowned with a Tiara and says:)

Down with imposture, down with crime. (Candidate does the same, repeating the same words, Thrice Puissant Grand Master then passes with the candidate to the skull wreathed with laurel, and kneeling down with him says:)

Candidate Stabbing the Skulls.

"Everlasting glory to the immortal martyr of virtue." May his death be a lesson to us. Let us unite to crush tyranny and imposture.

Thrice Puissant Grand Master—(Rises, orders the candidate to do the same, and passing on to the skull surmounted with a regal crown, he stabs it, saying:)

"Down with tyranny! Down with crime!" (Candidate repeats both the acts and the words.)

Thrice Puissant Grand Master—My brother, you will now read aloud the inscription on the transparency. (Candidate reads as follows:)

"Whoever shall overcome the dread of death, shall emerge from the bosom of the earth, and have a right to be initiated into the greater mysteries."

Thrice Puissant Grand Master—(With a solemn and melancholy voice.) It is not yet too late; reflect on the importance of your obligation and on the dreadful consequences which perjury might bring upon your head. Nothing could save you from the punishment which we would have full right to inflict. As already stated, we have no more to do with symbols of more or less significance, it is truth; it is reality we have now before us. Our statutes are dreadful! We demand of you nothing contrary to the laws of honor. But if you have discovered the object we have in view; if you have an idea of the end at which we aim, you will easily understand the importance of secrecy. You are now bound by your word of honor, and you may still retire. But one step more, and you are bound to us forever and at the peril of your life. (After a little silence.)

Thrice Puissant Grand Master—What have you decided?

Candidate—To proceed.

MUSIC.

['Thrice Puissant Grand Master's, torch is extinguished and the door is opened with great force.

Grand Marshal—(With his hat over his eyes; walks in with his sword erect and seizes the candidate by the arm.) *"Your rashness is great! You wish to proceed? Your doom is sealed!—Punishment awaits you!* (He hurries him into the second apartment, when the music stops.)

SECOND APARTMENT:—This apartment is hung with blue tapestry. At the end of the hall there are two altars. On one burns spirits of wine and perfumes on the other. This apartment receives its only light from the small pans in which burns spirits of wine. The President is here called Grand Pontiff. He is clothed in a long white robe, wears a long white beard and his face is veiled. On his head is a crown of oak leaves. He is standing and holds a vase and a shell-formed silver spoon wherewith to take the perfumes.

Grand Pontiff—(To marshal with candidate; in a calm and composed voice.) What does that man wish?

Grand Marshal—He is a Grand Scotch Knight of St. Andrew, of Scotland, who, after overcoming the terrors of death, goes in quest of truth.

Grand Pontiff—(To Grand Marshal.) You know Sir Knight the importance and holiness of our mysteries. Do you vouch for the discretion of this candidate?

Grand Marshal—Grand Pontiff, you may judge by the words he will pronounce with me. (Grand Marshal and candidate both pronounce aloud the word Nekamah.)

Grand Pontiff—Since the candidate submits to the fearful sentences of the tribunal of the Free Judges; since he is determined to go in search of truth, I will grant his request.

MUSIC.

Knight of Eloquence—(From his concealment behind the drapery in a grave tone.) All things whatsoever ye would that men should do unto you, do ye even so to them.

Do not unto another, what ye would not should be done unto you.

Worship the Supreme Being.

Help the destitute.

Be sincere and shun falsehood.

Be patient and bear the faults of your brethren.

Keep your engagements faithfully and remember that one of the chief virtues of a true philosopher is discretion.

Suffer with resignation the slings and arrows of outrageous fortune.

Love your brethren Kadosh as yourself.

Such are the duties of a philosopher, of a true Knight Kadosh. (Music stops, and Knight of Eloquence retires.)

Grand Pontiff—(To candidate.) You have already been informed that among the Knights Kadosh truth and reality take the place of symbols, and even now your sagacity will partly raise the curtain which cannot be entirely removed until you have sustained new trials. In all the preceding degrees you must have observed that the object of Scotch Masonry is to overthrow all kinds of superstition, and that by admitting in her bosom on the terms of the strictest equality, the members of all religions, of all creeds and of all countries, without any distinction whatever, she has, and indeed can have, but one single object and that is to restore to the Grand Architect of the Universe; to the common father of the human race those who are lost in the maze of impostures, invented for the sole purpose of enslaving them. The Knights Kadosh recognize no particular religion, and for that reason we demand of you nothing more than to worship God. And whatever may be the religious forms imposed upon you by superstition at a period of your life when you were incapable of discerning truth from falsehood, we do not even require you to relinquish them. Time and study alone can enlighten you. But remember that you will never be a true mason unless you repudiate forever all superstitions and prejudices.

However, until then, you will own that we have required of you nothing more than to acknowledge with us the sole, the only certain and undoubted point admitted as such by all the human race without exception. We mean the existence of a first great cause, whom we call God Almighty. Repeat then with me the usual oath of all who wish to proceed further and kneel before the altar of truth. (Candidate kneels.)

SECOND OATH, KNIGHT KADOSH.

I........solemnly and sincerely promise and swear wholly to devote myself to the emancipation of humanity; to practice toleration, in political and religious matters especially, toward all men. To strive unceasingly for the happiness of my fellow beings; for the propagation of light and for the overthrow of superstition, fanaticism, imposture and intolerance.

I furthermore solemnly promise and swear to help my brethren, even at the peril of my life, if they should be persecuted for their religion, for the holy cause of liberty, or as members of the higher masonic bodies. So help me God.

Grand Pontiff—(Having raised candidate and handed him the spoon.) My brother, you will now throw incense in the fire burning on the altar of perfumes. (Candidate obeys.)

Grand Pontiff—Almighty Father, Holy and Merciful. Oh! Thou, of whom we are the beloved children. accept this incense which we offer thee with our hearts, as a token of love and reverence. May thy kingdom come at last, and with it the end of all fanaticism, intolerance, imposture and superstition. Amen.

Grand Pontiff—And now my brother, proceed with courage on the journey which you have so rashly undertaken.

MUSIC.

(Candidate takes the hand of the Grand Pontiff, bows to him, then follows the Grand Marshal who conducts him to the door of the Areopagus or third apartment, whereat he knocks as a Grand Scotch Knight of St. Andrew of Scotland; 00 000 0000 After Knocking, the Grand Marshal leaves the candidate in charge of a Knight and proceeds to his post in the Areopagus.)

THIRD APARTMENT:—This apartment is styled Areopagus:*** It is hung with black tapestry, strewed with red flames. The banner of the Elect hangs over the head of the President, whose throne is on a platform seven steps high. The President is called Sovereign Grand Judge. He is clothed in a long trailing robe. In his hand is a long white rod. His face is concealed by a black hood. He wears a red collar without embroidery, at the end of which hangs a medallion bearing the number 1. Before the Sovereign Judge is an altar on which is a balance, a sword and three black candlesticks with three branches each. In each branch burns a candle of yellow wax.

The Areopagus is composed of seven members; never more. They are called Free Judges and are placed in a circle on the right and left of the Sovereign Grand Judge. Before each Free Judge is a triangular table,

Note 852.—"Areopagus. The third apartment in a Council of Kadosh is so called. It represents a tribunal, and the name is derived from the celebrated court of Athens."—Mackey's Encyclopædia of Freemasonry, Article Areopagus.

on which is a black candle stick with three branches. In each branch burns a candle of yellow wax.

The first and second Free Judges, together with the others members of the Areopagus wear a black robe. A black hood covers their faces. Each holds a long white rod.

Like the President, they have around their necks a red collar, without embroidery, at the end of which hangs also a medallion on which is engraved the respective number of each.

The Grand Marshal is here called the Grand Provost of Justice. He wears a black dalmatic, a hemlet with a visor, a sword and a poniard. He stands at the door of the Areopagus. The candidate wears a black veil.

Sovereign Grand Judge—(In answer to knocks on door.) Who knocks?

Grand Provost of Justice—A Grand Scotch Knight of St. Andrew of Scotland who wishes to proceed further and who, relying on the mercy of this dreaded tribunal, dares to ask admittance among the Knights Kadosh. His name is .... [give the name of the candidate] and hitherto his brethren have found no fault in him.

Sovereign Grand Judge—Permit him to enter. (The Grand Provost of Justice then opens the door and takes hold of the candidate.)

Sovereign Grand Judge—Grand Provost of Justice, is this man so rash as to dare the rigor of our tribunal? Is he so sure of the purity of his intentions, of his love for mankind, of his hatred for imposture, intolerance, fanaticism and superstition? Or have you neglected to inform him that he is now in the presence of those terrible Free Judges, whose unflinching justice has caused the most powerful to tremble?

Grand Provost of Justice—Sovereign Grand Judge,

the awe which the very name of this august tribunal causes among men has prompted me to conceal its rigorous duties from the candidate. But knowing his liberal opinions; having received the oath which he took on the holiest remains, and placing entire confidence in him after the reprobation with which I have seen him brand powerful, but infamous wretches I thought that I was justified in bringing him before his judges. (The Grand Provost of Justice then causes the candidate to kneel and extend his hand as if to take an oath.)

Sovereign Grand Judge—Now let him hear with due respect the sentence we have to pass upon him.

Sovereign Grand Judge—First and Second Free Judges proceed in silence to collect the votes. You are aware that one single negative vote is sufficient for exclusion. Let no favor or partiality have influence over you. (The first and second Free Judges proceed in silence to collect the votes, after which they make their report in a low voice to the Sovereign Grand Judge.)

Sovereign Grand Judge--Free Judges, one of you have voted in the negative and it is his wish to submit his reasons to the Areopagus. Let him state his objections.

A Free Judge—(Rising.) I have voted in the negative Sovereign Grand Judge. I have good reasons to believe, nay I know, that the candidate entertains anti-masonic opinions; that is to say, intolerant and sectarian principles, not only in religious but also in masonic matters. I know that his notions of politics and government are far from being liberal and it is now plain to me that the rapid progress he has made in the Masonic Hierarchy is owing merely to the unwise indulgence and weakness of his brethren. He knows nothing of our sublime institution and he would almost tax us with absurdity. I therefore request that he be commanded and enjoined to lay before us in writing, and over his own signature, his profession of faith, on masonic, religious and political matters.

All Free Judges—We concur with our colleague.

Sovereign Grand Judge—(To candidate.) You have heard the decision of the Areopagus. We must have your profession of faith, on masonic, political and religious matters before giving a decision on the fearful accusations brought against you. (Rise and obey.)

Sovereign Grand Judge—Grand Provost of Justice, do your duty.

MUSIC.

(The Grand Provost of Justice covers the head of the candidate and retires with him. When out of the Areopagus, the Grand Provost of Justice receives from the candidate the required profession of faith, whereupon the Grand Provost of Justice after leaving the candidate in charge of a Knight, returns to the Areopagus and delivers the profession of faith to the Sovereign Grand Judge, when the music stops and the Sovereign Grand Judge reads aloud the profession of faith.)

Sovereign Grand Judge—Free Judges, now that you have heard the profession of faith of the candidate, are you satisfied and do you deem him worthy of proceding further?

All Free Judges—Unanimously. Yes.

Sovereign Grand Judge—Grand Provost of Justice, introduce the candidate. (Order is executed.)

Sovereign Grand Judge—The profession of faith which you have submitted to this tribunal, is the only defence which you could oppose to the accusations brought against you. Whatever might have been your opinions, we have no right to doubt your good faith. This profession which you have written and signed with your own hand will remain forever in our archives. We believe it to be sincere, for we hold you to be a man of honor. These reasons, together with the fortitude which you have shown in the first trials of this illustrious degree, have prompted this Areopagus to allow you to proceed. But remember that this tribunal shows no mercy to traitors and perjurers and that it visits them with the severest punishment. Approach! You must take another oath. Kneel down and repeat with me. (Candidate kneels down.)

THIRD OATH, KNIGHT KADOSH.

[During the taking of this oath the Grand Provost of Justice holds the point of his sword to the heart of the candidate.]

I.......of my own free will and accord, do hereby solemnly and sincerely promise and swear to keep faithfully the secrets of the Sublime degree of Knight Kadosh and strictly to obey the statutes of the order.

I further solemnly promise and swear to protect innocence and to punish crime, to help all in distress, to do all in my power to crush oppressors and to defend the oppressed. Every Knight Kadosh shall be to me as if the ties of blood had united us.

I further solemnly promise and swear never to challenge a Knight Kadosh to mortal combat, before having previously submitted my motives to the Council assembled in its Areopagus, and if I were in a place where no Council existed, to take advice of at least two Knights Kadosh.

I furthermore solemnly promise and swear, never to slander a Knight Kadosh, and never to cause him any prejudice either by word or by action. And should I ever infringe or violate any of my obligations I now take, I do from this moment accept and consent to undergo the sentence which may be pronounced against me by this dreaded tribunal, which I hereby acknowledge as my Supreme Judge. All of which I promise to do, under the penalty of death. So help me God.

MUSIC.

[Sovereign grand Judge causes the candidate to kiss three times the cresslet of his sword which he brandishes three times, exclaiming: Justice! Justice! Justice! He then breaks his rod and throws the fragments thereof at the feet of the candidate. The Grand Provost of Justice then conducts the candidate to the first apartment, there to await the order to reappear.]

FOURTH APARTMENT:—In this apartment, the lodge is styled *Senate*. The President is called Thrice Puissant Grand Master, and represents Frederic'" Second, King

Note 353.—"The evidence of the connection of Frederick with the Institution in his latter days, and of his organization of the Ancient and Accepted Scottish Rite, are, it must be confessed, derived only from the assertions made in the Grand Constitutions of 1786, and from the statements of the earliest bodies that have received and recognized these Constitutions. If the document is not authentic, and if those who made the statements here have been mistaken or been dishonest, then the proof of Frederick's interest and labors in Masonry must fall to the ground. Yet, on the other side, the oppugners of the theory that in May, 1786, the King signed the Constitutions—which fact alone would be sufficient to establish his Masonic character—have been able to bring forward in support of their denial little more than mere conjecture, and, in some instances, perversions of acknowledged history. Brother Albert Pike, in the edition of the Grand Constitutions which he prepared for the use of the Supreme Council of the Southern Jurisdiction, and published in 1872, has most thoroughly investigated this subject with the learning of a scholar and the acumen of a lawyer. While unable to advance any new facts, he has collected all the authorities, and has, by the most irrefragible arguments, shown that the conclusions of those who deny the authenticity of the Constitutions of 1786, and Frederick's connection with them, are illogical, and are sustained only by false statements and wild conjecture. Brother Pike very candidly says:

"There is no doubt that Frederick came to the conclusion that the great pretensions of Masonry in the blue degrees were merely imaginary and deceptive. He ridiculed the Order, and thought its ceremonies mere child's play; and some of his sayings to that effect have been preserved. But it does not at all follow that he might not at a later day have found it politic to put himself at the head of an Order that had become a power; and, adopting such of the degrees as were not objectionable, to reject all that were of dangerous tendency, that had fallen into the hands of the Jesuits, or been engrafted on the Order by the Illuminati.'

"It is evident that the question of what active part Frederick took in the affairs of Masonry is not yet settled. Those who claim him as having been, to within a short period before his death, an active patron of and worker in the Order, attempt to sustain their position by the production of certain documents. Those who deny that position assert that those documents have been forged. Yet it must be admitted that the proofs of forgery that have been offered are not such as in an ordinary criminal trial would satisfy a jury."—Mackey's Encyclop dia of Freemasonry, Article Frederick the Great.

of Prussia. In some lodges the President is styled Grand Commander, in others Great Sovereign. The East is hung with black velvet, embroidered with silver and strewed with death's heads transpierced with a poniard. The throne is hung with black velvet, with large white stripes and silver fringe. Over the throne is a double-headed eagle crowned, with his wings open but not spread. He holds a sword in his claws. A death's head transpierced with a poniard, is sometimes used instead of an eagle.

The drapery of the canopy is strewed with red Teutonic crosses and brilliant stars. In the back of the canopy is a large Teutonic cross of red cloth. In each side of the throne is one of the standards of the order. The hall is illuminated by five candles of yellow wax. The West is hung with red tapestry. Towards the west end of the hall is a large mausoleum in the shape of a pyramid.

A funeral urn, covered with a black veil, is placed on the platform of the mausoleum. It is surrounded by a crown of laurel. On the right of the urn is a regal crown; on the left a popish tiara. At the upper angle of the mausoleum is a vase in which burns spirits of wine. On the right and left of the mausoleum there are small pans in which perfumes burn and create thick smoke which renders surrounding objects almost invisible. In the middle of the West, is an altar on which are placed a human skull inlaid with silver, a decanter of red wine and a loaf of white bread, all of which is covered by a white cloth which is removed at a certain period of the ceremony.

Between the East and the altar is the mysterious ladder which a black cloth conceals from the candidate till the moment specified in the ritual. On each side of the mausoleum and a little behind, is stationed a Knight armed with an axe. A meeting of five Knights Kadosh is called a Council. This mysterious ladder has two supporters of seven steps each. The first supporter on the right is called *Oheb Eloah.*[354]

The second supporter on the left is called *Oheb Karobo.*

The names of the steps, beginning at the bottom on first step are as follows, viz:

Tsedakah, Shor Laban, Mathoc, Emunah,[355] *Amal, Sagghi, Sabbal.* The seventh and last is called *Ghemul, Binah, Thebunah.*

The steps of the supporter on the left are as follows, beginning also at the bottom:

Astronomy, Music, Geometry, Arithmetic, Logic, Rhetoric, Grammar.

Master of Ceremonies—(Seven knocks on door; 00 00 00 0.) (Music stops.)

Thrice Puissant Grand Master—Sir Knight First Lieutenant Grand Master, who dares thus to interrupt our deliberations?

First Lieutenant Grand Master—Sir Knight Second Lieutenant Grand Master, who dares thus to interrupt our deliberations?

Second Lieutenant Grand Master—Sir Knight Captain of the Guards, inquire who dares thus to interrupt our deliberations?

Note 354.—"This and Oheb Karobo, Love of our Neighbor, are the names of the two supports of the Ladder of Kadosh. Collectively, they allude to that divine passage, 'Thou shalt love the Lord, thy God, with all thy heart, and with all thy soul, and with all thy mind. This is the first and great commandment. And the second is like unto it. Thou shalt love thy neighbor as thyself. On these two commandments hang all the law and the prophets.' Hence the Ladder of Kadosh is supported by these two Christian commandments."—Mackey's Encyclopædia of Freemasonry, Article Oheb Eloah.

Note 355.—"Sometimes spelled Amunah, but not in accordance with the Masoretic points. A significant word in the high degrees, signifying fidelity, especially in fulfilling one's promises."—Mackey's Encyclopædia of Freemasonry, Article Emunah.

N. B.—Previous to seating the Knights the Thrice Puissant Grand Master puts on the left foot of the candidate the spur of Knighthood. All resume their seats with the exception of the candidate and Master of Ceremonies.

Captain of Guard —(Opening the door a little.) Who dares thus to interrupt our deliberations?

Master of Ceremonies—It is a Grand Scotch Knight of St. Andrew of Scotland, who after having obtained from the illustrious Areopagus leave to proceed further craves the Grand Master's high influence for the purpose of being admitted into the holy order of which he is the supreme chief.

Captain of Guard—(After closing the door.) Sir Knight Second Lieutenant Grand Master, it is a Grand Scotch Knight of St. Andrew of Scotland, who after having obtained from the illustrious Areopagus leave to proceed further, craves the Grand Master's high influence for the purpose of being admitted into the holy order of which he is the supreme chief.

Second Lieutenant Grand Master—Sir Knight First Lieutenant Grand Master, it is a Grand Scotch Knight of St. Andrew of Scotland, who after having obtained from the illustrious Areopagus leave to proceed further, craves the Grand Master's high influence for the purpose of being admitted into the holy order of which he is the supreme chief.

First Lieutenant Grand Master—Thrice Puissant Grand Master, it is a Grand Scotch Knight of St. Andrew of Scotland, who after having obtained from the illustrious Areopagus leave to proceed further, craves your high influence for the purpose of being admitted into the holy order of which you are the supreme chief.

Thrice Puissant Grand Master—What is his name?

First Lieutenant Grand Master—What is his name?

Second Lieutenant Grand Master—What is his name?

Captain of Guard—(Opening the door a little.) What name? (Master of Ceremonies gives the candidate's name. Captain of the Guards then reports the name to the Second Lieutenant, he to the First Lieutenant, and this officer to the Thrice Puissant.)

Thrice Puissant Grand Master—(To First Lieutenant Grand Master.) What right has he?

First Lieutenant Grand Master—(To Second Lieutenant Grand Master.) What right has he?

Second Lieutenant Grand Master—(To Captain of the Guard.) What right has he?

Captain of Guard—(To Master of Ceremonies.) What right has he?

Master of Ceremonies—He possesses all the rights which he derives from the higher degrees, already conferred upon him, but the only one which he makes bold to appeal to, is that of being a man. His rights are expressed by *Michtar*.

Captain of Guard—He possesses all the rights which he derives from the higher degrees already conferred upon him, but the only one which he makes bold to appeal to, is that of being a man. His rights are expressed by *Michtar*.

Second Lieutenant Grand Master—He possesses all the rights which he derives from the higher degrees already conferred upon him, but the only one which he makes bold to appeal to, is that of being a man. His rights are expressed by *Michtar*.

First Lieutenant Grand Master—He possesses all the rights which he derives from the higher degrees already conferred upon him, but the only one which he makes bold to appeal to, is that of being a man. His rights are expressed by *Michtar*.

Thrice Puissant Grand Master—Permit him to enter.

First Lieutenant Grand Master—Permit him to enter.

Second Lieutenant Grand Master—Permit him to enter. (Captain of the Guards then opens the door and gives admittance to the Master of Ceremonies and the candidate, who place themselves in advance of the mausoleum.)

Thrice Puissant Grand Master—(To Master of Ceremonies.) Since you have ventured to introduce this intruder among us, and were so bold as to give him no other title than that of being a man, what do you und. r- stand by that word?

Master of Ceremonies—By "man" I understand a being divested of the prejudices and superstitions of his childhood, who is determined to follow unflinchingly in the path of truth. A being whom no puerile consideration can check in his glorious career.

Thrice Puissant Grand Master—If such be the disposition of the candidate, let him kneel and behold that mausoleum. (Master of Ceremonies causes the candidate to turn toward mausoleum, directs him to kneel and to extend his hand toward the urn on which are written the letters J.-B.-M.)

Thrice Puissant Grand Master—(To candidate.) When your rashness prompted you to enter this awful Sanctuary, you were no doubt informed of the danger which threatened you, and of the trials which still await you. Swear therefore, upon your word of honor, never to reveal what you have seen or heard hitherto. Remember however, that even now you are at liberty to withdraw in peace, if a timid conscience, if prejudices and superstition or any other reason, cause you to hesitate, but forget not that the slightest indiscretion will cost you your life. Are you still willing to proceed?

Candidate—Yes, and I solemnly take the oath you require.

Thrice Puissant Grand Master—(To candidate who is still on his knees.) Since you will proceed, we must unfold to you the mysteries and real object of Scotch Masonry. Rise and be seated. If the degrees which you have hitherto received have elicited your attention and study, you must certainly come to the conclusion that a great mystery is hidden under the various emblems which have been successively presented to you. And now shall be fulfilled the promise which has so often been made to you. In one word you shall receive the true light. Although the degree which is now being conferred upon you, is but the 30th of our Hierarchy, it is nevertheless the *Ne plus ultra* of Masonic knowledge.

In almost all the rituals of this degree, nothing but vengeance is spoken of. But this is an allegory without meaning, for this degree contains all the philosophy of our sublime institution, which is nothing more, nothing less, than the actual result of our Thrice Puissant Grand Master's philosophy, and philosophy discountenances vengeance. Virtue alone and good examples, patience and energy in opposing evil can ensure its triumphs. In this, no more than in the preceding degrees, have we to avenge the death of Hiram Abiff, or even the slaughter of the Knights Templars, and the murder of their Grand Master. And if the ceremonies of this degree recall to our minds the catastrophe resulting in the overthrow of an illustrious order, it is true nevertheless that the commemoration of the bloody tragedy of the 11th day of March 1314, has not for its object to perpetuate ideas of vengeance against its perpetrators, which would be absurd and anti-masonic, but to make us feel the necessity of union, the better to resist tyranny and unmask imposture, and ultimately to substitute for both, even by force of arms, if necessary, the reign of liberty, equality and fraternity. And indeed, these three words

contain the whole doctrine of our Thrice Puissant Grand
Master. Masonry is the history of mankind and we
must own that our fore-fathers acted wisely when in
order to illustrate the sublime teachings of our institution, they selected the most striking events in that
history, the better to impress upon our minds the fatal
results of discord which alone encourages usurpers in
their bloody and ungodly schemes. For if men, one
and all, had always been united by the ties of fraternity
and consequently by the duties they owe to their brethren, would there have been any possibility for the Jewish
hierarchs to have murdered our Thrice Puissant Grand
Master? For the French and Romish Hierarchs to have
slaughtered the Knights Templars? And in later days,
the Calvinists of France? Most undoubtedly not. If then
we wish order and peace to prevail on earth, we must be
united; we must have but one will, but one mind. Both
we find in the teachings of Masonry only, and against
that compact of unity, tyranny and usurpation, whether
religious or political, must fall subdued and powerless.
And now my brother, that by your courage, your resolution to discharge your duty as a man and as a Knight,
you have won our confidence, we will give you a pledge
of our regard. But you must go through a last and
necessary trial. Rise my brother!

Thrice Puissant Grand Master—Sir Knight Master
of Ceremonies, conduct the candidate to the mysterious
ladder. (Master of Ceremonies conducts the candidate
to the ladder, which is then uncovered.)

Thrice Puissant Grand Master—First and Second
Lieutenant Grand Masters, officers and Knights, form
a circle around the mysterious ladder. (Order is obeyed)

Thrice Puissant Grand Master—(To candidate.) M
brother, you will now ascend the first step of our mys-

terious ladder.   (Order is obeyed.)

Thrice Puissant Grand Master—My brother, the ladder before you has two supporters, the one on the right bears the Hebrew words *Oheb Eloah,* that is *Loving God,* the one on the left bears the Hebrew words *Oheb Karobo,* that is *loving his neighbor.*

There are seven steps on each side; each step has a word written upon it. The words on one side of the ladder are Hebrew, on the other side the words are English. The name of the first step on which you now stand is called *Tsedakah,* which means *Justice,* because upon justice must be based all our actions; because a true Knight Kadosh, even when called upon to punish, must not forget that justice is never to be violated.

Thrice Puissant Grand Master—(Strikes one with the pommel of his sword. Candidate then ascends the second step.) This second step is called *Shor-Laban,* that is *White Ox;* a figure to teach us that by constant and patient labor, and the purity of our intentions only, we may hope to witness the success of our cause.

Thrice Puissant Grand Master—(Strikes one. Candidate ascends third step.) This step is called *Mathoc,* that is *Meekness.* This virtue is so valuable in the profane world, it is still more necessary in the Knight Kadosh. For it is by this virtue only that we may hope to convince our erring brethren, and influence them to enter the path of true happiness and liberty.

Thrice Puissant Grand Master—(Strikes one. Candidate ascends fourth step.) This fourth step is called *Emunah,* that is *Fidelity, Steadiness.* You easily understand how precious this quality is in a Knight Kadosh. There can be no success for him if he is not faithful to his obligations, if he is luke warm in fulfilling his duty.

It is with these virtues especially that he will secure the triumph of that truth which must be the constant object of all his worship, and were truth banished from the hearts of all other men it ought ever to be found in the heart of a Knight Kadosh.

Thrice Puissant Grand Master—(Knocks one. Candidate ascends fifth step.) This fifth step is called *Amal-Sagghi*, that is *Great Labor*. And truly it is only by unceasing exertions; by great labor that we can attain the object we have in view. And if labor is necessary for man in all the walks of life, it is still more so for a Knight Kadosh, who neither can, nor must, take any rest so long as the welfare of humanity is not definitely secured.

We must have patience in adversity, live in perfect union among ourselves; and for that purpose, we must be very cautious and never admit among us any one of whom we are not sure, or whose will is not free, such as religious monks, kings, princes and lords of the world; for their ideas of liberty are in opposition to the doctrine of our Thrice Puissant Grand Master.

Thrice Puissant Grand Master—(Strikes one. Candidate ascends sixth step.) This sixth step is called *Sabbal*, that is *Burden*, to remind us of our task. We have to undergo many trials; many dangers threaten us and we must never be taken by surprise. We must always be united, and for that purpose, we must forgive our brethren their errors and their faults if we wish them to forgive ours.

Thrice Puissant Grand Master—(Strikes one. Candidate ascends seventh step.) This seventh step is called *Ghemul, Binah, Thebunah*, that is *Generosity, Intelligence* and *Prudence*. And indeed, my brother, this must

be the last step of perfection. A generous man is al
ways ready to sacrifice himself for the benefit of his
brethren. An intelligent man studies the secrets of
nature, and draws therefrom all that can promote human
happiness. A prudent man does not waste his resources
and never trusts to hazard. He is very cautious so that
when the time comes for execution, every circumstance
may contribute to the success of our holy cause. (A
pause.)

MUSIC.

(After a few moments the music stops.)

Thrice Puissant Grand Master—On the other side of
the ladder are written the names of those sciences which
all men sincerely desiring to help their fellow creatures
must study. Nothing can be expected from an ignorant
man. He is bound forever to be a dupe and consequently a slave. A well informed man is free for education
has expanded his intellect, enlarged his mind and has
borne him, as it were, to the very steps of the throne of
eternal truth. He sees, he understands, he knows.
Light is given to him. To his brethren he may be a
guide, a teacher. But an ignorant man is blind. He
staggers in the dark and falls a victim to imposture and
tyranny. And what is still worse; he very soon becomes
an instrument of oppression to ensnare his own brethren.
He knows not the extent of the mischief done by him.
His conscience speaks not, and, thanks to his ignorance,
humanity retrogrades to barbarism and idiocy. Study
then my brother, study without ceasing, and be always
guided by the noble ambition of teaching and directing
your brethren.

The word written on the last or seventh step, of the
other side of the ladder, is *Grammar;* that is the art of
speaking and writing correctly. He who is unacquaint-
ed with his own language excites the mirth of others,
and where ridicule exists, there can be no confidence.

The word written on the sixth step is *Rhetoric.* That

is, the art of speaking on any subject, with elegance, propriety and force. Rhetoric is the theory of eloquence. It is not *given* to every man to be eloquent, but every man should know the rules of eloquence. The power of speech is immense, and you certainly know, that in all the revolutions, by which the people have attempted to reconquer their liberty and their rights, speech has been the chief weapon used by their leaders to enlighten and guide the masses. The word written on the fifth step is *Logic.* That is the art of making use of reason, in our inquiries after truth and in the communication of it to others. It is indispensable. For Grammar and even eloquence itself would avail nothing if you failed to know how to draw conclusions in proof of what you assert, victory can be obtained only by the power and propriety of reasoning.

The word written on the fourth step is *Arithmetic.* That is, the science of numbers. It is useless here to demonstrate the necessity of this science, for it is the A∴B∴C∴ of the most common education.

The word written on the third step is *Geometry.* That is the art of .measuring space. Space has three dimensions, length, breadth and thickness. By means of Geometry, the Architect draws his plans, the General stations his army, the Engineer selects the spot where to make his entrenchments; his fortifications. By the means of geometry, geographers can measure the dimensions of the globe, the extent of the seas, the position of the several states, empires, kingdoms and provinces of this world. With the aid of geometry, astronomers have succeeded in making observations and in counting the periods of time, the return of seasons of years. In a word geometry is the basis of Arithmetic and the principles of mathematics.

The word written on the second step is *Music*. That is the science of harmony. Not only does harmony soften and polish the manners and awaken tender and kind feelings in the rudest hearts, but it is also indispensable in distributing all the works of man. The eyes are fascinated by symmetry and the ear by the sounds of harmony. It seems ever to invite the mind to further investigations in the vast fields of happiness.

The word written on the first step is *Astronomy*. That is the science of the motion, magnitude and position of the celestial bodies. The firmament is an open book, on the pages of which is written the word of God, in all its majestic splendor.

With the assistance of astronomy we can observe the motions, measure the distances, comprehend the magnitudes and calculate the periods and eclipses of the heavenly bodies. The study of astronomy furnishes us with unparalleled instances of the power, wisdom and goodness of our Father who dwells in heaven, and in the hearts of all good Masons. Astronomy is the religion of space, leading man through a starry peristyle, up to the religion of ideas.

My brother, all these several sciences, as you may easily understand, give a full sway to human intelligence and elevate it by study and meditation, to the very last degree of perfection, to which the genius of man can pretend. *Ne plus ultra.* (As these last words are uttered the ladder is suddenly lowered, and the candidate, supported by two Knights, finds himself on the floor.)

Thrice Puissant Grand Master—(To candidate.) This sudden fall, so unexpected, is the emblem of the misfortunes which may strike you, whatever may be the extent of your knowledge and your virtues. Whatever may be the degree of elevation to which you may have attained among men, a single breath can bring you down to a common level. Then you will know the value of sound philosophy, such as is taught by Scotch Masonry. Virtue, which you will have constantly practiced will be your refuge and your consolation; that strength of mind which you will find in the store-house of your heart and the elements of which we are happy to perceive in you, will enable you to suffer nobly the slings and arrows of outrageous fortune.

Thrice Puissant Grand Master—Order, Sir Knights! (All rise and place themselves under the sign of order.)

MUSIC.

(Thrice Puissant Grand Master leaves his seat and proceeds to mausoleum when music stops.)

Thrice Puissant Grand Master—Sir Knights, form a circle in front of the mausoleum. (Order is obeyed.)

Thrice Puissant Grand Master—Sir Knights, on your knees! (Members and candidate kneel.)

Thrice Puissant Grand Master—(Taking the hand of the candidate and pointing to the urn.) Noble victim whose name is concealed under the emblem of the $S.\cdot.$ $W.\cdot.$ of the first three degrees. Oh Thou, whose ashes were gathered from the pile on which two infamous tyrants have, by the most excruciating tortures, terminated thy glorious life. Oh Thou, whom we have ever glorified under the several names of *J.* $\cdot.$ *of B.* $\cdot.$ *and of M.* $\cdot.$ Thou, our illustrious Grand Master Jacobus Burgundus Molay. I here invoke thy great name and memory. I bring thee a disciple, aye, a disciple who will follow thy virtues, thy magnanimity. Be thou a witness to the oath he will now take. May he look with horror on the oppressors of humanity and help us ultimately to accomplish our noble labor. To punish crime and to protect innocence.

Thrice Puissant Grand Master—To candidate. Repeat with me!

FOURTH OATH, KNIGHT KADOSH.

I.......do most solemnly promise and swear, upon my word of honor and upon this urn which recalls to my mind the memory of a virtuous man who fell a victim to tyranny and imposture, to be faithful to all my former obligations; to pay due obedience to the statutes of the Grand Elect Knights Kadosh, and I hereby renew the oath which I have taken as a Knight Rose Croix.

I furthermore promise and swear constantly to strive to reach the true and grand object of a Knight Kadosh. To protect innocence and to punish crime, and from this day forward to devote myself to the holy cause of humanity.

I furthermore promise and swear to use every means in my power to crush tyranny, to unmask and confound imposture, to contribute with all my might to the diffusion of light and to the propagation of liberal ideas, wheresoever I may be.

I furthermore promise and swear to defend the public weal; to consider the oppressed as my brethren, and the oppressors as my enemies.

I furthermore promise and swear to free my fellow beings from the disgraceful yoke of tyranny and imposture under which they groan, and as much as in me lies, to secure for my brethren, according to their capacity and merit, the share to which they are legitimately entitled in the legal sovereignty of the people.

I henceforth devote and consign myself to disgrace and contempt, to the execration and punishment of the Grand Elect Knights Kadosh, if I ever fail in this my solemn obligation, or if I ever pass over to despots and imposters. *God by my witness, my shield! Amen. Amen. Amen.*

Thrice Puissant Grand Master—Rise, Sir Knights. (All rise and place themselves under the sign of order.)

Thrice Puissant Grand Master—(To candidate.) Let us do our duty and perform a solemn ceremony, the object of which is more fully to convey to your mind the necessity of ever keeping the sacred obligations which you have this day taken. (Removes the cloth from the altar on which is the skull.)

Thrice Puissant Grand Master—My brother, you are now convinced that the degree of Knight Kadosh is the apex of the Masonic edifice. It contains all the science of Masonry. You are rapidly approaching the end of its teachings, and as all in this degree assumes an appearance of actual reality, I will, as it is my duty, lay your finger on the terrible symbol of human equality. (He puts candidate's hand on the skull.) Are these the remains of the most powerful, or of the most humble of mortals? Who can answer this question? We all enter life in the same manner, and before death all rank and privileges disappear. This is the truth, acknowledged and proclaimed by the Knights Kadosh, and in order never to forget it, they all drink from the same cup, from the cup of equality. They all break together the bread of fraternity, the bread which is as necessary to the life of the poor, as to the life of the rich; as well to the life of the strong, as to the life of the weak; as well to the life of the tyrant, as to the life of the victim. (Thrice Puissant Grand Master then breaks the bread and distributes it among the Knights; then fills the cup, drinks and passes it to his neighbor, and he to his till all have drank.)

Thrice Puissant Grand Master—(Pointing to the regal crown.) This crown my brother, is the emblem of hypocrisy and tyranny. It represents the crown of

Philip the Fair, King of France, and the crown of all those, who under the name of kings and monarchs have usurped the power, exclusively belonging to the people and for that reason we trample it under foot, and we invite you to do the same. (Thrice Puissant Grand Master then throws the crown on the floor and tramples upon it. The candidate and all the Knights also trample on it, when all the Knights brandish their poniards and exclaim:)

All—Down with tyrants. May thus roll in the dust, the crown of every king and potentate.

Thrice Puissant Grand Master—(Passing over to the Tiara.) This represents the Tiara of the cruel and cowardly Pontiff, who sacrificed to his ambition the illustrious order of those Knights Templars of whom we are the true successors. A crown of gold and precious stones ill befits the humble head of one who pretends to be successor, the Vicar, of Jesus of Nazareth. It is therefore the crown of an imposter, and it is in the name of him who said "neither be ye called Masters," that we trample it under our feet.

Thrice Puissant Grand Master—(To candidate.) Are you disposed to do the same?

Candidate—I am. (Thrice Puissant Grand Master then throws the Tiara on the floor and tramples upon it, the candidate and all the Knights also trample on it, when all the Knights brandishing their poniards exclaim:)

All—Down with imposture!

Thrice Puissant Grand Master—(To candidate.) You have made good the hopes we entertained of you. You have discarded all stupid and vulgar prejudices. You now fully deserve to be Knighted Kadosh.

Thrice Puissant Grand Master—(Striking the shoulders of the candidate three times with the flat of his sword.) To the glory of the Grand Architect of the Universe, in the name and under the auspices of the Grand Consistory of.....Sublime Princes of the Royal Secret, 32nd degree of the....., Ancient and Accepted Scottish Rite, in and for the Sovereign and Independent State of......, under the jurisdiction of the Supreme Council for the northern jurisdiction of the United States of America, sitting at the city of New York, State of New York, and by virtue of the authority vested in me by......Council of Kadosh, No.....I receive and constitute you a Knight Kadosh, or Knight of the Black and White Eagle, and an active member of this Council of Kadosh. (Thrice Puissant Grand Master returns to the throne and takes his seat.)

Thrice Puissant Grand Master—(One knock with pommel of sword.) Be seated Sir Knights.

N. B.—Previous to seating the Knights the Thrice Puissant Grand Master puts on the left foot of the candidate the spur of Knighthood. All resume their seats with the exception of the candidate and Master of Ceremonies.

Thrice Puissant Grand Master—(To candidate.) We will now my brother, proceed to give you the signs, tokens and words of the degree of Knights Kadosh. (As the Thrice Puissant Grand Master explains the signs, the Master of Ceremonies causes the candidate to execute the motions.)

Sign of Kadosh.

SIGN OF KADOSH.

Place the right hand on the heart, the fingers separated. Let the right hand fall on the right knee. Bend and grasp the knee; then seize the poniard which is suspended from the ribbon, raise it to the height of the shoulder, as if to strike and say, *Nekam Adonai.*

SIGN OF ORDER.

Hold the sword in the left hand and place the right hand extended over the heart.

Sign of Order.
Knight Kadosh.

Token, Knight Kadosh.   Second Position.

TOKEN.

Place right foot to right foot, and knee to knee; present the right first, the thumb elevated, seize the thumb alternately, let it slip and step back a pace, then raise the arm as if to strike with the poniard. In doing this the first says, *Nekamah-bealim*, and the other answers, *Pharash-kol.*[356]

BATTERY :—Seven strokes, by three, two and one; 000 00 0.

HOURS OF MEETINGS—The Council opens at the beginning of night and closes at daybreak.   ———

Note 356.—"Pharazal. A significant word in the high degrees, and there said, in the old rituals. to signify 'we shall all be united.' Delauney gives it as pharas kol, and says it means 'all is explained.' "—Mackey's Encyclopædia of Freemasonry, Article Pharazal.

AGE:—The Knights Kadosh have no age; they have a century or more.

PASS WORD:—To enter, *Nekam.* Answer *Menahhem,* that is *Consolator.* To retire, *Phaal-Kol.* Answer *Pharash-Koh.*

SACRED WORD:—*Nekamah-bealim.* Answer *Pharash-Koh.* But more generally *Nekam-Adonai.* Answer *Pharash-Kol.*

MARCH:—Make three hurried steps, the hands crossed on the head. Kneel on one knee. Present the poniard, by the handle, to the President, who leaves his seat, raises the Knight and conducts him to the East. The word *Mishtar,* which expresses the rights of a Knight Kadosh, means that it is the duty of one who is commissioned to execute the decree of the Judge.

MUSIC.

[Thrice Puissant Grand Master leaves his seat and introduces the candidate to all the Knights, who shake hands with him, and a moment after the music stops when Thrice Puissant Grand Master returns to his seat.]

Thrice Puissant Grand Master—Sir Knight Master of Ceremonies, conduct the candidate to the seat of honor in the East. (Order is obeyed.)

Thrice Puissant Grand Master—Be seated, Sir Knights. Sir Knight of Eloquence, the floor is yours. (Knight of Eloquence rises, bows and delivers the following discourse:)

DISCOURSE.

Sir Knights, newly initiated. You have just passed through a most solemn, instructive and impressive ceremony. You rise from an intellectual repast, which will no doubt, furnish rich material for future reflection, and I feel confident that you will make a profitable application of the lessons you have received. By virtue of

the office which I have the honor to hold in this
Council, it is my duty as well as my privilege to address
you on this interesting occasion. Were the task self
imposed, I should consider that I was rendering myself
liable to the charge of temerity; as it is, I approach the
performance of it with diffidence, surrounded as I am
by so many bright and honored lights of our Hierarchy;
brothers who by their zeal, energy, intelligence and
well-directed researches, have shed additional lustre
upon our annals.

We will not now occupy your attention in the dis-
cussions of when or where Masonry first became a
distinct organization, neither will we pause to answer
the cavil of those who insist that all of Masonry is contained in the first three degrees; nor of those who are
pleased to call the higher degrees of Scotch Masonry
side degrees; ornamental degrees. Their argument is
the old one; that Masonry is unchangeable, and that
these degrees, not having been originally a part of the
system, cannot belong to it. They mistake progress for
change. When the spirit of God moved upon the face of
the waters; when the Great Jehovah ordained the creation of the world; when the first sun rose to greet with
its beams, the new morning and the august command
was uttered: "Let there be light," the lips of deity
breathed Masonry into existence and it must live forever more; for truth is eternal, and the principles of
truth are the foundation of Masonry.

Masonry is unchangeable, but it must of necessity in
the fulfillment of its mission keep pace with the advance
of civilization, the arts and sciences. It must lead and
not be lead by them. This is progress; it is not change.
Electricity is co-existent with matter. It is the same
now, and will be to the end of time, as it was at crea-

tion's dawn.

To our forefathers it was a dread inspiring mysteri-ous agent of destruction, and to this day it is compara-tively little understood. Your own great philosopher, the immortal Franklin, in the eighteenth century, first disarmed it of its terrors, reduced it to subjection to the will of man, and opened a way for further investigation. But it was reserved for our day to improve upon the work that he inaugurated, when; Oh wondrous achieve-ment of science; it is become the medium of instant communication between the most distant parts of the globe. A simple wire, wrought out of the bowels of the earth, carries with the velocity of imagination, invisible messengers. The pulse beats of London, Paris and St. Petersburg can be felt and counted on the shores of the Atlantic.

And is the principle of electricity changed? No, it is not changed, but the arts and sciences have combined to make it subservient to the wants of man.

What is Masonry? Is it not the pursuit of science; the practice of virtue, and the teaching of those sublime doctrines which tend to bind the whole family of men in fraternal union?

If this definition is correct, it remains for us only to proceed to make the application and to trace the means we shall employ in accomplishing its object. It is a task that we should all zealously undertake, as we shall all be sharers in the glory and prosperity of our united labors, if success attend our laudable efforts. I ask your indulgence therefore, whilst I address myself to the subject, which I shall briefly discuss under three heads.

The first, presenting general considerations of the objects of our institution, will conduct our minds to a

proper point, whence our work may go hand in hand
with our principles.

The second will treat of the instructions to be given
to candidates concerning our doctrines and precepts.

And the third, of the encouragement and recompense
which await those, who, by their zeal and labors, shall
prove themselves worthy.

Truth, Light and Liberty are the natural heritage of
man. But many who admit the correctness of this
axiom, in a general sense, exclaim that all cannot understand the truth, appreciate the light, or make a
proper use of the liberty which we assert is their birth-
right. A large portion of mankind arrogate to themselves the right to maintain in ignorance and slavish dependence, millions of their fellow creatures, the children
of the same great parent, created in his own image the
masterpiece of his handiwork. If those who possessed
the capacity and power had employed as much talent
and ingenuity, and expended as much treasure in the
cultivation of the minds and faculties of their species
as they have in blinding, deceiving and debasing them,
the noble family of man could at this day present a
spectacle of so much happiness, peace and contentment,
as to be worthy the regard of their creator, who being
good and just, certainly never intended that they should
exist in a state of ignorance and misery. The truth of
this you cannot but acknowledge, since it is the principle which gave birth to Masonry. No, we are not born
to remain in ignorance and misery. Masonry then is
destined to repair the injuries which society has sustained from the machinations of its enemies and to
make out the means whereby man may be restored to
his natural rights and dignity, as an intelligent being.

The degree of Knight Kadosh; that is to say, Sacred or Holy Knight, which is one of the most elevated in our order, presents great facilities for the accomplishment we have in view.

To explain this end, we must direct our attention rather to the consideration of what Masonry should be in our day, than to what it has been heretofore. We must, in a manner, draw a veil over the past, that our glimpse of the future may not be prejudiced.

We will not discuss further the origin or the history of Masonry. Each one has liberty to adopt the opinions that seem to him most reasonable. To suppose that its source was in Egypt or India; that it sprang from such a war; or such a sect; that it was the offspring of such a revolution, or such a system of astronomy or religion.

The Knights Kadosh will abandon for the present, the charms of erudition, for considerations of more immediate importance. I mean the application of the principles of Masonry to the accomplishment of our designs, and it is precisely for this purpose that they established such bodies as that which is now convened.

Already we have decreed our laws and regulations, and we are now about to commence our labors. We feel the necessity of putting into operation our lofty conceptions, but at the outset, the fear that our zeal may overrun our prudence calls up in our minds the question how are we to take part effectively in these labors? Who will be our guide, our teacher? Strange position which reveals in an instant, and notwithstanding our willingness, the obstacles and embarrassments which we must encounter. What shall we teach our disciples? What dogmas, what principles? In one word, how shall we most judiciously co-operate with each other for the

welfare of humanity? For you must be aware that this
is the aim of all our teachings, of all that you have
obligated yourselves to perform.

These questions, my bretheren, however important
and however embarrassing they may be, happily admit
of an easy and simple solution. Your only difficulty
will be in the selection, out of the different means which
may present themselves; and in order to enable you
more speedily to arrive at that choice, I have only to remind you of one thing, and that is, the solemn obligation which you have just taken, and which we tacitly renew every time that we reassemble. You have sworn to
combat fanaticism and superstition. Well, Sir Knights,
in this obligation you will find the source of all your
duties, and the possibility of performing them. It contains the dogmas and morality which you will present to
those who are worthy of being employed in the noble
works for which we are associated. To wage war against
fanaticism and superstition, seems to me to be one of
the most glorious human efforts of virtue, for it is an
enterprise fraught with difficulty and encompassed with
dangers, offering no other recompense than the approval
of your own conscience, or that of those true brothers
who find their sweetest enjoyments in the promotion of
the welfare of their fellows, and for those who can appreciate such recompense, it is the greatest that can be
given or enjoyed.

But what is fanaticism and what is superstition? will
perhaps be the question of the newly initiated, and how
can we combat them without causing disorders in the
body politic which they infect, without drawing on our
own heads the direful vengeance of those whose prosperity depends upon them? What then are fanaticism and

superstition?

Ah, my brethren, the heart sickens and pales at the mention of those words; the mind recoils with horror at the reflection, they give rise to. To endeavor to paint them, is to expose ones self to their fury. Merciful God; in thy holy name their blasphemous atrocities have been perpetrated. In the sacred name of religion they have polluted thy footstool. When they are mentioned we should drape our temples in mourning, and draw a veil over the name of the eternal. Ah! my brethren, vain would be the attempt to calculate the evils which they have engendered; to count the tears or measure the blood with which they have deluged this fair earth. Who can reckon the number of their victims? That which astonishes, while it consoles, is the admirable courage which you still display in entering the lists against those uncompromising foes of human rights, whom no earthly power has ever yet been able to subdue. Having conceived that there is some hope of success, you are resolved to make the attempt, and you query with yourself where are the weapons that you are to employ? These weapons exist my brethren; they are within your reach. It remains only for you to seize them and to use them with the force of resolution, strengthened only by the consciousness that your cause is just. These weapons are science, truth and humanity. Fanaticism is the offspring of ignorance. To ignorance, oppose knowledge, which springs from enlightened education. Instruct the masses; teach them truth. To knowledge add virtue, and the universe is saved.

There are no weapons more sure or more terrible than those which I propose. The veriest despots and tyrants tremble before them. Heaven has ordained no others.

But the monster is also begotten of ambition and fraud. Well, even against these, your weapons are the same. Your only resources are science and truth. Present unceasingly to the eyes and ears of all the world the melancholy results of deceit and ambition. The history of the past, spread as a map before them, will be your faithful ally in the contest. Select there examples and facts the most striking.

History speaks trumpet tongued of the many centuries of the degradation and misery of our race. History will speak for you. Its simple but affecting truths will touch the hardest hearts, and confound those of the most perverse. Show them countries invaded, devastated, desolated. Point them out valleys strewn with the whitening bones of God's children and mountains streaming with human gore. Show them that everlasting servitude; the tortures, the scaffold, the fagot or the lingering death in the dungeon. There exists still the wrecks of nations which bear faithful testimony to these frightful episodes, in their history, and whose children, even at this day, weep over the ruins of their cities and the blackened records of their countries.

Ask the unfortunate descendents of Idumea of whom Israelites is the ancient name. They can, better than any others, tell you the cost of ignorance and ambition, and to what deplorable excesses they lead.

Ask them how many millions of lives have been sacrificed to them, and at whose orders? Ask them why they burned their infants alive in sacrifice to Moloch, the very god of the people whom they had exterminated?

Ask them why their priests dethroned at will and murdered their own Monarchs, and why their Kings assassinated each other?

Demand of them under what circumstances the brother was obliged to slay his brother, the father, his son, his daughter, his wife, his friend, the most tender?

Under what circumstances they were compelled to give whole cities to the flames and exterminate every living thing, and butcher the men, the women and the helpless infants clinging to the breasts of their mothers?

Ask of the ancient Gauls for what reason they also burned their women and children as sacrifices to their god Teutates, and consulted the destinies of the future in their entrails?

Come down to more modern ages. Ask what caused the division and fall of the Roman Empire? Who murdered the Saxons, the Waldenses, the Albigenses? Who massacred the Aborigines of America, and half the people of Europe?

Listen to that bell; the peals say St. Bartholomew. Who caused the best and purest blood of France to rain like water over the land? Pass through the streets of the city of Paris and ask who has strewed them with corpses and gore? Do you see the head of the most virtuous of men; of Admiral Coligny? Tell us who struck it off? Who sent as a present the most acceptable to the High Priest of Rome, as a trophy in whose infamous revelries celebrated in token of a still more infamous victory? Who then perpetrated these crimes; these atrocious deeds? Answer I say! Is it not ambition? Is it not fanaticism, superstition and ignorance?

But my brethren, Heaven has not put entirely out of our reach a remedy for evils so grave. He who created the sun to give light to the universe, has also created reason, the sun of our human system, and furnished science to guide us through the labyrinth of unspeakable difculties and calamities. To contend against this fanaticism Heaven created men of talent, virtue and genius, and each age has given birth to a benefactor of his race contemporary with the most accursed of its enemies.

Heroes, sages, friends of humanity have appeared successively through all descending time, to enlighten, to comfort the earth.

Hail their august names, contemplate their divine precepts, their virtues, their sublime actions, and keep them unceasingly present to your recollection. The remembrance of them is sufficient to reanimate hope in despairing hearts, and you will prove that the good done by them can also be accomplished in our days.

Quote often the precepts of Zoroaster[???] and Confucius. Remind them of the devotion of Codrus and Leonidas, the virtues and maxims of Pythagoras[???] Sociates, of Plato[???] of Epictetus and of Marcus Aurelius. Say with Zoroaster: "Love your fellow men and succor them; pardon those who have offended you." Knights who would be faithful to your obligations, and who feel the importance of their vows to God and to virtue, have painful and arduous duties to perform; they have obstacles to surmount, errors to contend with, subtle adversaries to overthrow; a war eternal to wage against ignorance and fanaticism. A worthy Knight may fall into the snare of a traitor, under the accusation of an informer; of a hpyocrite, or perhaps

Note 357.—"The doctrine of pure Zoroastrianism was monotheistic. The Supreme Being was called Ahuramazda, and Haug says that Zoroaster's conception of him was perfectly identical with the Jewish notion of Jehovah. He is called 'the Creator of the earthly and spiritual life, the Lord of the whole universe, at whose hands are all the creatures.' He is wisdom and intellect; the light itself, and the source of light; the rewarder of the virtuous and the punisher of the wicked.
"The dualistic doctrine of Ormuzd and Ahrimanes, which has falsely been attributed to Zoroaster, was in reality the development of a later corruption of the Zoroasteric teaching."—Mackey's Encyclopædia of Freemasonry, Article Zoroaster.

Note 358.—"He taught the mystical power of numbers, and much of the symbolism on that subject which we now possess is derived from what has been left to us by his disciples; for of his own writings there is nothing extant. He was also a geometrician, and is regarded as having been the inventor of several problems, the most important of which is that now known as the forty-seventh problem of Euclid. He was also a proficient in music, and is said to have demonstrated the mathematical relations of musical intervals, and to have invented a number of musical instruments. Disdaining the vanity and dogmatism of the ancient sages, he contented himself with proclaiming that he was simply a seeker after knowledge, not its possessor, and to him is attributed the introduction of the word philosopher, or lover of wisdom, as the only title which he would assume."—Mackey's Encyclopædia of Freemasonry, Article Pythagoras.

Note 359.—"Academy, Platonic. Founded in 1480 by Marsilius Ficinus, at Florence, under the patronage of Lorenzo de Medicis. It is said by the Masons of Tuscany to have been a secret society, and is supposed to have had a Masonic character, because in the hall where its members held their meetings, and which still remains, many Masonic symbols are to be found."—Mackey's Encyclopædia of Freemasonry, Article Academy, Platonic.

become the victim of his own generous confidence. He should not expect to be exempt from the persecutions which are in reserve for those who are the zealous advocates of justice; the sworn enemies of falsehood. Is he not, if true and faithful, entitled to the gratitude, homage, friendship and consolation of his brethren? It becomes then, for them to prescribe the means they will adopt to do honor to his efforts; to crown his successes; to proclaim his virtues; to console him in disgrace and comfort him in misfortune; to visit him in sickness and relieve him in distress. And when he shall be no more, to strew with flowers and bedew with tears his last resting place, retaining a lively recollection of his virtues, and burying all his imperfections beneath the sod that rests upon his bosom.

In conclusion my brethren, Masonry is the love of truth and of humanity. The sun of truth will dissipate the clouds of error, that hang like a pall over our fellow-men. Live in hope and let your progress be onward. Our strength will be found in union. Be frequent in your attendance on your lodges. Visit your brethren. Be missionaries of virtue and truth. Hide not your light under a bushel. Demand, as the price of advancement, talents and good works. In your Councils be orderly, respectful and attentive so that the newly initiated may exclaim; "that which I have sought, I have found Science, Order and Light. I am proud to have been received into such a society."

His heart will be elevated, his mind will be enlightened. The sphere of his affection will be enlarged; our institutions will have for him a lasting charm. He will celebrate our good works, and Masonry, victorious over all adverse circumstances, will become the honored medium of uniting all mankind in one vast brotherhood.

Now my brethren, I must close. I thank you for your attention. I have endeavored to touch upon each subject of importance to the order. To impress upon your minds the chief aim of Scotch Rite Masonry. I desire to witness its triumph. I have endeavored to vindicate the means. I have reminded you of your obligation, traced your duties, pointed out the enemies against whom you have to contend. I have feebly pictured the evils caused by ignorance, fanaticism and superstition. These evils are great. If they touch your hearts; if you partake of the honor which they inspire, it will be for you to work out the means to diminish them. The remedy is in your power. Practice in the world the precepts you have learned here. The world will recompense you with its applause, and what is better still, you will have the applause of your own consciences.

Among your brethren beware of jealousy and strife. Be charitable in your conduct towards them. Be charitable in speaking of them. Forgive their errors and pardon their iniquities. If they wrong you, intercede kindly with them, remembering that to err is human, to forgive divine. And finally keep aloof from uniting yourselves with any sectional, political or sectarian religious organization whose principles can in any way bias your mind or judgment, or in the slightest degree trammel with obligations, the vows which you have just made. Remember that now and henceforth you are the champions of justice and human rights. Your battlefield is the world at large.

Thrice Puissant Grand Master—(Strikes one with pommel of sword.) Order, Sir Knights! (All rise and place themselves under the sign of order, when the Thrice Puissant Grand Master in the name of the Council compliments the Knight of Eloquence on his discourse and sits down.)

Thrice Puissant Grand Master—Be seated Sir Knights! Sir Knights, First and Second Lieutenant Grand Masters, inform the Knights on your respective valleys that they are permitted to address this Council, if they have anything to offer for the good of the order and of this body.

First Lieutenant Grand Master—Sir Knights on my valley, the Thrice Puissant Grand Master informs you that you are permitted to address this Council if you have anything to offer for the good of the order and of this body.

Second Lieutenant Grand Master—Sir Knights on my valley, the Thrice Puissant Grand Master informs you that are you are permitted to address this meeting if you have anything to offer for the good of this order and of this body. (Any Knights who wish make remarks.)

Second Lieutenant Grand Master—Sir Knight, First Lieutenant Grand Master, silence prevails on my valley.

First Lieutenant Grand Master—Thrice Puissant Grand Master, silence prevails.

Thrice Puissant Grand Master—Sir Knights, First and Second Lieutenant Grand Masters, inform the Knights on your respective valleys that the box of fraternal assistance is about to be presented to them.

First Lieutenant Grand Master—Sir Knights on my valley, the Thrice Puissant Grand Master informs you that the box of fraternal assistance is about to be presented to you.

Second Lieutenant Grand Master—Sir Knights on my valley, the Thrice Puissant Grand Master informs you that the box of fraternal assistance is about to be presented to you. (The Master of Ceremonies then pre-

GRAND ELECT KNIGHT KADOSH.

sents the box to each Knight, beginning with the Thrice Puissant Grand Master, the First and Second Lieutenant Grand Masters, Knight of Eloquence and other officers. When the collection has been taken, the box is returned to the Thrice Puissant Grand Master, who sums up the contents which he hands to the Treasurer through the Master of Ceremonies.)

CLOSING CEREMONIES

GRAND ELECT KNIGHT KODASH.[***]

Thrice Puissant Grand Master—(Strikes one with the pommel of his sword.) Sir Knight, First Lieutenant Grand Master, at what hour are the labors of the Knights Kadosh adjourned?

First Lieutenant Grand Master—(Striking one with the pommel of sword.) At day break, Thrice Puissant Grand Master.

Thrice Puissant Grand Master—Why do we adjourn our labors at day light?

First Lieutenant Grand Master—The better to conceal our schemes from the profane, Thrice Puissant Grand Master.

Thrice Puissant Grand Master—What are those schemes?

First Lieutenant Grand Master—Thrice Puissant Grand Master, to punish crime and to protect innocence?

Thrice Puissant Grand Master—What do you understand by punishing crime?

First Lieutenant Grand Master—Thrice Puissant

Note 360.—"Knight Kadosh, formerly called Grand Elect Knight Kadosb (Grand Elu du Chevalier Kadosch). The Knight Kadosh is the thirtieth degree of the Ancient and Accepted Scottish Rite, called also Knight of the White and Black Eagle. While retaining the general Templar doctrine of the Kadosh system, it symbolizes and humanizes the old lesson of vengeance. It is the most popular of all the Kadoshes.
"In the Knight Kadosh of the Ancient and Accepted Scottish Rite, the meetings are called Councils. The principal officers are, according to the recent rituals, a Commander, two Lieutenant Commanders, called also Prior and Precepter; a Chancellor, Orator, Almoner, Recorder, and Treasurer. The jewel, as described in the ritual of the Southern Supreme Council, is a double-headed eagle, displayed resting on a teutonic cross, the eagle silver, the cross gold enamelled red. The Northern Council uses instead of the eagle the letters J. B. M."—Mackey's Encyclopædia of Freemasonry, Article Knight Kadosh.

Grand Master, it is by resisting oppression and imposture by all available means, by calling down the hatred of the people on the head of tyrants and impostors, by undermining and overthrowing their power, even by force of arms, that we fulfill the obligation of punishing crime.

Thrice Puissant Grand Master—What do you mean by protecting innocence?

First Lieutenant Grand Master—Thrice Puissant Grand Master, it is by raising mankind from the degradation in which they are sunken; by diffusing abroad the blessings of education; by bringing our fellow beings to the highest degree of civilization to which humanity can pretend that we obey the command of our Thrice Puissant Grand Master, and that we attain the objects which the Knights Kadosh have in view to protect innocence.

Thrice Puissant Grand Master—Such indeed are our duties. Let us never forget them, either within or without this temple. Sir Knights, First and Second Lieutenant Grand Masters, request the members of this Council to assist me in adjourning the Senate.

First Lieutenant Grand Master—Sir Knights on my valley, the Thrice Puissant Grand Master requests you to assist him in adjourning this Senate.

Second Lieutenant Grand Master—Sir Knights on my valley, the Thrice Puissant Grand Master requests you to assist him in adjourning this Senate.

Thrice Puissant Grand Master—Order Sir Knights! (All rise and place themselves under the sign of order.)

Thrice Puissant Grand Master—Let us pray Sir Knights.

CLOSING PRAYER, KNIGHT KADOSH.

Our Father, who art in Heaven, in whom we live, move and have our being. Oh! Thou who willest that

man should enjoy all the benefits which Thy munificence holds out to him, may thy kindness help us in re-
moving the obstacles which tyranny and imposture have
set up against thy holy and ever just providence. Oh!
help us in setting our brethren free. In punishing the
oppressors of humanity, may we never pronounce in vain
our terrible motto, Nekam Adonai. Amen, so mote
it be.

(Led by the Thrice Puissant Grand Master, all make
the sign and say, Nekam Adonai. Then all, led by the
Thrice Puissant Grand Master strike seven, 00 00 00 0;
with the hands.)

Thrice Puissant Grand Master—To the glory of the
Grand Architect of the Universe, in the name and under the auspices of the Grand Consistory of the Ancient
and Accepted Scotch Rite, in and for the Sovereign
and Independent State of.........under the Jurisdiction of the Supreme Council for the Northern Jurisdiction of the United States of America, sitting at the City
of New York and State of New York, and by virtue of
the power in me vested by....Council of Kadosh, No..
I declare its labors adjourned. Sir Knights, you may
retire in peace. Be ever guided by prudence and swear
upon this sword not to reveal any of the transactions of
this day. (Thrice Puissant Grand Master leaves the
throne, proceeds to the West and presents the hilt of
his sword which he holds by the blade. All the Knights
pass successively before the Thrice Puissant Grand Master, extend the right hand over the hilt of the sword and
say: *"I swear,"* after which all retire in peace and silence.

PHILOSOPHICAL ANALYSIS

THIRTIETH DEGREE: GRAND-ELECT KNIGHT KADOSH; OR, KNIGHT OF THE WHITE AND BLACK EAGLE.

The "Ne plus ultra" of Masonic Falsehood—The Ritual Tinkered. Added to, and Amended—"Nothing but Vengeance is Spoken of."—Christians Ferociously Condemned as Bigots—Sham Pretence of a Universal Religion.

Kadosh is a Chaldee and Hebrew word, meaning "Holy," used in *Isaiah, 6, 3,* applied to God. This is, therefore, the degree of the Holy Knight. It is common to receive men into this degree, who have not taken all the preceding degrees. Thus, in the degree before this, the Grand Master, by mere authority, receives candidates into eleven degrees, which they have not taken, to enable them to receive the 30th, and become Knights Kadosh. This explains, how men of ordinary memories, and business occupations, can take 33 such degrees, *i. e.,* they don't take them.

This degree is called, in its ritual, the *"Ne plus ultra"* (no more beyond) of Masonic knowledge; (*page 276.*) "though but the Thirtieth degree." A careful reading of the ritual though, will convince thoughtful persons, that this statement is true; and that this degree is also the *"Ne plus ultra"* of Masonic falsehood, fraud, hypocrisy, treason, and general scoundrelism. The proofs of this extraordinary indictment are these:

1. "It is said to have been invented at Lyons in 1743," that is, 144 years ago. This makes it "ancient." (Note 345.)

Now, the ritual is the degree, and this ritual, (page 291.) contains the *telephone,* which is of yesterday; which proves, that this *ancient* degree has been tinkered, added to, and amended, from Ramsay to Albert Pike! This falsehood is a century and a half long.

2. The candidate is made to trample on the Pope's tiara, which bauble is worn in some fashion by every Grand Officer of lodges. This is hypocrisy.

3. Christ is complimented, and His prohibition: "Call no man master," is quoted. Yet Masons all have "Masters." This is hypocrisy.

4. This degree, and almost every other, professes to war on despotism. Yet Masonry is the completest despotism on earth; the edicts of a Grand Lodge must be "obeyed without examination." (*Mackey Lex.*) Taxation at discretion, without reason given, has been decided lawful by lodge-law. (See *Chase's Digest,* art, *Taxation.*) Why this very ritual gives the Master power to stop and adjourn any debate, by three raps with the pommel of his sword! No slaves on a Southern plantation were ever bound by the laws of property to a more abject, cringing obedience to their master, than these Masons are to theirs.

5. The candidate allows the Master, to put his (the candidate's) hand, on a human skull, as a "terrible symbol of human equality;" and they all drink with told: "This is the apex of the Masonic edifice." (Page him "the cup of devils" out of that skull; and they are

285.) And it is. For it is simple, absolute devil-worship. (See *1. Cor. 10, 20.*)

6. This degree quotes Christ's law of equal "love to our neighbor," and yet tells the candidate, after he is received: "The slightest indiscretion will cost you your life;" that is, they will kill him, if he lets out their secrets; tells the truth, by error, "indiscretion," or mistake. If this is not Masonic scoundrelism, what is scoundrelism? (See this on *page 275.*)

7. Yet the candidate is told: "In almost all the rituals of this degree, (*and there were seven Kadosh rituals, see note 348.*) nothing but vengeance is spoken of." But this degree is nothing but philosophy, and philosophy discountenances vengeance. (*Page 276.*) Now return to page 260, of this degree, and see the candidate and his Master, stabbing the dead enemies of the lodge! Is not this the meanest kind of vengeance, such as was practiced on Cromwell, by his enemies? Why, this degree swears this same candidate, to "punish crime," "which I promise to do under penalty of death." And this, forsooth, is no vengeance, but "philosophy." Is it wonderful, that the Bible throughout, calls these false worships, "whoredom?" There never was a drab, at East Cheap, in the days of Falstaff, or in the Five Points, New York, before Jerry McCauley, who could hold up her brazen front, and lie with such impudent coolness, as is practiced in this "Apex of Masonic knowledge."

8. Why, the very basis of the whole Scottish Rite,

that is, the pretended constitutions of Frederick, 1786, are pronounced, by one Masonic historian, *"the Grand Lie* of the order;" which is endorsed by Folger, and as good as endorsed by Mackey himself; (See *note 353.*) who says: "the question is not yet settled, whether there were any such constitutions signed by Frederick, or whether Morin forged them.

9. The Grand Pontiff (*page 263.*) tells the candidate that Scotch Masonry * * * admits to her bosom, on terms of the strictest equality, the members of all religions, of all creeds, and of all countries, without any distinction whatever. This is bad enough. To put beast-worship, child-murder, at the Ganges, and religious cannibalism, on a level, is to deny and exclude the religion which condemns false worships. The prophet Daniel would have been excluded, as a "sectarian bigot," for violating the broad charity of image-worship. But even this pretence is false. This degree was made and practiced in France, and now in the United States. None of the Asiatic, and other heathenisms, so praised by this degree, on page *298,* prevailed in France, or now exist here. Hence the bigots so ferociously condemned are Christians; those who corrupt and enslave the minds of their little children by teaching them the Lord's prayer, and "Now I lay me down to sleep." This degree, framed in 1748, was in its full glory when the street cry in Paris was: '*Tout L'Eveque a la lanterne!"* (*Every bishop to the lamp-*

post!)   Those were Christian bishops, and their crime was Christianity.   And the fierce and savage denunciations of "sectarians," who teach men religion to enslave them, mean Christians.   If not, whom do they mean? Even their sham pretence of a universal religion is violated by their hatred of Christ.

CHAPTER LVII

THIRTY-FIRST DEGREE, OR GRAND INSPECTOR INQUISITOR COMMANDER.[361]

DECORATIONS:—Hangings are white; as also the canopy under which is the throne of the President. There are ten gilded columns; one on each side of the President in the East; one on each side of the Councilors or Inspectors in the West; three on the south side of the room and three on the north, equi-distant from each other.

On the column on the right of the President is inscribed in large letters the word "Justitia" and the attributes of the first and third degrees. On that upon his left the word *"Equitas"* and the attributes of the eighteenth and thirtieth degrees, from the two columns springs a Gothic Arch, from the apex thereof is sus-

Note 361.—"Grand Inquisitor Commander. The 31st degree of the Ancient and Accepted rite. It is not an historical degree, but is simply administrative in its character; the duties of the members being to examine and regulate the proceedings of the subordinate lodges and chapters. The meeting is designated a 'Sovereign Tribunal,' and is composed of nine officers, viz.: A Most Perfect President, a Chancellor, a Treasurer, and six Inquisitors—one being elected to perform the functions of Inspecting Inquisitor. The decoration of the Lodge is white, with eight golden columns; on the dais above the presiding officer's throne are the letters J. E.; there is also an altar covered with white drapery. In the East, on a low seat, is placed a case containing the archives of the Order, covered with blue drapery, having on its front a large red cross; on the right of the altar is the table of the Chancellor, on the left that of the Treasurer. The floor of the Sovereign Tribunal is covered by a printing, the centre of which represents a cross, encompassing all the attributes of Masonry. There is no apron; the members wear a white collar, on which is embroidered a triangle with rays, having in its center the figures 31, to which is suspended the jewel—a silver Teutonic cross. In France the regulations direct a white apron, with aurora (yellow) flap, embroidered with the attributes of the degree."—Macoy's Encyclopedia and Dictionary of Freemasonry, Article Grand Inquisitor Commander.

pended over the head of the President, the Tetractys[***]
of Pythagoras, thus: .˙.   and under it a naked sword
and a balance, or .˙.˙ · the scales of justice. On
the column on the right of the Counsellors is inscribed
the word *"Lenitas"* and the attributes of the second and
fourteenth degrees, and on the column on their left, the
word *"Misericordia,"* and the attributes of the fourth
and fifteenth degrees. From these two columns springs
a Gothic Arch, from the apex whereof is suspended in
letters of gold the sacred word of the eighteenth degree.
On the three columns in the South, going from East to
West, are the busts of Moses, Zoroaster and Minos, with
the names of each inscribed on his column, and the
attributes of the ninth, thirteenth and twenty-second
degrees. On the columns on the North, also going from
East to West are the busts of Confucius, Socrates and
Alfred the Great, with the names of each inscribed on
his column and the attributes of the twenty-fifth,
twenty-eighth and twenty-ninth degrees.

In front of the President is an altar, on which are the
square and compasses, the plumb and level, a small pair
of scales, a naked sword, two poniards and the book of
constitutions.

Between the throne of the President and the altar is
a stand upon which is placed the coffer containing the
record of the Supreme Tribunal. In the centre of the

Note 362.—"Signifies literally, the number four, and is therefore synonymous with the quaternion; but it has been peculiarly aipplied to a
symbol of the Pythagoreans, which is composed of ten dots arranged in
a triangular form of four rows.
This figure was in itself, as a whole, emblematic of the Tetragrammaton, or sacred name of four letters (for tetractys, in Greek, means
four), and was undoubtedly learned byl Pythagoras during his visit to
Babylon. But the parts of which it is composed were also pregnant
ayimbols. Thus the one point was a symbol of the active principle or
creator, the two points of the passive principle or matter, the three of
the world proceeding from their union, and the four of the liberal arts
and sciences, which may be said to complete and perfect that world."—
Mackey's Encyclopaedia of Freemasonry, Article Tetractys.

GRAND INSPECTOR INQUISITOR COMMANDER. **313**

room are ten lights; in the East ten, and in the west ten; each ten being arranged by 1, 2, 3, 4, in the form of the Tetractys.

The altar is covered with a white cloth and on the front part thereof, towards the West, is painted or embroidered a pair of golden scales resting on the point of a naked sword.

TITLES, OFFICERS AND THEIR STATIONS:—The assembly is styled Supreme Tribunal and is composed of nine members and never more. If any more members are present they may be consulted but they cannot vote.

The presiding officer is styled Most Perfect President and sits in the East.

The Wardens are styled Councilors or Inspectors, and sit together in the West.

The Secretary, Keeper of the Seals and Archives is styled Chancellor and sits on the right of the President.

The Treasurer sits on the left of the President.

The Advocate is stationed in the South.

The Defender is stationed in the North.

The Master of Ceremonies is stationed in front of the Counsellor.

The Pursuivant or Usher, at the door of the Tribunal.

The Tyler is not included among the nine members, composing the Supreme Tribunal and is styled Inquisitor, he is stationed outside. All the members of the Supreme Tribunal except the President, are styled Most Enlightened.

CLOTHING, JEWELS, ETC:—No apron is worn in the Supreme Tribunal. In the inferior bodies, the Grand Inspectors Inquisitors wear one of entirely white sheepskin, with a Teutonic Cross embroidered in silver on the flap. The collar is white. On the breast at the point is a triangle emitting rays, embroidered in gold in the centre of which is the number 31 in Arabic figures.

In the inferior bodies, instead of a collar, a Grand Inspector Inquisitor Commander may wear around his neck a golden chain from which hangs the cross of the order. The links of the chain are formed of the interlaced attributes of the eight fundamental degrees of Masonry, viz: 1st, 2nd, 3rd, 4th, 14th, 15th, 18th and 30th.

The jewel of the degree is a Teutonic Cross of silver.

The members are all clothed in black and wear swords. During a reception [initiation] they wear black masks or veils. "This degree shall be conferred in the presence of three Sovereign Grand Inspectors General 33°."

Constitutions of 1786, Art. XI.

PREROGATIVES:—When a Grand Inspector Inquisitor Commander, wearing the proper insignia, visits a lodge of an inferior degree, he announces himself as a Grand Inspector Inquisitor Commander. He is proved in the ordinary manner and the report is made in the ear of the Master who causes all the members to be placed around the altar. He then sends the two Wardens to receive said Grand Inspector Inquisitor Commander who is conducted by them to the altar. The Master then leaves his seat and placing the three gavels upon the altar, he presents them to the visiting Grand Inspector Inquisitor Commander, who accepts and returns them to the Master and to each of the Wardens, after which he is conducted by the Master to the seat of honor.

The Supreme Council, or Grand Consistory, as the case may be, have alone the right to establish Supreme Tribunals in their jurisdiction. Each Supreme Tribunal is a distinct body, as a Chapter of Rose Croix or a Council of Kadosh, and it should have the exclusive privilege of conferring the 31°. But the custom has generally prevailed in this country that the Supreme Council or Grand Consistory, according to circumstances, should be opened as a Supreme Tribunal to confer the 31°. When the Supreme Council is to confer said degree, it is open in its Consistorial Chamber.

Illustrous Commander in Chief—(Still in the Consistory, business having been disposed of.) Sublime Princes, let us proceed to the Supreme Tribunal for the purpose of disposing of the business of the day. Illustrious Brother First Lieutenant Commander, give orders that the procession be formed.

First Lieutenant—Illustrious Brother Second Lieutenant Commander, it is the order of the Illustrious Commander in Chief that we repair to the Supreme Tribunal of Grand Inspectors Inquisitors Commanders. Cause the procession to be formed.

Second Lieutenant—Sublime Prince Grand Master of Ceremonies, it is the order of the Illustrious Commander in Chief, that we repair to the Supreme Tribunal of Grand Inspectors Inquisitors Commanders. Cause the procession to be formed.

Master of Ceremonies—Illustrious Brethren, Sublime Princes, by order of the Illustrious Commander in Chief, we are now to repair to the Supreme Tribunal of Grand Inspectors Inquisitors Commanders. Arrange yourselves in procession. (The procession is accordingly formed. The Grand Master of Ceremonies goes in front. Then the Grand Standard Bearer who is followed by the Illustrious Commander in Chief, with the Deputy Illustrious Commander in Chief on his left. Then the Grand Chancellor and Minister of State, carrying the coffer containing the records of the Supreme Tribunal. Next the two Lieutenant Commanders, and then the other officers and members. On entering the Supreme Tribunal, the Illustrious Commander in Chief, proceeds to the east of a place midway between the throne and the altar, where is a stand or small table on which to place the coffer containing the records He faces to the West, the Grand Chancellor and Minister of State place the coffer on the stand and take the right and left respectively of the Illustrious Commander in Chief and Deputy, also facing the West. The two Lieutenant Commanders stand opposite the Illustrious Commander in Chief, facing the East. The Grand Master of Ceremonies is on the North side facing the South. The Standard Bearer is on the South side facing the North. The Deputy Illustrious Commander in Chief, if present, stands between the Illustrious Commander in Chief and the Minister of State. The other officers and members complete the circle, the Coffer being in its centre. The Illustrious Commander in Chief is now the Most Perfect President. The Lieutenant Commanders are the Chancellors or Inspectors. The Minister of State, the Advocate. The Captain of the Guards, the Pursuivant or Usher.)

OPENING CEREMONIES

GRAND INSPECTOR INQUISITOR COMMANDER.[363]

Most Perfect President—(Ascending the throne.) Most Enlightened Brethren, the obligations of duty are eternal to the good Mason. See Brother Pursuivant, that the doors of this Supreme Tribunal are safely guarded and give orders that none be allowed to enter without our permission, that we may tranquilly perform our duty. Be seated my brethren. (All the officers now take their respective stations and the members occupy the seats on the North and South. Meanwhile the Pursuivant goes out, returns, gives the battery which is answered without and reports as follows:)

Pursuivant—Most Perfect President, the doors of the Supreme Tribunal are safely guarded.

Most Perfect President—Then we may safely proceed. Most Enlightened Brother Pursuivant what is your duty?

Pursuivant—To execute your orders, coming to me by the West and see the judgments of the Tribunal duly executed; to serve and return all processes, and to compel order, when the Supreme Tribunal is in session.

Most Perfect President—Most Enlightened Brother, Master of Ceremonies. What is your duty?

Note 363.—"Grand Inspector. Inquisitor Commander. The thirty-first degree of the Ancient and Accepted Scottish Rite. It is not an historical degree, but simply a judicial power of the higher degrees. The place of meeting is called a Supreme Tribunal. The decorations are white, and the presiding officer is styled Most Perfect President. The jewel of the degree is a Teutonic cross of silver attached to white watered ribbon." Mackey's Encyclopædia of Freemasonry, Article Grand Inspector, Inquisitor Commander.

Master of Ceremonies—(Rising.) Most Perfect President, to carry your orders within and without the Supreme Tribunal; in case of trial to introduce the accused and witnesses, and in case of reception to accompany the candidate during the ceremony of reception.

Most Perfect President—Most Enlightened Brother Defender, what is your duty in the Supreme Tribunal?

Defender—(Rising.) To defend all persons charged with offences and tried before this Tribunal, to see that no incompetent evidence is admitted against them, nor any that is competent in their favor rejected. To present the truth in their defence and to urge all circumstances of extenuation or of justification in their behalf.

Most Perfect President—Most Enlightened Brother Advocate, what is your duty here?

Advocate—(Rising.) To prefer charges against those who, under the jurisdiction of this Tribunal, have been guilty of offences against Masonic law and duty; to draft the acts of accusation, prepare the testimony, elicit the truth and present the whole case fairly, without misrepresentation or exaggeration to the Supreme Tribunal.

Most Perfect President—Most Enlightened Brother Chancellor, what is your duty?

Chancellor—(Rising.) To record the proceedings and judgments of the Supreme Tribunal.

Most Perfect President—Most Enlightened Brother Treasurer, what is your duty here?

Treasurer—(Rising.) To receive all moneys belonging to the Supreme Tribunal, to keep the same faithfully, and to pay out all warrants duly signed by the proper officers.

Most Perfect President—Most Enlightened Brother Junior Councilor, what is your duty?

Junior Councilor—(Rising.) To guard against all

violations of Masonic law, to give my advice on all proper occasions, to the Most Perfect President and to pronounce just and righteous judgments.

Most Perfect President—Most Enlightened Brother Senior Councilor, what is your duty?

Senior Councilor—(Rising.) That of my Junior, tempering justice with equity and ever remembering the dictates of mercy.

Most Perfect President—Most Enlightened Brother Senior Councilor, what is your duty of the Most Perfect President?

Senior Councilor—To preside in judgment and decide the law, to judge justly and to punish sternly, but ever remembering the frailty and imperfection of human nature, to pardon and forgive while there yet remains hope of reformation.

Most Perfect President—Most Enlightened Brother Senior Councilor, what is the duty of all the members of this Supreme Tribunal when sitting in judgment?

Senior Councilor—Careful investigation of all material facts, natural and charitable construction of acts and motives, calm and deliberate consideration, just judgment and utter disregard of persons, influence, rank and power.

Most Perfect President—I recognize my duty. My brethren see that you neither forget nor neglect those that devolve on you. You are now in the Holy Sanctuary of eternal Masonic justice and equity. Let us promise and most solemnly pledge ourselves to perform, so far as human frailty will permit the high duties that we have agreed to devolve upon us; to be ever faithful to the constitution, statutes and regulations of the order, and to be always and everywhere guided by justice and equity.

All—(Extending the right hand towards the coffer containing. the records.) We do solemnly promise and swear.

Most Perfect President—And now my brethren, let us implore the aid, the mercy and the protection of him who can alone give us strength to perform our promises. Order my brethren. On your knees! (All rise under the sign of order as given on page 192. and then kneel.)

PRAYER.

Hear us with indulgence, O infinite Deity, whose attributes are infinite yet infinitely harmonious! Thou of whose essence are justice, equity and mercy, intermingled into one infinite excellence. Thou of whom all thoughts and all actions of men are known, and visible as thine own! To whom the infinite past and infinite future are one now, and the infinitudes of space in all directions are here. Give us the wisdom and the will to judge justly, accurately and mercifully. Keep our feet from going astray; lead us by the hand of truth, close up to us all the paths and avenues of temptation. Strengthen our good resolves and free us from the empire of prejudice, partiality, error and passion. Help us to perform all our Masonic duties, to ourselves, to other men, and to Thee. Let the great flood of Masonic light flow in a perpetual current over the whole world and make Masonry the creed of all mankind. Pardon us when we offend. When we go astray, lead us back to the true path and help our feeble efforts to advance the cause of liberty and toleration; and when we come to be finally judged by Thee, do not thou judge us as in our feebleness and passion we may have judged others, but forgive us, and take us home to Thee. Amen.

All—So mote it be.

Most Perfect President—(Rising.) Rise my brethren. (All rise under the sign of order.)

Most Perfect President—Most Enlightened Brethren Grand Inspectors Inquisitors Commanders. Let us proceed to our ¹abors, that through our exertions our beloved order may prosper and our solemn obligations be complied with. Aid me my brethren and enlighten me with your counsel. To order, Most Enlightened Brethren!

First Sign.

FIRST SIGN.

Most Perfect President—(Making the first sign.) By crossing both hands, bring them to the navel, thumbs crossing each other and says Justice.

ANSWERING SIGN.

All—(Make the answering sign.) Cross both arms above your head, right outside, palms outward, and say Equity.

Answering Sign.

All—So mote it be.

Most Perfect President—(Gives the battery by one, three, four and one; 0 000 0000 0.)

All—(Give the battery.)

Most Perfect President—Most Enlightened Brother Senior Councilor, this Supreme Tribunal is now open. Let due proclamation thereof be made.

Senior Councilor—Most Enlightened Brother Junior Councilor, this Supreme Tribunal is now open. Let due proclamation thereof be made.

Junior Councilor—Most Enlightened Brother Pursuivant, make proclamation that this Supreme Tribunal is now open, and that all who demand its judgment may now draw near.

Pursuivant—(Opening the door.)   Hear ye, this Supreme Tribunal of Grand Inspectors Inquisitors Commanders is now open.   Whosoever hath been cited to appear or hath complaints or appeal to make or answer, let him draw near and he shall be heard. (Closes the door.)

Most Perfect President—(Strikes one.)   Most Enlightened Brethren, be seated.

Most Perfect President—Most Enlightened Brother Chancellor, arise and let us proceed to open the coffer containing the records of the Supreme Tribunal, and to take therefrom such as may be needed for our present labors.   (The Most Perfect President and Chancellor leave their seats and proceed to the coffer, each holding a key thereof, it having two locks. They open it and take out the record book of the Sovereign Tribunal and any other books or papers needed and return to their seats; the Chancellor carrying the book or books and papers)

Most Perfect President—(Strikes one.)   Most Enlightened Brethren, listen to the reading of the record of the last session of the Supreme Tribunal. Brother Chancellor, read the record! (Chancellor reads.)

Most Perfect President—Most Enlightened Brethren, if there be anything in the record to be added to or diminished, be pleased to make it known. (If any error or omission is pointed out, it is corrected and the record is then signed by the Most Perfect President and Chancellor. Then, if there be any papers to be acted on, they are read and considered.)

Most Perfect President—The record of our last session is approved and duly signed, all communications are disposed of and we may now proceed to other business.

CHAPTER LVIII

THIRTY-FIRST DEGREE, OR GRAND INSPECTOR INQUISI-TOR COMMANDER.[344]

INITIATION.

Most Perfect President—(Strikes one.) Most Enlightened Brethren, Grand Inspectors Inquisitors Commanders, the Grand Consistory of Sublime Princes of
the Royal Secret, has been pleased to designate the
Grand Elect Knight Kadosh, A....B, as worthy to receive the important degree of Grand Inspector Inquisitor Commander, and to become a member of this Supreme Tribunal of the 31st degree of the Ancient and
Accepted Rite of Masonry. But yet his initiation cannot proceed, if any lawful objection be made. If you
consent to confer upon him the said degree and to admit
him as a member here, inform me by giving the sign of
affirmation. (All who favor it raise the right hand
above their head.)

Most Perfect President—If any do not consent, let
them inform me by giving the negative sign. (This

Note 364.—"The thirteenth degree conferred in the Consistory of
Princes of the Royal Secret, Scotch Masonry, and the thirty-first upon
the catalogue of that system. It is otherwise termed Grand Inquiring
Commander. It has no historical allusions, being simply administrative
in its character. The assembly is entitled a Sovereign Tribunal. The
hangings are white. The officers are the Most Perfect President the
Wardens, who are termed Inspectors; the Secretary, who is called Chancellor. The members are styled Most Enlightened. There is no apron
worn in the Tribunal, but when visiting inferior bodies, the members
wear a white apron, with the Teutonic cross. Jewel, a silver Teutonic
cross. A white collar is worn, showing a triangle, with the figures 31 in
the center."—Morris's Masonic Dictionary, Article Grand Inspector, Inquisitor Commander, or Order of Five Brethren,

sign is made by stretching the right arm to the front,
the hand open and raised upwards as if repelling a person. If there be no objection, or if any objection be
made and overruled the Master proceeds.)

Most Perfect President—Most Enlightened Brother
Master of Ceremonies, repair to the ante-chamber of the
Supreme Tribunal and if the Grand Elect Knight
Kadosh whom we have determined to receive here, be in
attendance and you are satisfied of his identity, and of
his proficiency in all the degrees from the first to the
thirtieth inclusive, prepare him in such manner as our
usages require, bring him with you to the door of this
Supreme Tribunal and apply for his admission here by
the proper alarm. (The Master of Ceremonies withdraws and meets the candidate who is clothed in the
insignia and jewel of a Knight Kadosh. He examines
him in all the preceding degrees from the first up to the
thirtieth inclusive. He then blindfolds him and conducts him to the door and gives the alarm of the 30th
degree, 00 00 00 0.)

Pursuivant—Most Enlightened Brother Junior Councilor, the alarm of a Knight Kadosh resounds at the
door.

Junior Councilor—Most Enlightened Brother Senior
Councilor, the alarm of a Knight Kadosh resounds at
the door.

Senior Councilor—Most Perfect President, the alarm
of a Knight Kadosh resounds at the door.

Most Perfect President—Most Enlightened Brother
Senior Councilor, order the Junior Councilor to see
from whom the alarm proceeds.

Senior Councilor—Most Enlightened Brother Junior
Councilor, order the Pursuivant to inquire from whom
the alarm proceeds.

Junior Councilor—Most Enlightened Brother Pursuivant, open and inquire from whom the alarm proceeds.

Pursuivant—(Opening the door.) Who approaches the Supreme Tribunal, and what is his desire?

Master of Ceremonies—It is the Master of Ceremonies having in charge a Knight Kadosh, who seeks to obtain the 31st degree, and whom having examined and finding him duly qualified, virtuous, upright, eminent, he asks permission to introduce into this Supreme Tribunal.

Pursuivant—(Closing the door.) Most Enlightened Brother Junior Councilor, it is the Master of Ceremonies having in charge a Knight Kadosh, who seeks to obtain the 31st degree, and whom having examined and finding him duly qualified, virtuous, upright, eminent, he asks permission to introduce into this Supreme Tribunal.

Junior Councilor—Most Enlightened Brother Senior Councilor, it is the Master of Ceremonies having in charge a Knight Kadosh, who seeks to obtain the 31st degree, and whom having examined and finding him duly qualified, virtuous, upright, eminent, he asks permission to introduce into this Supreme Tribunal.

Senior Councilor—Most Perfect President, it is the Master of Ceremonies having in charge a Knight Kadosh, who seeks to obtain the 31st degree, and whom having examined and finding him duly qualified, virtuous, upright, eminent, he asks permission to introduce into this Supreme Tribunal.

Most Perfect President—What is his name?

Senior Councilor—What is his name?

Junior Councilor—What is his name?

Pursuivant—(Opening the door.) What is his name?

Master of Ceremonies—It is the Knight Brother. A....B. (The Pursuivant, Junior and Senior Councilors repeat the same.)

Most Perfect President—What is his occupation?

(The Senior and Junior Councilors and Pursuivant repeat, each in his turn.)

Master of Ceremonies—That of [liquor dealer] useful and honorable, as all work is in this world. (The Pursuivant, Junior and Senior Councilors repeat the answers successively.)

Most Perfect President—Hath he, by sufficient service and patient obedience as a Mason learned the first lesson in the art of governing? (The Senior and Junior Councilors and Pursuivant repeat the question.)

Master of Ceremonies—He hath. He has learned to govern himself. (The Pursuivant, Junior and Senior Councilors repeat the answer.)

Most Perfect President—Is he true and trustworthy? Is he honest, temperate, of equal temper, charitable of judgment and of merciful impulses? (The Senior and Junior Councilors and Pursuivant repeat the question.)

Master of Ceremonies—He is a Knight Kadosh, and his brethren have thought him not unworthy to be admitted here. (The Pursuivant, Junior and Senior Councilors repeat the answer.)

Most Perfect President—Most Enlightened Brother Senior Councilor give orders that the Most Enlightened Brother Master of Ceremonies and the Knight Kadosh, so vouched for be allowed to enter.

Senior Councilor—Most Enlightened Brother Junior Councilor, give orders that the Most Enlightened Brother Master of Ceremonies and the Knight Kadosh, so vouched for be allowed to enter.

Junior Councilor—Most Enlightened Brother Pursuivant, allow the Most Enlightened Brother Master of Ceremonies and the Knight Kadosh, so vouched for to enter.

Pursuivant—It is the order of the Most Perfect

President that you be allowed to enter. (The candidate enters, conducted by the Master of Ceremonies who leads him toward the East, and halts in front of the President. The door is then closed.)

Most Perfect President—My brother, you desire to take upon yourself an arduous and most responsible office. There is but one infallible, unerring judge. All human judgment is at best uncertain. The errors of the judge have consequences as serious as those of the crimes of other men, and they must often, however innocent and unintentional, produce when they are made known by that unrelenting censor, Time, regret and sorrow and sometimes remorse. It is not wise to seek to judge our fellow men. It is a stern duty and an unwelcome task, to be performed when it cannot in any wise be honorably avoided, and never a privilege to be desired and coveted.

Woe unto that man who assumes the power of judgment, and so to some extent usurps the prerogative of God, if he be not himself dispassionate, upright, impartial, just. Does your heart tell you that only proper motives lead you to seek that power and that you may with safety to yourself, take it into your hands?

Candidate—It does.

Most Perfect President—It is well my brother, if indeed you be not deceived. Go with your guide; heed well the lessons and the warnings you will receive and return again to me. (The Master of Ceremonies conducts him six times around the room halting in turn before each of the six columns in the North and South, and addressed by a brother at each as follows:

AT THE COLUMN OF ALFRED:—I was the just King Alfred, of Saxon England. I framed wise laws, made upright judges, independent of my will and that of the people; and caused just and speedy judgment to be given.

In all my realm, justice and right were sold to none, denied to none, delayed to none.

I slept little, I wrote much, I studied more, I reigned only to bless those over whom I had dominion. I have vanished into the past and many ages have marched in solemn procession by my grave. Yet I still live in the memory of men. They call me "Great King," "wise law giver," "just judge." Follow then my example, or fear to sit in judgment on thy fellows.

AT THE COLUMN OF SOCRATES:—I was Socrates the Athenian. I knew the holy mysteries and reverenced God in nature. In the sacred groves of Athens, I taught that God was one and the soul of man immortal. I taught obedience to the laws and decrees of the people of Athens and the Council of five hundred.

When I sat in the Court of the Areopagus, I swore by the paternal Apollo, by Ceres and by Jupiter the King, that I would give sentence uprightly and according to law, or when the law was silent, to the best of my judgment, and that I would not receive gifts, nor should any other for me, nor receive bribes from my own passion, prejudice or affection, nor allow any other person to do the like by any means, whether direct or indirect, to prevent justice in the court.

And when by an unjust judgment the same court condemned, I refused to flee away and escape, lest I should bring the laws into disrepute, holding the good citizen bound to submit to even the unjust judgment of the State. If thou wouldst fain become a judge of others, first prepare thyself by learning to obey the laws.

AT THE COLUMN OF CONFUCIUS:—I was Confucius, who read and interpreted to the people of Ancient China, the great laws engraved by the finger of God, in everlasting letters upon the pages of the many leaved book of nature. I said to them, desire not for your country any other benefit than justice. The great law of duty is to be looked for in humanity. Justice in equity; to render to every man that to which he is entitled. He who would stand above the ordinary level of men, must be exempt from prejudice, self-conceit and obstinacy, and be governed by the mandates of justice alone. Cultivate justice and piety, which great toward your parents and relations, should be greater toward your country.

Hear much, reflect much and say nothing superfluous. Let doubt of guilt be acquitted and presumption of innocence solid proof. So I taught, and my influence lived after me and was good and gave good fortune to my country, and yet controlled its destinies. That is the noblest recompense of human virtue. Do thou strive so to live and act, to obey and govern, and thou too mayst live in the good opinion of men after thou art dead and thy influences may make thee too a King over the minds of men.

AT THE COLUMN OF MINOS:—I was Minos, the law giver of Crete, I taught the Cretans that the laws which I enacted were dictated by Zeus the father, for all true and righteous laws and all human justice are but the developments of that eternal and infinite justice, that is of the essence of the Deity, he who assumes to judge his brethren, clothes himself with a power like that of God. To usurp a jurisdiction is to invade the territory of his prerogative. Act so that men may praise thy moderation, thy inflexibility, thy equity and thy integrity. And yet regard not alone the opinion and the judgment of the living, but seek the approval of those who shall live hereafter, whose verdict will be more just, even if more

severe. Woe unto thee, if being thyself vicious or criminal, thou dost assume to judge others and still more if
thou givest corrupt judgment. For then will thy memory be execrated, and in all time, it shall be the bitterest
reproach to an unjust judge to call him by thy name.

AT THE COLUMN OF ZOROASTER:—I was Zoroaster,
whose words became law to the Persians. I said, "He
is the best servant of God, whose heart is upright, who
is liberal, with due regard to what is just to all men;
who turns not his eyes towards riches and whose heart
wishes well to every thing that lives." So act towards
all men that when they die, thou shalt not have to regret their death, because thou hast done them wrong and
can no longer make reparation. He alone is just who is
charitable and merciful in his judgments and he alone
is wise who thinks *well* and not *evil* of other men.

Attempt not to break through the laws of providence,
nor impiously presume to correct the ways of God. Nor
measure the ocean of his wisdom with the tape-line of
thy little conceptions.

Neither cringe nor fawn, nor depend meanly; but
find thy happiness within thyself. Satisfy thine own
conscience and fear neither the outrages of fortune, nor
the injuries of enemies. Crime is not to be measured
by the issue of events, but by the bad intentions of the
doer. Study therefore the dominion of thyself and
quiet thine own commotions, and hold it the noblest
ovation, to triumph over thy passions. Let the long
train of thy trophies be within thee, and not without,
and when thou sittest in judgment on others, let malice
be manacled and envy fettered behind thy judgment seat.

AT THE COLUMN OF MOSES—I was Moses,'" the leader and lawgiver of the Israelites. I was initiated into
the mysteries and wisdom of ancient Egypt, and that
wisdom dictated the statutes by which Israel was governed. I said unto the people, "Thou shalt not wrest the
judgment of thy poor in his cause.

"Thou shalt take no gift, for the gift blindeth the
wise, and perverteth the words of the righteous.

"Ye shall do no unrighteousness in judgment. Thou
shalt not respect the person of the poor, nor honor the
person of the mighty.

"Ye shall hear the small as well as the great. Ye
shall not fear the face of man, for the judgment is
God's." (Candidate halts before the Councilors.)

Senior Councilor—Thou hast heard the words of the
great sages, lawgivers and philosophers of antiquity.
Remember now the sacred word of the 18th degree.
Hear the voice of one whom all Christendom regards
as the greatest lawgiver that has ever come among men;
and listen reverentially to his teachings.

"If ye forgive not men their trespasses, neither will
your Heavenly Father forgive your trespasses. But if
ye forgive men their trespasses, your Heavenly Father
will also forgive you. With what judgment ye judge,
ye shall be judged, and with what measure ye mete, it
shall be measured to you again.

"If thy brother trespass against thee, go and tell him
his fault between thee and him alone. If he shall hear

Note 365.—"Moses. Moses was learned in all the wisdom of the
Egyptians; he was initiated in all the knowledge of the wise men of that
nation, by whom the learning of antiquity had been retained and held
sacred; wrapped up from the eye of the wicked and vulgar in symbols
and hieroglyphics, and communicated to men of their own order only,
with care, secrecy, and circumspection. This secrecy is not in any wise
to be wondered at, when we consider the persecution which would have
followed a faith unacceptable to the ignorance of the nations who were
enveloped in superstition and bigotry."—Macoy's Encyclopædia and Dictionary of Freemasonry, Article Moses.

thee, thou hast gained thy brother. Judge not according to the appearance, but judge righteous judgment.

"If thy brother trespass against thee, rebuke him, and if he repent, forgive him, and if he trespass against thee seven times in a day, and seven times in a day turn again to thee saying 'I repent' thou shalt forgive him.

"Blessed are the merciful, for they shall obtain mercy."

Go now my brother, to the East, the seat of that justice which also is a ray of the great light separated from the others by the prism of Masonry. (Candidate is conducted to the East.)

Most Perfect President—Be seated my brother. You have heard the lesson of immortal wisdom, once uttered by mortal lips that have long since mouldered into dust. Through those lips God spake unto men, for from him alone cometh all wisdom. You desire to become a member of this Tribunal and a Supreme judge in Masonry. The Grand Consistory of Sublime Princes of the Royal Secret, satisfied of your capacity and qualifications; of your impartiality and justice has, in its wisdom, granted your request. When you shall have been received among us it will devolve on you to administer the high justice of the order, and in that the purest equity must be your guide. In every case submitted to your judgment, and whether the matters and the parties be Masonic or profane, you must hear affably, deliberate calmly and yield to no other influences than those of Justice and Equity, of Lenity and Mercy; the four sacred words that with their splendor light every Supreme Tribunal of Grand Inspectors Inquisitors Commanders.

You will not suspect, we trust, that to your title of Inquisitor will be attached that odious meaning which has made the name so fearful and detestable in all the countries in which toleration has found a domicile. In the name we bear, it means one who seeks and searches for, inquires after and investigates the truth, and the truth alone.

The punishment must ever be proportionate to the offence, and some must not be punished for doing things for which others are not so much as called to account. In punishing also, we must guard against passion and remember that there is no such thing in Masonry as vindictive justice.

When you maintain a cause in argument, in any form whatever; in the court, the market, or the fireside, you are never to forget, or offend against, the rules of courtesy and charity, or overpass the boundaries of moderation. There must be in your argument neither heat nor bitter words. If you have maturely reflected and are satisfied that the grounds you take are wholly right, maintain with firmness and express with frankness your own opinion, but not too positively or scornfully towards your antagonist, nor with the use of any words that can justly wound his feelings or startle his self respect. Suggestion often convinces more than assertion. And a modest and courteous demonstration will succeed when rude and positive logic will always fail.

Ever remember that being human, you must of necessity often err. That those who hold different opinions entertain them as honestly as you do your own. And that you have no right to deny or doubt their sincerity. Especially never harshly denounce an opinion that more experience and a more thorough investigation may some day compel you to adopt. And therefore always treat your opponents as if it were certainly at some time to happen, that their opinions could become your own.

If in his progress upward to this degree, the Mason has not learned wisdom, he has already advanced too far. And it is the doctrine of Masonry that no man is truly wise who is not kind and courteous; charitable in his construction of men's motives, lenient and merciful, and distrustful of his own ability to resist the allurement of temptation and the mighty influences of prejudice and passion. Remember that you represent the order; that you must maintain its dignity and glory, preserve its constitutions and act by its laws. And that all those things are committed to your fidelity. You are neither to be subordinate nor subservient, nor haughty, nor domineering, and ever to bear in mind that *"quod non vetat lex, hoc vetat fieri pudor."* What law's letter does not prohibit is often forbidden by propriety and fitness of things.

My brother, no one should assume a Masonic obligation unless he is convinced that he possesses sufficient resolution and moral strength to enable him faithfully to keep and perform it. It is unfortunately too true, that no cause of insincerity, prevarication and falsehood has been more powerful than the practice of administering oaths; and that attempts to strengthen the obligations of morality and duty, by oaths with exaggerated penalties, are generally found to have no tendency but to relax them.

You may judge by what you have heard, what are the duties which you will assume as a Grand Inspector Inquisitor Commander, and in what spirit and manner you must discharge them. Do you feel that it is in your power so to perform those duties?

Candidate—(Rising.) I do.

Most Perfect President—Are you ready to endeavor to renounce all passions and overcome all weaknesses that could lead you to do acts of injustice and give hasty and inconsiderate judgment?

Candidate—I am.

Most Perfect President—Do you believe that you can sacrifice your pride of opinion and love of self respect, to maintain the holy cause of justice and equity?

Candidate—I do.

Most Perfect President—Go then to our holy altar, in charge of our Most Enlightened Brother, the Master of Ceremonies and there kneel with sincerity and reverence, with no thought in your heart and no word on your lips but those of soberness and truth. (Master of Ceremonies conducts him to the altar, causes him to kneel on the right knee, and places in his left hand the scales of justice, laying his right hand on the book of constitutions.)

Most Perfect President—(Striking one and rising.) Order my brethren! Form the circle around the candidate. (All rise and suround the candidate, extending their left hands over him while they hold their swords in the right, and all repeat with him the responses; after which the Most Perfect President leaves his seat and meets the candidate.)

Most Perfect President—Kneeling at this altar of Masonry in token of humility and reverential awe of Deity; do you, upon these emblems of justice, equity, uprightness and the law's dread vengeance, most solemnly and sincerely swear that you will never reveal any of the secrets of Grand Inspector Inquisitor Commander to any person and under any circumstances in the world, unless duly permitted to do so by a Consistory of Sublime Princes of the Royal Secret.

Candidate and All—I do.

Most Perfect President—Do you furthermore promise

and swear that you will scrupulously observe and cause to be observed, the constitutions, statutes and regulations of this Supreme Tribunal so long as you remain a member thereof; that you will with zeal and energy propagate the doctrines of the Ancient and Accepted Rite of Masonry, and labor for its diffusion and prosperity, and that you will not consent to the admission of any person to the high degrees of the Rite who is not an intelligent man, of respectable acquirements and information, and of virtue and honor?

Candidate and All—I do.

Most Perfect President—Raise your right hand towards heaven. Do you most solemnly and sincerely swear, that you will carefully examine all cases in which you may be judge; listen attentively to every argument that may be urged therein and faithfully and impartially weigh both evidence and argument, being neither careless nor indifferent, partial nor prejudiced; nor wearying of investigation, with no other purpose than that of giving a true, just, equitable and merciful judgment?

Candidate and All—I do.

Most Perfect President—Do you solemnly and sincerely swear that you will never sit in judgment in any case where you may entertain feelings of enmity or ill-will toward a party therein, or any feelings of prejudice or dislike; nor in any case where from any cause whatever you doubt whether you can hear patiently, consider calmly, and decide impartially?

Candidate and All—I do.

Most Perfect President—Do you solemnly and sin- and swear that you will never allow rank and power, influence or money to sway your judgment, and that before you as a judge, all men shall stand on one common level, to be condemned if guilty; to be acquitted if innocent?

Candidate and All—I do.

Most Perfect President—Do you solemnly and sincerely swear that you will as a judge lay aside all pride of opinion, obstinacy and self will, and be governed absolutely by the dictates of law, justice equity and your own conscience, so far as the frailty of your nature will permit?

Candidate and All—I do.

Most Perfect President—Do you solemnly and sincerely swear that you will usurp no doubtful power; that you will strain no law so as to make it cover cases to which it does not plainly apply; that you will presume every man innocent until he is proven guilty, and that you will give to every one accused the benefit of all reasonable doubt, and of a charitable and natural construction of his actions; and remember that the Masonic law seeks punishment as a means only, and not as an end?

Candidate and All—I do.

Most Perfect President—Repeat then with me. (Candidate and all repeat the following:)

All this I do swear, expecting that God will so judge me, as I judge others, and consigning myself to the contempt of my brethren and to their just and terrible anger, to be visited upon my unprotected head, if I should willfully or through indifference violate this my solemn oath and obligation. So help me God.

All—Forgive us our tresspasses, O! Father, as we forgive those that trespass against us.

Most Perfect President—Witness the solemn oath my brethren, and let it be recorded.

All—We witness it.

Chancellor—And I record it. (As the last words are uttered, light is given to the candidate, the scales of justice are taken from him and placed on the altar.)

Most Perfect President—(Taking the candidate by the hand. (Rise my brother.) (Candidate rises and all the brethren sheath their swords.)

Most Perfect President—Most Enlightened Brother Master of Ceremonies, do your duty. (Master of Ceremonies divests the candidate of all his decorations and lays them on the altar.)

Most Perfect President—Sir Knight, we divest you of all your decorations, because the degree which you are now entering is above those you have already received, and in it you enter the judicial branch and leave the military branch of the order. Most Enlightened Brother Master of Ceremonies, teach the candidate the march of the Grand Inspectors Inquisitors Commanders and then bring him to me.

Most Perfect President—To your places Grand Inspectors Inquisitors Commanders! (The Most Perfect President, officers and members, return to their places. The Master of Ceremonies places the candidate under the sign of order. Then he causes him to step off one step to the front with the right foot, and then bring his feet together so as to form a square, at the same time uncrossing and crossing his arms. Then he steps off with the left foot one step and forms the square again, uncrossing and crossing his arms, and so on by alternation until he reaches the foot of the throne.)

Most Perfect President—(Invests him with the collar and jewel of the order.) I invest you with the white collar and jewel of this degree. See that the purity of the former and the lustre of the latter be never sullied or dimmed by your injustice, inhumanity or impurity. Return to the altar my brother, and kneel.

Most Perfect President—Order Most Enlightened Brethren! (All rise under the sign of order. Candidate goes to the altar and kneels.)

Most Perfect President—(Laying both hands on the candidate's head.) To the glory of the Grand Architect of the Universe, in the name and under the auspices of the Grand Consistory of Sublime Princes of the Royal Secret, 32nd degree of the Ancient and Accepted Rite of Masonry, for the State of——, under the jurisdiction of the Supreme Council of Sovereign Grand Inspectors General, 33rd degree for the Northern Jurisdiction of the United States of America, sitting at New York, and by virtue of the powers conferred on me by this Supreme Tribunal of Grand Inspectors Inquisitors Commanders, I do receive and constitute, create and acknowledge you a Grand Inspector Inquisitor Commander of the 31st degree of that rite, and a member of this Supreme Tribunal.

Arise Most Enlightened Brother. Take for a moment the two poniards which lie before you. They are weapons that you have carried before in Masonry, and we yet retain them because they were anciently given to the candidate that with one he might punish perjury and with the other protect innocence.

Put them down my brother! They do not belong to a Grand Inspector Inquisitor Commander, who is a judge and not a soldier. The moral force of the law and the Tribunal is more potent than a thousand daggers. Perjury like any other crime, is punished by law, or by the general contempt and execration, and innocence is not now protected by the poniard.

Most Enlightened Brother Master of Ceremonies, this newly received Grand Inspector Inquisitor Commander has laid aside forever the steel which is symbolic of violence. Give him therefore, the signs, words and tokens of the degree. Be seated my brethren. (The Most Perfect President returns to the throne and takes his seat. All the members seat themselves and the Master of Ceremonies gives the candidate the signs, words and tokens of the degree, as the same are explained by the Most Perfect President.)

First Sign.

SIGN.

Cross both hands over the navel, the left over the right.

ANSWER.

Cross them over the head, the fingers extended and separate, and the palms upward.

Answering Sign.

Token.

TOKEN.

Place right foot to right foot, and right knee to right knee, take each other by the left hand, and with the right hand strike a gentle blow on the other's right shoulder.

SACRED WORD:—One says justice the other answers equity. Both together say: So mote it be.

BATTERY:—Nine. By one, three, four and one.

Master of Ceremonies—Most Perfect President, the signs, words and tokens are made known to our newly initiated brother.

Most Perfect President—Order Most Enlightened Brethren Grand Inspectors Inquisitors Commanders! (All rise under the sign of order.)

Most Perfect President—I do hereby proclaim the Most Enlightened Brother A....B, a Grand Inspector Inquisitor Commander 31st degree of the Ancient and Accepted Rite of Masonry, regularly made and created, and I do commend him as such to all Freemasons of that Rite over the surface of the globe and require them to receive and acknowledge him as such. Most Enlightened Brother Master of Ceremonies, conduct our newly proclaimed brother to the seat of honor. (Master of Ceremonies conducts him to the right hand of the President.)

Most Perfect President—Be seated my brethren. (Order is obeyed.)

Most Perfect President—Most Enlightened Brother Advocate, be pleased further to instruct this our newly received brother, in regard to the principles of this degree. (Advocate rises and delivers the discourse.)

DISCOURSE BY ADVOCATE.

My brother, this degree was instituted when anarchy reigned among the rites of Masonry. It was evidently indispensible to establish a special body that should see to the maintenance of principles and the regularity of Masonic forms.

The Tribunal of Grand Inspectors Inquisitors Commanders was thus created, and invested with the power, as it was charged with the duty of visiting the different bodies and inspecting their work; of taking care that caution should be observed in the selection of candidates; of compelling a strict observance of the ritual in the higher degrees. To these powers were added by degrees, that of judging differences between the brethren and of trying those guilty of offences against Masonic law.

These powers and this jurisdiction are now defined, and the mode of proceeding regulated by the supreme authority.

To hear patiently, to weigh deliberately and dispassionately, and to decide impartially; these are the chief duties of a judge. After the lessons you have received, I need not further enlarge upon them. You will be ever eloquently reminded of them by the furniture upon our altar, and the decorations of our Tribunal.

The book of constitutions will remind you of your obligations, and that he alone who faithfully observes the law has a right to enforce it upon others.

In the scales of justice you are to weigh the facts and the law alone, nor place in neither scale personal friendship, or personal dislike, neither fear nor favor, and when reformation is no longer to be hoped for, you are to smite relentlessly with the sword of justice, ever remembering that as you judge here below, so you will be yourself judged hereafter by one who has not to submit like an earthly judge, to the sad necessity of inferring the motives, intentions and purposes of men, (of which all crime essentially consists) for the uncertain and often unsafe testimony of their acts and words, as men in thick darkness grope their way, with hands outstretched before them, but before whom every thought, feeling, impulse and intention of every soul that now is, or ever was, or ever will be on earth, is, and ever will be through the whole infinite duration of eternity, present and visible.

The square and compasses the plumb and level are well known to you as a Mason. Upon you as a judge, they peculiarly inculcate uprightness, impartiality, careful consideration of facts and circumstances, accuracy in judgment, and uniformity in decision.

As a judge, too, you are to bring up square work, and square work only. Like a temple erected by the plumb, you are to lean neither to one side nor to the other. Like a building well squared and levelled, you are to be firm and steadfast in your convictions of right and justice.

Like the circle swept by the compasses, you are to be true. The peculiar and principal symbol of this degree is the Tetractys of Pythagoras, suspended in the East. Where ordinarily the sacred word or letter glitters, and like it, representing the Deity. Its nine external points from the Triangle,

the chief symbol in Masonry, with many of the meanings of which you are familiar.

To us its three sides represent the three principal attributes of the Deity, which created, and now as ever support, uphold and guide the Universe in its eternal movement; the three supports of the Masonic temple, itself an emblem of the Universe. Wisdom, or the infinite divine intelligence; strength or power, the infinite divine will; and beauty, or the infinite divine harmony; the eternal law, by virtue of which the myriads of suns and worlds flash ever onward in their ceaseless revolutions, without clash or conflict in the infinite space, and change and movement, are the law of all created existence.

To us, as Masonic judges, the triangle figures for the pyramids, which planted firmly as the everlasting hills and accurately adjusted to the four cardinal points, defiant of all assaults of men and time teach us to stand firm and unshaken as they, when our feet are planted upon the solid truth.

It includes a multitude of geometrical figures, all having a deep significance to Masons. The triple triangle is peculiarly sacred, having ever been among all nations, a symbol of the Deity. Prolonging all the external lines of the hexagon, which also it includes, we have six smaller triangles, whose bases cut each other in

Triple Triangle

the central point of the Tetractys, itself always the symbol of the generative power of the universe, the Sun.

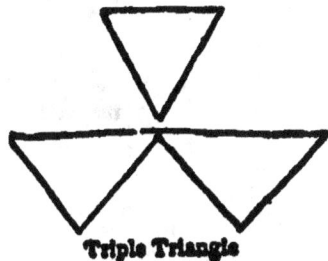

Brahama'''' Osiris,''' Apollo, Bel'''' and the Deity himself.

Thus too, we form twelve still smaller triangles, three times three of which compose the Tetractys itself.

I refrain from enumerating all the figures that you may trace within it; but one may not be passed unnoticed. The Hexagon itself faintly images to use a cube, not visible at the first glance, and therefore the fit emblem of that faith in things, which, though invisible are nevertheless real, and the existence of which may be proved by reason and logic. The first perfect solid and reminding you of the Cubical Stone'''' that sweated

Note 866.—"In the Vedic hymns all the powers of nature are personified, and become the objects of worship, thus leading to an apparent polytheism. But, as Mr. J. F. Clarke (Ten Great Religions, p. 90), remarks, 'behind this incipient polytheism lurks the original monotheism; for each of these gods, in turn, becomes the Supreme Being.' And Max Muller says (Chaps, i. 9), that 'it would be easy to find in the numerous hymns of the Veda passages in which almost every important deity is represented as supreme and absolute.' This most ancient religion—believed in by one-seventh of the world's population, that fountain from which has flowed so much of the stream of modern religious thought, abounding in mystical ceremonies and ritual prescriptions, worshipping, as the Lord of all, 'the source of golden light,' having its ineffable name, its solemn methods of initiation, and its symbolic rites—is well worth the serious study of the Masonic scholar, because in it he will find much that will be suggestive to him in the investigations of the dogmas of his Order."—Mackey's Encyclopædia of Freemasonry, Article Brahmanism.

Note 867.—"The Osirian mysteries consisted in a scenic representation of the murder of Osiris by Typhon, the subsequent recovery of his mutilated body by Isis, and his deification, or restoration to immortal life. Julius Firmicus, in his treaties On the Falsity of the Pagan Religions, thus describes the object of the Osirian mysteries: 'But in those funerals and lamentations which are annually celebrated in honor of Osiris, the defenders of the Pagan rites pretend a physical reason. They call the seeds of fruit, Osiris; the earth, Isis; the natural heat, Typhon; and because the fruits are ripened by the natural heat and collected for the life of man, and are separated from their natural tie to the earth, and are sown again when winter approaches, this they consider is the death of Osiris; but when the fruits, by the genial fostering of the earth, begin again to be generated by a new procreation, this is the finding of Osiris.' This explanation does not essentially differ from that already given in the article Egyptian Mysteries. The symbolism is indeed precisely the same—that of a restoration or resurrection from death to life."—Mackey's Encyclopædia of Freemasonry, Article Osiris, Mysteries of.

Note 868.—"Bel, is the contracted form of Baal, and was worshiped by the Babylonians as their chief deity. The Greeks and Romans so considered and translated the word by Zeus and Jupiter. It has, with Jah and On, been introduced into the Royal Arch system as a representative of the Tetragrammaton, which it and the accompanying words have sometimes ignorantly been made to displace."—Mackey's Encyclopædia of Freemasonry, Article Bel.

Note 869.—"Every stone of the temple was formed into a square, containing five equilateral triangles, each equilateral triangle being equal to a cube, and each side and base of the triangles being equal to a plumb line."—Macey's Encyclopædia and Dictionary of Freemasonry, Article Cubical Stone.

blood, and of that deposited by Enoch, it teaches justice, accuracy and consistency.

The infinite divisibility of the triangle, teaches the infinity of the universe, of time, of space and of the Deity, as do the lines that diverging from the common centre ever increase their distance from each other, as they are infinitely prolonged.

As they may be infinite in number, so are the attributes of Deity, infinite and as they emanate from one centre and are projected into space, so the whole universe has emanated from God.

Remember also, my brother, that you have other duties to perform than those of a judge. You are to inquire into and scrutinize carefully the work of the subordinate bodies in Masonry.

You are to see that recipients of the higher degrees are not unnecessarily multiplied; that improper persons are carefully excluded from membership, and that in their life and conversation, Masons bear testimony to the excellence of our doctrines, and the incalculable value of the institution itself.

You are to inquire also into your own heart and conduct, and keep careful watch over yourself that you go not astray. If you harbor ill-will and jealousy; if you are hospitable to intolerance and bigotry, and churlish to gentleness and kind affections, opening wide your heart to one, and closing its portals to the other, it is time for you to set in order your own temple, or else you wear in vain the name and insignia of a Mason, while yet uninvested with the Masonic nature.

Everywhere in the world there is a natural law, that is, a constant model of action, which seems to belong to the nature of things; to the constitution of the universe. This fact is universal. In different departments we call this mode of action by different names, as the law of matter, the law of mind, the law of morals, and the like. We mean by this, a certain mode of action, which belongs to the material, mental or moral forces; the mode in which commonly they are found to act and which it is their ideal to always act. The ideal laws of matter, we only know from the fact that they are always obeyed. To us the actual obedience is the only evidence of the ideal rule; for in respect to the conduct of the material world, the ideal and the actual are the same. The laws of matter we learn only by observation and experience. Before experience of the fact, no man could foretell that a body falling towards the earth would descend sixteen feet the first second, twice that the next, four times the third, and sixteen times the fourth. No mode of action in our consciousness anticipates this rule of action in the outer world. The same is true of all the laws of matter. The ideal law is known because it is a fact. The law is imperative. It must be obeyed without hesitation. Laws of crystallization, laws of proportion in chemical combination; neither in these nor in any other law of nature is there any margin left, for oscillation or disobedience. Only the primal will of God works in the material world, and no secondary, finite will.

There are no exceptions to the great general law of abstraction, which binds atom to atom in the body of a ratifier, visible only by aid of a microscope; orb to orb, system to system; gives unity to the world of things, and rounds these systems of worlds to a universe.

At first there seem to be exceptions to this law, as in growth and decomposition and in the repulsions of electricity, but at length all these are found to be especial cases of the one great law of attraction, acting in

various modes. The variety of effect of this law, at first
surprises the senses, but in the end, the unity of cause
astonishes the cultivated mind. Looked at in reference
to this globe, an earthquake is no more than a chink that
opens in a garden walk in a dry day in summer.

A sponge is porous, having small spaces between the
solid parts. The solar system is only more porous, having larger room between the several orbs. The universe
yet more so, with spaces between the systems, as small
compared to infinite space, as those between the atoms
that compose the bulk of the smallest invisible animalcule, of which millions swim in a drop of salt water.
The same attraction holds together the animalcule, the
sponge, the system and the universe. Every particle of
matter in that universe is related to each and all the
other particles, and attraction is their common bond.
In the spiritual world; the world of human consciousness, there is also a law and ideal mode of action, for the
spiritual forces of man. The law of justice is as universal an one as the law of attraction though we are very
far from being able to reconcile all the phenomena of
nature with it. The lark has the same right, in our
view, to live, to sing, to dart at pleasure through the
ambient atmosphere, as the hawk has to ply his strong
wings in the summer sunshine, and yet the hawk
pounces on and devours the harmless lark, as it devours
the worm, and as the worm devours the animalcule. And
so far as we know, there is nowhere, in any future state
of animal existence, any compensation for this apparent
injustice. Among the bees, one rules while the others
obey; some work while others are idle. With the small
ants, the soldiers feed on the proceeds of the workmen's
labor. The lion lies in wait for and devours the ante-
lope, that has apparently as good a right to life as he.

Among men, some govern, some serve. Capital commands and labor obeys. And one race superior in intellect, avails itself of the strong muscles of another that is inferior. And yet, for all this, no one impeaches the justice of God. No doubt all these varied phenomena are consistent with one great law of justice, and the only difficulty is that we do not, and no doubt we cannot, understand that law. It is very easy for some dreaming and visionary theorist to say that it is most evidently unjust for the lion to devour the deer, and for the eagle to tear and eat the wren, but the trouble is that we know of no other way, according to the frame, the constitution and the organs which God has given them, in which the lion and the eagle could manage to live at all. Our little measure of justice is not God's measure. His justice does not require us to relieve the hard-working millions of all labor; to emancipate the serf or slave, unfitted to be free, from all control. No doubt underneath the little bubbles which are the lives, the wishes, the wills and the plans of ten hundred millions or more of human beings on this earth, (for bubbles they are, judging by the space and time they occupy in this great and age-outlasting sea of human-kind). No doubt, underneath them all resides one and the same eternal force, which they shape into this or the other special form. And over all the same paternal providence presides, keeping eternal watch over the little and the great, and producing variety of effect, from unity of force.

It is entirely true to say that justice is the constitution, or fundamental law of the moral universe; the law of right, a rule of conduct for man, (as it is for every other living creature). In all his moral relations, no doubt all human affairs, (like all other affairs) must be subject to that, as the law paramount. And what is right

igrees therewith and stands, while what is wrong conflicts with it and falls. The difficulty is what we ever
erect our notions of what is right and just, into the law
of justice, and insist that God shall adopt that as his
law; instead of striving to learn by observation and reflection what his law is, and then believe that law to be
consistent with his infinite justice, whether it corresponds with our limited notion of justice, or does not so
correspond. We are too wise in our own conceit, and
ever strive to enact our own little notions into the universal laws of God. It might be difficult for man to
prove, even to his own satisfaction, how it is right or
just for him to subjugate the horse and ox to his service, giving them in return only their daily food, which
God has spread out for them on all the green meadows
and savannahs of the world. Or how it is just that we
should slay and eat the harmless deer, that only crop
the green herbage, the buds and the young leaves and
drink the free running water that God made common
to all; or the gentle dove, the innocent kid, the many
other living things that so confidently trust to our protection. Quite as difficult perhaps, as to prove it just
for one man's intellect, or even his wealth, to make another's strong arms his servants, for daily wages or for
a bare subsistence.

To find out this universal law of justice is one thing;
to undertake to measure off something, with our own
little tape-line, and call that God's law of justice, is another.

The great, general plan and system, and the great
general laws enacted by God, continually produce what,
to our limited notions, is wrong and injustice, which
hitherto men have been able to explain to their own
satisfaction, only by the hypothesis of another existence,
in which all inequalities and injustices in this life will
be remedied and compensated for. To our ideas of jus-

tice, it is very unjust that the child is made miserable for life by deformity or organic disease, in consequence of the vices of its father, and yet that is part of the universal law.

The ancients said that the child was punished for the sins of its father. We say that its deformity, or disease, is the consequence of its father's vices, but so far as concerns the question of justice, or injustice, that is merely the change of a word.

It is very easy to lay down a broad general principle, embodying our own idea of what is absolute justice, and insist that everything shall conform to that. To say, all human affairs must be subject to that, as the law paramount, and what is right agrees therewith and stands; what is wrong conflicts and falls. Private cohesions of self-love, of friendship or of patriotism, must all be subordinate to this universal gravitation toward the eternal right.

The difficulty is that in this universe of necessities, God created; of sequences; of cause and effect, and of life evolved from death; this interminable succession and aggregate of cruelties, will not conform to any such, absolute principle or arbitrary theory, no matter in what sounding words and glittering phrases it may be embodied.

Impracticable rules in morals are always injurious, for, as all men fall short of compliance with them, they turn real virtues into imaginary offences against a forged law.

Justice as between man and man, and as between man and the animals below him, is that which, under, and according to the God created relations existing between them, and the whole aggregate of circumstances surrounding them, is fit and right, and proper to be done, with a view to the general as well as to the individual interest. It is not a theoretical principle by which the very relations that God has created and imposed on us, are to be tried, and approved or condemned.

God has made this great system of the universe and enacted general laws for its government. Those laws environ everything that lives, with a mighty net-work of necessity. He chose to create the tiger, with such organs that he cannot crop the grass, but must eat other food or starve.

He has made man carniverous also, and the smallest singing bird is as much so as the tiger. In every step that we take, in every breath we draw, is involved the destruction of a multitude of animated existence, each, no matter how minute, as much a living creature as ourselves. He has made necessary among mankind, a division of labor, intellectual and moral. He has made necessary the varied relations of society and dependence; of obedience and control. What is thus made necessary cannot be unjust, for if it be, then God, the great lawgiver, is himself unjust.

The evil to be avoided, is the legalization of injustice and wrong, under the false plea of necessity.

Out of all the relations of life grow duties, as naturally and as undeniably, as the leaves grow upon the trees. If we have the right, created by God's law of necessity, to slay the lamb that we may eat and live, we have no right to torture it in so doing, because that is in no wise necessary. We have the right to live, if we fairly can, by the legitimate exercise of our intellect, and hire or buy the labor of the strong arms of others, to till our ground, to toil in our manufactories; but we have no right to over-work or under-pay them.

It is not only true that we may learn the moral law

of justice; the law of right, by experience and observation, but that God has given us a moral faculty, our conscience, which is able to perceive this law directly and immediately, by intuitive perception of it. And it is true that man has, in his nature, a rule of conduct higher than he has ever yet come up to; an ideal of nature that shames his actual history, because man has ever been prone to make necessity; his own necessity, the necessities of society, a plea for injustice. But this notion must not be pushed too far. For if we substitute this ideality for actuality, then it is equally true, that we have within us an ideal rule of right and wrong, to which God himself, in his government of the world, has never come and against which he (we say it revenentially) every day offends. We detest the tiger and the wolf, for their rapacity and love of blood, which are their nature.

We revolt against the law, by which the crooked limbs and diseased organism of the child, are the fruits of the father's vices. We even think that a God, omnipotent and omniscient, ought to have permitted no pain, no poverty, no servitude. Our ideal of justice is more lofty than the actualities of God. It is well as all else is well.

He has given us that moral sense, for wise and benificent purposes. We accept it, as a significant proof of the inherent loftiness of human nature, that it can ascertain an ideal so exalted, and we should strive to attain it, so far as we can do so consistently with the relations which he has created, and the circumstances which surround us and hold us captive.

If we faithfully use this faculty of conscience; if applying it to the existing relations and circumstances we develop it and all its kindred powers, and deduce the duties that out of these relations and those circumstances, limited and qualified by them, arise and become obligatory upon us, then we learn justice; the law of right; the divine rule of conduct for human life. But if we undertake to define and settle the mode of action, that belongs to the indefinitely perfect nature of God and to set up an ideal rule beyond all human reach, we soon come to judge and condemn his work, and relations which it has pleased him in his infinite wisdom to create.

A sense of justice belongs to human nature and is a part of it. Man can find a deep, permanent and instinctive delight in justice, not only in the outward effects, but in the inward cause, and by his nature love this law of right; this reasonable rule of conduct, this justice, with a deep and abiding love. Justice is the object of conscience, and fits it as light fits the eye and truth the mind. Justice keeps just relations between men. It holds the balance between nation and nation; between a man and his family, tribe, nation and race; so that his absolute rights and theirs do not interfere, nor their ultimate interests ever clash, nor the internal interests of the one prove antagonistic to those of all, or of any other one. This we must believe, if we believe that God is just. We must do justice to all, and demand of all. It is a universal human debt; a universal human claim. But we may err greatly in defining what that justice is. The temporary interests, and what to human views are the rights of many, do often interfere and clash. The life interests of the individual, often conflict with the permanent interests and welfare of society; and what may seem to be the natural rights of one class or race, with those of another.

It is not true to say that one man, however little, must not be sacrificed to another, however great; to a majority, or to all men. That is not only a fallacy, but a most dangerous one. Often one man, and many men, must be sacrificed, in the ordinary sense of the term, to the interest of the many. It is a comfortable fallacy to the selfish; for if they cannot, by the law of justice, be sacrificed for the common good, then their country has no right to demand of them self-sacrifice; and he is a fool who lays down his life, or sacrifices his estate, or even his luxuries, to ensure the safety or prosperity of his country. According to that doctrine, Curtius was a fool, and Leonidas an idiot, and to die for one's country is no longer beautiful and glorious, but a mere absurdity. Then it is no longer to be asked that the common soldier shall receive, in his bosom, the sword or bayonet thrust, which otherwise would let out the life of the great commander, on whose fate hang the liberties of his country, and the welfare of millions yet unborn.

On the contrary, it is certain that necessity rules in all the affairs of men, and that the interest, and even the life of one man, must often be sacrificed to the interest and welfare of his country. Some must ever lead the forlorn hope. The missionary must go among savages, bearing his life in his hand. The physician must expose himself to pestilence, for the sake of others. The sailor, in the frail boat upon the wide ocean, escaped from the foundering and burning ship, must step calmly into the hungry waters, if the lives of the passengers can be saved, only by the sacrifice of his own. The pilot must stand firm at the wheel, and let the flames scorch away his own life, to ensure the common safety of those whom the doomed vessel bears. The mass of men are always looking for what is just. All the vast machinery which makes up a State—a world of States—is, on the part of the people, an attempt to organize, not that ideal justice which finds fault with God's ordinances, but that practical justice, which may be attained in the actual organization of the world. The minute and wide-extending civil machinery, which makes up the law and the courts, with all their officers and implements, on the part of mankind, is chiefly an effort to reduce to practice the theory of right.

Constitutions are made to establish justice. The decisions of Courts are reported, to help us judge more wisely in time to come. The nation aims to get together the most just men in the State, that they may incorporate into statutes, their aggregate sense of what is right.

The people wish law to be embodied in justice, administered without passion. Even in the wildest ages, there has been a wild, popular justice. But always mixed with passion and administered with hate; for justice takes a rude form with rude men, and becomes less mixed with hate and passion in more civilized communities. Every progressive state revises its statutes and revolutionizes its constitution from time to time, seeking to come closer to the utmost, possible, practical justice and right, and sometimes, following theorists and dreamers, in their adoration of the ideal, by erecting into law positive principles of theoretical right, works practical injustice and then has to retrace its steps.

Literary men, always look for practical justice, and desire that virtue should have its own reward, and vice its appropriate punishment. They are ever on the side of justice and humanity, and the majority of them have an ideal justice better than the things about them. Juster than the law, for the law is ever imperfect, not attaining even to the utmost practicable degree of perfection. And no man is as just as his own idea of possible and practicable justice. His passions and his necessities ever cause him to sink below his own ideal. The ideal justice, which men ever look up to and strive to rise toward, is true, but it will not be realized in this world. Yet we must approach as near to it as practicable, as we should do toward that ideal democracy that now floats before the eyes of earnest and religious men; fairer than the Republic of Plato or Moore's Utopia, or the golden age, or fabled memory; only taking care that we do not, in striving to reach and ascend to the impossible ideal, neglect to seize upon and hold fast to the possible actual. To aim at the best, but be content with the best possible, is the only true wisdom. To insist on the absolute right, and throw out of the calculation the important and all-controlling element of necessity, is the folly of a mere dreamer.

In a world inhabited by men with bodies, and necessarily with bodily wants and animal passions, the time will never come when there will be no want, no oppression, no servitude, no fear of man, but only love. That can never be, while there are inferior intellects, indulgence in low vice, improvidence, indolence, awful visitations of pestilence and war and famine, earthquake and volcano, that must of necessity cause men to want, serve, suffer and fear.

But still, the plowshare of justice is ever drawn through and through the field of the world, uprooting the savage plants. Ever we see a continual and progressive triumph of the right. The injustice of England, lost her America, the fairest jewel of her crown.

The injustice of the French aristocracy and clergy, bore them to the ground more than the revolution of 1789 did, and exiled them to foreign lands, there to pine away and die; their fate a warning to bid mankind be just.

We intuitively understand what justice is better than we can depict it. What it is in a given case depends so much on circumstances, that definitions of it are wholly deceitful. Often it would be unjust to society to do what would, in the absence of that consideration, be pronounced just to the individual. General propositions of man's right to do this or that are ever fallacious, and not unfrequently it would be most unjust to the individual himself, to do for him what the theorist, as a general proposition, would say was right and his due.

We should ever do unto others what, under the same circumstances, we ought to wish, and have the right to wish, they should do unto us.

There are many cases, cases constantly occurring, where one man must take care of himself, in preference to another, as where two struggle for the possession of a plank that will save one but cannot uphold both. Or where assailed he can save his own life, only by slaying his adversary. So one must prefer the safety of his country to the lives of her enemies, and sometimes to insure it to those of her own innocent citizens.

The retreating general may cut away a bridge behind him to delay pursuit, and save the main body of the army, though he thereby surrenders a detachment, a battalion, or even a corps of his own force, to certain destruction.

These are not departures from justice, though like other instances where the injury or death of the individual is the safety of the many, where the interest of one individual class or race, is postponed to that of the public, or of the superior race. They may infringe some dreamers ideal rule of justice.

But every departure from real, practical justice, is no doubt attended with loss to the unjust man, though the loss is not reported to the public. Injustice, public or

private, like every other sin and wrong, is inevitably
followed by its consequences. The selfish, the grasping,
the inhuman, the fraudulently unjust; the ungenerous
employer and the cruel master, are detested by the great
popular heart, while the kind master, and liberal employer, the generous, the humane and the just, have the
good opinion of all men, and even envy is a tribute to
their virtues. Men honor all who stand up for truth
and right, and never shrink. The world builds monuments to its patriots. Four great statesmen, organizers
of the right, embalmed in stone, look down upon the lawgivers of France, as they pass to their hall of legisla-
tion; silent orators to tell how nations love the just. How
we revere the marble lineaments of those just judges,
Jay and Marshall that look so calmly towards the living
bench of the Supreme Court of the United States! What
a monument Washington has built in the heart of
America and all the world, not because he dreamed of
an impracticable, ideal justice, but by his constant efforts
to be practically just. But necessity alone, and the
greatest good of the greatest number, can legitimately
interfere with the dominion of absolute and ideal justice.

Government should not foster the strong at the expense of the weak, or protect the capitalist and tax the
laborer. The powerful should not seek a monopoly of
development and enjoyment. Not prudence only and
the expedient for to-day should be appealed to by statesmen, but conscience and the right. Justice should not
be forgotten in looking at interest, nor political morality
neglected for political economy. We should not have
national housekeeping instead of national organization
for the basis of right.

We may well differ as to the abstract right of many
things; for every such question has many sides, and few

men look at all of them; many only at one. But we all readily recognize cruelty, unfairness, inhumanity, partiality, over-reaching, hard-dealing, by their ugly and familiar lineaments.

We do not need to sit as a court of errors and appeals to revise and reverse God's providence, in order to know and to hate and despise them. There are certainly great evils of civilization at this day, and many questions of humanity long adjourned and put off. The hideous aspect of pauperism; the debasement and vice in our cities tell us, by their eloquent silence, or in inarticulate mutterings, that the rich and the powerful and the intellectual, do not their duty by the poor, the feeble and the ignorant. And every wretched woman that lives, heaven scarce knows how, by making shirts at sixpence each, attests the injustice and inhumanity of man.

There are cruelties to slaves, and worse cruelties to animals, each disgraceful to their perpetrators, and equally unwarranted by the lawful relation of control and dependence which it has pleased God to create.

In human affairs, the justice of God must work by human means. Men are the instruments of God's principles. Our morality is the instrument of his justice, which, incomprehensible to us, seems to our short vision, often to work injustice, but will at some time still the oppressor's brutal laughter. All the justice we mature will bless us here and hereafter, and at our death we shall leave it, added to the common store of human kindness. And every Mason, who, content to do that which is possible and practicable, does and enforces justice, may help deepen the channel of human mortality in which God's justice runs. And so the wrecks of evil that now check and obstruct the stream, may be the sooner swept out and borne away by the restless tide of omnipotent right. Let us my brother, in this as in all else, endeavor always to perform the duties of a good Mason and a good man.

Most Perfect President—(Striking one.) Grand Inspectors Inquisitors Commanders, members of this Supreme Tribunal, if any one has any remarks to offer, to enforce the obligations of justice and equity, or for the good of Masonry, the Supreme Tribunal will be pleased to hear him. (If there is no answer.)

Senior Councilor—Most Perfect President, silence prevails.

Most Perfect President—Grand Inspectors Inquisitors Commanders, the box of fraternal assistance will now be presented to you. (Collection is taken.)

Most Perfect President—Most Enlightened Brother Chancellor, read the minutes of this day's proceedings. (Chancellor reads the minutes.)

Most Perfect President—Grand Inspectors Inquisitors Commanders, if any one has any observation to make in regard to the minutes now read, he has permission to do so.

Senior Councilor—Most Perfect President, silence prevails.

Most Perfect President—The minutes of this day's labor, as recorded during our present sitting, are adopted. (Chancellor puts record with other books and papers in the coffer.)

Chancellor—Most Perfect President, I await your pleasure. (The Perfect President goes to the coffer, and with the Chancellor locks it.)

CLOSING CEREMONIES

Grand Inspector Inquisitor Commander.

Most Perfect President—Most Enlightened Brother Senior Councilor, what is the hour for rest for true Masons?

Senior Councilor—Most Perfect President, the hour when all their duties are performed.

Most Perfect President—Has that hour arrived my brother?

Senior Councilor—As nearly as in this life it ever comes to mortals, since none perform all their duties, and our Masonic labors end only at the grave.

Most Perfect President—Most true, my brother. Remains there yet any complaint unheard, wrong unredressed or known offence unpunished, that requires action from this Tribunal?

Senior Councilor—None, Most Perfect President.

Most Perfect President—It is permitted then that this Supreme Tribunal shall be closed, that we may return to the Sacred Asylum of Sublime Princes of the Royal Secret. Join me my brethren in the concluding ceremony. Order Grand Inspectors Inquisitors Commanders! (All rise under the sign of the order.)

Advocate—(Striking one.) From all errors and mistakes in opinion and conclusion:

Senior Councilor—(Striking three.) From all impatience and inattention to evidence and argument; from all petulance and peevishness, all carelessness and indifference; from all harsh and uncharitable constructions of act or motive:

Senior Councilor—(Striking four.) From all partiality and prejudice, from all obstinacy and pride of opinion, and all wilful adherence to error; from all usurpations of power and unwarrantable assumptions of jurisdiction; from all improper influences that prevent man's judgment:

Most Perfect President—(Striking one.) From all false judgment and intentional injustice, keep us free, our Father, who art to judge us at the end of our earthly pilgrimage.

All—And as we judge others, so do thou in mercy judge us. Amen.

Most Perfect President—(Making the first sign.) "Justice."

All—(Making the answering sign.) "Equity."

All—So mote it be.

All—(Led by Most Perfect President, give the battery.)

Most Perfect President—Most Enlightened Brethren, Grand Inspectors Inquisitors Commanders, let us now form the procession and proceed to the Sacred Asylum of Sublime Princes of the Royal Secret. (The Most Perfect President then leaves the throne and the procession is formed as in opening, and the brethren proceed to the Grand Consistory. If the newly admitted brother is at once to receive the 32°, he remains in the hall with a brother until the consistory is prepared to receive him. Otherwise he is allowed to retire.)

STATUTES FOR THE GOVERNMENT OF ALL TRIBUNALS OF THE THIRTY-FIRST DEGREE.

ARTICLE I.

1. Every Tribunal of the 31st degree, when sitting in judgment, shall be composed of ten members, and no more, not including the Advocate and Defender.

2. When trying a case, in which a Sovereign Prince of the Royal Secret is a party, all the members must have attained the 32nd degree, and in all other cases, at least five must have attained it viz: President, Councilors, Secretary and Treasurer, and the others must have attained the 31st degree.

ARTICLE II.

1. Tribunals of the 31st degree have exclusive jurisdiction to hear, try and determine all offences against Masonic law, or the statutes, constitutional provisions, rules and regulations of the Supreme Council of the 33rd degree, committed by brothers who have attained any degree above the 18th, and of appeals from all judgments of all Chapters of Rose Croix within their jurisdiction. But as to offences committed by Knights of the Rose Croix, attached to regular Chapters, and for the punishment thereof, the statutes of such Chapters have made provision, their jurisdiction shall be concurrent; and in such cases, the body first having possession of the case shall proceed and the other desist.

2. The Tribunals of the 31st degree, shall also have jurisdiction in all cases ordered by the Chapters to be

transmitted to them for trial, and to decide all questions certified to them by the Chapters and by Councils of Princes of Jerusalem and Lodges of Perfection, their decision being in all cases final and conclusive.

ARTICLE III.

1. Any Mason knowing of the commission, by a brother of rank above the 18th degree, of any offence against Masonic law, may make known the fact to any Grand Inspector Inquisitor Commander, by communication in writing, stating the offence, its nature and circumstances and the time of its commission, which shall be delivered by such Commander to the Illustrious Advocate, who shall prepare and prefer the act of accusation.

2. Each Commander shall also in like manner make known to the Illustrious Advocate every violation of Masonic law within his knowledge, and the Advocate shall prepare and prefer acts of accusation in all such cases, and in every case where the facts come otherwise to his knowledge.

3. Upon the act of accusation being preferred, the Chancellor shall issue a citation under the seal of the Tribunal, which shall be served by copy in writing by the Pursuivant, or by any other Mason at a distance, to whom the Chancellor may direct and transmit it, by which the accused shall be cited to appear before the Tribunal, at a certain time and place, and answer the charge. The nature of such charge shall not be specified, but a copy of the act of accusation shall be delivered to the accused in person, whenever he applies for it.

4. If it is known that the accused is not to be found or when the citation is returned that he is not found, a copy thereof shall be put up in the place where he last resided, in the lodge room of the Council, or other Masonic body of which he was last a member, or in any

lodge room, if he was a member of none, or if there be no such room, then in any public place, and the facts returned upon the citation.

5. The day fixed for appearance shall be at least ten days after the actual or constructive service.

6. Upon the day fixed, if the accused appear, he shall make full answer to the charge, stating, if he pleases, any extenuating circumstances, and detailing the facts as particularly as he pleases.

The Defender is charged with the duty of preparing his defence.

7. And if he does not appear, or when he has answered, a day shall be fixed for trial, and written evidence may in the meantime be taken on both sides.

8. The testimony of persons not Masons must be given on oath, and that of Masons upon their highest Masonic obligations, and either may be taken in writing or orally.

ARTICLE IV.

1. At the time fixed for trial, unless the Tribunal grants further delay, as it may do at its discretion, the testimony taken in writing shall be read, and the witnesses heard, the accused having the right to be present, fully to examine and cross-examine the witnesses, and to be heard by himself or the defender, or both. He or his defender shall also have the right to conclude the argument.

2. After the case is heard, argued and submitted, the accused and witnesses shall withdraw, and the Tribunal shall deliberate.

3. After deliberation the members shall vote upon the different specifications in the act of accusation, each member voting in turn, beginning with the youngest member, and the officers following according to rank, from lowest to highest. The Advocate and Defender shall vote.

4.   Two-thirds of those present shall concur, to find the accused guilty of any specification.

5.   The punishment shall be fixed by a like vote, a majority determining its nature and extent.

6.   The accused shall then be called in, and informed of the result. If he be found guilty, the sentence shall be communicated by the Chancellor, to all Masonic bodies of which he is a member, and the punishment shall be imposed according to the sentence, and the laws, statutes and regulations governing the case.

7.   If the trial proceeds in the absence of the accused, the Defender shall represent him, and perform all the duties of Council for him to the best of his ability.

ARTICLE V.

1.   Appeals from judgment of Chapters of Rose Croix, shall be sent up in writing, with all the papers, a simple notice of appeal being alone necessary to give the Tribunal jurisdiction.

2.   Every appeal shall be suspensive.

3.   If the appeal be on the facts, the Tribunal shall try it *de novo*. If it involve only a question of law, they shall decide it, and affirm, reverse, demand or grant a new trial, or altogether quash and annul, as may be proper and in accordance with Masonic law.

4.   In case the Tribunal tries the case *de novo*, the proceedings at the trial shall be the same as in cases of original jurisdiction.

5.   Any Subordinate body may submit a question or questions to the Tribunal for its decision, upon order to that effect, and the Tribunal shall take jurisdiction, upon a certificate of the Recorder or Secretary of such inferior body, stating the question and its reference, shall decide, and transmit a certificate of its decision, and upon the decision of such questions, that of the ma-

jority shall stand as the decision of the whole, and no dissent be made known; but any Commander who dissents may present his opinion in writing, with the reasons for it, and have it filed for reference.

6. A record of all such decisions, and of the decisions on points of Masonic law, shall be kept by the Chancellor in a book for that purpose, under appropriate headings.

ARTICLE VI.

1. No trial whatever for offences shall be had in any consistory of Sublime Princes of the Royal Secret.

2. The Tribunals of the 31st degree shall also have a jurisdiction to issue mandates, to require Subordinate bodies to proceed to judgment or otherwise, to do whatever acts they ought to do in order to give to a brother his Masonic rights, as also mandates requiring them to desist from proceeding in proper cases, and mandates to bring up their proceedings, when alleged to be against law, to be examined and affirmed, or quashed, as law and right may require.

3. They shall also have jurisdiction to issue mandates, to bring before them questions of right to office in Subordinate lodges and bodies, and to hear and determine the same.

4. And mandates to suspend, or supersede any judgment or action of such inferior body.

5. The said Tribunal shall usurp and assume to themselves no powers not granted by these statutes, or not following as necessary incidents or corollaries from the powers hereby granted.

6. They may act as Tribunals of conciliation or decision, in all matters of difference, dispute or dissension

between Masons of the same or different degrees, when such matters are either referred to them by subordinate bodies, or by the parties themselves, or one of them, or by other Masons, and shall examine into and weigh the facts, merits, and give and enforce such judgment and decision as shall in their view be just, right and equitable in the premises.

ARTICLE VII.

1.   All mandates and process of the Tribunal shall be signed by the Chancellor and sealed with the seal of the Tribunal.

2.   A record shall be faithfully kept of all the proceedings and judgments of the Tribunal, and all depositions and other papers shall be filed and carefully preserved

PHILOSOPHICAL ANALYSIS

THIRTY-FIRST DEGREE; OR, GRAND INSPECTOR INQUISITOR COMMANDER.

Filled With Vain Repetitions—Republican Appointment of a Masonic Rebel—Claims to Rule Judicially the Masonic Order—The Ways of the Lodge Are Movable.

This degree covers sixty pages, so dull, prolix, and humdrum, that they remind one of the "vain repetitions" of the heathen, which Christ forbade. Nineteen pages are filled by the "Illustrious Advocate," with a tedious compound dessertation on the metaphysics of "justice," "ideal," and "actual," leading nowhere, and teaching nothing. Indeed, knowing that Masons who run lodges are neither fools, nor blockheads, but sly, keen men; one would be at a loss for the motive which has produced such solemn humbuggery, but for the fact that pickpockets practice similar arts to amuse the crowd, while feeling for their purses; and Mormons and other religious impostors teach wonderful things, to awe the ignorant, and keep them still, while devils mesmerize them.

In this thirty-first degree, for which the writers give neither date nor origin, nine men erect themselves into a "Sovereign Tribunal," or Supreme Court, to rule Masons! Their "Advocate" (page 343) speaks of it as "created," but says not when, where, or by whom. Who could "create" them into a tribunal, when there was no higher power to create them; and in Masonry, no appeals to the people are ever made. *Mackey* and *Macoy* simply remark: "It is not a historical degree."

Unless the nine got together, and initiated themselves

into this degree, they must have been appointed by the Jew Inspector Morin, who was appointed by the "Council of Emperors," at Paris, in 1761, to inspect lodges in the New World, confer their degrees, and report to them. *Morin* set up for himself, and his employers denounced him as an "audacious juggler;" recalled his patent, and appointed a weak *Brother Martin* in his place. Little cared *Morin* for that. He appointed sixteen other Inspectors, thirteen of whom were Jews. These created a *degree* of Inspectors, which is this 31st degree! And when *Morin* had made money enough by the sale of Masonic degrees and dignities, he disappeared from history, and Masonic writers say they know not where he lived, or when he died! But his work lived after him. His "Inspectors," in 1801, became the present Supreme Council, Southern Jurisdiction, Charleston, S. C.; added eight degrees to the twenty-five committed by "the Emperors" to Morin; altered, stretched, and modified the twenty-five, and made *"The Ancient, Accepted Scottish Rite"* of thirty-three degrees, which now rules the Masonic world; of which *Albert Pike,* of Washington is now (1887) Sovereign Grand Inspector General, with a salary of $1,000 a month, *"ad vitam;"* (for life) with access to Masons of both parties in Congress, who gave his son a clerkship under Hayes' (Republican) administration; with a salary of $2,000 a year. Gen. Pike was a rebel secessionist.

If these facts, taken wholly from the highest Masonic authorities, are true, the "Ancient, Accepted Scottish Rite" is as liable to indictment for swindling, getting money under false pretenses, and gambling practices, as mock auctions, lotteries, Faro Banks, and Three Monte men. And if the Masonic charters granted by Congress and the State Legislatures, can be withdrawn, the laws will treat the lodges as they are now handling the institutions of Mormonism. The two institutions are morally and legally the same.

The jewel of this thirty-first degree is a "Teutonic cross;" the jewel of an order, or degree, which both Mackey and Macoy say was unfit to be put into the *Ancient and Accepted Scottish Rite;* and that it was only admitted to fill up a gap. And the members who are judges, wear no aprons, which are badges of labor. They are above it. (Note 361.)

But these are trifles. Here in this thirty-first degree we have a *"Sovereign Tribunal,"* or Supreme Court; meeting in magnificent court-rooms, with court officers, "Advocate," and "Defender;" claiming to rule, judicially, the Masonic order; and aspiring to rule all secret orders; which draw more, far more money from the people of the United States, than the Civil Government. It administers its own oaths; issuing its own decrees; and swearing its subjects to obey them, on pain of death; and that in the preceding degree, (*Knight of Kadosh*) which claims to be softened and modified from the seven old Kadoshes which breathed, says the ritual: "Nothing but vengeance;" and our own Court, and Legislative records show, not only "breathed vengeance," but executed it. And so powerful have these secret lodges become, at times, and so dire their secret "vengeance," that every nation in Europe has, at times, suppressed them in self-defense. And now, England and Sweden, and Denmark live by sufferance of the lodges; adopting the compliance which the devil demanded of Christ, *viz.,* practicing their secret worships!

This is sufficiently horrible. But if this were all, the

National Christian Association never would have existed. This very degree, as indeed do all the others,
pretends to honor Christ, by quoting His words, and
lauding Him as a human law-giver, (see *page 332*) and
yet fills its pages with the teachings of *Brahma, Osiris,
Apollo,* and *Bel,* (see Page 346, and the degrees generally) as equally authoritative with Christ's. It lauds
Moses, on the same page with Christ, (332) and, in
a degree or two back, assails Moses' teachings with
a savage bitterness equal to that of the coarsest infidel
the United States ever produced. The Bible says of
the harlot: "Her ways are movable, that thou canst
not know them." (*Prov. 5, 6.*) And false religion is
the "Great whore that sitteth on many waters." And
Masonry, or the secret lodge system, is the "image" of
that beast. And the ways of the lodge are "movable,"
like those of the "mother of harlots!" This is what calls
on every child of God, on every patriot, every philan-
thropist, who does not wish to see the religion of Egypt
transferred from the Nile to the Mississippi, to rise,
and call on God for deliverance from this *"Ancient and
Accepted Rite;"* which, in this thirty-first degree, and in
all its degrees, puts the mysteries of *Osiris* on a level
with the revelations of Jesus Christ!!

CHAPTER LIX

THIRTY-SECOND DEGREE, OR SUBLIME PRINCE OF THE ROYAL SECRET.'"*

DECORATIONS:—Bodies of this degree are styled Consistories. The lodge is held in a high place, the second story of a building at least. The hangings are black, strewed with tears of silver, skeletons, etc., death's heads and cross bones.

In the East is a throne, to which you ascend by seven

Note 870.—"Sublime Prince of the Royal Secret. The 32nd degree of the Ancient and Accepted rite, and for many years, or until the institution of the 33d degree, this was the highest degree, or ne plus ultra of Masonry. The body is styled a Consistory, and should be held in a building of two stories. The officers are, a Thrice Illustrious Commander, First and Second Lieutenants, a Minister of State, a Grand Chancellor, a Grand Treasurer, a Grand Secretary, and a Grand Captain of the Guard. In the East a throne, elevated on seven steps, which is the seat of the Thrice Illustrious Commander, who wears a robe of royal purple, and he and the Lieutenants, wear swords. The collar of this degree is black, lined with scarlet, and in the center, at the point, a double-headed eagle, of silver or gold, on a red Teutonic cross. The apron is of white satin, with a border of gold lace, one inch wide, lined with scarlet; on the flap is a double-headed eagle, on each side of which is the flag of the country in which the body is located, the flag of Prussia and the Beauseant of the Kadosh degree; on the apron is the camp of the Crusaders, which is thus explained; it is composed of an enneagon, within which is inscribed a heptagon, within that a pentagon, and in the center an equilateral triangle, within which is a circle. Between the heptagon and pentagon are placed five standards, in the designs of which are five letters, which form a particular word. The first standard is purple, on which is emblazoned the ark of the covenant, with a palm tree on each side; the ark has the motto Laus Deo. The second is blue, on which is a lion, of gold, couchant, holding in his mouth a golden key, with a collar of the same metal on his neck, and on it is the device, Ad majorem Dei gloriam. The third is white, and displays a heart in flames, with two wings; it is surmounted by a crown of laurels. The fourth is green, and bears a double-headed black eagle, crowned, holding a sword in his right claw, and a bleeding heart in his left. The fifth bears a black ox, on a field of gold. On the sides of the enneagon are nine tents, with flags representing the divisions of the Masonic army; on the angles are nine pinions, of the same color as the flag of the tent that precedes it. The hall of the Consistory is hung with black, strewed with tears of silver. The jewel is a double-headed white and black eagle, resting on a Teutonic cross, of gold, worn attached to the collar or ribbon. The members are called Sublime Princes of the Royal Secret. The moral of the degree teaches opposition to bigotry, superstitition, and all the passions and vices which disgrace human nature."—Macoy's Encyclopædia and Dictionary of Freemasonry, Article Sublime Prince of the Royal Secret.

steps. It is a chair of state, lined with black satin like the hangings, but strewed with flames, not tears.

Before the throne is an altar covered with black satin, strewed with tears. In front of the altar, the black cover falls to the floor and on it are painted or embroidered a death's head and two cross bones. Over the death's head is the letter J∴ and under the cross bones the letter M.

On this altar are the books of constitution and statutes of the order, a naked sword, a sceptre and a balance. In the West are the two Wardens. In front of each is a table covered with crimson cloth, lined and edged with black and strewed with tears. The cover of each table hangs to the floor in front, and on each cover, in front, the four letters N∴K∴——M∴K∴, each two if in Hebrew, being read from right to left. On each table are two naked swords, crossed. The hall is divided into two parts, by a railing or balustrade. The East is in the rear of this, and the West in front of it. In the West is a representation of the camp of the Princes.

OFFICERS AND TITLES:—The Master is styled Sovereign of Sovereigns, Great Prince, or which is more usual and far better, Illustrious Commander in Chief. He is said to represent Frederick the Second, King of Prussia. The two Wardens are styled Lieutenant Commanders. The Orator, Minister of State.

Besides these officers, there are a Grand Chancellor, a Grand Secretary, a Grand Keeper of the Seals, and Archives, a Grand Treasurer, a Grand Architect, or Engineer, a Grand Hospitaller, and Surgeon, a Grand Standard Bearer, a Grand Master of Ceremonies, a Grand Captain of the Guards, and a Grand Tyler. In some localities, there are also an Illustrious Deputy Commander in Chief and an Assistant Grand Tyler. The Grand Secretary, Grand Chancellor and Grand Keeper of the Seals and Archives, are sometimes separate officers, and sometimes the three offices are combined in one, that of Grand Chancellor.

In the Consistory the Officers are seated as follows

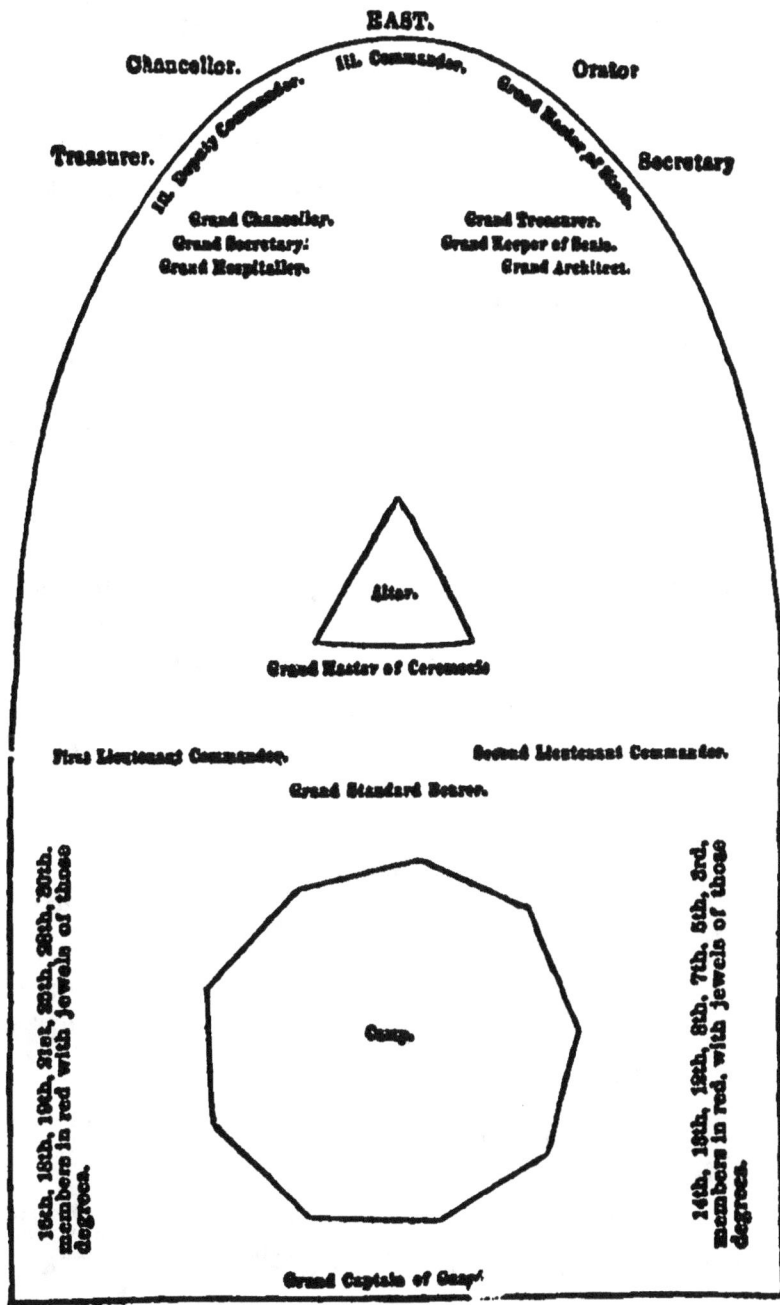

EAST.

Chancellor.   Ill. Commander,   Orator

Ill. Deputy Commander.   Grand Master of Seals.

Treasurer.   Secretary

Grand Chancellor.   Grand Treasurer.
Grand Secretary: Grand Keeper of Seals.
Grand Hospitaller.   Grand Architect.

Altar.

Grand Master of Ceremonie

First Lieutenant Commander.   Second Lieutenant Commander.

Grand Standard Bearer.

Camp.

16th, 18th, 19th, 21st, 29th, 28th, 20th, members in red with jewels of those degrees.

14th, 18th, 18th, 8th, 7th, 5th, 3rd, members in red, with jewels of those degrees.

Grand Captain of Camp.

And on the outside of the door is the Grand Tyler, or in his absence, the Assistant Grand Tyler, thus the number of officers in that body would be sixteen, but the Secretary and Keeper of the Seals and Archives being generally replaced by the Grand Chancellor and the Assistant Grand Tyler, being appointed only to supply the Grand Tyler when absent, are not counted among the officers, whose number is not to exceed thirteen, as will be seen hereafter.

There are also in the hall, west of the officers, on the right and left, fourteen members clothed in red, without aprons, and each having on his breast, suspended from a black ribbon, worn as a collar, the jewel of one of the degrees, to wit, numbering these members from one to fourteen, they wear respectively the jewels of the 30th, 28th, 25th, 21st, 19th, 18th, 16th, 14th, 13th, 10th, 8th, 7th, 5th and 3rd degrees.

The first five are the Standard Bearers of the corps, that encamp around the Pentagon; and the last nine are the Commanders of the corps, that encamp around the Nonagon, in the camp hereafter described:

The names of the first five are as follows:

1st.	Bezaleel, for the standard,	"T."
2nd.	Aholiab,[371] for the standard,	"E."
3rd.	Mah[372] Shim, for the standard,	"N."
4th.	Garimont, for the standard,	"G."
5th.	Amariah, for the standard,	"U."

The names of the others are:

Note 371. "Aholiab. A skilful artificer of the tribe of Dan who was appointed, together with Bezaleel, to construct the tabernacle in the wilderness and the ark of the covenant."—Mackey's Encyclopædia of Freemasonry. Article Aholiab.

Note 372.—"It is a component part of a significant word in Masonry. The combination mahhah, literally 'what! the,' is equivalent, according to the Hebrew method of ellipsis, to the question, What! is this the —— ?' "—Mackey's Encyclopædia of Freemasonry, Article Mah.

1st.	Malachi,[373] for the tent,	"S."
2nd.	Zerubbabel, for the tent,	"A."
3rd.	Nehemiah, for the tent,	"L."
4th.	Johaben, for the tent,	"I."
5th.	Phaleg, for the tent,	"X."
6th.	Jehoiada, for the tent,	"N."
7th.	Aholiab, for the tent,	"O."
8th.	Joshua, for the tent,	"N."
9th.	Ezra,[374] for the tent,	"I."

These fourteen names must certainly appear arbitrary and without meaning. The rituals and other Masonic works say nothing of the meaning and reason why these names were selected. All that is to be done is to study and perhaps that reason will be found.

But we have no right to leave out these or other names or words, because these, as a slender thread, may lead us to the discovery of what we are now ignorant of. Otherwise the names and words, being left out, the real meaning would never be discovered. However, for a reception, in ample form, there should be present twenty-seven officers and members, including the fourteen Standard Bearers and Commanders above mentioned.

THE CAMP:—Is a nonagon enclosing a heptagon, that

Note 373.—"Malachi or Malachias. The last of the prophets. A significant word in the thirty-second degree of the Scottish Rite."—Mackey's Encyclopædia of Freemasonry, Article Malachi or Malachias.

Note 374.—"Ezra. There are two persons named Ezra who are recorded in Scripture. 1. Ezra, a leading priest among the first colonists who came up to Jerusalem with Zerubbabel, and who is mentioned by Nehemiah; and 2, Ezra, the celebrated Jewish scribe and restorer of the law, who visited Jerusalem forty-two years after the second Temple had been completed. Calmet, however, says that this second Ezra had visited Jerusalem previously in company with Zerubbabel."—Mackey's Encyclopædia of Freemasonry, Article Ezra.

enclosing a pentagon, that an equilateral triangle, and that a circle. On the side of the nonagon are nine tents with a flag, pennon, and letter to each. Each tent represents an entire camp, and the several sides of the nonagon are thus assigned by our present rituals, to the Masons of the several degrees, from the first to the eighteenth as follows:

S. Flag and pennon white, sprinkled lightly with crimson. That tent indicates the camp of the Knights Rose Croix, Knights of the East and West, and Princes of Jerusalem, 18th, 17th and 16th degrees. The Commander Malachi.

A. Flag and pennon light green. That tent indicates the camp of the Knights of the East or Sword, 15th degree. The Commander Zerubbabel.

L. Flag and pennon red. That tent indicates the camp of the Grand Elect Perfect and Sublime Masons, 14th degree. Commander Nehemiah.

I. Flag and pennon black and red. That tent indicates the camp of the Knights of the Royal Arch and Grand Master Architects, 13th and 12th degrees. Commander Joabert or Johaben.

X. Flag and pennon black. That tent indicates the camp of the Sublime Knights Elected, Illustrious Elect of Fifteen and Elected Knights of Nine, 11th, 10th and 9th degrees. Commander Phaleg.

N. Flag and pennon red and black in lozenges. That tent indicates the camp of the Intendants of the Building, 8th degree. Commander Jehoiada.

O. Flag and pennon, red and green. That tent indicates the camp of the Provost and Judges, and Intimate Secretaries 7th and 6th degrees. Commander Aholiab.

N. Flag and pennon green. That tent indicates the camp of the Perfect Masters and Secret Masters, 5th and 4th degrees. Commander Joshua.

I. Flag and pennon blue. That tent indicates the camp of the Masters, the Fellow Crafts and Apprentices of Symbolic Masonry and Volunteers, 3rd, 2nd and 1st degrees. Commander Ezra.

On each of the external angles of the pentagon, is a great standard, each designated by a letter, and each supposed to indicate the camp of a corps of Masons, occupying a side of the pentagon. The standards are described as follows, in the language of Heraldry, and indicate the following degrees:

T. Purple. On it is the Ark'" of the Covenant, in gold, between two palm trees, vert, and two lighted torches or candlesticks, gold motto at the base, *"Laus Deo."* Around this standard are stationed the Knights Kadosh, and the Grand Scottish Knights of St. Andrew, 30th and 29th degrees. Standard Bearer is Bezaleel.

E. Azure. On it is a lion couchant in gold, holding in his mouth a key in gold, and a gold collar around his neck, with the figures 525 on the collar. Motto at the

---

Note 375.—"The Ark of the Covenant or of the Testimony was a chest originally constructed by Moses at God's command. (Exod. xxv. 16.) In which were kept the two tables of stone, on which were engraved the ten commandments. It contains, likewise. a golden pot filled with manna, Aaron's rod, and the tables of the covenant. It was at first deposited in the most sacred place of the tabernacle, and afterwards placed by Solomon in the Sanctum Sanctorum of the Temple, and was lost upon the destruction of that building by the Chaldeans. The later history of this ark is buried in obscurity."—Mackey's Encyclopedia of Freemasonry Article Ark of the Covenant.

base, *Custos Arcani,* and in some rituals, *Ad Majorem Dei Gloriam.* The latter is the motto of the Jesuits. Around this standard are stationed the Knights of the Sun, the Commanders of the Temple and the Princes of Mercy, 28th, 27th and 26th degrees. Standard Bearer is Aholiab.

N. Argent."'* On it is a flaming heart, gules, wings sable, crowned with laurel, vert. Motto at the base *Ardens Gloria Surgit.* Around this standard are stationed the Knights of the Brazen Serpent, the Princes of the Tabernacle and the Chiefs of the Tabernacle, 25, 24th and 23rd degrees. Standard Bearer is Mah-Shim.

G. Vert.* On it is an eagle, with two heads displayed, sable armed, gold; ensigned with an imperial crown of gold, resting on both heads; holding in his dexter claw a sword, point in base; in his sinister claw a bloody heart. Motto at the base, *Corde, Gladio Potens.* Around this standard are stationed the Princes of Libanus and the Knights Noachite or Prussian Knights, 22nd and 21st degrees. Standard Bearer Garimont.

U. Or.† On it is an ox statant, sable. Motto at base, *Omnia Tempus Alit.* Around this standard are stationed the Masters ad vitam and the Grand Pontiffs, 20th and 19th degrees. Standard Bearer Am·riah.

At the angles of, and inside the triangle are supposed to be encamped the Princes of the Royal Secret and the Grand Inspectors Inquisitors Commanders, with such Knights of Malta as, having proved themselves true and faithful, may have been received among us. At each corner of the triangle is one of the following birds: A raven, a dove and a phoenix.

CLOTHING, JEWEL, ETC :—The Illustrious Commander

Note 276.—"Argent. French for silver. An heraldic term used in describing coats of arms, thus: The arm of the Company of Freemasons in the reign of King Henry IV. 'Azure, on a chevron, between three castles, Argent.''—Macoy's Encyclopaedia and Dictionary of Freemasonry, Article Argent.

*In Heraldry a green color.
*Or, in Heraldry, means gold or gold color.

in Chief is clothed in the modern costume of Royalty, of crimson stuff. He is armed with a sword and shield. On the table, in front of him, lie his sceptre and a balance. The Lieutenant Commanders are also armed with sword and shield, and wear their hats. The other officers, and at least six members, should be clothed in crimson, and remain in the eastern portion of the Consistory. Neither the officers nor members, when in costume, wear any apron, but only the collar, to which is suspended the jewel of the order. The collar is black, edged with silver; on the point is embroidered in red a teutonic cross, and in the centre of the cross an eagle, with two heads of silver. The collar is lined with scarlet silk, and on the lining is embroidered a teutonic cross, in black. The girdle is black, with silver fringe, and on the front of it is embroidered a red cross. The jewel is a teutonic cross of gold. The apron is white, lined and edged with red. On the flap is embroidered a red cross, relieved with silver around the edges. In the middle of the apron is embroidered the plan of the camp of the Princes.

According to the constitutions of 1786, Art. XI, the 32nd degree is not to be conferred, unless three Senior Grand Inspectors General are present.

The diploma of a Sublime Prince of the Royal Secret is styled Patent; and the charter of the Consistory, The Constitutions.

STATED MEETINGS:—The stated meetings of a Consistory shall be held on the 21st of March, 25th June, 21st September and 27th December in each year.

OFFICERS OF A CONSISTORY.

1. Illustrious Commander in Chief.
2. Illustrious Deputy Commander in Chief.
3. First and Second Lieutenant Commanders.
4. Grand Minister of State.
5. Grand Chancellor.
6. Grand Treasurer.

7. Grand Secretary.
8. Grand Keeper of Seals and Archives.
9. Grand Hospitaller and Surgeon.
10. Grand Architeect and Engineer.
11. Grand Master of Ceremonies.
12. Grand Standard Bearer.
13. Grand Captain of the Guards.
14. Grand Tyler.
15. Assistant Grand Tyler.

When the Illustrious Commander in Chief addresses a subordinate officer, or a member, and when such offcer or member addresses the Illustrious Commander in Chief, the officer or member will rise and salute with his sword; bring it to the carry, then to the present and then, dropping the point to the ground, to the right and a little in front of himself, the arm fully extended downwards; in which position he remains until the colloquy is concluded, and then comes again to the present and then to the carry.

OPENING CEREMONIES

SUBLIME PRINCE OF THE ROYAL SECRET.["]

Illustrious Commander in Chief—(Strikes one with pommel of his sword.)

First Lieutenant Commander—(Strikes one with pommel of his sword.)

Second Lieutenant Commander—(Strikes one with

Note 377.—"This is the thirty-second degree of the Ancient and Accepted Rite. There is abundant internal evidence, derived from the ritual and from some historical facts, that the degree of Sublime Prince of the Royal Secret was instituted by the founders of the Council of Emperors of the East and West, which body was established in the year 1758. It is certain that before that period we hear nothing of such a degree in any of the Rites. The Rite of Heredom or of Perfection, which was that instituted by the Council of Emperors, consisted of twenty-five degrees. Of these the twenty-fifth, and highest, was the Prince of the Royal Secret. It was brought to America by Morin, as the summit of the High Masonry which he introduced, and for the propagation of which he had received his Patent. In the subsequent extension of the Scottish Rite about the beginning of the present century, by the addition of eight new degrees to the original twenty-five, the Sublime Prince of the Royal Secret became the thirty-second.

Bodies of the thirty-second degree are called Consistories, and where there is a superintending body erected by the Supreme Council for the government of the inferior degrees in a State or Province, it is called a Grand Consistory.

The clothing of a Sublime Prince consists of a collar, jewel, and apron. The collar is black edged with white. The jewel is a Teutonic cross of gold. The apron is white edged with black. On the flap are embroidered six flags, three on each side the staffs in saltier, and the flags blue, red, and yellow. On the centre of the flap, over these, is a Teutonic cross surmounted by an All-seeing eye, and on the cross a double-headed eagle not crowned. On the body of the apron is the tracing-board of the degree. The most important part of the symbolism of the degree is the tracing-board, which is technically called 'The Camp.' This is a symbol of deep import, and in its true interpretation is found that 'royal secret' from which the degree derives its name. This Camp constitutes an essential part of the furniture of a Consistory during an initiation, but its explanations are altogether esoteric. It is a singular fact, that notwithstanding the changes which the degree must have undergone in being transferred from the twenty-fifth of one Rite to the thirty-second of another, no alteration was ever made in the Camp, which retains at the present day the same form and signification that were originally given to it.

The motto of the degree is 'Spes mea in Deo est,' i. e., My hope is in God."—Mackey's Encyclopaedia of Freemasonry, Article Sublime Prince of the Royal Secret.

pommel of his sword.)

Illustrious Commander in Chief—Valiant Captain of the Guards, see that the Sentinels are stationed, and advise them that we are about to open this Grand Consistory, that they may allow no one to approach, who hath not the words and signs of a Prince of the Royal Secret. (The Captain of Guards goes out, executes the orders of the Illustrious Commander in Chief, returns and salutes on entering.)

Captain of Guards—Illustrious Commander in Chief, the Sentinels are stationed and duly instructed; we are secure against intrusion.

Commander in Chief—Sublime Princes, First and Second Lieutenant Commanders, it is not enough for us to be protected, we must also be certain that none but friends are gathered under our colors. Visit the several camps, inspect the several corps of the army, and satisfy yourselves that no spy or enemy has intruded himself among us. Order Sublime Princes! (All rise under the sign of order. The two Lieutenant Commanders leave their stations and proceed from West to East, one on the right the other on the left, to receive the pass-word from each member present, including the Illustrious Commander in Chief, after which they return to their stations.)

Second Lieutenant Commander—Sublime Prince, First Lieutenant Commander, there is no spy or enemy in my camp.

First Lieutenant Commander—Illustrious Commander in Chief, there is no spy or enemy among us. We have met none but friends and brethren, ready to act as soon as the signal is given.

Commander in Chief—Be seated my brethren. (All resume their seats.)

Commander in Chief—Sublime Prince, Valiant First Lieutenant Commander, at what hour are we to act?

First Lieutenant Commander—At the fifth hour after sunset, Illustrious Commander in Chief.

Commander in Chief—And for what reason, Sublime Prince, can we not act before?

First Lieutenant Commander—Illustrious Commander in Chief, because if our actions were premature, our enemies might learn and defeat the plans we have formed for the regeneration of humanity. (At this moment, a brother in the ante-room strikes five blows on a drum; one by itself, and four at equal distances, and in quick succession, imitating the report of a cannon.)

Illustrious Commander in Chief—Sublime Prince, Second Lieutenant Commander, what's the hour?

Second Lieutenant Commander—Illustrious Commander in Chief, the gun has just fired, and tells us that five hours have elapsed since sunset.

Commander in Chief—Then the hour for action has come, and as all is ready in both your camps, Sublime Princes, Valiant First and Second Lieutenant Commanders, inform your brave companions, that I shall proceed to perform my duty.

First Lieutenant Commander—Valiant Companions of my camp, the Illustrious Commander in Chief informs you that he is about to proceed to perform his duty.

Second Lieutenant Commander—Valiant Companions of my camp, the Illustrious Commander in Chief, informs you that he is about to proceed to perform his duty.

Commander in Chief—(Rising.) Order Sublime Princes! (All rise under the sign of order.)

Commander in Chief—(Striking one with the pommel of his sword.) *Salix.*

First Lieutenant Commander—(Strikes one.) *Noni.*

Second Lieutenant Commander—(Strikes one.) *Tengu.*

All—(Led by Commander in Chief give sign, and say three times:) *Laus Deo.*

Commander in Chief—Sublime Prince, Captain of the Guards, advance and receive the watch-word of the day. (The Captain of Guard advances to the throne and receives from the Illustrious Commander in Chief the watch-word of the day, and the response. He then goes round and gives the watch-word to each member, each returning him the answer.)

Captain of Guard—Illustrious Commander in Chief, all the members present have the watch-word.

Commander in Chief—Attention Sublime Princes! Present swords! (All bring their swords to a present with the Commander in Chief.)

Commander in Chief—To the glory of the Grand Architect of the Universe, in the name and under the auspices of the Supreme Council of the 33rd degree, for the Northern Jurisdiction of the United States of America, sitting in the valley of New York, and by virtue of the powers in me vested, as Commander in Chief of this Grand Consistory of Sublime Princes of the Royal Secret, 32nd degree of the Ancient and Accepted Rite, for the State of......, I do hereby declare this body to be in session, for the advancement of the interests of humanity and the cause of virtue.

Commander in Chief—Carry swords! Together my brethren! (Led by the Commander in Chief, all bring their swords to a carry and pass them under left arm, point to the rear, and give the battery with their hands, after which they again bring their swords to a carry, then to a present and sheath them.)

Commander in Chief—Be seated Sublime Princes. Sublime Grand Chancellor, are you prepared to read the baluster of the last session of this Grand Consistory?

Commander in Chief—(If answered affirmatively.) Valiant Princes, First and Second Lieutenant Commanders, request the Sublime Princes in your respective camps, to listen attentively to the reading of the baluster of the last session of this Grand Consistory.

First Lieutenant Commander—Sublime Princes of my camp, the Illustrious Commander in Chief requests you to listen attentively, to the reading of the baluster of the last session of this Grand Consistory.

Second Lieutenant Commander—Sublime Princes of my camp, the Illustrious Commander in Chief requests you to listen attentively, to the reading of the baluster of the last session of this Grand Consistory.

Commander in Chief—Sublime Prince, Grand Chancellor, read the baluster of the last session of this Grand Consistory. (Baluster is read.)

Commander in Chief—Sublime Princes, First and Second Lieutenant Commanders, inform the Sublime Princes of your respective camps, that this Grand Consistory will listen to, and act upon any remarks they may have to offer, in relation to the baluster which has now been read.

First Lieutenant Commander—Sublime Princes of my camp, the Illustrious Commander in Chief informs you that this Grand Consistory will listen to and act upon, any remarks you may have to offer, in relation to the baluster which has now been read.

Second Lieutenant Commander—Sublime Princes of my camp, the Illustrious Commander in Chief informs you that this Grand Consistory will listen to, and act upon, any remarks you may have to offer, in relation to the baluster which has just been read.

Second Lieutenant Commander—(If there are no remarks.) Sublime Prince, First Lieutenant Commander, silence prevails prevails in my camp.

First Lieutenant Commander—Illustrious Commander in Chief, silence prevails in both camps.

Commander in Chief—Such being the case, the baluster of your last session is adopted. (The Grand Chancellor signs the records and the Grand Master of Ceremonies presents it to the Illustrious Commander in Chief for his signature, after which the Illustrious Commander in Chief orders the Grand Master of Ceremonies to visit the avenues and ascertain whether there be any brethren visitors; if any, they are introduced with the usual forms and ceremonies. Then the Grand Chancellor lays before the Illustrious Commander in Chief the *"Order of the Day,"* which is disposed of as in other degrees.)

CHAPTER LX

THIRTY-SECOND DEGREE, OR SUBLIME PRINCE OF THE ROYAL SECRET.'''

INITIATION.

When the Grand Consistory is prepared to proceed with the reception, a message to that effect is sent by a brother to the Grand Master of Ceremonies, who is with the candidate. The Grand Master of Ceremonies then gives the alarm of a Grand Inspector Inquisitor Commander at the door, 0 000 0000 0.

Commander in Chief—Sublime Prince, First Lieutenant Commander, ascertain the cause of that alarm.

First Lieutenant Commander—Sublime Prince, Captain of the Guards, ascertain the cause of that alarm.

Captain of Guard—Opening the door. What is the cause of that alarm?

Master of Ceremonies—The Grand Master of Ceremonies desires to gain admission, to present to the Illustrious Commander in Chief a worthy Grand Inspector

Note 878.—"Sublime Prince of the Royal Secret. [Scotch Masonry.] —The fourteenth degree conferred in the Consistory of Princes of the Royal Secret, Scotch Masonry, and the thirty-second upon the catalogue of that system. The assembly is called a Sovereign Consistory. The historical allusions are to the origin of masonry in general, and embrace an explanation of the preceding degrees. The officers are a Sovereign Grand Commander, representing Frederick II., of Prussia; two Illustrious Lieutenant Grand Commanders, Minister of State, Grand Chancellor, Grand Treasurer, Grand Secretary, Grand Architect, Grand Standard Bearer, Grand Captain of the Guards, Grand Master of Ceremonies, Expert Brother, Sentinel and two Guards. The hangings are black, strewed with tears. The apron is white, lined and trimmed with red, displaying the tracing-board of this degree; the movable part has a double-headed eagle. Jewel, a Teutonic Cross. The tracing-board is complicated. The outer figure is a nonagon; within this a heptagon; within this a pentagon; within this an equilateral triangle, and within the last a circle. On the lines of the pentagon are five standards, U. G. N. E. T., being respectively, golden yellow, green, white, azure, and purple. The sides of the nonagon represent the divisions of the masonic army, with the letters I. N. O. N X. I. L. A. S. Hour of departure, fifth hour after sunset."—Morris's Masonic Dictionary, Article Sublime Prince of the Royal Secret.

Inquisitor Commander, who desires to receive the last
secrets of the Ancient and Accepted Rite of Masonry.

Captain of Guard—Sublime Prince, First Lieutenant Commander, the alarm is caused by the Grand Master of Ceremonies, who desires to gain admission, to
present to the Illustrious Commander in Chief a worthy
Grand Inspector Inquisitor, who desires to receive the
last secrets of the Ancient and Accepted Rite of Masonry.

First Lieutenant Commander—Has he well considered and understood the lessons which he has received
in the preceding degrees, Valiant Captain of the Guard?

Captain of Guard—Illustrious Grand Master of Ceremonies, has he well considered and understood the lessons which he has received in the preceding degrees?

Master of Ceremonies—He has.

Captain of Guard—Sublime Prince, First Lieutenant
Commander, he has.

First Lieutenant Commander—Is he willing to unite,
with all his heart, in the great cause in which we are
now engaged?

Captain of Guard—Illustrious Grand Master of Ceremonies, is he willing to unite with all his heart, in the
great cause in which we are now engaged?

Master of Ceremonies—He is.

Captain of Guard—Sublime Prince, First Lieutenant Commander, he is.

First Lieutenant Commander—Does he know that
none are wanted here, except earnest and sincere men,
who are not selfish, and whose philanthropy is not a
mere name but a practical reality, and is he such an one?

Captain of Guard—Illustrious Grand Master of Ceremonies, does he know that none are wanted here,
except earnest and sincere men, who are not selfish, and
whose philanthropy is not a mere name, but a practical
reality, and is he such an one?

Master of Ceremonies—He does, and he is; I vouch for him.

Captain of Guard—(Closing the door.) He does and he is. The Sublime Prince, Grand Master of Ceremonies vouches for him.

First Lieutenant Commander—Illustrious Commander in Chief, the alarm is caused by the Sublime Prince, Grand Master of Ceremonies, who desires to gain admission, to present to you a worthy Grand Inspector Inquisitor Commander, who desires to receive the last Secrets of the Ancient and Accepted Rite of Freemasonry; one who has well considered and understood the lessons he has received in the preceding degrees; who is willing to unite with all his heart in the great cause in which we are engaged; who knows that we want none but earnest and sincere men, who are not selfish, and whose philanthropy is not a mere name, but a practical reality, and for whom the Sublime Prince, Grand Master of Ceremonies vouches, that he is such a man.

Commander in Chief—We rely with great confidence upon the assurances of the Sublime Prince, our Grand Master of Ceremonies, in regard to the qualifications and merits of the brother whom he brings with him. Sublime Princes, Grand Hospitaller and Engineer, you will now retire and prepare this Grand Inspector Inquisitor Commander, to receive the last secrets of the Ancient and Accepted Rite of Masonry. (They go out and invest the candidate with the decorations and jewel of the 31st degree, and place a poniard in each of his hands. They also tie a cord around his body, and conduct him to the door, one holding the end of the cord, the other having a hand upon his shoulder.)

Master of Ceremonies—(Knocks 0 000 0000 0; and then retires behind the candidate and two brothers.)

Commander in Chief—Who knocks, Sublime Prince, First Lieutenant Commander?

First Lieutenant Commander—Who knocks, Valiant Captain of the Guard?

Captain of Guard—(Opening the door.) Who knocks?

Master of Ceremonies—We conduct the Grand Inspector Inquisitor Commander, whom the Illustrious Commander in Chief has promised to enter. (Grand Captain of the Guards then shuts the door.)

Commander in Chief—Sublime Princes, I am willing to see this brother introduced among us, because we cannot enlist too many champions of our sacred cause. The Sublime Prince, our Grand Master of Ceremonies has vouched for him in such terms as our usages require, and we are therefore authorized to believe that he will do Masonry good service, in the war which she is waging against the ancient enemies of the human race.

Captain of Guard—Remove the barrier, and let the Grand Master of Ceremonies enter with the brother. (The door is opened, the candidate is introduced and made to halt in front of the Illustrious Commander in Chief, between the camp and the two Lieutenant Commanders.)

Commander in Chief—Who is this that comes as if reluctantly, or as a criminal, into this holy sanctuary?

Master of Ceremonies—It is a lover of wisdom, and an apostle of liberty, equality and fraternity, as understood by true Masons. He seeks to unite with those who labor for the emancipation of mankind.

Commander in Chief—What has he done hitherto toward that mighty work?

Master of Ceremonies—He has advanced in regular gradation, from the degree of Entered Apprentice to that of Grand Inspector Inquisitor Commander, and in all, his merits and his good works have obtained him the approbation and good opinion of his brethren.

Commander in Chief—By what principles, above all others, does he now profess to be governed?

Master of Ceremonies—By those of justice and equity.

Commander in Chief—What is it he now desires?

Master of Ceremonies—To be admitted a Prince of this Grand Consistory, that he may the more effectually aid in the great struggle for which Masonry is preparing, the second war against the giants, in which the liberty and happiness of humanity are at stake.

Commander in Chief—What means does he possess, and with what arms is he supplied, that can render him an efficient soldier in our ranks?

Master of Ceremonies—He has courage and pure intentions.

Commander in Chief—Are they enough?

Master of Ceremonies—No! He needs further instructions to have the veil finally removed, that has so long interposed between him and the true Masonic light; to attain the summit of the mountain up whose slopes he commenced to toil as an Entered Apprentice, and above all, the aid of him in the hollow of whose hand are victory and disaster, and who alone can give us strength to overcome.

Commander in Chief—We rejoice to receive the answers. My brother your motives are worthy of all praise, and if you are sincere; if you adopt as your own what the Grand Master of Ceremonies answered in your name, your claim to be admitted among us is legitimate and valid. Have you heard and understood all that he has answered for you, before and since your entrance here?

Candidate—I have.

Commander in Chief—And do you adopt and now

reiterate the same in all its parts, in the spirit as well as in the letter, as fully as if dictated by your heart and every sentence had been uttered by your own lips?

Candidate—I do.

Commander in Chief—Then your hopes of admission here, and of ultimate victory in the great contest that approaches are well founded. We are satisfied as to the purity of your motives and that you possess the requisite resolution and courage; but you are aware that more is needed, in him who would be invested with the highest rank, and take upon himself the responsibilities of Command. To wear that honor worthily and perform efficiently the duties it imposes, you must possess intellect, the talent to command and ample information.

We demand of you that proof. My brethren, free this aspiring brother from his bonds, and bid him lay his poniard on the altar. (The candidate places his two poniards on the altar, the cord is taken off and the two brothers retire to their places, the Grand Master of Ceremonies remaining alone with the candidate.)

Commander in Chief—My brother, the cause to which you desire to devote yourself is a noble one. Their devotion to it, has made all the great patriots and philanthropists, of all ages of the world illustrious, and their names and memories the richest inheritance of the human race. It is most honorable in you to seek to follow their example, and so to be the benefactor of your kind.

His is a poor ambition who does not long to do some good, that shall last beyond the limits of his own brief life.

If you have learned all that the Ancient and Accepted Rite has offered you the means of learning, you are prepared. We must know that you have at least endeavored to do so. Have you learned the first lesson? Have you fitted yourself to command, by first learning how to obey? Are you ready now, and always hereafter, to obey the lawful orders of this Grand Consistory and its Illustrious Commander in Chief for the time being; and to peril your life in the great battle that is to be fought against the enemies of God, and the foes of human liberty and human progress? Do you dare to do and suffer, and have you a hand to burn, like Scaevola, for your country or your friend? Can you, and do you answer these questions in the affirmative?

Candidate—I can and I do.

Commander in Chief—Then let your vows be sacred, and your promises made upon the altar of your heart.

Go now and study the symbolism of this degree, and learn its meaning, that you may be prepared to do what further we shall require of you. Sublime Prince Grand Master of Ceremonies, conduct the candidate to the camp of the Masonic army, and halt first at the quarters occupied by the Masons of the symbolic degrees. (The Grand Master of Ceremonies conducts the candidate to the tent numbered nine.)

Master of Ceremonies—My brother, the 32nd degree of the Ancient and Accepted Rite, which we are now conferring on you, is the military organization, as the 31st degree is the judicial organization, of the order.

The camp which you are entering and its several parts are all symbols, the meaning of which we will hereafter endeavor to explain to you.

As you pass around and through this symbolic camp, we will give you the necessary explanations as to its external features, and recall briefly to your mind the characteristics of the several degrees, whose standards float over the camp, to aid you in hereafter understanding the esoteric meaning of the whole. You will then perhaps see that whatever in Masonry seems arbitrary incongruous; mere empty words, and idle images and pictures, has in reality a profound meaning; that a great idea is embodied in this degree, of which its organization, and the disposition and details of the camp are the utterances, scientifically and skillfully arranged, and that in every thing it proceeds with precision and order to develop the idea, and insure the success of the noble and holy cause for which it is armed and organized.

The external lines of the camp form a nonagon, or a

figure of geometry with nine equal sides. You perceive that on each side of the nonagon is a tent, with a flag and pennon that each flag and its pennon are of a different color from the others, and that each tent is designated by a letter. Each represents a camp, and the several sides of the nonagon are thus assigned by our rituals, to the Masons of the different degrees, from the first to the eighteenth, of which each Commander in turn will give you an explanation.

Master of Ceremonies—Illustrious Commander Ezra, be pleased to communicate to our brother, the esoteric explanation of the tent No. 9.

Ezra—You are now at the ninth tent, the letter of which is I.∴. Its flag and pennon are blue, and here are said to be encamped the Apprentices, Fellows Crafts and Masters of the Blue or Symbolic degrees, and the volunteers. The commanding officer represents Ezra.

THE FIRST DEGREE:—Shows you man, such as nature has made him, with no other resources than his physical strength. But each symbol and ceremony of Masonry, has more than one meaning; one enveloped as it were, within the other, and all not developed or made known at once. The inmost meaning of the first degree is man subjugated and struggling toward freedom, blinded by superstition, destitute of knowledge, defenceless, and with the chains of despotism round him.

He knocks timidly at the door of Masonry, is received, sworn to secrecy and made to stand upright in the middle of the lodge, as a man; as a man!

It is his first lesson. Before then he was half naked, and half clad, neither barefoot nor shod, half freeman and half serf.

THE SECOND DEGREE:—Shows the necessity and holiness of labor, and consequently of knowledge. Man perceives here that to supply his physical wants, his organs are but the instruments of intellect, the expansion of which, or knowledge can alone constitute him a freeman and a king over creation.

THE THIRD DEGREE:—Teaches us that our inviolable destiny is death, but at the same time, in the ceremony and in the very name of Hiram it shadows forth the great doctrine of another life, and the immortality of the soul. The word Hiram[19] in Hebrew, means, "He who was, or shall be raised alive or lifted up," and it also symbolizes

Note 379.—"Hiram Abif. There is no character in the annals of Freemasonry whose life is so dependent on tradition as the celebrated architect of King Solomon's Temple. Profane history is entirely silent in respect to his career, and the sacred records supply us with only very unimportant items. To fill up the space between his life and his death, we are necessarily compelled to resort to those oral legends which have been handed down from the ancient Masons to their successors. Yet, looking to their character, I should be unwilling to vouch for the authenticity of all; most of them were probably at first symbolical in their character; the symbol in the lapse of time having been converted into a myth, and the myth, by constant repetition, having assumed the formal appearance of a truthful narrative. Such has been the case in the history of all nations."—Mackey's Encyclopaedia of Freemasonry, Article Hiram Abif.

the people, rising from the death of vassalage and ignorance, to the life of freedom and intelligence.

Commander in Chief—Sublime Prince Grand Master
of Ceremonies, conduct the candidate to the next tent.
(Order is obeyed:)

Master of Ceremonies—Illustrious Commander
Joshua, be pleased to communicate to our brother the
esoteric meaning of the tent No. 8.

Joshua—The tent which you have now reached is the
eighth, the letter of which is N.·. Its flag and pennon
are green, and here are supposed to be encamped the
Secret Masters and Perfect Masters, or the Masons of
the 4th and 5th degrees. The commanding officer represents Joshua.

THE FOURTH DEGREE:—Teaches truth and consequently the existence of one God, and the relations existing
between man and his Heavenly Father.

THE FIFTH DEGREE:—Teaches us the love of God for
the human race, and the magnitude of divine attributes.

Commander in Chief—Sublime Prince Grand Master
of Ceremonies, conduct the candidate to the next tent.
(Order is obeyed.)

Master of Ceremonies—Illustrious Commander *Aholiab*, be pleased to communicate to our brother the
esoteric meaning of the tent No. 7.

Aholiab—The tent which you have now reached is
the seventh, the letter of which is O.·. Its flag and pennon are red and green. Here are supposed to be encamped the Intimate Secretaries and Provosts and
Judges, or the Masons of the 6th and 7th degrees. The
commanding officer represents Aholiab.

THE SIXTH DEGREE:—Develops and fully proves the
sublime and consoling doctrine of the immortality of
the soul.

THE SEVENTH DEGREE:—Teaches justice as the necessary consequence of the relations between God and man

Commander in Chief—Sublime Prince, Grand Master of Ceremonies, conduct the candidate to the next tent. (Order is obeyed.)

Master of Ceremonies—Illustrious Commander *Jehoiada*, be pleased to communicate to our brother the esoteric meaning of the tent No. 6.

Jehoiada—The tent which you have now reached is the sixth, the letter of which is N.:. Its flag and pennon are red and black, in lozenges. Here is supposed to be encamped the Intendants of the Building, or the Masons of the 8th degree. The commanding officer represents Jehoiada.

THE EIGHTH DEGREE:—Teaches the necessity of order, without which, society cannot exist.

Commander in Chief—Sublime Prince Grand Master of Ceremonies, conduct the candidate to the next tent. (Order is obeyed.)

Master of Ceremonies—Illustrious Commander Paleg, be pleased to communicate to our brother the esoteric meaning of the tent No. 5.

Paleg—The tent which you have now reached is the fifth, the letter of which is X.:. Its flag and pennon are black. Here are supposed to be encamped the Knights Elect of Nine, the Illustrious Elect of Fifteen, and the Sublime Knights Elected. The commanding officer represents Paleg.

THE NINTH DEGREE:—Teaches us that no one has the right to take the law into his own hands. That the interests of society require that the administration of justice should be entrusted to a certain number of pure and upright men, for the benefit of all, and that true Masonry discountenances all acts of violence.

THE TENTH DEGREE:—Teaches that it does not consist with the good of society, that all should pretend to command, and that the administration of order, or the executive power, like that of justice, or the judicial power, must be confided to a few of the wisest and most experienced of the citizens.

THE ELEVENTH DEGREE:—Teaches us that the laws which are to govern a community must be elaborated, or the legislative power exercised, by the most able and honest citizens, and that to such men only it belongs, to represent the people in the legislative assemblies, there to maintain the rights and freedom of the people.

Commander in Chief—Sublime Prince Grand Master of Ceremonies, conduct the candidate to the next tent. (Order is obeyed.)

Master of Ceremonies—Illustrious Commander Joabert, be pleased to communicate to our brother the esoteric meaning of the tent No. 4.

Joabert—The tent which you have now reached is the fourth, the letter of which is I.:. Its flag and pennon are black and red. Here are supposed to be encamped the Grand Master Architects and the Knights of the Royal Arch, or the Masons of the 12th and 13th degrees. The commanding officer represents Johaben.

THE TWELFTH DEGREE:—Teaches that by labor alone we can obtain happiness, for our fellow beings and ourselves, and that to whatever degree of civilization mankind may attain, a true Mason will never cease to labor, that he may thereby make more complete the condition of his brethren.

THE THIRTEENTH DEGREE:—Teaches the utility of study, as the only means of drawing nearer to our Heavenly Father, and practicing true religion, the object of which is to attain a knowledge of the perfections and unbounded munificence of God, and thereby to become more and more perfect, by imitating his kindness in our relations with our brethren.

Commander in Chief—Sublime Prince Grand Master of Ceremonies, conduct the candidate to the next tent. (Order is obeyed.)

Master of Ceremonies—Illustrious Commander Nehemiah, be pleased to communicate to our brother the esoteric meaning of the tent No. 3.

Nehemiah—The tent you have now reached is the third, the letter of which is L.·. Its flag and pennon are red. Here are supposed to be encamped the Grand Elect Perfect and Sublime Masons of the 14th degree. The Commanding officer represents Nehemiah.

THE FOURTEENTH DEGREE:—You receive the reward of your labors. You were admitted to the sacred vault where you saw the end of all mystic forms, which the ignorance of mankind has made necessary. You then saw the future destiny of Freemasonry, that is of man, who enters upon the inheritance given him by his Heavenly Father. God is no longer to be feared, but to be loved with all the heart, mind and strength.

Commander in Chief—Sublime Prince Grand Master of Ceremonies, conduct the candidate to the next tent. (Order is obeyed.)

Master of Ceremonies—Illustrious Commander Zerubbabel, be pleased to communicate to our brother the esoteric meaning of the tent No. 2.

Zerubbabel—The tent which you have now reached is the second, the letter of which is A. Its flag and pennon are light green. Here are supposed to be encamped the Knights of the East, or of the Sword, or the Masons of the 15th degree. The commanding officer represents Zerubbabel.

THE FIFTEENTH DEGREE:—Teaches hope and faith in the new Era which dawns upon mankind, when men will be emancipated from dead forms and ceremonies, and when the whole power of man's intellect will be exerted to obtain a perfect knowledge of truth, and of the laws that flow from it.

Commander in Chief—Sublime Prince Grand Master of Ceremonies, conduct the candidate to the next tent. (Order is obeyed.)

Master of Ceremonies—Illustrious Commander Malachi, be pleased to communicate to our brother the esoteric meaning of the tent No. 1.

Malachi—The tent which you have now reached is the first, the letter of which is S.·. Its flag and pennon are white, sprinkled lightly with crimson. Here are supposed to be encamped the Princes of Jerusalem, the Knights of the East and West, and the Knights Rose Croix de Herodem, or the Masons of the 16th, 17th and 18th degrees. The commanding officer represents Malachi.

THE SIXTEENTH DEGREE:—Teaches that every religion, of mere forms and ceremonies and external practices, must eventually crumble to pieces, for it is a dead body without a soul, and that the Masonry of the Ancient and Accepted Rite, founded on the simple and pure doctrine of love, toleration and reason, must be eternal, because it is true and a reality, and being positively that which the Master from Nazareth taught, and every true child of our Heavenly Father may well adopt and profess it.

THE SEVENTEENTH DEGREE:—Teaches that every good and intelligent Mason must look upon himself as a pioneer, preparing the way for greater and better men to come after him, and that he must be content to work and do his duty, whether the results of his labor are manifest and visible during his life, or not; to sow no matter who reaps. Soldier of truth, he must always march straight onward, following the route which she indicates, to every loyal man. Death alone must make him pause.

Age gives no discharge from her service, and every true Mason may be certain, that if he manfully toils and fights in her cause, he will, whether the effect of his labors be seen by his mental eyes or not, leave to others who come after him, a noble heritage, ever to increase, as Mason follows Mason, in uninterrupted succession until men shall succeed each other in this world no longer.

THE EIGHTEENTH DEGREE:—Illustrates, by example, the truth of this doctrine of accumulation of intellectual wealth by inheritance, for in it are exhibited all the sublime truths, the axioms of ethics and philosophy, discovered and uttered by all former intellects, whose names, shining in the past, are so many resplendent proofs of the perfectibility of mankind, gathered and combined, in the sublime teachings of the Master from Nazareth, who was the possibility of the race made real.

He passed away in doing good, and we are rich with the splendid inheritance he left us. His death teaches us civil and religious toleration, and that, short as is our mental vision, and limited as our knowledge of the great mysteries of God and nature must ever be, we must never persecute, or ever become a stranger, to our brethren, because the opinions which they enunciate, conflict with those that we entertain, or are accustomed to hear. For in this degree the new law of love is taught, and the chief pillar among the three, with which are here replaced the ancient pillars of the temple, is charity, which not only relieves the wants, but is tolerant of the errors and mistaken opinions of other men. The degree is open to men of all creeds, who believe in the fundamental doctrines of the Ancient and Accepted Rite of Masonry. Every man who endeavors to teach at all, has a mission to perform. God tolerates him and allows him to teach, and we may well do the same.

For after all, the will of God governs, and the doctrine that is true will prevail, while what is false will not. What is persecuted grows, but if error be combatted, with no other weapons than those of Masonry, the total regeneration of humanity will come in God's good time.

Master of Ceremonies—You have now passed around the nonagon, and a full explanation has been given you of each tent by its commander. Within this you perceive is traced a heptagon, or a figure of geometry with seven equal sides, and within that a pentagon, or one with five equal sides. On each of the external angles of the pentagon is a great standard, designated by a letter and supposed to indicate the camp of a corps of Masons, occupying externally a side of the pentagon. I will now conduct you to the fifth standard.

Master of Ceremonies—Amariah, be pleased to communicate to the candidate the esoteric meaning of the fifth standard of the pentagon.

Amariah—My brother, the fifth standard, before which you now stand, has for its letter, U. . Its armorial bearings are thus described in the language of Heraldry: Or,* An ox-statant. Sable. Motto at the base. *Omnia Tempus Alit.* Time gives growth and strength to all things. Here are supposed to be encamped the Grand Pontiffs and Masters, *ad vitam,* or the Masons of the 19th and 20th degrees. The commanding officer represents Amariah.

†Or, in Heraldry, means gold or gold color.

THE NINTEENTH DEGREE:—Teaches us that, as true apostles of the doctrine of civil and religious toleration, we must, as it were, bridge the abyss that divides us from our brethren, who adhere to the old law and ceremonial observances of the past, and win them over to us by kindness and reason. When man is no longer a slave, we must appeal to his heart and intellect, if we would bring about the reign of peace, harmony and science. There are no other means by which an intelligent man can be convinced, however he may be compelled.

THE TWENTIETH DEGREE:—Teaches us the necessity of caution, in addition to energy and daring, that those who tread upon and live by the propagation of false creeds, may not defeat our plans for the emancipation of human intellect.

Commander in Chief—Sublime Prince Grand Master of Ceremonies, conduct the candidate to the 4th standard. (Order is obeyed.)

Master of Ceremonies—Garimont, be pleased to communicate to the candidate the esoteric meaning of the fourth standard.

Garimont—The standard which you have now reached is the fourth, the letter is G.∴. Its armorial bearings: vert; an eagle, with two heads displayed, sable, armed or ensigned with an imperial crown, or resting on both heads, holding in his dexter claw a sword, point in base; in his sinister claw a bloody heart. Motto at the base *Corde Gladio Potens.* Mighty of heart and with the sword. Here are supposed to be encamped the Noachites or Prussian Knights, and the Knights of the Royal Axe, or Princes of Libanus, or the Masons of the 21st and 22nd degrees. The commanding officer represents Garimont.

THE TWENTY-FIRST DEGREE:—Teaches you to strive earnestly to learn the means necessary to vindicate the power of truth, in bringing together all God's children, whatever their religious and political opinions. That means to raise man to the consciousness of what he is, and will soon become; what he ought to be.

THE TWENTY-SECOND DEGREE:—Teaches you that even after succeeding in that object, you would still need to be ever watchful and always on the alert, to bar the way of entrance against sectarianism.

Commander in Chief—Sublime Prince Grand Master of Ceremonies, conduct the candidate to the third standard. (Order is obeyed.)

Master of Ceremonies—Mah Shim, be pleased to communicate to the candidate the esoteric meaning of the third standard.

Mah-Shim—My brother, the standard which you have now reached is the third, its letter is N.∴. Its armorial bearings: *Argent.* A flaming heart, gules, winged, sable, crowned with laurel, vert. Motto at the base: *Ardens Gloria Surgit.* Inflamed with glory, it ascends. Here are supposed to be encamped the Chiefs of the Tabernacle, the Princes of the Tabernacle, and the Knights of the Brazen Serpent, or the Masons of the 23rd, 24th and 25th degrees. The commanding officer represents Mah-Shim.

THE TWENTY-THIRD DEGREE:—Teaches that after firmly establishing the institution of the Ancient and Accepted Rite, we should profoundly study the doctrine of the master from Nazareth, and expound to our brethren of the old law its practical and sublime lessons. The old law has not effected the happiness of mankind, nor have the old philosophies.

THE TWENTY-FOURTH DEGREE:—Teaches how arduous is the task of a true Mason, who endeavors to oppose sectarianism, for the sectarian will always obstinately maintain his own, narrow and exclusive creed, as the absolute and only truth, and such creeds will long continue to hold a large portion of mankind in bondage.

THE TWENTY-FIFTH DEGREE:—Teaches us to maintain the doctrine of liberty, equality and fraternity, as the only means of gathering around us the intelligent and good men of every lineage, creed and opinion, to repel and defeat the encroachments of idle theorists and kingly and priestly usurpers.

Commander in Chief—Sublime Prince Grand Master of Ceremonies, conduct the candidate to the second standard. (Order is obeyed.)

Master of Ceremonies—Aholiab, be pleased to communicate to the candidate the esoteric meaning of the second standard.

Aholiab—My brother, the standard which you have now reached is the second. Its letter is E.·. Its armorial bearings: *Azure*. A lion couchant, or holding in his mouth a key, or and collared, or with the figure 525 on the collar. Motto at the base, *Custos Arcani*. Keeper of the secret. Here are supposed to be encamped the Princes of Mercy, or Scottish Trinitarians, the Grand Commanders of the Temple and the Princes Adept, or Knights of the Sun, or the Masons of the 26th, 27th and 28th degrees. The commanding officer represents Aholiab.

THE TWENTY-SIXTH DEGREE:—Teaches us how a sincere and lasting alliance may be effected between the three intellectual classes of men: The disciples of the natural law and of philosophy; those of the law of Moses, and the other ancient faiths, and those who follow the doctrine of the Ancient and Accepted Rite, or the law taught by the Grand Master from Nazareth. However crude, defective and erroneous men's opinions may be, they will always listen to the voice of mercy, benevolence and affection.

THE TWENTY-SEVENTH DEGREE:—Teaches that the noblest reward, of him who has proved himself the apostle and champion of universal peace and toleration; who has aided fraternity to overcome and annihilate all formulas that stood in his way, will be to enjoy the fruits of his toil, among those who were once divided, but by his exertions have been brought to remember that they are brethren. Knowing this, the Mason's thirst for knowledge increases, and he learns that only by profound study, can he solve the great problem of the ultimate destiny in store for humanity.

The twenty-eighth degree solves that problem and shows the ultimate result of the doctrine of our Master; of that doctrine which is the way, the truth and the life. It is, that mankind are at last to become one single peaceful family, whose father and head is the eternal God, infinite in love.

Commander in Chief—Sublime Prince Grand Master of Ceremonies, conduct the candidate to the first standard. (Order is obeyed.)

Master of Ceremonies—Bezaleel, be pleased to communicate to the candidate the esoteric meaning of the first standard.

Bezaleel—My brother, you have now reached the first standard. Its letter is T.:. Its armorial bearings; purple, the ark of the covenant, or between two palm trees, vert, and two lighted candlesticks. Motto at the base, *Laus Deo;* praise be to God. Here are supposed to be encamped the Grand Scottish Knights of St. Andrew, or Patriarchs of the Crusades and the Knights Kadosh, or the Masons of the 29th and 30th degrees. The commanding officer represents Bezaleel.

THE TWENTY-NINTH DEGREE:—Teaches you how much can be effected in a righteous cause by perseverance. When the Ancient and Accepted Rite of Masonry shall have accomplished its mission, men will rest in the true Edeno in a realm where peace and fraternity will reign.

THE THIRTIETH DEGREE:—Teaches us to organize that army of tried and veteran Masons, that is to defend the rights of mankind against unlimited regal despotism, sacerdotal usurpation and intolerance, and the monopolies of rank, caste and privilege, and cause these usurpers to tremble, like the Babylonian king, when (according to the legend) an awful hand wrote the word of judgment on the wall of his banquet chamber.

Master of Ceremonies—My brother, you have now passed around the pentagon, and a full explanation has been given you of each Standard Bearer.

Enclosed in this pentagon you observe an equilateral triangle. At its angles, it is said, are encamped the Princes of the Royal Secret, the Grand Inspectors Inquisitors Commanders and such Knights of Malta, as having proved themselves true and faithful, have been accepted and received among us. Within the triangle is a circle, in which are said to be the quarters of the Sovereign Grand Inspectors General, of the 33rd degree, who serve as Lieutenant Commanders, under the Most Puissant Sovereign, Grand Commander. It is said in some rituals, and appears in most of the engraved tracing boards, that within the circle is a cross, sometimes with five arms of equal length, on which were to be the quarters of the five Princes, who, as Lieutenant Commanders, were in turn to be second in command, and whose standards float at the five angles of the pentagon.

Commander in Chief—Sublime Prince Grand Master of Ceremonies, let the candidate advance in front of the camp and face the East. (Order is obeyed.)

Commander in Chief—My brother, if you have assumed in good faith the obligations of the preceding degrees, the general features of which have now been summarily recited to you, and if you have studied and understood the doctrines which they teach, and the principles which they inculcate, you are entitled to our regard and esteem, and are fitted to do the duties of a good Mason, for you have bound yourself to do all that virtue, honor and manhood can require, and you have learned all that ancient and modern philosophy can teach in regard to the great mysteries of God and the universe.

Remember what you have been told in regard to the tracing-board or camp of this degree, that you may the better understand the explanation to be hereafter given. if in the test which you are to undergo, you prove yourself worthy to receive it.

First, however, as some evidence that you have not forgotten the teachings of the previous degrees, in the work of which we should examine all candidates, you must show that you remember that of the one through which you have so recently passed.

Commander in Chief—Why come you hither with weapons unfit for a judge, emblems of rude violence? For what purpose do you bring hither two poniards?

Candidate—I was told that one was intended to punish perjury and the other to protect innocence.

Commander in Chief—And you were also told that perjury was no longer punished by the dagger, but by the law and general contempt, and that innocence was now protected otherwise than by the poniard. Have you again assumed them of your own accord?

Candidate—I have not, they were placed in my hands?

Commander in Chief—It is well. Give them to our brother, the Grand Master of Ceremonies. They suit a Prince of the Royal secret no better than they suit a judge. (Candidate takes them from the altar and gives them to the Grand Master of Ceremonies.)

Commander in Chief—What was placed in your left hand when you assumed the obligation of the 31st degree?

Candidate—A pair of scales.

Commander in Chief—What lesson was it meant to teach you?

Candidate—That in all my judgments and opinions of men, I should be guided solely by justice and equity.

Commander in Chief—What is the pass-word of the 31st degree?

Candidate—There is none.

Commander in Chief—What are the sacred words.

Candidate—Justice and equity.

Commander in Chief—What words follow these two?

Candidate—So mote it be.

Commander in Chief—Give the token of that degree to the Sublime Prince Grand Master of Ceremonies? (It is given.)

Master of Ceremonies—Illustrious Commander in Chief, the token is correct.

Commander in Chief—Receive from our brother the Grand Master of Ceremonies, in lieu of the weapons which you have given up, that of a Knight and Prince of Masonry, especially appropriate for one who is to command. (Grand Master of Ceremonies hands the candidate a sword.)

Commander in Chief—(Rising.) Order my brethren! Sublime Prince Grand Master of Ceremonies, conduct the candidate to the altar. (All rise under the sign of order. The Illustrious Commander in Chief, leaves his seat and meets the candidate at the altar.)

Commander in Chief—My brother, if you would advance further, you must assume the obligation of this degree. That you may be certain that we are all bound to you, by ties as strong as those that will bind you to us, kneel at our altar, lay your hands and sword upon the book of constitutions and repeat after me:

OBLIGATION.

I......of my own free will and accord, in the presence of the Grand Architect of the Universe and of this Grand Consistory of Sublime Princes of the Royal Secret, and faithful guardians of the sacred treasure, do hereby and hereon, most solemnly and sincerely swear, under all the penalties of my former obligations in Masonry, that I will never, directly or indirectly, reveal or make known, to any person or persons whomsoever, any; even the least, of the secrets of this degree, unless to one duly qualified and entitled to receive them, and to such persons only, as I shall find to be after due and strict trial.

I furthermore vow and swear, that I will punctually obey all due signs and summonses, handed or forwarded to me, by the regular officer or officers of this Grand Consistory, so long as I remain within its jurisdiction, sickness, great distance, my duty to my family, or other over-ruling cause alone excusing me.

I furthermore vow and swear, always to conform to, and obey the statutes and regulations of the order, and to demean and behave myself, as one should who has been deemed worthy to be honored, with so high a degree, that no part of my conduct may in the least reflect discredit on the Grand Consistory, or disgrace myself.

I furthermore vow and swear, never to visit or recognize any spurious, irregular, illegitimate or clandestine body pretending to be Masonic, if I know it to be such, but will always denounce and discountenance all such, and to hold no Masonic intercourse with any member or members of any such bodies, and may God keep me just, equitable and charitable. Amen! Amen! Amen! Amen!

Commander in Chief—Rise my brother, you have still a solemn duty to perform, by certain journeys, symbolical of the warfare you are ever hereafter to wage, against the chief foes of human progress. You will thus give us the most solemn pledge of your sincerity and resolution, and prove to us that you recognize God as our common father, and all men his children.

Commander in Chief—(After returning to his station.) Be seated Sublime Princes. (All are seated except the candidate and Master of Ceremonies.)

Commander in Chief—My brother, be prepared. Remember that we shall accept each journey as your most solemn pledge, given to us in the sight of God, that the enemy of humanity, against whom you symbolically march, you will ever hereafter actively and energetically war against, with all lawful weapons and by all legitimate means. (At this moment five guns are heard firing.)

Commander in Chief—My brother, you have heard the signal. The hour has come when you must march upon the first of those campaigns, which every true Mason and Prince must ever be ready to make, for the relief of his suffering brethren. You are inexperienced, and will need a guide, and we entrust you to our tried brother, the Grand Master of Ceremonies, who has been with you from the beginning. (Illustrious Commander in Chief, now leaves his seat and goes to the candidate.)

Commander in Chief—Give your sword to the Grand

Master of Ceremonies my brother. A sword is a common weapon, worn alike by oppressors and their victims.
Before we return yours, it and yourself must be purified,
for a Prince and Commander in Masonry must have
none but pure motives, nor ever use his weapon, except
to protect the weak and the oppressed, and to keep within the bounds of law, if not of justice and equity, those
who still retain usurped powers. Do you swear and
swear so only to use it?

Candidate—I do. (In the meantime a laver**** is set
on a table in front of the nonagon, and filled with pure
water, and a napkin of white linen is laid near the laver.
The Illustrious Commander in Chief takes the right
hand of the candidate and dips it in the water and then
wipes it with the napkin, after which he also dips the
hilt of the sword in the water, wipes it, and returns it
to the candidate.)

Commander in Chief—(To candidate.) My brother,
you are now purified, by your oath and by this water,
which, with all our Ancient and Oriental Masters, was
an emblem of purity, both of body and soul. Your sword
is also without spot or stain, because the arm that wields
it will henceforward be guided by justice and true honor
alone. Remember that if you, at any time hereafter,
act unworthily, as a Mason and a Knight, by striking a
blow in an unjust cause, or failing when it is your duty
to strike a blow in a just one, you will be guilty of
violating your solemn oath.

And we now warn you, that many eyes will hereafter
be upon you, and will watch jealously, to see how you
keep and perform that and your other obligations. (The

Note 350.—"In the ancient mysteries the laver with its pure water
was used to cleanse the neophyte of the impurities of the outer world,
and to free him from the imperfections of his past or sinful life. It
is a necessary article in many of the higher degrees, for the ablution
of the candidate in his progress to a higher and purer system of
knowledge."—Macoy's Encyclopaedia and Dictionary of Freemasonry.
Article Laver.

Illustrious Commander in Chief resumes his seat, and at this moment a gun is fired.)

Commander in Chief—Order, Sublime Princes! (All rise.) Draw swords! Carry swords! Present swords! Salute! Proceed on your journey my brother with the kind brother whose experience will guide you. During your journey we will pray for you. (Candidate commences his journey.)

PRAYER.

Kind and indulgent Father of the great family of man. Supreme Intelligence; author of light and life, aid us in our efforts to make this world more worthy of Thee, and bless with thy favor our brother who marches to restore to light those who have forgotten Thee, and thy truth. For thy infinite love Thou bearest to thy suffering children, aid him and us in our warfare against ignorance; against those who mislead, impose upon and deceive thy people, and make the light of knowledge shine in all the corners of the earth. Amen! Amen! Amen! Amen!

Commander in Chief—Attention, Sublime Princes! Recover swords! Return swords! Be seated!

Master of Ceremonies—Illustrious Commander in Chief, the candidate has returned in safety from his first campaign.

Commander in Chief—My brother, we have already informed you that these journeys are the symbols of the several struggles to be made by Masonry, in the accomplishment of its holy mission, and by you as one of her soldiery. The first enemy that we have to contend against is ignorance. It is the child of despotism and the capital of the demagogue.

It has, in most countries, degraded the masses of mankind to a level with the beasts of burden; has made them bow their necks to wear the yoke, and hug the chains and manacles that dishonor them. It is the potent auxiliary of tyrants and hypocrites, by which they keep in bondage the souls and bodies of the children of God, who need but education to inform them that they are not of an inferior stock, nor born to toil, that power and craft may live in luxury, and rank and privilege be paid and pensioned by the public.

Let us then labor to eradicate ignorance, and to expose those who deceive and delude the people, and our Father in Heaven will smile upon our efforts. (At this moment a second gun is fired.)

Commander in Chief—The signal is again given. Courage, my brother, and march upon your second campaign. We will in silence offer up our prayers for your success. (The candidate is again conducted, by the Grand Master of Ceremonies, three times round the camp, and again halts, facing the Illustrious Commander in Chief.)

Master of Ceremonies—Illustrious Commander in Chief, the candidate has returned in safety from his second campaign.

Commander in Chief—The second formidable enemy, against which Masonry has to contend, is superstition, side by side with which ever marches its twin-brother fanaticism. Superstition is the offspring of ignorance, and nothing has more contributed to the degradation of our race. By its influence alone, nations once resplendent with civilization, and from which, as centres, science and arts, and all that enlightens and elevates man, flowed abroad into all the countries of the world, are now sunken in stupid somnolence and asphyxia, or have become almost idiotic.

The spirit of fanaticism still lives, and is active and

vigorous everywhere. It seems almost to be an essential element of human nature.

Against those ancient enemies of the light, we make war, panoplied with the armour of the doctrine of the great teacher of Nazareth, which is the doctriie of Masonry.

These doctrines must ultimately conquer, all intelligences, and Masonry will eventually rule the world, because its only arms are charity and persuasion and that intelligent logic, of which your sword is the symbol, and because it rebukes and disallows intolerance and persecution. (At this moment a third gun is fired.)

Commander in Chief—The signal is again given. Depart my brother, on your third campaign, while we again pray in silence for your success. (The candidate is again conducted three times around the camp, and halted again facing the Illustrious Commander in Chief.)

Master of Ceremonies—Illustrious Commander in Chief, the candidate has returned in safety from his third campaign.

Commander in Chief—My brother, if you had actually, instead of symbolically, undertaken this third campaign, for the purpose of measuring your strength against despotism and ambition, you would not have returned to us in safety. For while despotism, upon its ancient thrones, guarded by ignorance, superstition, fanaticism, privilege and rank, is too formidable to be so overthrown, it is, at the same time, timid and cowardly, and therefore merciless. It forgives no attempt against itself. The influence that will ultimately overthrow it must gain ground by slow and imperceptible degrees. The tree of liberty grows everywhere, watered by the blood of patriots. Alone you can do little, nor is it now in the power of Masonry to lead revolutions, and by arms establish free institutions. When we widen too much the circle of our exertions, we simply invite our initiates to do nothing, because what we tell them they are to do is impracticable. Our object on the contrary is to effect some practical good, within the limits of that circle in which our influences may be felt. When men and nations are fitted to be free, they will be so, and a great living example of freedom, based on law and order, is, in its calm, silent dignity of strength and peace, the mightiest antagonist of despotism, and arbitrary power. We must take care that we do not make the object of our order unreal and chimerical. (At this moment a fourth gun is fired.)

Commander in Chief—The signal is given again. Depart my brother, on your fourth campaign, while we again pray in silence for your success over the enemy, even baser than the former, against which you are now to march. (The candidate is again conducted three times around the camp, and halted, facing the Illustrious Commander in Chief.)

Master of Ceremonies—Illustrious Commander in Chief, the candidate has returned in safety from his fourth campaign.

Commander in Chief—My brother, among the enemies of true fraternity, one of the most potent is the love of wealth and greediness for gain.

The desire for a competency and even for wealth, to be liberally and generously used, is laudable and the parent of many virtues, but carried to excess and made the sole object of a man's life, it is hostile to the best interest of humanity; closes the hand and heart and sets self-interests in opposition to the large and benevolent plans of Masonry, which it regards as visionary expensive and absurd; wherefore this inordinate longing after wealth is an enemy against which Masonry has to contend. (At this moment a fifth gun is fired.)

Commander in Chief—The last signal is now given, you must make your fifth and last campaign against the most obstinate enemy of all, after which, your struggles being over, and victory having crowned you with its laurels, their purity unstained by a single drop of blood, you will take possession of your patrimony, reconquered for yourself and your brethren, and God will bless your labors, and through them advance the cause of true Masonry.

We shall soon meet again, but before you set forth, I will give you certain signs and words whereby we may recognize each other, and whereby you will be enabled to detect such traitors as, after their defeat, may attempt to introduce themselves to you; and among your brethren you must be cautious and prudent.

Commander in Chief—Sublime Prince Grand Master of Ceremonies, give to the candidate the sign, pass-word and sacred word of the 32nd degree. (It is done as follows:)

Sign Sublime Prince of the Royal Secret.

SIGN.

Place the right hand open on the heart; extend it forward, the palm downwards and then let it fall by the right side.

PASS WORDS:—One says Phaal-Kol, which means separated. The other answers Pharash Kol, which means reunited. Then the first says Nekam Makah which means blow or calamity or revenge. Both then pronounce together the word Shaddai, which means the strong, the mighty, a name of deity.

SACRED WORDS—The first is Salix[301] the answer to which is Noni, and then both together say, Tengu.[302] The first two words are formed by the letters designating the tents on the sides of the nonagon, and the third by those of the standard of the pentagon.

Master of Ceremonies—Illustrious Commander in Chief, the candidate has the sign, pass-word and sacred-words, of the 32nd degree.

Commander in Chief—My brother, before you set forth on your first campaign, we purified your heart by the solemn oath which you took between our hands and we also purified your hand and sword by water, the emblem of purity. Our object then was to bind you to act upon the principles of justice and equity, and not upon those of revenge and cruel reprisals against unrighteous enemies. You were to vindicate the rights of man and you have done so. God has smiled upon your exertions for he has so far given you the victory, and the holy land of our inheritance is in sight. You are now to take posession of it, but full in your way stands a three-fold enemy that cannot be avoided, but must be met and

Note 301.—"Salix. A significant word in the high degrees. Invented, most probably, at first for the system of the Council of Emperors of the East and West, and transferred to the Ancient and Accepted Scottish Rite. It is derived, say the old French rituals, from the initials of a part of a sentence, and has, therefore, no other meaning."—Mackey's Encyclopaedia of Freemasonry, Article Salix.

Note 302.—"Tengu. A significant word in the high degrees of the Scottish Rite. The original old French rituals explain it, and say that it and the two other words that accompany are formed out of the initials of the words of a particular sentence which has reference to the 'Sacred treasure' of Masonry."—Mackey's Encyclopaedia of Freemasonry, Article Tengu.

overcome. To succeed in that contest, you need to be still further purified, by fire and incense. Do you consent to submit to this trial?

Candidate—I do. (In the meantime the table and laver will have been removed, and replaced by a pan containing burning coals and a censer containig incense. The Illustrious Commander in Chief then leaves his seat and goes to the pan containing burning coals.)

Commander in Chief—(At altar of incense.) Advance my brother! (Candidate and Grand Master of Ceremonies advance to the altar when Illustrious Commander in Chief throws on the burning coals a few grains of incense, and while it burns he passes the right hand of the candidate five times over the fire; candidate holding his sword in his left hand.)

Commander in Chief—This arm is purified and devoted to justice and equity for ever. Give me your sword! (Takes sword from candidate and passes it five times over the fire.)

Commander in Chief—This weapon is also purified and devoted like its master. May God bless them, if they are guided by justice and honor. May both be disgraced if their deeds are unholy.)

Commander in Chief—Order; Sublime Princes! (All rise.) Draw swords! Carry swords! Present swords! Salute! Depart now my brother on your last campaign, and we will offer up our prayers for your success.

PRAYER.

Our Father, who are in Heaven, have mercy on our weakness. If it be thy will that we should direct and guide our brethren, preserve us from anger, vanity, temerity and error. Let us not fall into temptation, and seek to usurp those powers that belong in common to all thy children, and which we have so long struggled to restore to their hands. Let no criminal action; no base word, evil thought, or unholy feeling ever defile the temple which we have builded to Thee in our hearts. Enable us, with the aid of this candidate, to prevail against the selfishness, the apathy and the indifference of the world around us, and to overcome the same in our own natures, and so remove the last and greatest obstacle to the final triumph of the new land of love, and the universal dominion of the true principles of Masonry. Amen! Amen! Amen! Amen! Amen!

Commander in Chief—Be seated my brethren! (The three circuits being completed, the Grand Master of Ceremonies halts with the candidate facing the throne.

Master of Ceremonies—Illustrious Commander in Chief, the candidate has returned in safety from his fifth and last campaign.

Commander in Chief—My brother, we congratulate you upon your safe return among us. The three-fold enemy against whom you last marched, is found in Masonry, in our own bosoms as well as in the world. We incur no personal hazard in encountering this triune evil spirit, but it is the more obstinate and almost unconquerable, because it is passive, stationary and inert. It is the spirit of selfishness, apathy and indifference. Could we but overcome it, and substitute *in its place* zeal, ardour and disinterestedness, the victory over the giant wrongs and injustices, would be certain and speedy.

It is difficult to rouse even Masons to energetic action. It is difficult to convince them that there is anything in Masonry beyond the mere work of the lodge. If, remembering your pledge now given us, you do not fall into this apathy—indifference, but are faithful to your obligations, Masonry will profit by your labors and the *result of your experience. Sublime Prince Grand Mas-*

ter of Ceremonies, invest the candidate with the token, battery, etc., of this degree.

Token, Sublime Prince of the Roya Secret, 1st Position.

TOKEN.

Seize the sword with the right hand; unsheath it and carry it up to the right side, the hilt resting on the right hip, the point upwards. Place the right foot behind the left, so as to form a square, leaving a small distance between the feet thus arranged. Raise the left arm, the hand open and extended, as if to repulse an attack. Seize each other's left hand, the fingers interlaced. Then draw close to each other and embrace. One says Hochmah, (that is wisdom or philosophy) and the other answers Tsedakah, that is, truth, justice and equity. (In some rituals these-two words are said to be the sacred and pass of the degree.)

BATTERY.

Is five strokes, by one and four: 0 0000.

Token, 2nd Position.

HOURS OF LABOR:—The hour for the marching of the army is the fifth after the setting of the Sun.

MARCH:—The march is five steps, starting alternately with the right and left foot, and bringing the feet together at each step.

WATCH-WORDS:⁖⁘—There are seven watch words, one for each day in the week, and seven other words are given in answer to each watch-word, and are as follows:

Monday, watch-word, Darius, answer, Daniel.

Tuesday, watch-word, Xerxes, answer, Habakkuk.

Wednesday, watch-word, Alexander, ans. Zephaniah.

Thursday, watch-word, Philadelphus, answer, Haggai.

Friday, watch-word, Herod, answer Zachariah.

Saturday, watch-word, Hezekiah, answer, Malachi.

Sunday, watch-word, Cyrus, answer Ezekiel.

(The manner in which the watch-words are to be given and the answers received, has already been stated at the opening. During the explanations given by the Illustrious Commander in Chief, the Grand Master of Ceremonies causes the candidate to execute the movements.)

Commander in Chief—Be seated my brother, while we endeavor to explain to you the esoteric meaning of the camp, or tracing-board of this degree. However, before we proceed to give you those explanations, we deem it necessary to call your attention to the *two most* prominent systems in the Ancient and Accepted Rite. The first was promulgated in 1762, by nine commissioners appointed by the Council of Emperors of the East and West, and by the Council of the Princes of the Royal Secret. The first named body was created at Paris in 1758, the latter instituted in 1759, at Bordeaux, by said Council of Emperors.

Note 383.—"Watchwords. Used in the thirty-second degree of the Ancient and Accepted Scottish Rite because that degree has a military form, but not found in other degrees of Masonry."—Mackey's Encyclopaedia of Freemasonry, Article Watchwords.

Up to 1762 the great number of Scottish degrees had created much confusion, hence the necessity of settling the regulations of the "Masonry of Perfection." Such was then the name borne by our Rite, and of classifying the degrees of the system adopted by the Council of Emperors of the East and West. Those regulations, consisting of thirty-five articles, and the list of degrees, twenty-five in number; the last of which was the Sublime Commander of the Royal Secret, were promulgated on the 21st of September, 1762.

The camp before you was evidently made for that system. Adapted to our present one, it is arbitrary. Now in 1786, Frederick Second, King of Prussia, who according to many was at the head of the order in Europe, framed, or rather approved it is said, a new constitution of our rite in eighteen articles, changing the name of Rite of Perfection into that of Ancient and Accepted Scottish Rite, and adding eight new degrees to the old system thus extending the number of degrees to thirty-three, the last of which is Sovereign Grand Inspector General. My brother, we here give you a full list of the degrees of each system:

In 1762.	In 1786.
1. Entered Apprentice.	Entered Apprentice.
2. Fellow Craft.	Fellow Craft.
3. Master Mason.	Master Mason.
4. Secret Master.	Secret Master.
5. Perfect Master.	Perfect Master.
6. Intimate Secretary.	Intimate Secretary.
7. Intendant of the Building.	Provost and Judge.
8. Provost and Judge.	Intendants of the Building.
9. Elected Knight of Nine.	Elected Knight of Nine.
10. Elected Knight of Fifteen.	Elected Knight of Fifteen.
11. Chief of the Twelve Tribes.	Sublime Knight Elected.
12. Grand Master Architect.	Grand Master Architect.
13. Royal Arch.	Royal Arch.

14.	Ancient Grand Elect.	Ancient Grand Elect.
15.	Knights of the Sword.	Knights of the East.
16.	Prince of Jerusalem.	Prince of Jerusalem.
17.	Knights of the E. and W.	Knights of the East and West.
18.	Knights of Rose Croix.	Knights of Rose Croix.
19.	Grand Pontiff.	Grand ·Pontiff.
20.	Grand Patriarch.	Gr. Mas. of all Symbolic.
21.	Grand Master of the Key.	Noachite or Prussian Kni'ts.
22.	Knight of the Royal Axe.	Kt. of R. A. or Pr. of Libanus.
23.	Prince Adept.	Chief of the Tabernacle.
24.	Com. of the W. & B. Eagle.	Prince of the Tabernacle.
25.	Com. of the Royal Secret.	Knight of the Brazen Serpent.
26.		Prince of Mercy.
27.		Sov. Com. of the Temple.
28.		Knights of the Sun.
29.		Gr. Scotch Kt. of St. Andrew.
30.		Gr. Elect Knight Kadosh.
31.		Gr. Ins. Inq. Commander.
32.		Sub. Pr. of Royal Secret.
33.		Sov. Gr. Inspectors General.

EXPLANATION OF CAMP:—We read in almost all the rituals of this degree, that Frederic the Second, or the Great King of Prussia, being at the head of the Masonic fraternity on the continent of Europe, projected a league of the union of the brethren, Companions, Knights, Princes and Commanders of Masonry, for the purpose of rescuing Jerusalem and the Sepulchre of Jesus of Nazareth from the hands of the Turks, by a new crusade, in which it was his intention to command in person. It is said that he prepared a plan, by which the army was to encamp, which is the same now represented to you, and which is also perpetuated on the tracing-board and apron of this degree.

But it is not at all probable that Frederic the Great ever thought seriously of invading Palestine, and waging a new crusade. He was far too busily engaged in the affairs of his own kingdom, and too much of a philosopher to have thought of so chimerical a project. Nor had he any control whatever over the Masonic fraternity, elsewhere than in Prussia, nor even was he Grand Master of Masons there, and if he had intended a crusade, he was too accomplished a general ever to have fixed upon such a plan, for a real encampment. It is contrary to all rule. It would be wholly impracticable in the field, and it is entirely evident that it is merely an imaginary plan, never meant to be put to actual use.

It is equally evident that if Frederic had expected to gather any army of Masons, which he could not seriously have done, the number of Masons of the different degrees would not have been so proportioned as to admit of their encamping by the plan proposed. Of some of the degrees there would have been but a handful, and the Apprentices, Fellow Crafts and Masters, to whom only one of the nine sides of the nonagon is assigned, would have outnumbered all the rest.

The camp being therefore, impracticable, and even absurd as an actuality, we must either conclude that the inventor was a man of no sense, or that it is an allegory and a symbol. We are certain of the latter.

The camp, which is so prominent a feature in this degree, must originally have had a meaning, for it cannot be supposed that a man of intellect ever seriously occupied himself with making a beautiful figure on paper, arranging it as a camp and adopting arbitrary letters and names without any deeper meaning than that which you have thus far discovered. It is an elaborate, complicated and intricate symbol. Its meaning was no doubt originally explained, only orally, and that alone would be reason and cause sufficient why that meaning should in time be lost. For that cause alone has cost Masonry the true meaning of many, even

of its simpler symbols and substituted, strained, un-
natural and common place interpretations in their
place.

The figure is a five-armed cross, enclosed by a circle,
that by a triangle, that by a pentagon, that by a heptagon, and that by a nonagon. On the lines of the nonagon, are the camps of those from the 19th to the 30th
degrees inclusive. On the triangle, those of the 31st
and 32nd degrees. It is evident that the distribution of
these degrees is now nearly arbitrary. While eighteen
degrees occupy the nonagon, being double the number
of its sides, twelve occupy the pentagon and two the
triangle. It is true that Knights of Malta are added
to make three bodies for the triangle, but this is evidently a mere make-shift, for they are not Masons,
and to introduce them destroys the whole idea at once.

The seventeen sides of these three figures in no way
suit the present number of the degrees. Then again,
there are no camps at all on the heptagon, and so it becomes a perfectly useless part of the figure. The dis-
crepancies in the rituals, as to the distribution of the
first eighteen degrees, show that the arrangement is
arbitrary, and there is no attempt made to connect the
letters of the camp, or of the standards, in any way,
with the degrees to which they are assigned. They
would seem to have been taken at random, like the
names of the Commanding officers, which offer the
most singular and incongruous mixture.

As if further to increase the difficulty, the rituals differ as to the standards to which the respective letters
Y∴E∴N∴G∴U∴are to be assigned. These devices
of these standards are not apparently connected with
the degrees in either arrangement, nor is any attempt
made to explain their meaning, or show from whence
part of them came. Then we are told of three birds,

one in each corner of the triangle; ι Raven, a Dove[***] and a Phœnix.[***] No one vouchsafes to tell us where they came from; or the palm-trees on each side of the ark; or the meaning of the inflamed or winged heart; or of the five armed cross in the circle. And if any attempt to explain these things has been made, it is painful to a man of intellect to read the miserable and trivial stuff to which sensible men are expected respectfully to listen. The reason for selecting geometrical figures is obvious. The circle is unity, and it with others represent the five sacred Masonic numbers, 1, 3, 5, 7, and 9.

We have deeply studied these emblems, reflected upon them, and made many researches in the hope of fathoming their meaning. What we have discovered we propose to communicate to you. It is our own discovery. We have not received it by tradition. Besides the cause already mentioned, there is we believe, another that has lead to the intentional denatu-realization of this symbol, and that has probably destroyed the possibility of ever receiving the whole meaning. Whether the partial explanation we shall give you is

Note 384.—"This bird was the diluvian messenger of peace, and hovered over the retreating waters like a celestial harbinger of safety. Thus a lunette floating on the surface of the ocean, attended by a dove with an olive branch in its mouth, and encircled by a rainbow, form a striking and expressive symbol which needs no explanation. If Freemasonry has allowed this bird to occupy a high situation amongst its hallowed symbols, the reasons for such an appropriation are fully com petent to justify the proceeding. The dove was an agent at the creation, at the deluge, and at the baptism of Christ."—Macoy's Encyclopaedia and Dictionary of Freemasonry, Article Dove.

Note 385.—"Phoenix. The old mythological legend of the Phoenix is a familiar one. The bird was described as of the size of an eagle, with a head finely crested, a body covered with beautiful plumage, and eyes sparkling like stars. She was said to live six hundred years in the wilderness, when she built for herself a funeral pile of aromatic woods, which she ignited with the fanning of her wings, and emerged from the flames with a new life. Hence the phoenix has been adopted universally as a symbol of immortality. Higgins (Anacalypsis, ii. 441,) says that the phoenix is the symbol of an ever-revolving solar circle of six hundred and eight years, and refers to the Phenician word phen, which signifies a cycle. Aumont, the first Grand Master of the Templars after the martyrdom of De Molay, and called the 'Restorer of the Order,' took, it is said, for his seal, a phoenix brooding on the flames, with the motto, 'Ardet ut vivat'—She burns that she may live."—Mackey's Encyclopaedia of Freemasonry, Article Phoenix.

right or not, you must yourself judge. It is not given you as sacramental.

Prior to 1786 at least, the Ancient and Accepted Rite consisted of only twenty-five degrees. The first eighteen were the same as at present. That you may fully understand what is to be said hereafter, we subjoin, the degrees above the eighteenth, as they then existed.

1762.

19. Grand Pontiff, Master ad vitam.
20. Grand Patriarch, Noachite.
21. Grand Master of the Key of Masonry.
22. Prince of Libanus, or Knight of Royal Axe.
23. Prince Adept.
24. Commander of the White and Black Eagle.
25. Commander of the Royal Secret.

1786.

19. Grand Pontiff.
20. Grand Master ad vitam.
21. Noachite or Prussian Knights.
22. Prince of Libanus.
23. Chief of the Tabernacle.
24. Prince of the Tabernacle.
25. Knight of the Brazen Serpent.
26. Prince of Mercy.
27. Grand Commander of the Temple.
28. Knight of the Sun.
29. Grand Scotch Knight of St. Andrew.
30. Knight Kadosh.
31. Grand Inspector Inquisitor Commander.
32. Sublime Prince of the Royal Secret.

In other words, our 19th and 20th degrees were then in one, the 19th. Our 21st was the 20th; our 22nd was then the 22nd; and our 28th was then the 23rd; *our*

30th or a degree like it, was then the 24th; our 32nd was then the 25th, and there was no degree above that; and our 23rd, 24th, 25th and 26th, as well as the 33rd were not then known. The 27th was a detached degree, and the 29th was part of another system. The regulations and constitutions, said to have been made at Bordeaux, by the Princes of the Royal Secret in 1762, give the list of the degrees and require 81 months; that is 9 times 9, by 1, 3, 5, 7, to be occupied in obtaining them. They are divided into seven classes of 3, 5, 3, 3, 5, 3, 3, degrees respectively; the time required for obtaining the degrees, in each class respectively 9 and 15, or three times five months. The regulations term these the mysterious numbers, and there is in article two a paragraph in regard which is translated as follows:

"All these degrees, in which one must be initiated in a mysterious number of months, to arrive in succession at each degree, form the number of 81 months; $8+1=9$; as 8 and 9 express 89, and as 9 times $9=81$; all of which are perfect numbers and very different from 1 and 8 which make 9 and 1 and 8 compose 18, for these are imperfect numbers, and this combination is imperfect." But a true Mason, who has completed his time, gathers at last the Masonic rose.

Now taking the numbers of the different figures of the camp: Of the circle, or unity, the triangle, pentagon, heptagon and nonagon, we have $1+3+5+7+9$, which added together make 25, the number of degrees in 1762, and placing the Commanders of the Royal Secret in the circle, it leaves one degree for each side of all the right hand figures. Thus the number of degrees corresponds with the figures; the heptagon ceases to be useless, and the arrangement of the degrees ceases to be arbitrary.

We conclude, at once, that this tracing-board was

settled when there were but twenty-five degrees, prior
to 1786, and we see at once that cause, additional to
time and the treachery of memory which has lost us
the full explanation of this collection of symbols. It is
that after the degrees had been increased to the 33rd,
the figures had too few sides, and it became necessary
to rearrange the degrees, and distribute them anew
among the camps. This displaced the letters; assigned
one letter to more than one degree; displaced the standards and caused the disuse of the heptagon, and made
the whole arrangement arbitrary and inexplicable. This
is the key to the mystery; or if it be not, we do not
believe there is any key, and with this key we proceed
to unlock that mystery as far as we can; knowing that
we can only partially do so, and only hoping to put
others and more learned investigators on the right
track and so be instrumental in the ultimate entire development of these interesting symbols. We again observe that the degrees of the two scales are identical up
to the 18th degree assuming as a reasonable supposition,

that the lower degrees
were originally assign-
ed to the lines of the
camp furthest from
the centre, because that
is natural, because the
general feature would
in all probability not
be changed in the re-
arrangement which
the increased number
of the degrees made
necessary, we at once find that the nonagon, offering us

nine sides, accommodates the first nine degrees, beginning with the Apprentice and ending with the Elect of Nine, and that the heptagon, completing with its seven sides the number 16, accommodates those from the tenth to the sixteenth, or Prince of Jerusalem inclusive, and thus, as the regulations do, puts these Princes at the head of the Masons of those sixteen degrees, and this agrees with the regulations of 1762, which declares them to be the Most Valiant Chiefs of the Renovated Masonry, and gives them control over all lodges of the Royal Perfection and Council of Knights of the East. See constitutions of 1762, Art. 31. Above the 16 degrees then, by the system of 1762, are the following which we number as they stand in both scales:

17. Knights of the East and West.   17
18. Sovereign Prince of Rose Croix.   18
19. Grand Pontiff and Master ad vitam   19 and 20
20. Grand Patriarch, Noachite.   21
21. Grand Master of the Key of Masonry.
22. Prince of Libanus, or Knight of Royal Axe. 22
23. Sovereign Prince Adept or Knight of the Sun.28
24. Grand Commander of the Black Eagle.   30
25. Sovereign Prince of Royal Secret.   32

Now it is obvious that the five sides of the pentagon accommodate the five degrees from the 17th to the 21st inclusive, and if we assign the Princes of the Royal Secret to the circle, as we must do to make the number correspond, we have for the triangle the three following degrees.

22. Prince of Libanus or Knight of Royal Axe.
23. Sovereign Prince Adept or Knight of the Sun.
24. Grand Commander of the Black Eagle.

To have placed an inferior degree on the triangle and one of these three on the pentagon, and thus further from the centre, would have been to disarrange and interrupt the regular order and succession of the degrees. From circumference to centre and this we do not think the inventors of the symbol would have done, even if it required a little forcing to make the emblems correspond; because one irregularity of that kind would have destroyed the harmony and symmetry of the whole system, and the idea on which it was framed. Now to the triangle three birds are assigned, apparently in the present system without any meaning.

We have seen an attempt to explain them, or give them a symbolical meaning, the success of which, if it aimed at being common place and trivial, was most encouraging. The Raven is the Black Eagle of the 24th degree; that is the Kadosh or Knight of the White and Black, of which degree the old jewel was a Black Eagle.

That fabulous bird, the Phœnix, of which only one, it is said, existed at a time, was in Arabia, sacred to the Sun, and an emblem of that Orb. It was said to burn itself upon a funeral pile when it grew old, and to spring in renewed youth from its own ashes, and hence it figured in Alchemy[306] that search after the Elixer that was to give immortality. Of course it was peculiarly appropriated to the degree of Knight of the Sun, or Prince Adept, which originally was an Alchemical degree, as the very word "Adept" and its pass-word,

Note 386.—"Freemasonry and alchemy have sought the same results. (the lesson of Divine Truth and the doctrine of immortal life,) and they have both sought it by the same method of symbolism. It is not, therefore, strange that in the eighteenth century, and perhaps before, we find an incorporation of much of the science of alchemy into that of Freemasonry. Hermetic rites and Hermetic degrees were common, and their relics are still to be found existing in degrees which do not absolutely trace their origin to alchemy, but which show some of its traces in their rituals. The 28th degree of the Scottish Rite, or the Knight of the Sun, is entirely a hermetic degree, and claims its parentage in the title of 'Adept of Masonry,' by which it is sometimes known."— Mackey's Encyclopaedia of Freemasonry, Article Alchemy.

"Stibiums or Antimony," supposed to be the universal solvent show and as appears also by its old ritual and lecture.

The Dove[887] was a sacred bird in Syria, and the only one employed for religious purposes, among the Hebrews. One was, according to the legend, sent out three different times with intervals of seven days between each mission by Noah from the Ark, as well as by Deucalion, and Noah is the first sacred word of the 22nd degree or Prince of Libanus.

We do not say that these explanations are correct, but they are at least reasonable and probable.

To each angle and side of the pentagon, as we have seen, is assigned a standard, designated by a letter and a particular device. The rituals differ however as to the letters belonging to the particular standards. They give them in these two ways.

T.·. The Ark and Palm Tree.   The Lion and Key.

E.·. The Lion and Key.   The Inflamed Heart.

N.·. The Inflamed Heart.   The Eagle with 2 Heads.

G.·. The Eagle with 2 heads.[888]   The Black Ox.

Note 887.—"In the Arkite rites, which arose after the dispersion of Babel, the dove was always considered as a sacred bird, in commemoration of its having been the first discoverer of land. Its name, which in Hebrew is ionah, was given to one of the earliest nations of the earth; and, as the emblem of peace and good fortune it became the bird of Venus. Modern Masons have commemorated the messenger of Noah in the honorary degree of 'Ark and Dove,' which is sometimes conferred on Royal Arch Masons."—Mackey's Encyclopaedia of Freemasonry, Article Noah.

Note 888.—"The double-headed eagle was probably first introduced as a symbol into Masonry in the year 1758. In that year the body calling itself the Council of Emperors of the East and West was established in Paris. The double-headed eagle was likely to have been assumed by this Council in reference to the double jurisdiction which it claimed, and which is represented so distinctly in its title. Its ritual, which consisted of twenty-five degrees, all of which are now contained in the Ancient and Accepted Scottish Rite, was subsequently established in the city of Berlin, and adopted by the Grand Lodge of the Three Globes. Frederick II., king of Prussia, who was the head of the Ancient and Accepted Scottish Rite, is said to have merged this body into his own Rite, adding to its twenty-five degrees eight more, so as to make the thirty-three degrees of which that Rite is now composed. The double-headed eagle was then adopted as the symbol of the thirty-third and ultimate degree. The whole Rite being considered as a representative of the Holy Empire, as is indicated by the titles of two of its officers, who are still called the Secretary and the Treasurer of the Holy Empire, the double-headed eagle, which was the ensign, as it has been seen, of that empire, was appropriately adopted as the symbol of the governing degree of the Rite."—Mackey's Encyclopaedia of Freemasonry, Article Eagle, Double-Headed.

$U.\cdot.$ The Black Ox.   The Ark and Palm Trees.

Applying these devices to the five degrees, 17th, 18th, 19th, 20th and 21st degrees, the Lion and Key would seem to be appropriate enough to the 21st degree, or the Grand Master of the Key of Masonry.

The crowned double-headed Eagle, which is the arms of Prussia, to the 20th degree, or the Noachites or Prussian Knights.

The Ark of the Covenant, of which the High Priest had the especial charge, to the 19th degree or Grand Pontiff and Master ad Vitam.

The inflamed winged heart, emblematical of the sufferings and glory of the Master from Nazareth, to the 18th degree, or Sovereign Prince of Rose Croix, and the Ox an Egyptian and Jewish symbol, displayed on one of the Standards of the four principal tribes to the 17th degree, or Jewish Knights of the East and West.

It is likely that these devices have a still deeper meaning and a mysterious reference to an ancient religion and its mysteries, but we have, as to this, ourselves succeeded in obtaining but a few hints, and we can therefore communicate no more to you. They will perhaps, give you the key to the esoteric meaning of these symbols and you cannot do better than to occupy your time and exercise your intellect in discovering that meaning.

The Ancient Persian[***] mysteries were sacred to the

Note 389.—"From the statement of this Persian Mason it appears that nearly all the members of the Persian Court belong to the mystic Order, even as German Masonry enjoys the honor of counting the emperor and crown prince among its adherents. The appearance of this Mohammedan Mason in Berlin seems to have excited a little surprise among some of the brethren there, and the surprise would be natural enough to persons not aware of the extent to which Masonry has been diffused over the earth. Account for it as one may, the truth is certain that the mysterious Order was established in the Orient many ages ago. Nearly all of the old Mohammedan buildings in India, such as tombs, mosques, etc., are marked with the Masonic symbols, and many of these structures, still perferct, were built in the time of the Mogul Emperor Akbar, who died in 1605. Thus Masonry must have been introduced into India from Middle Asia by the Mohammedans hundreds of years ago."—Mackey's Encyclopaedia of Freemasonry, Article Persia.

God, Mithras[***] *"Deo Soli Invicto Mithras"* to the sun god Mithras the Invincible, also called the Mediator, the fertilizer of deserts, the slayer of the dragon, and of evil spirits. He was worshipped among the Ethiopians and Egyptians in Greece, after the time of Pompey at Rome. He is represented in the sculptures as a young man mounted on the Equinoctial Bull, and plunging into its flank a sword, whose hilt terminated at the upper end in two heads of an Eagle or a Hawk. He is represented as at the mouth of a cavern, with a figure on each side bearing a lighted torch. He is accompanied by Eorosch, the Celestial Raven, and the dying bull is consoled by Taschtar, the dog-star, the harbinger of his resurrection. The bull was regarded as a symbol of the power that produces vegetation and life. He makes, the Zendavesta said, "the grass to grow abundantly and gives all fruitfulness to the earth." Hence the motto of the standard on which he figures *"Omnia Tempus Alit."* So in Egypt, Mnevis, the black Ox of Heliopolis, was dedicated to Osiris and they worshipped a black Bull, which they called Onuphis.

The lion, the sign of the Summer Solstice, and domicile of the Sun was the symbol of that orb. The figures in the mithriac monuments, and the second degree of the Prussian mysteries was called the degree of the Lion. The initiates were called Eagles, Hawks and Ravens. In a very curious Roman marble, the drawing

Note 390.—"Mithras, Mysteries of. There are none of the Ancient Mysteries which afford a more interesting subject of investigation to the Masonic scholar than those of the Persian god Mithras. Instituted, as it is supposed, by Zeradusht or Zoroaster, as an initiation into the principles of the religion which he had founded among the ancient Persians, they in time extended into Europe, and lasted so long that traces of them have been found in the fourth century. 'With their penances,' says Mr. King (Gnostics, p. 47,), 'and tests of the courage of the candidate for admission, they have been maintained by a constant tradition through the secret societies of the Middle Ages and the Rosicrucians down to the modern faint reflex of the latter—the Freemasons."—Mackey's Encyclopaedia of Freemasonry, Article Mithras, Mysteries of.

of which was published by Gronovius in his Latin edition of Agostini, representing Mithras, with one foot on the body and the other between the horns of a Bull, are seen a Lion's head and two palm trees just putting out their leaves, a Raven and an Eagle on a palm tree holding a thunderbolt in his claws. It is this thunderbolt which has been, in our symbol, corrupted into a sword, with a crooked and wavy blade.

Mithras himself was often represented with the head of a lion.

The palm tree was not only an emblem of virtue and truth, but it was also consecrated to the celestial movements, and above all, the annual revolutions of the Sun.

Among the Hebrews, it will be remembered, the lion was borne on the crimson standard of the tribe of Judah. The Ox, on the green standard of Ephraim. The Eagle on the green standard of Dan, and the ship on the purple standard of Zebulon. Perhaps the Ark of the Covenant is really the Ark of the Deluge, or the ship of Zebulon.

The inflamed winged heart is probably the winged globe or sun, a common symbol in Egyptian temples and an emblem of immortality.

The figure 525 on the golden collar of the lion had originally, no doubt, a meaning connected with the number of degrees or perhaps with an Epoch in the annals of Masonry, but for the present at least, that meaning is lost.

Nor have we been able to discover the origin of the several letters which designate the tents of the nonagon and the standards of the pentagon. Others possessed of more extensive learning may hereafter succeed in doing so, and also in unveiling the hidden meanings of the names of the commanding officers. We might pretend to do so, and give you, as others have done, arbitrary and perhaps unmeaning explanations, without any warrant but that of our own imagination. There has been too much of that in Masonry, and we prefer to be satisfied with the little that we know, and to leave the rest for future investigation.

It will be noticed that the seven watch-words for the different days of the week, all of them names of persons, correspond with the number of sides of the heptagon, and that if they were assigned to command there, they would make the number of commanders complete. These seven names are curiously enough, those of three Persian kings, Darius, Xerxes and Cyrus. The Macedonian conqueror Alexander, Ptolemy Philadelphus, one of his successors, Herod, the tributary Roman king in Judea, and Jewish king, Hezekiah, while all the answers are the names of Jewish prophets. The name of Herod and those of Xerxes and Ptolemy Philadelphus seem wholly out of place in Masonry.

The names of the Commanders of the nonagon; one Phaleg goes back to the building of the tower of Babel; one Aholiab, to the building of the first tabernacle, one Joshua, is the name of the successor of Moses, one Johaben, is fictitious, one Jehoiada, is that of the Jewish High Priest, in the time of Jehoash and Athaliah, and three, Zerubbabel, Ezra and Nehemiah, refer to the rebuilding of the temple, while the one remaining is the name of the last prophet.

Of the names of the five Chiefs of the standards, two Bezaleel and Aholiab, were those of the Architects of the tabernacle of the desert, Mahuzen or Masshin, which means in Latin, "Haesintantes" that is, hesitating, it is not the name of a person. Amariah was a common Jewish name, or if it be Emerk, the meaning is not known, and Garimont or Guarimond, was the Patriarch of Jerusalem, between whose hands the first

Templars took their oaths.

We may also observe, without any attempt to explain, that the name of Aholiab appears twice, once as a Commander of the nonagon and once as a Standard Bearer of the pentagon. The words of the degree offer quite as singular a mixture and among them is one that may perhaps be found to have a peculiar significance. It is a Hebrew word, "Hochmah." The word means "Wisdom" and particularly the wisdom of the Deity, or in the Kabbala,[*] the second "Dephirah' or Emanation from the Deity, the same as the mind, wisdom and word of Plato. This is perhaps an indication that the camp is altogether a Kabbalistic or Gnostic symbol, and if so, its meaning is to be found in the Kabbalistic writings, in which, so far, we have sought for it in vain, but we know the general meaning of the symbol, and one of the lessons, at least, which it was intended to teach us and to all Masons. The key to that is found in two words of the degreee, which we have already given you.

Phaal-Kol, it is said, means "separated." Separated as Masons have been for many years, by intestine dissensions, the jealousies of rival rites, and the efforts of illegitimate bodies to exercise usurped powers. Separated as mankind has been for ages by differences of religious belief, by the ambition and interests of kings by natural lines or mere imaginary boundaries that

Note 391.—"The Kabbala may be defined to be a system of philosophy which embraces certain mystical interpretations of Scripture. and metaphysical speculations concerning the Deity. man, and spiritual beings. In these interpretations and speculations, according to the Jewish doctors. were enveloped the most profound truths of religion, which, to be comprehended by finite beings, are obliged to be revealed through the medium of symbols and allegories. Buxtorf (Lex. Talm.) defines the Kabbala to be a secret science, which treats in a mystical and enigmatical manner of things divine, angelical, theological, celestial, and metaphysical; the subjects being enveloped in striking symbols and secret modes of teaching. Much use is made of it in the high degrees, and entire Rites have been constructed on its principles. Hence it demands a place in any general work on Masonry."—Mackey's Encyclopaedia of Freemasonry, Article Kabbala.

have made one people haters of another, and kept the
world miserable with wars. Separated as men have been
from truth and knowledge, by the arts and crafts of a
scheming and selfish priesthood. Separated as man has
been from his God by his passions and his vices, as well
as his ignorance.

And Pharash-Kol, it is said, means reunited. That
union of Masons, of all rites and degrees, of which the
camp is the apt and fitting symbol, to accomplish the
great ends of Masonry, to heal all dissensions within,
and produce peace and harmony without, to reconcile
all rites and make toleration and charitable judgment
universal; to elevate the masses of mankind and to
teach them their true interests, to substitute equality
and brotherhood in the place of despotic power and
usurped privilege; to dethrone anarchy and license and
canonize law and order, and in the place of smoking
altars of fanaticism and superstition, of bigotry and
sectarianism, to set up those of true Masonry, garland-
ed with flowers and sending up toward Heaven, mingled
with the perfumes of their incense, the thanks and
gratitude of the human race to a beneficent father, who
loveth all the children he has made.

That my brother is the Jerusalem of which the army
of Masonry hopes to take possession; the heritage
which our father intended his children to enjoy. No
particular spot on this earth, but the blessings of free
thought, free conscience and free speech, everywhere
common as the light and air, and everywhere good government, education and order.

The place of rendezvous of the army, you will find in
all the rituals of this degree to be at Naples, Rhodes,
Cyprus, Malta and Joppa. But they are merely sym-

bolical of the different periods of the world's progress towards that fortunate and happy state. The revolt of intellect against forms, under the lead of Luther, was the firing of the first gun, the assertion of America, of the principle proclaimed by the French philosophers of the 18th century, that all human government derives its authority from the will of the people, was the second and the proclamation in France of the doctrines of liberty, equality and fraternity was the third. The roar of the others will be heard in God's good time, and every man may do something to accelerate the coming of the day of final victory and triumph. For nothing that is done in this world is without its results, and every man may effect something in his own sphere and immediate circle. The whole globe is the field of our labors, but each runs his furrow and sows the good seed in his own little corner of it, and every one who does a brave deed, or says a wise thing, helps the coming of the great day and final enfranchisement of humanity. Wherever Masonry is practiced and honored, there let Masons organize for the relief of their less fortunate brethren.

The doctrines of Masonry are on the lips of many, but in the hearts of few. He who would teach it, must first practice it, and let his example, his generosity, his charity and his toleration commend it to the consideration of others.

Commander in Chief—(Striking one.) Sublime Prince Grand Master of Ceremonies, conduct our brother to the throne, there to be received and constituted and to be invested with the regalia of this degree.

Commander in Chief—Order my brethren! (All rise under the sign of order and form themselves in a circle around the candidate, who has been conducted by five steps to the foot of the throne, where he kneels. The members draw their swords, pass them to their left hands and direct the points towards the heart of the candidate, replacing the right hand in its former position.

Commander in Chief—In the name of God, and under the auspices of the Supreme Council of Sovereign Grand Inspectors General, 33rd and last degree of the Ancient and Accepted Rite for the jurisdiction of the United States of America, sitting at New York, State of New York, with the consent and sanction of the Sublime Princes of the Royal Secret here present, and by virtue of the powers with which I am vested as Illustrious Commander in Chief of this Grand Consistory, I do receive and constitute you a Sublime Prince of the Royal Secret and faithful guardian of the Sacred Treasure, to the end that you may have and enjoy all the rights, franchises and privileges and prerogatives appertaining to the degree and dignity now conferred on you. (Illustrious Commander in Chief then strikes with the blade of his sword five light blows on the shoulder of the candidate.)

Commander in Chief—Rise my brother.!

Commander in Chief—Sublime Princes, Carry Swords! Return Swords!

Commander in Chief—Receive the collar or sash. Its color is an emblem of sorrow and mourning for the miseries and sufferings of humanity. You have worn the same color in other degrees and are familiar with it. We yet wear it because our efforts have not yet secured the happiness of our brethren, and the higher we ascend in Masonry, the more we feel and deplore the miseries of the people.

Receive also and wear this Teutonic cross of gold, the jewel of the order. Deserve it by your services, which you shall hereafter render to the good cause in

which you now claim to be a chief and leader. Sublime
Prince Grand Master of Ceremonies, conduct this the
youngest of the Princes under the banner of the order,
and let his brethren look upon him and he upon them.
(Candidate is conducted by the Grand Master of Ceremonies under the banner and placed fronting the
brethren:)

Commander in Chief—Sublime Princes of this Royal
Grand Consistory, I proclaim our Illustrious brother
A.·.B.·.a Sublime Prince of the Royal Secret, 32nd
degree of the Ancient and Accepted Rite, and an honorary member of the Grand Consistory for the State of
....and I require you and all Sublime Princes of the
Royal Secret everywhere to acknowledge and recognize
him as such.

83—Second Masonic   RASSMAN

Commander in Chief—Sublime Prince Grand Master
of Ceremonies, conduct the candidate to the seat of
honor. (Grand Master of Ceremonies conducts candidate to left hand of Illustrious Commander in Chief.)

Commander in Chief—I congratulate you my brother, for myself and in the name of this Grand Consistory on your reception as a Sublime Prince of the
Royal Secret, and on your admission as a member of our
body, and I beg you to accept our sincere assurances of
brotherly affection and esteem.

Commander in Chief—Sublime Princes, return
swords! Be seated!

Commander in Chief—Sublime Prince Grand Minister of State, you have the floor. (Grand Minister of
State delivers an address.)

Commander in Chief—(Strikes one with the Pommel
of his sword.)

First Lieutenant Commander—(Strikes one.)

Second Lieutenant Commander—(Strikes one.)

Commander in Chief—Sublime Princes Valiant First
and Second Lieutenant Commanders, inform your brave

companions that this Grand Consistory will listen to, and act upon any remarks they may have to offer for the interest of this body, or of the order in general.

First Lieutenant Commander—Sublime Princes and companions of my camp, the Illustrious Commander in Chief informs you that this Grand Consistory will listen to, and act upon any remarks you hay have to offer for the interest of this body or of the order in general.

Second Lieutenant Commander—Sublime Princes and companions of my camp, the Illustrious Commander in Chief informs you that this Grand Consistory will listen to and act upon any remarks you may have to offer for the interest of this body or of the order in general.

Second Lieutenant Commander—(If no one responds.) Sublime Prince First Lieutenant Commander, silence prevails in my camp.

First Lieutenant Commander—(If no one rises to speak.) Illustrious Commander in Chief, silence prevails in both camps.

Commander in Chief—Sublime Princes, Valiant First and Second Lieutenant Commanders inform your brave companions that the box of fraternal assistance is about to be presented to them.

First Lieutenant Commander—Sublime Princes and companions of my camp, the Illustrious Commander in Chief informs you that the box of fraternal assistance is about to be presented to you.

Second Lieutenant Commander—Sublime Princes and companions of my camp, the Illustrious Commander in Chief informs you that the box of fraternal assistance is about to be presented to you. (The Hospitalier then takes the box of fraternal assistance to each member, beginning with the Illustrious Commander in Chief, First and Second Lieutenant Commanders, etc.)

Commander in Chief—Sublime Prince Hospitaller, you will hand the contents of the box to the Grand Treasurer.

CLOSING CEREMONIES

Commander in Chief—(Strikes one with pommel of his sword.)

First Lieutenant Commander—(Strikes one with pommel of his sword.)

Second Lieutenant Commander—(Strikes one with pommel of his sword.)

Commander in Chief—Sublime Princes, let us not like ungrateful children be thankless to our Heavenly Father, for the many blessings which, in his loving kindness, he has bestowed upon us. The poorest of us enjoy a thousand blessings, and is quit of a thousand calamities, the former of which God could have denied him and the 'atter cast upon him. He has enabled us to do some goo', and by his aid we may hope to do still more and we appear nearest to him, when we confer benefits on all men. Let love, gratitude and adoration ever burn brightly towards our Father in Heaven, on the altar of our hearts, and as words are powerless to express all that we ought to feel toward him, let us adopt the expressive symbol of our ancient brethren and offer him the perfumes of the purest incense.

Commander in Chief—Order Sublime Princes, and under arms! (All rise, draw their swords and come to a carry, the Illustri us Commander in Chief then passes his sword under his left arm, the point to the rear, and downwards, leaves iis seat and proceeds towards the altar of perfumes which must always be prepared for the occasion.)

PHILOSOPHICAL ANALYSIS

THIRTY-SECOND DEGREE; OR, SUBLIME PRINCE OF THE ROYAL SECRET.

The French Revolution—Jacobins Like Chicago Anarchists—Lodge and Romish Despotism—Denials that Masonry is a Religion—Proof that Masonry is a Religion—Made Twofold More the Child of Hell—Freemasonry Confessedly Deistic—Deism is Practical Atheism—Adopts the Motto of the Jesuits—"They Shall Be Rooted Up."

This degree originated thirty years before the French Revolution of 1789, and was active in producing it. The lodge-theory was that of the anarchists of today, that, if institutions or religion, and government were abolished, human passions. like fluids, would find their level in universal peace and happiness. Communists guillotined their king, and hung their bishops to lampposts; proclaimed "liberty and equality;" and put their religious creed over the gate of their cemetery: *"There is no God! Death is an eternal sleep."* The last degree of their system required the candidate to stab his brother, or nearest friend, as a traitor to the lodge, and amid the brother's groans, and pleadings for his life, they laid the candidate's gloved hand on the beating heart of a lamb. And, if he stabbed, they removed the blinder, and swore him to vengeance against Church and State. This was *"The Royal Secret."* This explains the vengeance sworn in this and other degrees of that day. (*See Robison's Conspiracy*, p. 299.) But, in this country, and at this day, this degree is senseless, and worthless. Its bluster about freeing the people, is meaningless, and itself not worth reading.

But how happens this once *"Ne plus ultra"* degree to be so prolix and stupid as to be scarce worth reading?

The answer is this: when formed by Jacobin Jesuits, in 1754, in the Jesuits' College of Clermont, Paris, it was *"the Military Organization,"* as the candidate was told. (See *page 397.*) It then crowned the Rite of Perfection of 25 degrees, which was adopted by "the Council of Emperors," four years later; that is, in 1758. (See *note 377.*) The Jacobins, like the Chicago anarchists lately hung were then secretly swearing to do what they afterwards did, *viz.,* wage war on the government. Hence this 32nd grade was not called a *degree,* but an *"organization,"* as it was. But when adopted by *Morin's* Sovereign Inspectors, at Charleston, S. C., in 1801, no war was then contemplated, but by Aaron Burr, and he was soon tried by Jefferson, for his life. The country was then peaceful, and satisfied and pleased with their free constitution, adopted in 1789, only twelve years before. Of course, no fighting was contemplated. True French sympathizers elected Jefferson that year; but the French revolution had reacted, and the Monroe doctrine was soon adopted, to keep the United States free from foreign entanglements. Masonry now did not mean *fight,* but *money,* and false worship.

What then were *Dalcho, Mitchell* and *Provost* to do? They had resolved on an "Ancient and Accepted Scottish Rite," to rule the false worships of Masonry throughout the world. They adopted a scale of thirty-two degrees; and placed this Military degree at the head: because, it had been, as the *notes* and ritual say: *"the Ne Plus Ultra degree,"* and it would not do to leave it out. They therefore stretched it, and stuffed it into its present shape, prolix enough. Hence the hotchpotch flummery of a camp of nine sides, with stupid Masonic explanations for every corner.

But the one "mission and object" (Mackey) of Masonry is kept steadily in view; which is the worship of
the god of this world, who is Satan, as the *"Grand
Architect of the Universe;"* and to accomplish this by
inventing "a religion in which all mankind agree;" and
this, by putting all earth's religions upon a level, and
uniting them together in Masonic worship, which is
boldly avowed in rituals, lexicons, and philosophical
degrees. This is, (in *Revelation, 13, 14,*) called: the
image of the beast, made by "them, that dwell on the
earth;" that is, everybody; every creed, and no creed,
all who join secret lodges. But this world-religion
must have some form and shape, to hold together; and
be taxed; hence, it takes the form, or image, of the
beast. Lodge despotism is as absolute as Romish
despotism, and is the image of it; and it is made, as we
have seen, by the lamb-dragon beast, which is Popery;
"that great city, (Rome) *which reigneth over the kings
of the earth."* (*Rev, 17, 18.*)

Note now the profound craft, by which this is to be accomplished, *viz.,* Masonry promises men salvation by
ceremonies invented by men, administered by priests,
and inhabited by devils. This is the sum and substance
of all the false religions on earth, and will ultimately
unite them against Christ. (See *Rev. 20, 9.*) But the
only opponents Masonry dreads, is Christ, who refused
to worship Satan, and his followers. If there were no
Christians in lodges, Masonry would not live an hour.
Hence, though Christ is wholly omitted, in the lower
degrees, He is taken into the lodges, made by Jesuits
and Jews, as a tool of incantation, but He is not permitted to be worshiped there, except by worships which
are paid to devils. In the next and last degree, of the
world's ruling rite, the 33rd, Christ is twice called *"our*

Sovereign;" (See *pp. 476-7.*) but none are baptized in
His name, nor do they celebrate His death. The bread
is eaten and the wine drunk from human skulls, in
honor of devils, not Christ; and though Christ is called
sovereign, they trample on His law. Why, then, do
they pay Him these empty compliments? Plainly, to
draw in ignorant, weak, and worldly Christians, and
this is what they achieve.

Nothing is more common, than the denial that Freemasonry is a religion. This denial is made by many
Masons, and by all Jack-Masons, who bear the burdens
of the lodge, while claiming merit for not joining it.
But the many distinct avowals, that *"Masonry is a religious institution,"* made by the highest Masonic authorities, have been given in their own words. The
diabolical craft of the system appears in this; that
while "traditions," which are man-made religions, crucified "the Son of God," they worship the cross, the
tool by which they tortured Him, to make believe they
were opposed to His crucifixion and torture, as if the
assassin should kneel before the dagger, with which he
stabbed his victim. Nor is this all, or the worst:
claiming that they unite all religions in one, they renounce and exclude the God and religion of the Bible,
as "bigoted" and narrow. They work only in Christian
lands, not in barbarous and savage countries; and they
denounce as "bigoted" the religion of the lands where
they work. And to crown their falsehood with felony,
they steal and falsely appropriate the principles and
fruits of the Gospel of Christ. The quotations which
we give below, not only prove that Masonry claims to be
a religion, but the true religion, and that its thistles produce figs, that its heathen ritual regenerates, sancti-

fies, and saves men.   To begin with the Entered Apprentice:

"There he stands without our portals, on the threshold of this new Masonic life, in darkness, helplessness and ignorance.   Having been wandering amid the errors, and covered over with the pollutions of the outer and profane world, he comes inquiringly to our doors, seeking the new birth, and asking a withdrawal of the veil which conceals divine truth from his uninitiated sight. * * * There is to be not simply a change for the future, but also an extinction of the past; for initiation is, as it were, a death to the world, and a resurrection to a new life." *Mackey's Ritualist, pp. 22-3.*

This is Satan's travesty and burlesque of Bible conviction of sin, and seeking religion.   The Fellow Craft is still compassing Mt. Sinai.   Then follows the new birth, or regeneration, not "by the Holy Ghost," but by the third, or Master's degree:

"This has very properly been called the *sublime degree of a Master Mason,* as well for the solemnity of the ceremonies which accompany it, as for the profound lessons of wisdom which it inculcates.   The important design of the degree is to symbolize the great doctrine of the resurrection of the body, and the immortality of the soul; and hence it has been remarked by a learned writer of our Order, that the Master Mason represents a man saved from the grave of iniquity, and raised to the faith of salvation."—*Mackey's Ritualist, p. 109.*

Then follows the Masonic lying-in, in which the devil acts as midwife.   The hoodwink falls, the lodge claps and stamps, and the weary, badgered and befooled candidate experiences such a 'change of heart,'"

as Saul and Judas Iscariot did after Satan entered
them. (See 1 *Sam. 16, 14*; and *Jno. 13, 27.*)

"THE SHOCK OF ENTRANCE is then the Symbol of the
disruption of the candidate from the ties of the world,
and his introduction into the life of Masonry. It is the
symbol of the agonies of the first death, and of the
throes of the new birth."—*Mackey's Ritualist, p. 24.*

This change is not imaginary, but real. The testimony of Christ, concerning such priest-made proselytes
is: "They become *twofold more the child of hell, than
before.*" (*Math. 23, 15.*) Witness Saul's attempt to
murder David and Jonathan, and Arensdorf's murder
of Haddock, of Sioux City. But not all Masons experience this fearful change of heart. The average
of Masons who attend lodge-meetings regularly, is only
one in five. Only those, who believe in and practice
lodge-worship, become "possessed" by the god of the
lodge. After Morgan's murder, three-fourths of the
lodges of the United States gave up their charters.
The remaining one-fourth, deliberately became acces-
sories to the horrible inhuman murder of Morgan, before or after the fact. They relished, and adhered to
Masonic "work," or worship; and "their foolish hearts
were blinded."

Of the fact that Masons who are thus bewitched with
sorcery, regard and believe it to be a religion, the proof
is abundant. Thus their ablest writer says:

"Speculative Masonry is the application and sanctification of the working tools and implements, the rules
and principles of operative Masonry, to the veneration
of God and the purification of the heart. The speculative Mason is engaged in the construction of a spiritual temple in his heart, pure and spotless, fit for the

dwelling place of Him who is the author of purity."—
Mackey's Ritualist, p. 89.

What is professing religion, if this is not? Then
also the same writer says of the Shock of Enlightenment, or Rite of Illumination:

"This mental illumination,—this spiritual light,
which, after his new birth, is the first demand of the
new candidate, is but another name for Divine Truth,—
the truth of God and the soul,—the nature and essence
of both,—which constitute the chief design of all Masonic teaching."—*Mackey's Ritualist, p. 33.*

We add the following, not because needed to prove
Masonry a religion, but to show that it is organized
deism:

"Every important undertaking in Masonry is both
begun and completed with prayer. The prayers given
in the hand-books of the Blue Lodge, are such, as all
Masons, whatever their religious faith, may unite in.
In the orders of knighthood the prayers are, as a matter
of course, strictly and intensely Christian. In the third
degree a sublime prayer, adapted from the 14th chapter
of Job, is made in American lodges an essential part
of the ritual of Raising."—*Morris' Dictionary Art.
Prayer.*

It is evident from the above quotations that *Freemasonry claims to be a religion.*

Now let Masonic authorities tell us what kind of a
religion it is.

"The truth is, that Masonry is undoubtedly a religious institution,—its religion being of that universal
kind in which all men agree, and which, handed down
through the long succession of ages, from that ancient
priesthood who first taught it, embraces the great tenets
of the existence of God, and of the immortality of the

soul; tenets, which by its peculiar symbolic languages, it has preserved from its foundation, and still continues in the same beautiful way to teach. Beyond this for its religious faith, we must not and cannot go."—*Mackey's Masonic Jurisprudence, page 95.*

"The religion then, of Masonry, is *pure theism*, on which its different members *engraft* their own peculiar opinions, but they are not permitted to introduce them into the lodge, or to connect their truth or falsehood with the truth of Masonry."—*Mackey's Lexicon, Art. Religion.*

"All the ceremonies of our order are prefaced and terminated with prayer, because Masonry is a religious institution and because we thereby show our dependence on, and our faith and trust in God."—*Mackey's Lexicon, Art. Prayer.*

"This is the scope and aim of its ritual. The Master Mason represents man when youth, manhood, old age, and life itself have passed away as fleeting shadows, yet raised from the grave of iniquity, and quickened into another and better existence. By its legend and all its ritual it is implied that we have been redeemed from the death of sin and sepulchre of pollution!"—*Mackey's Ritualist, p. 109.*

These and the like quotations might be continued to any extent and from different authors. But these will suffice to settle the question with all rational and intelligent readers. And if once the ministry and churches of this country can be possessed of these facts, there will be raised to God one general cry; as when President Lincoln called the American people to unite in prayer for deliverance from the curse of the slavery war. Deism is practical atheism. For the infinite God cannot be reached by finite minds, but only through a merciful Mediator.

But the key to the importance of this 32nd degree, is its Motto: *"Ad majorem Dei gloriam."* Note 370. This is the motto of the Jesuits; who, with the apostate Ramsay, made these French degrees, falsely called Scottish. This motto was adopted by their founder, *Ignatius Loyola;* and is still the motto of the order which he founded, in an underground chapel of the Holy Martyrs in 1534, seventeen years after *Luther* nailed his Theses to the church door at Wittenberg, in 1517. The reformation had only fairly begun, and this underground, secret order of Jesuits met the Reformation, and has turned it back. Some principalities in Germany, once Protestant, are now under Popish princes! That order now rules Popedom, though once prohibited by it, as Masonry is now. The reader will find the above motto on page *14,* of the introduction, and the founding of the order on page 9 of the *"History of the Society of Jesus."* *Baltimore,* 1878. And on pages 12 and 13 he says, that in the village of Lasorta, near Rome, while praying, he was "dazzled by a brilliant light;" and "the entire history of the order," says the historian, "is but a development of that vision."

Now, if that light had been from God, as was that which shone around Paul, at his conversion, Loyola's life would have borne the same fruit which Paul's did, instead of the ignorance, superstition, and persecution which has tracked Papacy ever since; and now furnishes saloon-keepers for our cities, and carries their votes to license pauperism, crime, blasphemy, and woe. But if that light was from Satan, who is Christ's rival and counterfeit, then we should expect the fruits, which we see follow the Papacy everywhere. Then that supernatural light was Masonic light, whose fruits are the same. And our Savior has told us: *"By their fruits ye shall know them."* These lodges are not of God's planting, and we have the word of Christ, that *"they shall be rooted up."* (*Math. 15, 13.*) Let us look to Him for the fulfillment of that glorious promise.

CHAPTER LXI

THIRTY-THIRD DEGREE, OR SOVEREIGN GRAND INSPEC-
TOR GENERAL.[881]

OFFICERS OF THE SUPREME COUNCIL 33RD DEGREE
ANCIENT AND ACCEPTED RITE.

1st. The Most Puissant Sovereign Grand Commander.

2nd. The Puissant Lieutenant Grand Commander.

3rd. The Illustrious Grand Orator and Minister of
State.

4th. The Illustrious Grand Chancellor, Grand Secretary General of the H.∴ E.∴ and Keeper of the Seals
and Archives.

5th. The Illustrious Grand Treasurer General of the
H.∴ E.∴

6th. The Illustrious Grand Master General of Ceremonies.

7th. The Illustrious Grand Marshal General.

8th. The Illustrious Grand Standard Bearer.

Note 892.—"Sovereign Grand Inspector General. The 33rd and ultimate degree of the Ancient and Accepted rite. It is not certainly known
when or where this grade originated. The theory which ascribes it to
the King of Prussia has long since been discarded by intelligent Masons.
The number of Inspectors in a kingdom or republic must not exceed
nine. These organized in a body, constitute the Supreme Council, which
claims jurisdiction over all the Ineffable and Sublime degrees. The presiding officer is styled Sovereign Grand Commander. The sash is white,
edged with gold, and suspended from the right shoulder to the left hip.
At the bottom is a red and white rose, and on the part crossing the
breast is a delta, with rays transversed by a poniard, and in the center
the number 33. The jewel is a black, double-headed eagle, crowned, and
holding a sword in his claws. The beak, claws, crown and sword are
of gold. The motto of the degree is 'Deus meumque jus,' 'God and my
right.' " Macoy's Encyclopaedia and Dictionary of Freemasonry, Article
Sovereign Grand Inspector General.

9th. The Illustrious Grand Captain of the Guards.

There shall be appointed a Grand Seneschal who must be a Deputy Inspector General but not a Constituent of this Supreme Council.

DECORATIONS:[""]—Hangings purple with skeletons, death's heads, cross bones, etc., painted or embroidered thereon. In the East a magnificent throne; over it a purple canopy trimmed with gold. Beneath the canopy is a transparency representing a delta, in the centre of which are seen the ineffable characters, near the centre of the room is a quadrangular pedestal covered with scarlet cloth, on which rests a naked sword. On the north side of the council chamber is a skeleton erect, holding the white banner of the order, opposite which, in the South is a flag of the country. Over the interior portion of the entrance is a blue scarf bearing the device "Deus Meumque Jus." On the East is a candelabra with five branches, in the West one with three branches, in the North one with a single branch, and in the South another with two branches 5+3+1+2 (11) lights.

The sword above mentioned rests on an open Bible the point of the sword pointing towards the southeast. The members are all seated on the south side of the room. The Council Chamber is shaped thus: The candidate does not wear any regalia or jewel tunics or gowns. The Master of Ceremonies carries a burning torch in his right hand during the first section of the ceremonies.

Note 393.—"Decorations. A lodge room ought, besides its necessary furniture, to be ornamented with decorations which, while they adorn and beautify it, will not be unsuitable to its sacred character. On this subject Dr. Oliver, in his Book of the Lodge (ch. v., p. 70), makes the following judicious remarks: 'The expert Mason will be convinced that the walls of a Lodge room ought neither to be absolutely naked nor too much decorated. A chaste disposal of symbolical ornaments in the right places, and according to propriety, relieves the dullness and vacuity of a blank space, and, though but sparingly used, will produce a striking impression, and contribute to the general beauty and solemnity of the scene.' "—Mackey's Encyclopaedia of Freemasonry, Article Decorations.

OPENING CEREMONIES

Most Puissant Sovereign Grand Com.—(Drawing his sword.) Puissant Lieutenant Grand Commander, are you satisfied that all within this sacred asylum are Grand Inspectors General?

Puissant Lieutenant Grand Com.—Most Puissant Sovereign Grand Commander, I will assure myself.

Puissant Lieut. Grand Com.—Illustrious Grand Master General of Ceremonies, satisfy yourself that all present have been exalted to the last degree of Sublime Masonry. (The Grand Master General of Ceremonies passes around the Council Chamber and being satisfied that all present are Grand Inspectors General, causes the Grand Seneschal to secure the door.

Grand Master General of Ceremonies—Puissant Lieutenant General Commander, none but Chiefs of Exalted Masonry are present. This Sacred Asylum is secure

Note 394.—"The only degree conferred in the Supreme Council, Scotch Masonry, and the thirty-third and last upon the catalogue of that system. It has no historical allusions, being purely administrative. There is no apron. The jewel is the black, double-headed eagle of Prussia, with golden beaks, crowned with an imperial crown of gold, and holding a naked sword in its claws. The badge is a white sash, four inches broad, edged with gold fringe, having at the bottom a red and white rose, and on the breast, a golden triangle, surrounded by the sun, and displaying within, the figures '33.' On each side of the triangle, at the distance of two inches, is a naked dagger. The motto of the degree is Deus meumque jus—God and my right. The assembly is termed a Supreme Council. The lights are eleven. The hangings are purple. The officers are: Most Puissant Sovereign Grand Commander, representing Frederick II., of Prussia; Puissant Lieutenant Grand Commander, Secretary General, Treasurer General, Grand Minister of State, Grand Master of Ceremonies, Grand Captain of the Guard, Grand Marshal and Grand Standard Bearer. Hours of work, from the time when the word of the order is given until the morning sun begins to illume the Council."—Morris's Masonic Dictionary, Article Sovereign Grand Inspector General.

and the Grand Seneschal is carefully guarding our portals.

Puissant Lieut. Grand Com.—Most Puissant Sovereign Grand Commander, all present are Supreme Chiefs of Exalted Masonry and we are well secured by the Grand Scneshal.

Most Puissant Sov. Grand Com.—'Tis well. From whence came you?

Puissant Lieut. Grand Com.—From the cradle, passing through life towards our common lot—the grave.

Most Puissant Sov. Grand Com.—Your duty?

Puissant Lieut. Grand Com.—To aid the suffering of humanity upon the road of life.

Most Puissant Sov. Grand Com.—What is the hour?

Puissant Lieut. Grand Com.—It is the hour for this Supreme Council to devote to its duties.

Most Puissant Sov. Grand Com.—And those duties are to God, our country and the order. Illustrious Grand Master General of Ceremonies receive the watchword. (The Grand Master General receives the watchword.) *"Deus Meumque Jus,"* and the answer, *My God and my Right* from each member, and standing at the altar pronounces it aloud.

Most Puissant Sov. Grand Com.—"My God and My Right." The watch-word being correct and our Sacred asylum secure, I proclaim by the mystic numbers, that this Supreme Council of the thirty-third and last degree of the Ancient and Accepted Scottish Rite for the United States of America, its territories and dependencies, will open for the glory of God. Let us implore his assistance in our struggle for justice and right. (Strikes 00000 000 0 00; with the hilt of his sword, which he then sheaths.)

Puissant Lieut. Grand Com.—(Strikes 00000 000 0 00; in the same manner.)

Most Puissant Sov. Grand Com.—Peers and Illustrious Brethren to order! (All rise under sign of order.)

Most Puissant Sov. Grand Com.—Let us pray. (All kneel facing East.)

OPENING PRAYER.

Almighty God; Father of light and life and love, who from thy throne above bestowest thine innumerable blessings upon the human race, we implore thy bounteous mercy upon this assemblage. Impart to us the knowledge of thy word. Protect this Council and its work. Grant us strength to continue our journey through life in the propagation of truth and justice, that we may be enabled to benefit those oppressed by the workers of iniquity, enlighten the ignorant, strengthen the weak, and comfort the suffering. And to Thee the most powerful, the most holy the everlasting Adonai, be the honor and glory forever and forever. Amen.

Most Puissant Sov. Grand Com.—Order, Peers and Illustrious Brethren! (All rise under sign of order.)

Sign of Order.

SIGN OF ORDER.

Left hand over the heart, fingers extended and close together.

Most Puissant Sov. Grand Com.—(With pommel of sword; 00000 000 0 00.)

Puissant Lieut. Grand Com.—(In same manner, 00000 000 0 00.)

Most Puissant Sov. Grand Com.—Peers and Illustrious Brethren, this Supreme Council of the thirty-third and last degree for the United States of America, its territories and dependencies is now open in the name of God. Be seated. (Business is transacted and minutes are here read.)

CHAPTER LXII

Thirty-Third Degree, or Sovereign Grand Inspector General.[395]

INITIATION.

Preparation of Candidate, 33rd Degree.

The candidate is prepared by being divested of his shoes and hat; clothed in a black robe without sword or regalia; a lighted taper in his right and a black cable tow around his neck, the ends of which are held by the Illustrious Grand Master General of Ceremonies, at the proper time.

The Illustrious Grand Marshal retires to the Chamber of Reflection, and all being ready he strikes on the door of the Council Chamber.

Note 395.—"Sovereign Grand Inspector General. The thirty-third and last degree of the Ancient and Accepted Scottish Rite. The Latin Constitutions of 1786 call it 'Tertius et trigesimus et sublimissimus gradus,' i. e., the thirty-third and most sublime degree'; and it is styled 'the Protector and Conservator of the Order.' The same Constitutions, in Article I. and II., say:

" 'The thirty-third degree confers on those Masons who are legitimately invested with it, the quality, title, privilege, and authority of Sovereign [Supremorum] Grand Inspectors General of the Order.

" 'The peculiar duty of their mission is to teach and enlighten the brethren; to preserve charity, union, and fraternal love among them; to maintain regularity in the works of each degree, and to take care that it is preserved by others; to cause the dogmas, doctrines, institutes, constitutions, statutes, and regulations of the Order to be reverently regarded, and to preserve and defend them on every occasion; and, finally, everywhere to occupy themselves in works of peace and mercy.'

"The body in which the members of this degree assemble is called a Supreme Council.

"The symbolic color of the degree is white, denoting purity.

"The distinctive insignia are a sash, collar, jewel, Teutonic cross, decoration, and ring.

"The sash is a broad, white-watered ribbon, bordered with gold, bearing on the front a triangle of gold glittering with rays of gold, which has in the center the numerals 33, with a sword of silver, directed from above, on each side of the triangle, pointing to its center. The sash, worn from the right shoulder to the left hip, ends in a point, and is fringed with gold, having at the junction a circular band of scarlet and green containing the jewel of the Order."—Mackey's Encyclopaedia of Freemasonry, Article Sovereign Grand Inspector General.

Ill. Grand Marshal—00000 000 0 00.)

Ill. Grand Capt. of Guard—Puissant Lieutenant Grand Commander, there is an alarm at the door of the Council.

Puissant Lieut. Grand Com.—Most Puissant Sovereign Grand Commander, there is an alarm at the door of the Council.

Most Puissant Sov. Grand Com.—Illustrious Grand Master General of Ceremonies, ascertain who dares to interrupt our labors.

Grand Master Gen. of Cer.—(Opening door.) Who dares to interrupt our labors?

Grand Marshal—(Outside.) Brother.........., a Sublime Prince of the Royal Secret, who is sincerely devoted to God, his country, and our holy order; grieving for the sufferings of humanity, he humbly solicits admission into this Supreme Council, where he hopes, with the assistance of Divine Wisdom, to accomplish his duty to God and his brethren.

Grand Master Gen. of Cer.—(Closing the door.) Puissant Lieutenant Sovereign Grand Commander, the alarm was made by our Illustrious Grand Marshal, on behalf of brother..........., a Sublime Prince of the Royal Secret, who is sincerely devoted to God, his country and our holy order; grieving for the sufferings of humanity, he humbly solicits admission into this Supreme Council, where he hopes with the assistance of divine wisdom, to accomplish his duty to God and his brethren.

Puissant Lieut. Grand Com.—Most Puissant Sovereign Grand Commander, the alarm was made by our Illustrious Grand Marshal on behalf of brother......, a Sublime Prince of the Royal Secret, who is sincerely devoted to God, his country and our holy order; grieving for the sufferings of humanity, he humbly solicits admission into this Supreme Council, where he hopes with the assistance of divine wisdom, to accomplish his duty to God and his brethren.

Most Puissant Sov. Grand Com.—Admit him.

Grand Master Gen. of Cer.—(Opening door.) It is the order of the Most Puissant Sovereign Grand Commander that the Illustrious Prince of the Royal Secret be admitted into the presence of this Supreme Council of Exalted Masonry. (Music plays, and the candidate is led into the Supreme Council by the Grand Master General of Ceremonies and the Grand Marshal General who holds the cable tow in his left hand. The candidate holding taper in right hand with head bowed is under the sign of the Good Shepherd and placed in the West.

Most Puissant Sov. Grand Com.—My brother your devotion to God, your country and our holy order, your grief for the sufferings of humanity, are your titles of admittance to this Council. Illustrious Grand Master General of Ceremonies, conduct the brother by five, three, one and two journeys, that he may travel and reflect upon his duties to God and his brethren. (The Grand Master General of Ceremonies conducts him in silence five times around the Chamber and stops in the West.)

Most Puissant Sov. Grand Com.—Sublime Prince, this your first journey in this degree is to remind you of your first step in the Masonic career. Then you were weak, helpless and in darkness. Ever remember that, when called upon to conduct those whom you have left behind; that you were once like them, weak and helpless. Reflect that from God we came and to him we must return. All our thoughts, all our actions must have but one object; the glory of our heavenly Father. He is the first of all. The great uncreated creator; origin of nature. Be not proud of thy exaltation, for misfortune can most easily attack the great. Brother, being assured that you are devoted to your country, behold its flag. Are you prepared to take an obligation to protect and defend this emblem of your nation?

Candidate—(Answers.)

Most Puissant Sov. Grand Com.—Then, with your right hand upon this sword and your left holding this flag, repeat after me your

FIRST OBLIGATION.

SOVEREIGN GRAND INSPECTOR GENERAL.[***]

In the name of God our Heavenly Father; in his presence and that of these Illustrious Princes of Exalted Masonry, I do solemnly promise and vow to be true and faithful to my country and its flag, and that I will defend both with my purse, my sword and with my life! So help me God. Amen.

Most Puissant Sov. Grand Com.—As a token of your fidelity, salute with a kiss this emblem of knightly honour. (Candidate kisses sword.)

Most Puissant Sov. Grand Com.—Kneel my brother. You have proved your right to the crown I now place upon your brow. True 'tis but a wreath of oak leaves, but it is to a Mason more priceless than the diadems of kings. It is the civic crown of the Roman Republic,

---

Note 398.—"The collar is of white-watered ribbon fringed with gold, having the rayed triangle at its point and the swords at the sides. By a regulation of the Southern Supreme Council of the United States, the collar is worn by the active, and the sash by the honorary members of the Council.

"The jewel is a black double-headed eagle, with golden beaks and talons, holding in the latter a sword of gold, and crowned with the golden crown of Prussia.

"The red Teutonic cross is affixed to the left side of the breast.

"The decoration rests upon a Teutonic cross. It is a nine-pointed star, namely, one formed by three triangles of gold one upon the other, and interlaced from the lower part of the left side to the upper part of the right a sword extends and in the opposite direction is a band of (as it is called) Justice. In the center is the shield of The Order, azure charged with an eagle like that on the banner, having on the dexter side a Balance or, and on the sinister side a Compass of the second, united with a Square of the second."—Mackey's Encyclopaedia of Freemasonry, Article Sovereign Grand Inspector General.

which was only awarded to those who had saved the life of a fellow creature. By becoming a Mason, you have also become a benefactor of mankind.

Most Puissant Sov. Grand Com.—(To Grand Master General of Ceremonies.) Let the second journey be made. (The Grand Master General of Ceremonies conducts him thrice around, while the Most Puissant Sovereign Grand Commander repeats:)

Most Puissant Sov. Grand Com.—Let us worship, in all humility and veneration the divine wisdom, of him who so bountifully regulates the universe. We must ever glorify labor; for by its means only can you obtain that true light which you foresaw in the doctrine of him who gave his life for the glory of his father and the emancipation of his brethren.

Behold the banner of our beloved order! Are you prepared to swear fidelity to this banner and our order?

Candidate—I am. (Music plays. The Grand Master of Ceremonies leads him to the North, where a skeleton with a wreath of cypress in one hand and the banner of the order in the other and a skull with wine in are now unveiled and the taper is taken from candidate.

Most Puissant Sov. Grand Com.—Then take in one hand this skull, from this emblem of mortality, while with the other you support the flag of our beloved order and repeat after me. (Candidate obeys).

SECOND OBLIGATION.

In presence of the Supreme Architect of the World and calling on these Illustrious brethren present as witnesses, I————do solemnly and sincerely swear, without prevarication or mental reservation, that I will be for ever faithful to the banner of the order, will follow it wherever it leads and will always defend it; allowing no danger to deter me therefrom.

I furthermore solemnly swear that I will hold **true** allegiance to the Supreme Council of the United States of America, its territories and dependencies. And that I will never acknowledge any body or bodies of men as belonging to the Ancient and Accepted Scottish Rite, claiming to be such, except such as hold allegiance to this Supreme Council, or those who recognize this Council. To all these I do most solemnly swear, calling upon the Most High God to ratify my oath. And s h o u l d I knowingly or willfully violate the same, may this wine I now drink, become a deadly poison to me, as the hemlock juice drank by Socrates. (Drinks wine out of skull.) And may these 'cold arms forever encircle me. Amen. (Skeleton's arms enfold him.)

Most Puissant Sov. Grand Com.—Your third journey reminds you, that in the high office you are now about to fulfill, you must never fail to fulfill your duty to God, your brethren and our order. Even now, though you know it not, you need the aid of your brethren, as others in time will require your assistance.

That torch which a brother holds before you, you will be called upon to bear for the benefit of others who seek light.

Your head is uncovered—your feet bare, to remind you that you must ever be prepared to assist brethren in need, and free them from the yoke of oppression, which is symbolized by the black cabletow around your neck.

Most Puissant Sov. Grand Com.—Kneel! Once again I crown you; now with this wreath of cypress, emblem of death and of immortality.

Most Puissant Sov. Grand Com.—Conduct the brother upon his third journey. (Candidate is led once around.)

Most Puissant Sov. Grand Com.—The object of all the degrees of the Ancient and Accepted Scottish Rite, is light, wisdom, tolerance, freedom, courage. As a proof that you possess that courage which you may be called upon to exert against your enemies; and that you hold danger and even death in contempt, we now call upon you, as a proof that you will never hesitate to obey the orders of those who have sworn that *"Justice"* shall rule the world, to plunge your hand into this vase of molten lead and pluck forth this golden ring. (The Most Puissant Sovereign Grand Commander drops the ring into the vase of mercury and the candidate snatches it out.)

Most Puissant Sov. Grand Com.—'Tis well! No harm awaited you. You knew it. But remember, all the ceremonies of Masonry are but faithful representations of the realities of life; and that you may be ever ready to lay down your life for the triumph of the principles of our Rite. Illustrious Grand Master General of Ceremonies, let the brother make the last journey. (Candidate is led twice around the room.)

Most Puissant Sov. Grand Com.—The object of this last trial was to teach you that no consideration; no danger must stop you, when justice and the rights of your brethren require your assistance. Your Masonic

labors; the liberal ideas you entertain; your devotedness and zeal for the propagation of our doctrines, en-
title you to the high dignity with which we are about to
invest you. (Candidate stops in the West.)

Most Puissant Sov. Grand Com.—Sublime Prince, the
Ancient and Accepted Rite recognizes and adopts none
of the religions of the world. We respect the creeds of
all men, because God alone is the Supreme Judge of his
children. Each of our brethren has full right to maintain his own faith and worship our Heavenly Father,
according to the dictates of his own conscience. What
is your religion?

Candidate—(Answers.)

Most Puissant Sov. Grand Com.—Sovereign Grand
Inspector Grand Orator, place upon the altar of Masonry the sacred book of our brother's religion. (This
is done.)

Most Puissant Sov. Grand Com.—And now, if of
your own free will you voluntarily assume the last and
most serious obligation of our order, advance and kneel
at the sacred altar of Masonry, resting your hands upon
the book of your religion. (This is done.)

Most Puissant Sov. Grand Com.—To order Sovereign
Grand Inspectors! Draw Swords!

Lieutenant Grand Com.—(Repeats order. All form
around altar pointing swords at candidate's breast.)

Most Puissant Sov. Grand Com.—Sublime Prince,
repeat after me and the brethren.

OBLIGATION SOVEREIGN GRAND INSPECTOR GENERAL.

In the presence of Almighty God and of the Illustrious members of this Supreme Council 33rd degree for
the United States of America, its territories and dependencies I ...., a Sublime Prince of the Royal
Secret, do hereby solemnly promise and swear, on the
holy book of my religion, never directly, or indirectly

to reveal the secrets and mysteries of the 33rd and last degree of the Ancient and Accepted Scottish Rite to any but a brother, legally and lawfully possessed of this dignity; and to obey and cause to be obeyed, the constitution, statutes and regulations of the order.

I furthermore solemnly promise and swear to be true and faithful to God, our common parent; to the holy order of which I have the honor of being a member, and to my beloved country.

I furthermore solemnly promise and swear, faithfully and punctually to fulfill all the obligations which I have taken in each of the degrees I have received, and strictly to comply with the duties imposed upon me as a Sovereign Grand Inspector General of the 33rd degree. Unceasingly to protect and defend the rights of my fellow beings, even at the peril of my life, and to use the authority in me vested with charity and equity, and for the glory of God and our order.

I furthermore solemnly promise and swear, faithfully to comply with my present obligation, waiving all equivocation or mental reservation, and the hope of being at any time relieved of the same, by any power whatsoever, under the penalties which I.........., of my own free will and accord impose upon myself; namely that of being disgraced among my fellow beings, to suffer the most cruel remorse of the soul. And may God heap upon my head the punishment in store for perjurers and all such as may violate their sacred obligations toward him. So help me God. Amen. Amen! Amen!

Most Puissant Sov. Grand Com.—Now my brother, salute with a kiss the sacred book of your religion. (He obeys.) Take this sword and remember to use it only against the enemies of our order and your country, and whenever you may be called upon to defend the rights of humanity.

Receive this ring*** (hands it to him) which is a sign of the Alliance you have this day made with us. You are forever bound to God, our order, and your country. Let your motto be *"Deus Meumque Jus."* "My God and my Right."

I will now communicate to you the secrets of this the last degree.

SIGN OF ORDER.

Place the left hand over the heart.

Sign of Order.

FIRST SIGN.

Kneel on left knee, cross the arms over the breast, then draw the sword, hold the point in the left hand and cross it with that of the opposite Inspector and give the

First Sign S. G. I. G.

Note 397.—''The ring is of plain gold one-eighth of an inch wide, and having on the inside a delta surrounding the figures 33, and inscribed with the wearer's name, the letters S∴G∴I∴G∴, and the motto of the Order, 'Deus meumque Jus.' It is worn on the fourth finger of the left hand.''—Mackey's Encyclopaedia of Freemasonry, Article Sovereign Grand Inspector General.

First Pass Word—"De Molay."
Answer—"Hiram Abiff."
Second Pass Word—"Frederick."
Answer—"Of Prussia."

SECOND SIGN.

Disengage swords, retain point in left hand, fall on both knees, kiss blade three times and give the
   Sacred Words—"*Micha, Macha, Bea-lim, Adonai.*"
"Who is like unto Thee, oh God."

Second Sign.

SIGN OF ENTRANCE.

Cross the arms on the breast, the head bowed down.
   Battery. 00000 000 0 00.
This is the decoration of the Sovereign Grand Inspector General, the insignia of the high office conferred on you by your brethren.
   Most Puissant Sov. Grand Com.—Puissant Sovereign Lieutenant Commander, pro-

of Entrance.

claim our beloved brother to be a Sovereign Grand Inspector General, 33rd and last degree and honorary member of this Supreme Council.
   Puissant Lieut. Grand Com.—I proclaim our beloved brother and Sublime Prince.........to be a Sovereign Grand Inspector General 33rd and last degree and an honorary member of this Supreme Council of the United States of America, its territories and dependencies.

Most Puissant Sov. Grand Com.—Illustrious Grand Master General of Ceremonies, conduct to the seat of honor the Sovereign Grand Inspector General. (Candidate is seated on the right of the Most Puissant Sovereign Grand Commander.)

Most Puissant Sov. Grand Com.—Peers and Illustrious brethren, let us award the honors of this exalted dignity to our latest created Grand Inspector General. (All salute candidate by 00000 000 0 00.)

Most Puissant Sov. Grand Com.—Be seated and listen to the lecture of the last degree.

LECTURE.

Illustrious Grand Minister of State—Illustrious brethren, by this time you will have learned that our object is not to rebuild the material temple of Solomon, but a moral temple, wherein truth and love shall dwell, and wherein must live as one brotherhood all those, who, having but one common parent, will abide by the laws of eternal equity and justice. We have not to avenge the murder of Hiram Abiff, for he represents that eternal wisdom, which ignorance and lust of power and falsehood had concealed from us, but we must go on, in search of those laws by which the moral world is regulated.

We have not persecuted the unfortunate nation of Judah, for having sentenced to death our beloved Sovereign, Jesus of Nazareth, the Apostle of the duties and rights of man, but we must crush forever superstition, fanaticism and intolerance. They, and not the children of Israel were guilty. Let us show them no mercy, and thereby secure the blessings of liberty of conscience. Each child of God must worship his father, according to his own conscience and enjoy those prerogatives of the heart and mind of which God alone is the Supreme Judge.

We have not to avenge the murder of Jacques de Molay and the Templars, but we must never allow, if in our power to prevent it any living man to possess sufficient power to accomplish another such a crime.

No man has a right to usurp a power which belongs to God alone. No man is above his brother, except by intellect, charity, good deeds and education.

To no man has God given authority to replace and represent him on earth, and all those who pretend to be his ministers and representatives must not be believed.

Our ignorance and selfishness alone give these usurpers the power, which they wield for the gratification of their impious schemes.

Our order is instituted to stop such encroachment and to prevent the renewal of the tragedy which ended in the murder of those Knight Templars, whose virtues and moral power caused such terror to the political and religious usurpers of that age, which is ever presented to our minds by the battery of this degree: five, three, one and two; significant to Sovereign Grand Inspectors of the year of the murder of those victims of intolerance kingcraft and priescraft, 5312.

We abhor the doctrine which teaches the murder of kings and priests, but as long as the weakness of mankind renders their usurpation unavoidable, we must prevent their exercising their power to oppress mankind and endeavor by degrees to enlighten our brother men and prepare their minds for the enjoyment of those rights and privileges which our Heavenly Father has guaranteed to his beloved children.

We have not to reconquer, by murder and bloodshed, that land, which the life and death of our Puissant Sovereign, Jesus of Nazareth made holy, but we have to reconquer our rights, and to substitute truth for error;

liberty and justice for despotism and iniquity. Then, and then only, shall we have reconquered the "Holy Land," the only true Holy Land that is the patrimony of love, intelligence and charity, which our father has given us.

Most Puissant Sov. Grand Com.—The Illustrious brethren can now offer any observations they wish for the benefit of this Supreme Council and our beloved order. (The business is now transacted.)

Most Puissant Sov. Grand Com.—Illustrious Grand Master of Ceremonies present to the Sovereign Grand Inspectors General the box of fraternal assistance. Collection is taken.)

CLOSING CEREMONIES

Sovereign Grand Inspector General.

Most Puissant Sov. Grand Com.—Puissant Sovereign Lieutenant Grand Commander, your duty?

Lieutenant Grand Com.—To combat for God, for my country and for the sacred principles of our holy order!

Most Puissant Sov. Grand Com.—What is the hour?

Lieutenant Grand Com.—The morning sun lights our Council.

Most Puissant Sov. Grand Com.—Since the morning sun has risen and shines over our Council, let us arise also Illustrious Brethren, and diffuse the light of knowledge over those minds darkened by ignorance. (Strikes 000. All rise under the sign of order.)

Most Puissant Sov. Grand Com.—Puissant Sovereign Lieutenant Grand Commander, inform the Illustrious brethren that I am about to close this Supreme Council by the mystic numbers.

Lieutenant Grand Com.—Peers and Illustrious brethren, take notice that the Most Puissant Sovereign Grand Commander is about to close this Supreme Council by the mystic numbers.

Most Puissant Sov. Grand Com.—(Strikes with sword 00000 000 0 00.)

Lieutenant Grand Com.—(Repeats the same.)

Most Puissant Sov. Grand Com.—Let us pray.

> Oh thou whose power o'er moving worlds presides,
> Whose voice created and whose wisdom guides!
> On darkling man, in pure effulgence shine,
> And cheer the clouded mind with light divine.
> 'Tis thine alone to calm the pious breast
> With silent confidence and holy rest.
> Father, from thee we spring to thee we tend
> Path, Motive, Guide, Original and End.

Response—Amen. Amen. Amen.

Most Puissant Sov. Grand Com.—Illustrious brothers retire again to the busy haunts of life, do your duty and prove to the world that we are worthy of our missions. This Supreme Council is closed. God be with us now and forever.

PHILOSOPHICAL ANALYSIS

THIRTY-THIRD DEGREE, OR SOVEREIGN GRAND INSPECTOR GENERAL.

Apex to Falsehood, Fraud and Ambition—Denies the Inspiration of the Bible—Fought Like Wolves Over a Carcass—Southern Lodges Worked up the Rebellion—Conclusion.

The origin of this degree is hidden; concealed, doubtless, lest its motive should appear with its birth, and its antiquity prove a burlesque. The thirty-first degree gave us a *"Sovereign Tribunal;"* and this second degree beyond, gives us another, a *"Supreme Council,"* whose jurisdiction is to be final and Universal in the world of Masonry. It is based (Note 395.) on Constitutions of 1786, which a Masonic French historian, *Kloss,* who knew, pronounces *"the Grand Lie of the order!"* (*Folger's Ancient and Accepted Scottish Rite,* page 60, Doc.) But whether invented to furnish another degree, to sell; or to keep the supreme control in Charleston, S. C., it is all one. It is a brief apex to falsehood, fraud, and imposition. In previous degrees the Savior is given no more exalted title than "the Master from Nazareth." But in this degree, He is once called *"our beloved Sovereign,"* (page 476.) and once *"our Puissant Sovereign. Jesus of Nazareth;"* (page 477.) which phrases used in an ordinary lodge, would make the speaker liable to be rapped down. No Jew would use such words of Christ, unless moved by what caused that Jew to hail Him as his Master, and kiss Him in the warden, *viz.,* money.

Those who glance through the ritual of the present

ruling rite, falsely called "Scottish," will see that this thirty-third degree has been preceded by a degree, called, and intended to be, the last, or "ultimate" of Masonry; from the Master Mason's or third degree, up. This 33rd degree may continue to be "ultimate," till its framer, *Albert Pike*, dies; who is now, in 1888, *seventy-nine* years old. And it may, indeed, prove to be "the last." For the deluge of dark orders from the mouth of the dragon, is a sign that the return of Christ is near. (*Rev. 12, 12.*) But if the accursed system continues to vex the earth, and destroy souls, this rite of 33rd degrees will fade out, and give way to other inventions. These degrees have been altered and added to, by *Pike*, who has translated the *Zendavesta* (page 439) as seen in the 32nd degree, of which this 33rd is a mere elongation, and filling out. No other Mason has ever translated the *Zend*, but Pike.

In these last degrees of the *rite*, the drag-net, of antiquity is drawn over all the old, lost nations; and alchemy, sun-worship, the worship of beasts and birds, trees, etc., are given on pages 435-42, as the sources of the mysteries of Masonry. And the mysteries and symbols of the Bible, are drawn from these, instead of *The Holy Ghost*, by whom inspired men *"spake as they were moved."* (*2 Pet. 1, 21.*) And having thus denied the source of the Bible as coming from God, Pike proceeds to put the worship of 'the black ox," "phœnix," etc., etc., which has sunk Egypt from the list of nations; on a level with the worship of our Savior, Christ; in Europe and America! There are his words: p. 443 "The great ends of Masonry" are, "to reconcile all rites, and make charitable judgment and toleration universal;" * * * and in the place of the smoking altar of fanaticism and superstition, of bigotry and sectarianism, to set up those of true Masonry." Etc., etc.! This is explicit: to destroy Christianity, and make Masonry the religion of the Globe!

This is not enough. He excuses the Jews for murder·
ing our Savior, Christ; who is nothing but a French
"Apostle of the rights of man;" (page 477) and, on the
next page, he declares: "To no man has God given the
right to represent Him on earth;" not even the man
Christ Jesus. And, on the same page: "We have not
to reconquer, by murder and bloodshed, that land made
holy by our Puissant Sovereign, Jesus of Nazareth."
Here he not only insults Christ by making Him a Masonic "Puissant Sovereign," but he justly brands the
conquest of Palestine, by the *Crusaders,* as *"murder and
bloodshed;"* while this whole fabric of the 33rd rite is
professedly based on those very Crusades, and derives
from them its honors, titles, and eclat! Surely, "whom
the gods will destroy, they first make mad."

But the force of this 33rd degree by no means lies in
the stupid quackery of its learning. In it

"More is meant, than meets the eye."

Note 392 explains the object of this otherwise weak
degree. It was made to reduce the governors of the
Masonic world to *"nine"* men, meeting in the little
slave-holding city of Charleston, S. C., with Albert
Pike for their "Sovereign Commander." This was the
world's first Supreme Council, opened by Mitchell and
Dalcho, in 1801. But this 33rd degree, with Pike at its
head, did not then exist; and it was weak and wavering.
Twelve years later, *i. e.,* in 1813, a "Supreme Council,"
Northern Jurisdiction, was located in New York, and
wolves never fought over a carcass more savagely, than
these secret swindlers of the people quarreled over the
spoils of lodgery. If the reader consults *Folger's*
History of the Scottish Rite, from page 15 onward, he
will see, and say, that the wolves, not the Masons, suffer by the comparison. While this fight between rival

bodies in New York and Boston was raging, the slave-holders sprung this 33rd degree upon them. Its motto: *"Deus et Meumque Jus,"* was Albert Pike's, on his sign at Washington, D. C., on his Southern Jurisdiction building, near the Avenue; and as *Note 293* says: "It claims jurisdiction over all the ineffable and sublime degrees." And though made within the memory of men now living, we read, in the same Note by Macoy: "It is not certainly known, when or where this degree originated;" that is to say, its origin is concealed. This is the most infamous Masonic act, next to burning their records of fifty-nine years before the war, to hide treason. But slavery then ruled the country, and this 33rd Charleston degree ruled the lodge. And the Southern lodge-rooms worked up the most unjustifiable and infamous war on record. The Southern people were dragooned into it, by leaders secretly sworn to obey Masonic leaders, or have their throats cut.

But that red sea of blood is crossed. And if the American ministry and churches can be rescued from the lodge-worships of Satan, the god of war; we shall take a long stride towards the Millenium of *"Peace on earth, and good will to men."*

CONCLUSION.

AMERICANS! We have spoken in faithfulness. Let us part in peace. No candid person can look, though slightly, over these pages, and not see:

1. That the *notes,* all taken from the highest Masonic authorities, prove the truth of the ritual.

2. That "the Ancient, Accepted Scottish Rite" is a tissue of fearful falsehood; that it is French, not Scotch: modern, not ancient; that it insults Christ. as Byron

did his wife, by seating a harlot by her side; that its
higher degrees were invented by **Jesuits** and **Jews**;
that its oaths are sinking our Court-houses into popular
contempt; and that by boldly avowing respect for, **and**
citing with equal reverence, the gods of idolatry, **and**
the God of the Bible, it denies all that Christ and **His**
apostles taught concerning heathenism: and pours a
steady stream of villification on Christianity, and on
Christ, its author; as "bigoted," and "sectarian," because they teach that men must "be born again," or
they cannot see the kingdom of heaven; that, while it
lauds liberty, it establishes absolute subjugation of man
to man; treading on crowns and tiaras, of kings and
priests, it seats its rulers on "thrones," clothes them
with "royal purple," and puts candidates on their knees
before them; and makes swarms of priests, who are
counterfeit, contemners, and rivals of Christ. And
by teaching salvation by its priests; and superseding,
and setting aside the laws of God, and the laws of the
land, in favor of its own, it shields all vice; destroys all
virtue; and by honoring the gods of heathenism, and
establishing their secret worships, they are putting in
operation causes in the United States. and in Europe,
which have ruined the old nations of Asia,

——and their decay
Has dried up realms to deserts.

But we know that Jesus Christ will yet reign on this
earth; and that to Him every knee shall bow, and every
tongue confess to the glory of God, the Father. AMEN.

CHAPTER LXIII

MASONIC SECRETS ILLUSTRATED.
THE EMBLEMS AND SECRETS OF THIRTY-THREE DEGREES.[*]

PREPARATION FOR FIRST OR ENTERED APPRENTICE DEGREE.

The candidate having satisfactorily answered the questions given on pages 95-6 and paid the initiation fee, is prepared for initiation as follows.

The Deacons or Stewards strip him to his shirt and drawers, and his drawers must be exchanged for a pair furnished by the lodge which fasten with strings. The *left* leg of these is rolled up above the knee. If his shirt does not open in front it is turned around, and if there are metal buttons or studs on it they are removed.

The *left* sleeve of his shirt is rolled up above the elbow, and the *left* side of his shirt is tucked in; so that the left leg, left foot, left arm and left breast are bare. A slipper is put on his *right* foot, a hoodwink over his eyes, and a small rope called a cable tow is put once around his neck.

Candidate duly and truly prepared, Entered Apprentice Degree.

*The first three Masonic degrees, termed Blue Lodge or Ancient Craft Masonry, are common to all the various Masonic Rites, and are fully and accurately given in "FREEMASONRY ILLUSTRATED," which is also published by Ezra A. Cook, at 40cts. for paper covered and 75cts. for cloth bound volume of three degrees (376 pages); only the emblems and secrets of the first three degrees are given here.

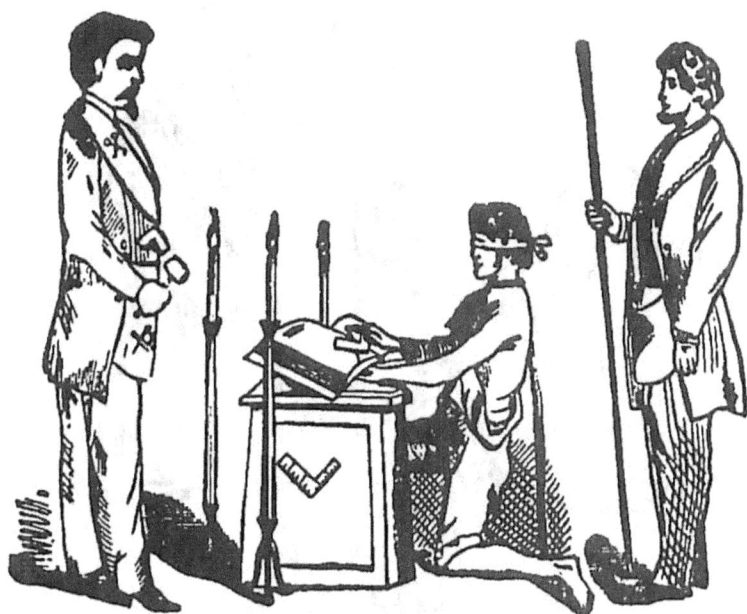

Candidate taking Entered Apprentice Obligation. See page 107.

"Every Mason is under an obligation to obey the laws of the lodge and the Grand Lodge. * * * It is the obligation which makes the Mason, and the difference between one Mason and another, consists simply in the fact that *one keeps his obligations better than another.*

"An obligation is an essential part of a degree."— *Morris's Dictionary, Art. Obligation.*

Shock of Enlightenment or Rite of Illumination, Entered Apprentice Degree

DUE-GUARD OF AN ENTERED APPRENTICE.

Hold out left hand, with palm up, a little in front of the body, height of hips; next place right hand horizontally over the left, two or three inches above it. [See cut.]

Due-Guard, Entered Apprentice.

Sign of Entered
Apprentice.

SIGN OF AN ENTERED APPRENTICE.

Made from due-guard by dropping left hand to side, and at same time raise right arm, with hand still open, and draw hand quickly across the throat, the thumb being next to the throat, then hand drops to side. [See cut.]

ENTERED APPPENTICE SIGN WITHOUT DUE GUARD.

Draw open right hand across the throat, thumb next to throat.

Entered Apprentice Grip.

ENTERED APPRENTICE GRIP.

Grasp hands as in ordinary hand-shaking, and press ball of thumb hard against the knuckle-joint of each other's fore-finger.

ENTERED APPRENTICE WORD.

Boaz, which is the name of the grip. For mode of giving this "word" see page 113.

"THE WORKING TOOLS OF AN ENTERED APPRENTICE

Are the *Twenty-four Inch Gauge* and *Common Gavel.*

"THE TWENTY-FOUR INCH GAUGE

Is an instrument used by operative masons to measure and lay out their work; but we, as Free and Accepted Masons, are taught to make use of it for the more noble and glorious purpose of dividing our time. It being divided into twenty-four equal parts, is emblematical of the twenty-four hours of the day, which we are taught to divide into three equal parts; whereby are found eight hours for the service of God and a distressed worthy brother, eight for our usual vocations, and eight for refreshment and sleep."—*Mackey's Ritualist, page 38.*

"THE COMMON GAVEL

Is an instrument made use of by operative masons to break off the corners of rough stones, the better to fit them for the builder's use; but we, as Free and Accepted Masons, are taught to make use of it for the more noble and glorious purpose of divesting our hearts and consciences of all the vices and superfluities of life; thereby fitting our minds as living stones for that spiritual building, that house not made with hands, eternal in the heavens."—*Mackey's Ritualist, page 38.*

JEWELS OF A LODGE.

"A Lodge has six Jewels; three of these are immovable and three movable.

"The immovable jewels are the *Square, Level and Plumb.*

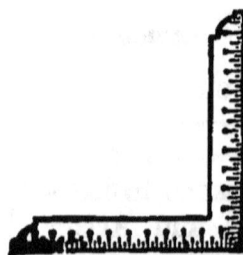
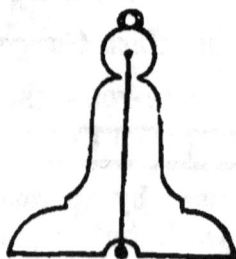
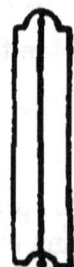

Square.   Level.   Plumb.

"THE *Square* inculcates morality;   the *Level* equality; and the *Plumb*, rectitude of conduct.

"They are called immovable jewels, because they are always to be found in the East, West and South parts of the Lodge, being worn by the officers in those respective stations."—*Mackey's Ritualist, page 57.*

"THE MOVABLE JEWELS

Are the *Rough Ashlar,* the *Perfect Ashlar* and the *Trestle-Board.*"

Rough Ashlar.   Perfect Ashlar.   Trestle-Board.

"The rough ashlar is a stone as taken from the quarry in its rude and natural state.

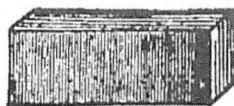

"The perfect ashlar is a stone made ready by the hands of the workmen, to be adjusted by the working tools of the fellow craft.

"The trestle-board is for the master workman to draw his designs upon.

"By the rough ashlar we are reminded of our rude and imperfect state by nature; by the perfect ashlar, that state of perfection at which we hope to arrive by a virtuous education, our own endeavors, and the blessing of God; and by the trestle-board we are also reminded that, as the operative workman erects his temporal building agreeably to the rules and designs laid down by the master on his trestle-board, so should we, both operative and speculative, endeavor to erect our spiritual building agreeably to the rules and designs laid down by the Supreme Architect of the Universe, in the great books of nature and revelation, which are our spiritual, moral, and Masonic trestle-board."—*Mackey's Ritualist, page 58.*

"Lodges were anciently dedicated to King Solomon, [who was said to be our first Most Excellent Grand Master] but Masons professing Christianity dedicate theirs to St. John the Baptist and St. John the Evangelist, who were two eminent patrons of Masonry; and since their time, there is represented, in every regular and well-governed lodge a certain point within a circle, the point representing an individual brother, the circle the boundary line of his conduct to God and man, beyond which he is never to suffer his passions, prejudices, or interest to betray him, on any occasion. This circle is embordered by two perpendicular parallel lines, representing those saints, who were perfect parallels in Christianity, as well as in Masonry; and upon the vertex rests the Holy Scriptures, which point out the whole duty of man. In going around this circle we necessarily touch upon these two lines, as well as upon the Holy Scriptures; and while a Mason keeps himself thus circumscribed, it is impossible that he should err."—*Sickels's Monitor, page 50.*

The Point within a Circle.

Preparation Fellow Craft Degree.

PREPARATION FOR FELLOW CRAFT DEGREE.

Candidate is prepared much the same as in the first degree. The *right* leg, *right* arm, *right* breast, and *right* foot being bare, a slipper on *left* foot and the cable tow twice around his naked right arm near shoulder.

A small white apron with bib turned up and he is "duly and truly prepared" to be made a Fellow Craft.

Candidate taking Fellow Craft
Obligation.

"Increased privileges and honors thus encircling the profession of Fellow Craft, weightier and more numerous responsibilities are superadded.

Powerful obligations, impelling him to be secret obedient, honest and charitable, guide and restrain him. * * *

"He is subject to the discipline of his mother-lodge, and to all the penalties of Masonry."— *Morris's Dictionary, Art. Fellow Craft.*

DUE-GUARD OF A FELLOW CRAFT.

Hold out right hand, palm down, height of hips, and raise left hand to point perpendicularly upward, fore-arm forming a right angle with arm. [See cut.]

Due-Guard, Fellow
Craft.

SIGN OF A FELLOW CRAFT.

Made from due-guard by dropping left hand carelessly to side while raising right hand to left breast, fingers a little crooked; then draw hand quickly across the breast; then drop hand to side. [See cut.]

Sign of a Fellow
Craft.

PASS GRIP OF A FELLOW CRAFT.

Grasp right hands as in ordinary hand shaking and press ball of thumb hard between knuckles of first and second fingers.

Pass Grip of Fellow Craft

PASS OF A FELLOW CRAFT—*Shibboleth;* the name of the grip.

GRIP OF A FELLOW CRAFT.

Grasp right hands in the usual way and press thumb on knuckle joint of second finger.

"THE WORKING TOOLS OF A FELLOW CRAFT

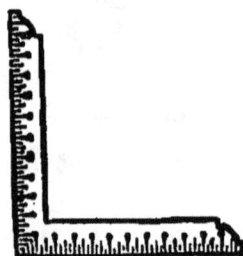

Plumb. Square. Level.

Are the *Plumb*, the *Square*, and the *Level*.

"The *Plumb* is an instrument made use of by operative masons to raise perpendiculars; the *Square*, to square their work; and the *Level*, to lay horizontals; but we, as Free and Accepted Masons, are taught to make use of them for more noble and glorious purposes; the plumb admonishes us to walk uprightly in our several stations before God and men, squaring our actions by the square of virtue, and remembering that we are traveling upon the level of time to that undiscovered country from whose bourne no traveler returns."-*Mackey's Rit. p. 78.*

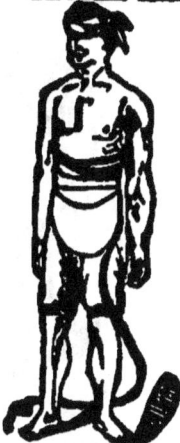

Preparation of Candidate
Master Mason's Degree

PREPARATION OF CANDII .TE, MASTER MASON'S DEGREE

The candidate is stripped. a .n previous degrees, but in this "*Subl·me Degree*," both breasts, both arms both feet and legs are bare. He is hood-winked and the cable-tow is put three times around his body.

Candidate taking Master Mason's Obligation. See page

Due-Guard, Master Mason.

DUE-GUARD OF A MASTER MASON.

Extend both hands, in front of the body, height of hips, palms down, thumbs nearly touching each other. [See cut.]

SIGN OF A MASTER MASON.

Made from due-guard, by dropping left hand and drawing right hand across the jewels to the right, thumb toward the body, eight of hips. [See cut.]

Sign of a Master Mason.

Real Grip of a Master Mason.

PASS GRIP OF A MASTER MASON.

Grasp hands naturally and press thumb between knuckles of second and third fingers.

STRONG GRIP OF A MASTER MASON OR LION'S PAW.

Hands joined as shown in cut, thumb and fingers pressing hard on hand and wrist of each other.

PASS OF A MASTER MASON *Tubal Cain;* name of grip.

"THE COMPASSES

Are peculiarly consecrated to this degree, because within their extreme points, when properly extended, are emblematically said to be inclosed the principal tenets of our profession, and hence the moral application of the Compasses, in the third degree, is to those precious jewels of a Master Mason, Friendship, Morality, and Brotherly Love."— *Mackey'. Ritualist, page 110.*

Are all the implements of masonry indiscriminately but more especially the *Trowel.*

"The *Trowel* is an instrument made use of by Operative Masons to spread the cement which unites a building into one common mass; but we, as Free and Accepted Masons, are taught to make use of it for the more noble and glorious purpose of spreading the cement of brotherly love and affection; that cement which unites us into one sacred band, or society of friends and brothers, among whom no contention, should ever exist, but that noble contention or rather emulation; of who can best work and best agree."—*Mackey's Rit. p. 111.*

THE TRAGEDY OF THE THIRD DEGREE.

PLAYING MURDER AND RESURRECTION IN TEN SCENES.

SCENE I.—PLAYING MURDER Assault by "*Jubela*" on the Candidate, alias "Grand Master Hiram Abiff."

SCENE II: PLAYING MURDER —"Jubela" draws 24 inch gauge across his throat.

SCENE III: PLAYING MURDER.—Assault by "Jubelo" on the Candidate.

SCENE IV: PLAYING MURDER.—"Jubelo" strikes him with the square on left breast.

SCENE V: PLAYING MURDER.—Assault by "Jubelum" on the Candidate.

SCEND VI. PLAYING MURDER.—"JUBELUM" kills him with the Setting Maul and tumbles him into the Canvas.

GRAND HAILING SIGN OF DISTRESS.

First Position.   Second Position.   Third Position.

SCENE VII: PLAYING DISTRESS.—Mourning for "our Grand Master Hiram Abiff."

Raise hands and arms as shown in first cut, and if in the ceremony of "raising" or in the dark, the words in brackets may be used, otherwise not. [O Lord.] Bring arms from first to second position, [My God,] bring arms to third position [is there no help for the widow's Son?] bring arms to side.

in the dark, when in distress, the words are "O Lord, my God is there no help for the widows son?" In the ceremony of *"raising"* after the second attempt and failure to raise the body, first by the Entered Apprentice's Grip and then by the Fellow Craft's when this sign is given the words are, "O Lord my God! O Lord my God! O Lord my. God! I fear the Master's word is forever lost."

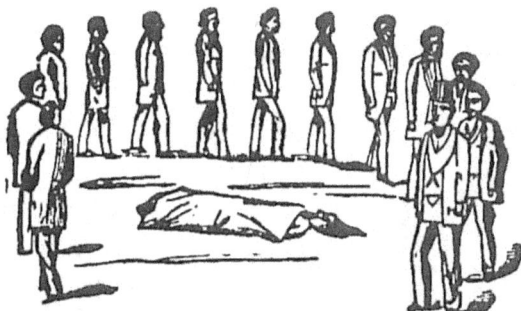

Scene VIII: Playing Distress.-Procession Singing Dirge for "our Grand Master Hiram Abiff."

Scene IX: Playing Resurrection—Praying at Mock Resurrection of Candidate alias "our Grand Master Hiram Abiff."

FIVE POINTS OF FELLOWSHIP.

Foot to foot, knee to knee, breast to breast, hand to back and cheek to cheek, or mouth to ear, when they whisper: *Mah-huh-bone*, which is the Master's word.

SCENE X: PLAYING RESURRECTION—Candidate Raised on the Five Points of Fellowship.

EMBLEMS[383] OF THE MASTER MASON'S DEGREE.

"THE THREE STEPS

Usually delineated upon the Master's carpet, are emblematical of the three principal stages of human life, viz: *youth, manhood,* and *age,*. In youth as Entered Apprentices, we ought industriously to occupy our minds in the attainment of useful knowledge; in manhood, as Fellow Crafts, we should apply our knowledge to the discharge of our respective duties to God, our neighbor, and ourselves; that so in age, as Master Masons, we may enjoy the happy reflection consequent on a well-spent life, and die in the hope of a glorious immortality.

NOTE 383.—"Under the term Emblems, writers include those conveying both the exotery and exotery of Masonic knowledge."—*Morris's Dictionary, Art. Emblems.*

"THE POT OF INCENSE

Is an emblem[384] of a pure heart, which is always an acceptable sacrifice to the Deity; and as this glows with fervent heat, so should our hearts continually glow with gratitude to the great and beneficent Author of our existence, for the manifold blessings and comforts we enjoy.

"THE BEE HIVE

Is an emblem of industry, and recommends the practice of that virtue to all created beings, from the highest seraph in heaven to the lowest reptile of the dust [etc.

"THE BOOK OF CONSTITUTIONS GUARDED BY THE TYLER'S SWORD

Reminds us that we should be ever watchful and guarded in our thoughts, words and actions, particularly when before the enemies of Masonry; ever bearing in remembrance those truly Masonic virtues, silence and circumspection.

"THE SWORD POINTING TO A NAKED HEART

Demonstrates that justice will sooner or later overtake us; and although our thoughts, words and actions may be hidden from the eyes of man, yet that

NOTE 384—"Everything in the esotery of the society is written down, or engraved upon durable objects by Symbols. Each of these has a public and private meaning, the latter communicated only by suitable restrictions to proper persons. These Symbols form a large part of the universal language of Masonry."—Morris's Dictionary, Art. Symbol.

"ALL-SEEING EYE,

Whom the Sun Moon and Stars obey, and under whose watchful care even comets perform their stupendous revolutions, pervades the inmost recesses of the human heart, and will reward us according to our merits.

"THE ANCHOR AND ARK

Are emblems of a well-grounded *hope*, and a well-spent life. They are emblematical of that divine *ark*, etc.

"THE FORTY-SEVENTH PROBLEM OF EUCLID.

This was an invention of our ancient friend and brother, the great Pythagoras, who, in his travels through Asia, Africa and Europe, was initiated into the several orders of priesthood, etc.

"THE HOUR GLASS

Is an emblem of human life. Behold! how swiftly the sands run, and how rapidly our lives are drawing to a close! etc.

"THE SCYTHE

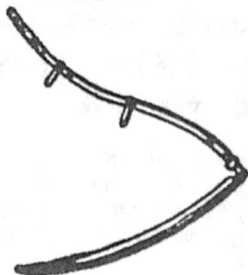

Is an emblem of time, which cuts the brittle thread of life, and launches us into eternity. Behold! what havoc the scythe of time makes among the human race! If by chance we should escape," [etc. See p. 311.] —*Sickels's Monitor, pages 113-119.*

THE SETTING MAUL, SPADE AND COFFIN.

"The second class of emblems are not monitorial, and therefore their true interpretation can only be obtained within the tyled recesses of the lodge. They consist of the Setting Maul, the Spade, the Coffin, and the Sprig of Acacia. They afford subjects of serious and solemn reflection to the rational and contemplative mind."—*Mackey's Ritualist, page 131.*

FOURTH, OR SECRET MASTER'S DEGREE.

PREPARATION OF CANDIDATE.

The candidate is prepared as a Master Mason with an apron tied over his eyes, and a square on his forehead, Master of Ceremonies then leads him to the door of the lodge and knock seven times; 000-000-0.

Preparation of Candidate.

TOKEN OF A SECRET MASTER.

First give the Master's Grip, and then slip the hand to each other's elbow, and balance seven times; at the same time bring the foot and knee in contact.

Pass Word—Zi-Za. (resplendent.)

Sacred Word—Adonai.

Token

SIGN OF SILENCE.

Sign—Is that of silence, which is made by placing the first two fingers of the right hand on the lips, which is answered by the first two fingers of the left.

FIFTH OR PERFECT MASTER'S DEGREE

PREPARATION OF CANDIDATE.

Zerbal proceeds to the Ante-chamber, and having prepared the candidate as a Secret Master, leads him by the green cord, which he

Sign of Silence.

puts around his neck, to the door of the lodge, and there knocks four.

SIGN OF RECOGNITION.

PERFECT MASTER'S DEGREE

Preparation of
Candidate.

Advance each the toes of the right foot until they meet bring the right knees together place one hand on the other heart, then bring the hand towards the right side and form a square.

Sign of Recognition.

SIGN OF ADMIRATION.

Raise the hands and eyes to heaven, then let the arms fall across the abdomen and look downwards.

Sign of Admiration.

TOKEN.

Place one the left hand on the other's right shoulder, seize each other's right hand, the thumb separate.

First Token.

Second Token.

SECOND TOKEN.

Interlace the forefingers of the right hands, thumbs upright, pressing against each other, forming a triangle.

Third Token.

THIRD TOKEN.

Clinch each other as in Master's grip, carry left hand between each other's shoulders, and press four times hard with the fingers in the back, and give the Master's Word [mah-hah-bone].

BATTERY :—Four equi-timed strokes; 0000

MARCH :—Make a square by walking four steps and bring the feet together at each step.

PASS WORD :—Acacia.

SACRED WORD :—Jehovah.

Sign Intimate Secretary.

INTIMATE SECRETARY'S SIGN.

Raise the right hand, then draw it from the left shoulder to the right hip, thus indicating the fall of a scarf.

Cross the arms horizontally, raise them to the height of the breast and then let them fall towards the hilt of the sword, while raising the eyes to heaven.

Token Intimate Secretary.

TOKEN.

Join right hands; the first one turns the other's hand and says, *Berith*, the other reversing the hand again says, *Neder,* then the first one resuming the first position, says, *Shelemoth.*

These three words might be interpreted: *Promise of a complete alliance.*

PASS WORD:—*Joabert* (the name of the candidate).

Answer—*Zerbal* (the name of the Captain of the Guards).

SACRED WORD:—J∴E∴H∴O∴V∴A∴H∴

SEVENTH DEGREE OR PROVOST AND JUDGE.

Grip of Provost and Judge.

GRIP.

Lock the two little fingers of the right hands with the forefinger, one of the other, and give seven light blows with the thumb of the right hand on the palm of the same.

SIGN, PROVOST AND JUDGE.

Place the two first fingers of the right hand on the nose.

ANSWER.

Place the first finger of the right hand on the top of the nose, and the thumb of the same under the chin, forming a square.

Sign, Provost and Judge.

PASS WORD:—*Tilo, Civi, Ky.*

SACRED WORD:—*Jachinai*, which is the plural of the word *Jachin.*

GRAND WORDS:—*Izrach-Jah, Jehovah, Hiram, Stolkin, Geometrass* and *Architect.*

Answer to Sign.

EIGHTH DEGREE OR INTENDANT OF THE BUILDING

SIGN OF SURPRISE.

Place the thumbs on the temples, the hands open so as to form a square, step backwards two paces, step forward two paces, then place the hands over the eyes and say, *Ben Korim*

SIGN OF ADMIRATION,

INTENDANT OF THE

BUILDING.

Interlace the fingers of both hands, turn the palms upwards, let the hands fall on the waist, look upwards and say, *Akar.*

Sign of Surprise,
Intendant of Building.

Sign of Admiration.

SIGN OF GRIEF.

INTENDANT OF THE BUILDING.

Place the right hand on the heart, the left on the hip, balance thrice with the knees; one says *Jai,* the other says *Jah.*

Sign of Grief.

Token, Intendant of Building.

TOKEN, INTENDANT OF BUILDING.

Strike one with the right hand over the other's heart; pass the right hand under the left arm, then seize the right shoulder with the left hand; one says *Jachinai*, the other, *Judah*.

NINTH DEGREE, OR MASTER ELECT OF NINE.

SIGN MASTER ELECT OF NINE.

First one raises the poniard and makes the motion of striking the other on the forehead; the other places his hand on his forehead as if to examine the supposed wound.

Second raises the arm, strikes at the other's breast as if with a poniard, and says, *Nekam*.

Answer.

ANSWER.

Place your right hand on your heart and say *Nekah*.

Sign, Master Elect of Nine.

Token

TOKEN.

Clinch the fingers of your right hand, and at the same time elevate your thumb. The second seizes your thumb with the right hand, at the same time elevating his thumb; signifying the nine elected, eight close together and one by itself.

PASS WORD:—*Begoal-Kohl.*

SACRED WORD:—*Nekam;* answer, *Nekah.*

SIGN, MASTER ELECT OF FIFTEEN.

Place the point of the poniard under the chin, and draw it downward to the waist, as if in the act of ripping open the abdomen.

Sign, Master Elect of Fifteen.

ANSWER.

Give the sign of an Entered Apprentice, with the fingers clinched and the thumb extended.

Answer

TOKEN, MASTER ELECT OF FIFTEEN.

Interlace each other's fingers of the right hand.

PASS WORD: — *Elignam* or *Eliam.*

SACRED WORD: — *Zerbal;* answer, *Benjah.*

Token.

ELEVENTH DEGREE OR SUBLIME KNIGHTS ELECTED.

SIGN, SUBLIME KNIGHTS ELECTED.

Cross the arms on the breast, the fingers clinched, and the thumbs elevated.

TOKENS, SUBLIME KNIGHTS ELECTED.

First — Present to each other the thumb of the right hand, the fingers clinched. One seizes the thumb of the other and reverse thrice his wrist. One says Berith, the other one says Neder; the first then says Shelemoth.

Sign, Sublime Knight Elected.

First Token.

Second Token.

Second—Take one the right hand of the other, and with the thumb strike thrice on the first joint of the middle finger.

PASS WORD:—*Stolkin;* (running of Water.)

SACRED WORD:—*Adonai.*

TWELFTH DEGREE OR GRAND MASTER ARCHITECT.

SIGN, GRAND MASTER ARCHITECT.

Sign Grand Master. Architect.

Slide the right hand into palm of the left as if holding a pencil in one hand, and in the other a tracing board; make the motion of tracing a plan on the palm of the left hand, every now and then directing the eyes toward the Grand Master as if drawing by dictation.

TOKEN.

Join right hand to the other's left, interlacing the fingers; place the left hand on the hip, the brother will do the same with his right hand.

PASS WORD:—*Rab-banaim*

SACRED WORD:—*Adonai.*

Token

FIRST SIGN, ROYAL ARCH.

Admiration; raise the hands to heaven, the head leaning on the left shoulder; fall on the right knee.

First Sign, Royal Arch.

SECOND SIGN.

Adoration; fall on both knees.

Second Sign, Royal Arch.

ROYAL ARCH TOKENS.

Place your hands beneath the other's arms, as if to help him to rise, saying at the same time, Be of Good Cheer.

The other returns the token, saying *Jabulum.*

Token.

SIGN OF OBLIGATION.

Place the right hand on the left side of the abdomen and draw it quickly and horizontally across the body to the right side.

Sign of Obligation
G. E. P. and S. Mason.

FIRST TOKEN.

Join the right hands, reverse them thrice. The first brother says, "Berith" the second says, "Neder," the first then says, "Shelemoth."

First Token Grand Elect, Perfect and Sublime Mason.

WORDS.

First Pass Word—Shibboleth.
First Covered Word—Jabulum.

Sign of Fire.

SIGN OF FIRE.

Raise the right hand open to the left cheek the palms outward, at the same time grasping the elbow with the left hand.

Second Token.

SECOND TOKEN.

Give the Master's Grip, one says, can you go further?

Answer, Second Token.

ANSWER.

The other slips his hand along the other's forearm up to the elbow. Each then places his left hand on the other's right shoulder and balance thrice, the legs crossed from the right.

WORD.

Second Covered Word—Makobim, Interpreted,"That's he! He is dead."
Second Pass Word—El-Hhanan.

SIGN OF ADMIRATION.

Raise both hands opened to heaven, the head inclined, the eyes directed upwards, afterward place the first two fingers of the right hand on the lips.

Sign of Admiration.

THIRD TOKEN.

Seize each other's right hand, grasp each other's right shoulder with the left hand and then pass left hands behind each other's back as if to bring one another closer.

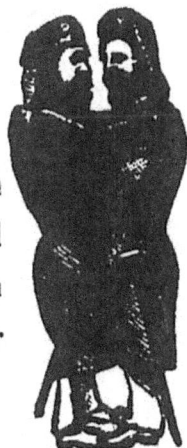

Third Token.

WORD.

Third Covered Word—Adonai.
Third Pass Word—Bea Makeh, Bamearah, interpreted, "Thank God we have found."

FIFTH SIGN.

Interlace all your fingers, hands raised over the head, palms outward (this sign serves to call a brother.)

SIXTH SIGN.

Admiration (see p.516).

ANSWER.

Look over your shoulders alternately.

SEVENTH SIGN.

Clap your hands on your thighs.

EIGHTH SIGN.

Put your hands, shut, to your mouth, as if to pull out your tongue, then place on your heart.

NINTH SIGN.

Raise right hand as if you had a poniard in it to strike a brother's forehead, to show that vengeance is completed.

Fifth Sign.

Answer.

FIRST TOKEN.

Eighth Sign.

Ninth Sign.

That of Intimate Secretary, B.∴N. ∴S.∴ which signifies promises of a complete alliance (see p.348.)
SECOND TOKEN.
Circumspection:

Token of Circumspection.

advance hands reciprocally first to the master t o k e n, then to the wrist, then to the elbow, and t h e w o r d i s *Gabaon.*

THIRD TOKEN.

Defiance, Resistance and *Remembrance.* Advance reciprocally, the hands as in the fourth degree, drawing them to each other three times; then place the left hand on the brother's back, then on his neck, as if to raise him.

PASS WORDS.

There are three principal ones: the first is *Shibboleth,* three times with an aspiration. The second is *El-Hanan.* The third is most essential to be known, and is *Bca-Makeh, Bamearah,* which is interpreted, "thank God we have found it."

Token of Resistance and
Remembrance.

COVERED WORDS.

The first is *Guiblim* or *Jabulum.* The second is *Makobim,* which, interpreted: "That's he! He is dead!" The third is *Adonai,* Supreme Lord of all.

FIFTEENTH DEGREE, OR KNIGHTS OF THE EAST OR SWORD.

SIGN.

Raise the right hand to the left shoulder and move it downward to the right hip, with a serpentine motion as if to represent the motion of the waters of a river; then draw the sword and bring it to the guard as if to fight.

Sign Knights of the East or Sword.

Token.

TOKEN.

Seize mutually the left hands, the arms lifted and extended as if to repulse an attack; at the same time make with the right hand the motion of clearing the way; then point the swords to each other's heart.

ONE SAYS *Judah*, THE OTHER ANSWERS *Benjamin*.

PASS WORD:—*laaborou hammuin*, OR LIBERTY OF PASSAGE.

GRAND WORD:—*Shalal, Shalom, Abi*, in Latin *Restoravit pacem patri*. He restored peace to his country.

SACRED WORD:—*Ruph-c-dom*.

SIXTEENTH DEGREE OR PRINCES OF JERUSALEM.

SIGN, PRINCES OF JERUSALEM.

Present yourself boldly with your left hand resting on your hip, as if ready for a combat.

Sign Princes of Jerusalem.

ANSWER.

Extend the arm at the height of
the shoulder, as if to begin the combat, the right foot forming a square
with the toe of the left.

Answer

TOKEN.

Join right hands, placing the
thumb on the joint of little finger;
with the thumb strike on that joint
5 times, by 1, by 2 and by 2, at same
time join right feet by the toes so
as to form a straight line, touch the
knee. Lastly place the left hand
open on the shoulder, one of the
other. One says twenty, the other
twenty-three.

Token

BATTERY.—Five, in some Councils five times five.

MARCH:—One slow step on the tip of the toes, sometimes five are made under the sign thus: Slide the left
foot forward, bring up the right foot to the toe of the
left, make a short pause and so on until the five steps
are made.

SEVENTEENTH DEGREE OR KNIGHTS OF THE EAST AND WEST.

PREPARATION OF CANDIDATE.

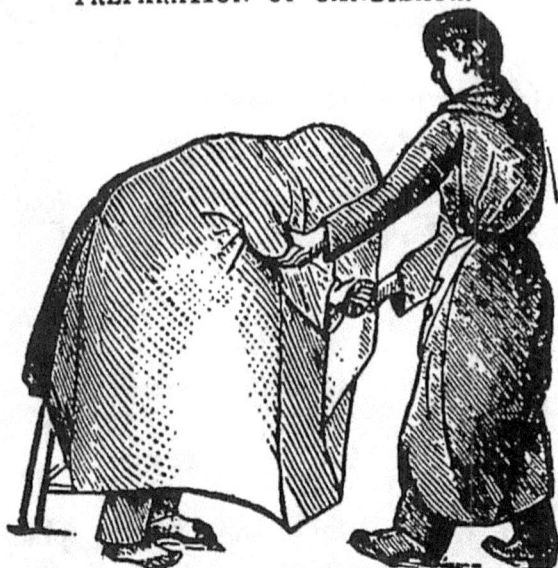

Master of Ceremonies prepares candidate in an ante-room hung with red and lighted by seven lights by clothing him with a long white robe, and brings him barefooted to the door of the Council.

Sign and Answer.

SIGN, KNIGHTS OF THE EAST AND WEST.

Look at your right shoulder and say, *Abaddon.*

ANSWER.

Look at left shoulder and say, *Jubulum.*

FIRST TOKEN.

Place left hand in each other's right hand, closing the fingers.

First Token.

SECOND TOKEN.

A touches B's left shoulder with right hand and B, answering touches A's right shoulder with left hand.

SIGN ON ENTERING COUNCIL.

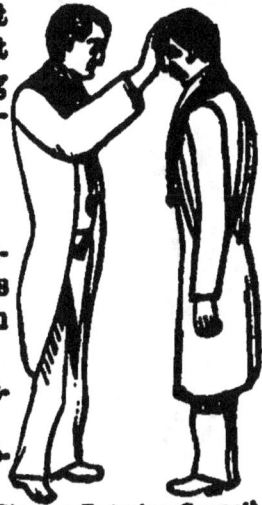

Touch Tyler's forehead, when he answers by putting his hand on your forehead.

PASS WORD:—*Jubulum.*

SACRED WORD:—*Abaddon.*

Second Token.

Sign on Entering Council.

EIGHTEENTH DEGREE OR SOVEREIGN PRINCE OF ROSE CROIX.

SIGN OF THE GOOD SHEPHERD.

Cross the arms on breast, with hands extended and eyes raised to heaven.

SIGN OF RECONCILIATION.

Raise right hand and with index finger point upward.

ANSWER.

Point downward with index finger of right hand.

Sign of the Good Shepherd.

Sign of Reconciliation.

EIGHTEENTH DEGREE OR SOVEREIGN PRINCE OF ROSE CROIX.

SIGN OF HELP, SOVEREIGN PRINCE OF ROSE CROIX.

Cross the legs, the right behind the left

Sign of Help.

ANSWER.

Same, except left leg behind the right.

TOKEN, SOVEREIGN PRINCE OF ROSE CROIX.

Give the sign of the Good Shepherd; face each other; bow; place reciprocally crossed hands on breast and give the fraternal kiss and pronounce the password

PASS WORD: *Immanuel.*

Answer.

NINETEENTH DEGREE OR GRAND PONTIFF

SIGN OF GRAND PONTIFF.

Extend horizontally the right arm; the hand is also extended· bring down the three last fingers perpendicularly.

TOKEN.

Each places the palm of his right hand on the other's forehead; one says, Alleluia, the other answers, Praise the Lord; the first then says, Immanuel, the other, God speed you. Both say, Amen.

Sign, Grand Pontiff Degree.

TWENTIETH DEGREE OR GRAND MASTER OF ALL SYMBOLIC LODGES.

FIRST SIGN, GRAND MASTER.

Token, Grand Pontiff.

Form four squares; first by placing the right hand on the heart, the fingers close together, the thumb separate, which makes two squares; second by placing the left hand on the lips, the thumb separate, which makes a third square; third, by bringing the heels together, the feet open on a square.

First Sign, Grand Master's Degree.

SECOND SIGN.

Kneel down, place the elbows on the floor, the head downwards and a little inclined to the left.

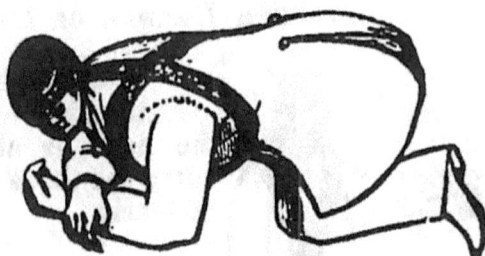

Second Sign, 20th Degree.

THIRD SIGN.

Cross the arms on the breast, the right arm over the left, the fingers extended and close together, the thumb forming a square, heels touching, which makes five squares.

Third Sign, 20th Degree.

N. B.—In some rituals only one sign is given instead of the first two, and this is to kneel on the right knee, the left hand being raised, which forms two squares; then place the left elbow on the left knee, fingers extended and closed, the thumb forming the square, the head downwards, somewhat inclined to the left.

SIGN OF INTRODUCTION.

The sword elevated, or if no sword is worn, the right arm raised before the head as if to ward off a stroke. In coming together, cross swords and form the arch of steel.

Token, 20th Degree.

TOKEN.

Take one the other's right elbow, with the right hand; press it four times; then slide the hand along the forearm down to the wrist; lastly, press the wrist-joint with the first finger only.

TOKEN OF INTRODUCTION.

[Given after the sign of introduction.]

Take each other's right hand, the first finger on the wrist joint; then as you retire slide the hand along the other's hand down to the tip of the fingers.

Token of Introduction.

N. B.—Some in the last token squeeze on the other's wrist, each drawing the other nine times alternately, and repeating each time the word Cyrus.

BATTERY:—The battery is three strokes, by one and two; 0 00.

MARCH:—Nine steps, each forming a square.

PASS WORD:—Jekson.

ANSWER:—Stolkin.

SACRED WORD:—Razah-belsijab

Lieutenant Commander—Arise my brother and receive the sign, token and words of this degree.

Sign of Order, Noachite Degree.

SIGN OF ORDER.

Raise the arms to heaven, the face toward the East, where the moon rises.

SIGN OF INTRODUCTION.

One raises three fingers of the right hand, the other seizes those fingers with his right hand, a n d says, Frederick the Second. He then presents his three fingers, which the first one seizes in the same manner, saying Noah.

Sign of Introduction, Noachite Degree.

Second Sign of Introduction.

SECOND SIGN, PRUSSIAN KNIGHT.

Seize one the first finger of the other's right hand and press it with the thumb and first finger, saying Shem.

The other gives the same token, saying Ham; then the first gives the same token, saying Japheth.

PASS WORD:—Peleg, Peleg, Peleg.

SACRED WORD: — Shem, Ham, Japheth.

TWENTY SECOND DEGREE, OR PRINCE OF LIBANUS.

SIGN, PRINCE OF LIBANUS.

Make the motion of lifting an axe with both hands. and striking as if to fell a tree.

ANSWER.

Raise both hands to the height of the forehead, the fingers extended, and then let the hands fall, thus indicating the fall of a tree.

Sign, Prince of Libanus.

Answer to Sign, *Prince of Libanus.*

TOKEN.

Seize each other's hands and cross the fingers as a sign of good faith.

PASS WORDS:—Japhet, Aholiab, Lebanon.

SACRED WORDS:—Noah, Bezaleel, Sadonias.

Token.

TWENTY-THIRD DEGREE, OR CHIEF OF THE TABERNACLE.

HIGH PRIEST.

The High Priest wears a large red tunic, over which is placed a shorter one of white without sleeves; on his head is a close mitre of cloth of gold, on the front of which is painted or embroidered a Delta, enclosing the Ineffable name in Hebrew characters. Over the dress he wears a black sash with silver fringe from, which hangs, by a red rosette, a dagger; the sash is worn from left to right. Suspended on his breast is the Breast Plate.

DRESS OF CANDIDATE.

A white tunic and white drawers, sandals on his feet and a white cloth over his head, covering his eyes, so as to prevent him from seeing.

High Priest, Chief of Tabernacle Degree.

Preparation of Candidate, Chief of the Tabernacle Degree.

SIGN, CHIEF OF THE TABERNACLE.

Advance the left foot; make with the right hand the motion of taking the Censer, which is supposed to be in the left hand.

Sign, Chief of Tabernacle.

TOKEN.

Seize each other by the left elbow with the right hand, bending the arm so as to form a kind of circle.

Token, Chief of Tabernacle.

BATTERY:—Seven strokes, by six and one, or thus: 00 00 00 0.

PASS WORD:—Uriel.

Sign of Recognition,
Prince of the Tabernacle.

Grand Sign, Prince
of the Tabernacle.

SIGN OF RECOGNITION.

Place the right hand open over the eyes, as if to protect them from a strong light, the left hand on the breast, then raise the right hand to the left shoulder, and bring it down diagonally to the right side. This is called the sign of the scarf.

GRAND SIGN.

Place both hands open upon the head, join the two thumbs and the two forefingers by their extremities so as to form a triangle.

N. B.—The token, battery and word are the same as in the preceding degree.

Sign of Order. Knights
of the Brazen Serpent.

TWENTY-FIFTH DEGREE, OR KNIGHTS OF BRAZEN SERPENT.

SIGN OF ORDER, KNIGHTS OF THE BRAZEN SERPENT.

Incline the head downwards, and point to the ground with the forefinger of right hand.

Sign of Recognition.
Knights of Brazen
Serpent.

SIGN OF RECOGNITION.

Form a cross upon yourself.

Token, Knights of Brazen Serpent

TOKEN.

Place yourself on the right of the brother, and take his left wrist with your left hand.

ANSWER.

He then takes your right wrist with his right hand.

PASS WORD:—I∴N∴R∴I∴, lettered only.

COVERED WORD:—*Johannes Ralp.*

SACRED WORD:—*Moses;* this word must be spelled.

Preparation of Candidate, Prince of Mercy Degree.

PREPARATION OF CANDIDATE.

The candidate is prepared by the Senior Deacon in a plain white robe, reaching from the neck to the feet, barefooted, hoodwinked, so as to prevent his seeing, with a rope passed three times around his body.

SIGN OF ENTRANCE.

Place the right hand open, so as to form a triangle above the eyes, as if to be protected against a strong light.

Sign of Entrance, Prince of Mercy.

Sign of Character, Prince of Mercy.

SIGN OF CHARACTER.

Form a triangle with the two thumbs, and the two forefingers; join them by the extremities, place the hands in front of, and touching the body.

SIGN OF HELP.

Cross both arms above the head, the hands open, palms outwards and say: To me, the children of Truth.

Sign of Help,
Prince of Mercy.

SIGN OF ORDER.

Stand up, the right hand resting on the hip.

Sign of Order.
Prince of Mercy.

TOKEN.

Place both hands, each on the other's shoulders, press them slightly thrice and say, Gomel.

PASS WORD:— *Gomel.*

COMMON WORDS: — Ghiblim and Gabaon.

SACRED WORDS:—Jehovah, Jachin.

SUBLIME WORD: — *Ednl-pen-cagu*, that is, do as you would be done by.

Token.

Twenty-seventh Degree, or Commander of the Temple.

Candidate taking Obligation, Commander of the Temple Degree.

SIGN OF RECOGNITION.

Form on your forehead a cross, with the thumb of your right hand, the fingers clinched.

ANSWER.

Kiss the place where the cross was made (This sign is used in the Court only.)

ANSWER.

(Out of Court.) Place first two fingers of the right hand on the mouth, the other fingers closed, the palm of the hand turned outward.

Sign of Recognition, Commander of the Temple.

Answer.

SIGN OF ORDER.

(In the Court.) Extend your right hand on the round table, thumb separate so as to form a square. When standing, place the right hand on the body below the breast, forming also a square.

Sign of Order, Commander of the Temple.

TOKEN.

Give three light blows with right hand on the other's left shoulder.

ANSWER.

He takes your right hand and gives it three light shakes.

Token, Commander of the Temple.

PASS WORD:—Solomon.

SACRED WORD:—I∴N∴R∴I∴, lettered.

TWENTY-EIGHTH DEGREE, OR KNIGHTS OF THE SUN.

SIGN, KNIGHTS OF THE SUN.

Place the right hand flat upon the heart, the thumb separate, so as to form a square.

ANSWER.

Raise the right hand, and with the index, point to heaven.

Sign, Knights of the Sun.

Answer.

PREPARATION OF CANDIDATE.

Brother Truth prepares the candidate as follows: A bandage over his eyes, a sword in his right hand; invests him with a ragged and bloody robe, puts a mask on his face, fetters binding his arms, a crown on his head, a purse in his left hand, etc.

TOKEN, KNIGHTS OF THE SUN.

Take in your hand those of the brother and press them gently; kiss him on the forehead and say Alpha. He returns the kiss and says Omega. But this is not much used.

PASS WORD:—Stibium.

Candidate.

Token, Knights of the Sun.

TWENTY-NINTH DEGREE, OR KNIGHTS OF ST. ANDREW.

First Sign, Knight
of St. Andrew.

FIRST SIGN; THAT OF EARTH.

Wipe your forehead with the back of the right hand, the head somewhat inclined forward.

FIRST TOKEN.

Seize each successively the first, then the second, and lastly the third joint of the other's index finger of the right hand, each spelling alternately the word of the first degree. (Boaz.)

First Token, Knight of St. Andrew.

2nd Sign, Water.

SECOND SIGN, THAT OF WATER.

Place the right hand upon the heart; extend it horizontally at the height of the breast; let it fall on the right side, as if to salute with the hand.

SECOND TOKEN.

Seize each successively the first, then the second, and lastly the third joint of the other's middle finger, as indicated for the index in the first token, each spelling the sacred word of the second degree, (Shibboleth.) For mode of giving it see page 184, Freemasonry Illustrated.

THIRD SIGN, THAT OF ASTONISHMENT AND HORROR.

Turn the head to the left, looking downwards; raise both hands clasped to heaven, a little towards the right.

Sign of Horror.

Sign of Fire.

FOURTH SIGN, THAT OF FIRE.

Join both hands, the fingers inter-laced and cover the eyes therewith, the palms outwards.

Answer to Sign of Fire.

ANSWER.

Give the sign of Air. Extend for-ward the right arm and hand at the height of the shoulder.

THIRD TOKEN.

Seize each successively the index finger of the other's right hand by the first joint. Each pronounce alternately one of the three syllables of the sacred word of the third degree. (Mah-hah-bone.)

FIFTH SIGN, THAT OF ADMIRATION.

Raise the eyes and hands to heaven, the left arm somewhat lower than the right, the heel of the left foot slightly raised, so that the left knee forms a square with the right leg.

Sign of Admiration.

SIXTH SIGN, THAT OF THE SUN.

Place the thumb of the right hand upon the right eye; raise the index finger so as to form a square, then bring it on a line, as if to indicate an object in view, saying: "I measure the sun itself."

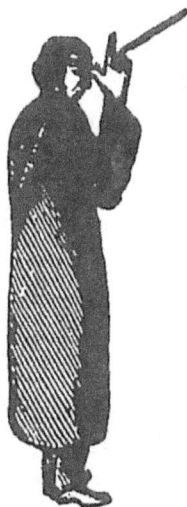

Sign of the Sun.

General Sign, Knight
of St. Andrew.

SEVENTH SIGN; GENERAL SIGN.

Form, on the breast, a cross of St. Andrew with the two arms, the hands upwards.

GENERAL TOKEN.

Seize one the last joint of the index finger of the other's right hand; the first one says *Ne*, the other *Ka*. Then seize the last joint of the little finger; the first one says *Mah*, the other, giving the whole word, says *Nekamah*.

General Token, Knight of
St. Andrew.

PASS WORDS.

Ardarel, or *Ardriel*,	*The Angel of Fire.*
Casmaren, or	" " " *Air.*
Talliud, or	" " " *Water.*
Furlac, or	" " " *Earth.*

Thirtieth Degree; Grand Elect Knight Kadosh, or Knight of the White and Black Eagle.

Candidate Stabbing the Skulls.

Sign of Kadosh.

SIGN OF KADOSH.

Place the right hand on the heart, the fingers separated. Let the right hand fall on the right knee. Bend and grasp the knee; then seize the poniard, which is suspended from the ribbon, raise it to the height of the shoulder, as if to strike, and say *Nekam Adonai.*

THIRTIETH DEGREE, OR GRAND ELECT KNIGHT KADOSH.

SIGN OF ORDER.

Hold the sword in the left hand and place the right hand extended over the heart.

Sign of Order.
Knight Kadosh.

TOKEN.

Place right foot to right foot, and knee to knee; present the right first, the thumb elevated, seize the thumb alternately, let it slip and step back a pace, then raise the arm as if to strike with the poniard. In doing this the first says, *Nekamah-bealim*, and the other answers, *Pharash-kol.*

Token, Knight Kadosh.   Second Position.

PASS WORD:—To enter, *Nekam.*

ANSWER:—*Menahhem,* that is *Consolator.* To retire, *Phaal-kol.*

ANSWER:—*Pharash-koh.*

SACRED WORD:—*Nekamah bealim.*

ANSWER:—*Pharah-koh;* but more generally, *Nekam-Adonai.*

ANSWER:—*Pharash-kol.*

FIRST SIGN.

Cross both hands, bring them to the navel, thumbs crossing each other, and say Justice.

First Sign.

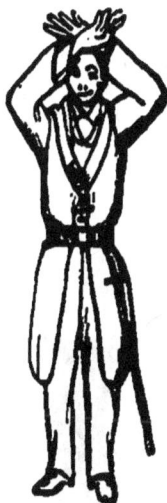

Answering Sign.

ANSWERING SIGN.

Cross both arms above your head, right outside, palms outward, and say Equity.

TOKEN, GRAND INSPECTOR INQUISITOR COMMANDER.

Place right foot to right foot, and right knee to right knee, take each other by the left hand, and with the right hand strike a gentle blow on the other's right shoulder.

SACRED WORD:—One says Justice, the other answers Equity. Both together say, So mote it be.

Token.

Camp. Sublime Prince of the Royal
Secret.

SIGN.

Place the right hand open on the heart; extend it forward, the palm downwards and then let it fall by the right side.

Sign Sublime Prince of the Royal Secret.

Token, Sublime Prince of the Roya Secret, 1st Position.

Token, 2nd Position.

TOKEN.

Seize the sword with the right hand; unsheath it and carry it up to the right side, the hilt resting on the right hip, the point upwards. Place the right foot behind the left, so as to form a square, leaving a small distance between the feet thus arranged. Raise the left arm, the hand open and extended, as if to repulse an attack. Seize each other's left hand, the fingers interlaced. Then draw close to each other and embrace. One says *Hochmah*, (that is wisdom or philosophy,) and the other answers *Tsedakah*. that is, truth, justice and equity. (In some rituals these two words are said to be the sacred and pass of the degree.)

BATTERY.

Is five strokes, by one and four; 0 0000.

THIRTY-THIRD DEGREE, OR SOVEREIGN GRAND

Preparation of Candidate, 33rd Degree.

PREPARATION OF CANDIDATE, SOVEREIGN GRAND INSPECTOR GENERAL.

The candidate is prepared by being divested of his shoes and hat; clothed in a black robe without sword or regalia; a lighted taper in his right hand and a black cable tow around his neck, the ends of which are held by the Illustrious Grand Master General of Ceremonies at the proper time. The Illustrious Grand Marshal retires to the Chamber of Reflection, and all being ready he strikes on the door of the Council Chamber.

Sign of Order.

SIGN OF ORDER.

Left hand over the heart, fingers extend'd and close together.

PENALTY, 33d DEGREE.

And should I knowingly or willfully violate the same, may this wine I now drink, become a deadly poison to me, as the hemlock juice drank by Socrates. (Drinks wine out of skull.) And may these cold arms forever encircle me. Amen. (Skeleton's arms enfold him.)

Skeleton Seizing Candidate when Taking Oath 33rd.

draw the sword, hold the point in the left hand and cross it with that of the opposite Inspector and give the

First Sign, S. G. L. G.

First Pass Word—"De Molay."²
Answer—"Hiram Abiff."
Second Pass Word—"Frederick."
Answer—"Of Prussia."

SECOND SIGN.

Disengage swords, retain point in left hand, fall on both knees, kiss blade three times and give the

Sacred Words—"Micha, Macha, Bealim, Adonai."

"Who is like unto Thee, oh God."

the breast, the head

www.ingramcontent.com/pod-product-compliance
Lightning Source LLC
Chambersburg PA
CBHW071822270326
41929CB00013B/1881